NHHT

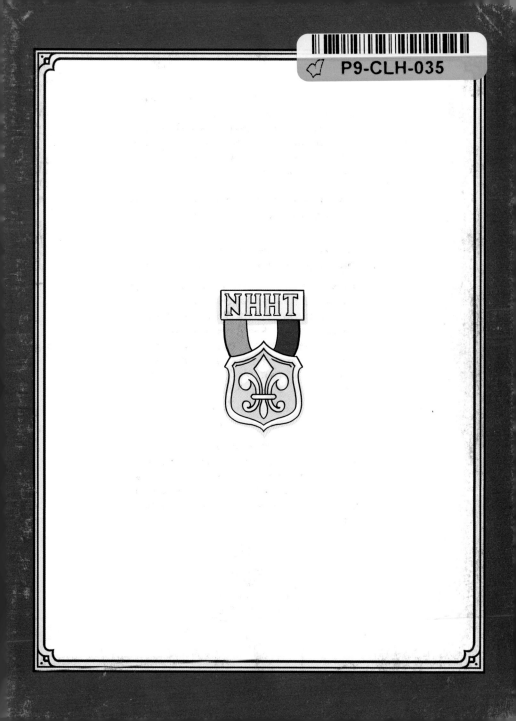

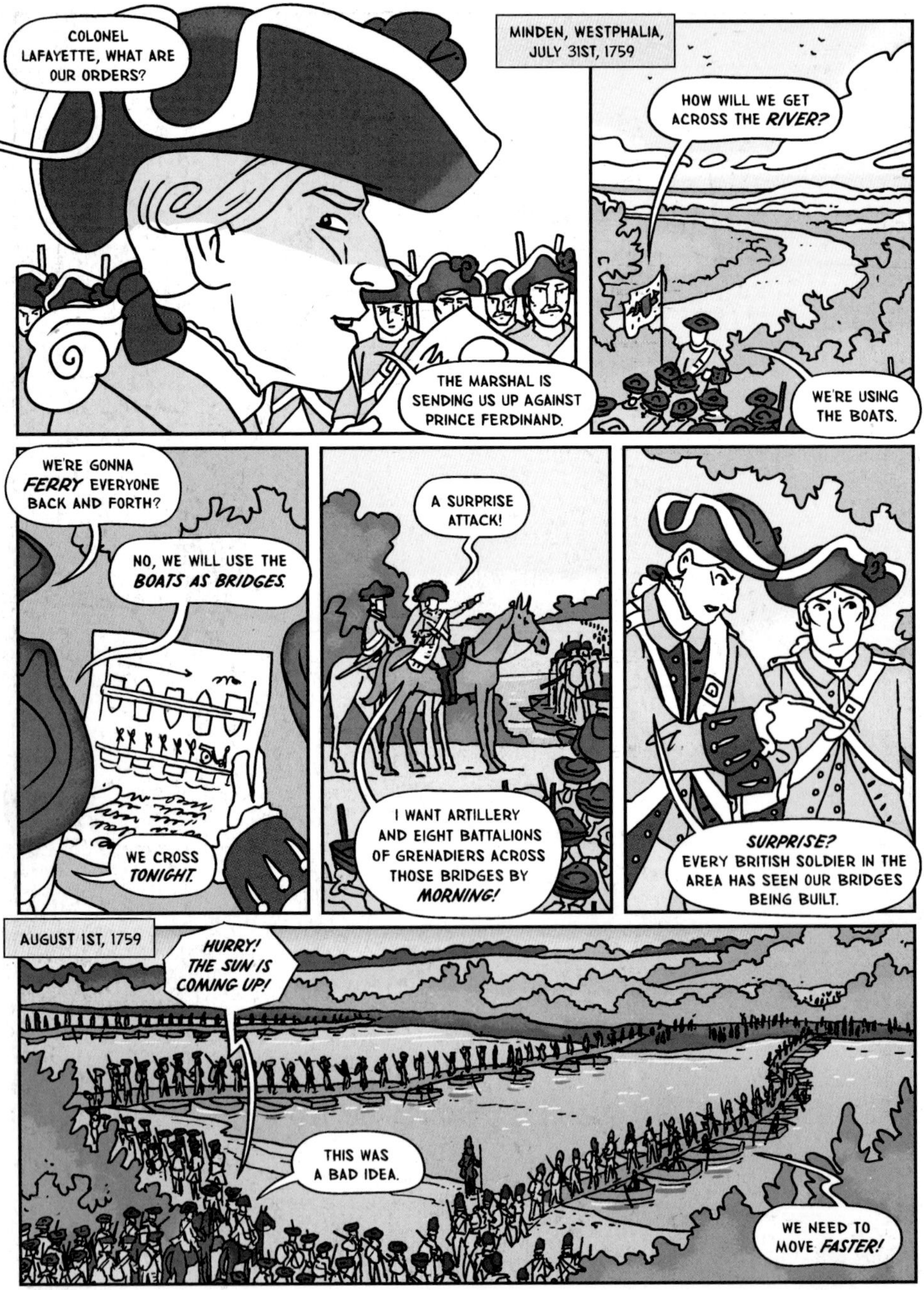
COLONEL LAFAYETTE, WHAT ARE OUR ORDERS?
MINDEN, WESTPHALIA, JULY 31ST, 1759
HOW WILL WE GET ACROSS THE RIVER?
THE MARSHAL IS SENDING US UP AGAINST PRINCE FERDINAND.
WE'RE USING THE BOATS.
WE'RE GONNA FERRY EVERYONE BACK AND FORTH?
NO, WE WILL USE THE BOATS AS BRIDGES.
WE CROSS TONIGHT.
A SURPRISE ATTACK!
I WANT ARTILLERY AND EIGHT BATTALIONS OF GRENADIERS ACROSS THOSE BRIDGES BY MORNING!
SURPRISE? EVERY BRITISH SOLDIER IN THE AREA HAS SEEN OUR BRIDGES BEING BUILT.
AUGUST 1ST, 1759
HURRY! THE SUN IS COMING UP!
THIS WAS A BAD IDEA.
WE NEED TO MOVE FASTER!

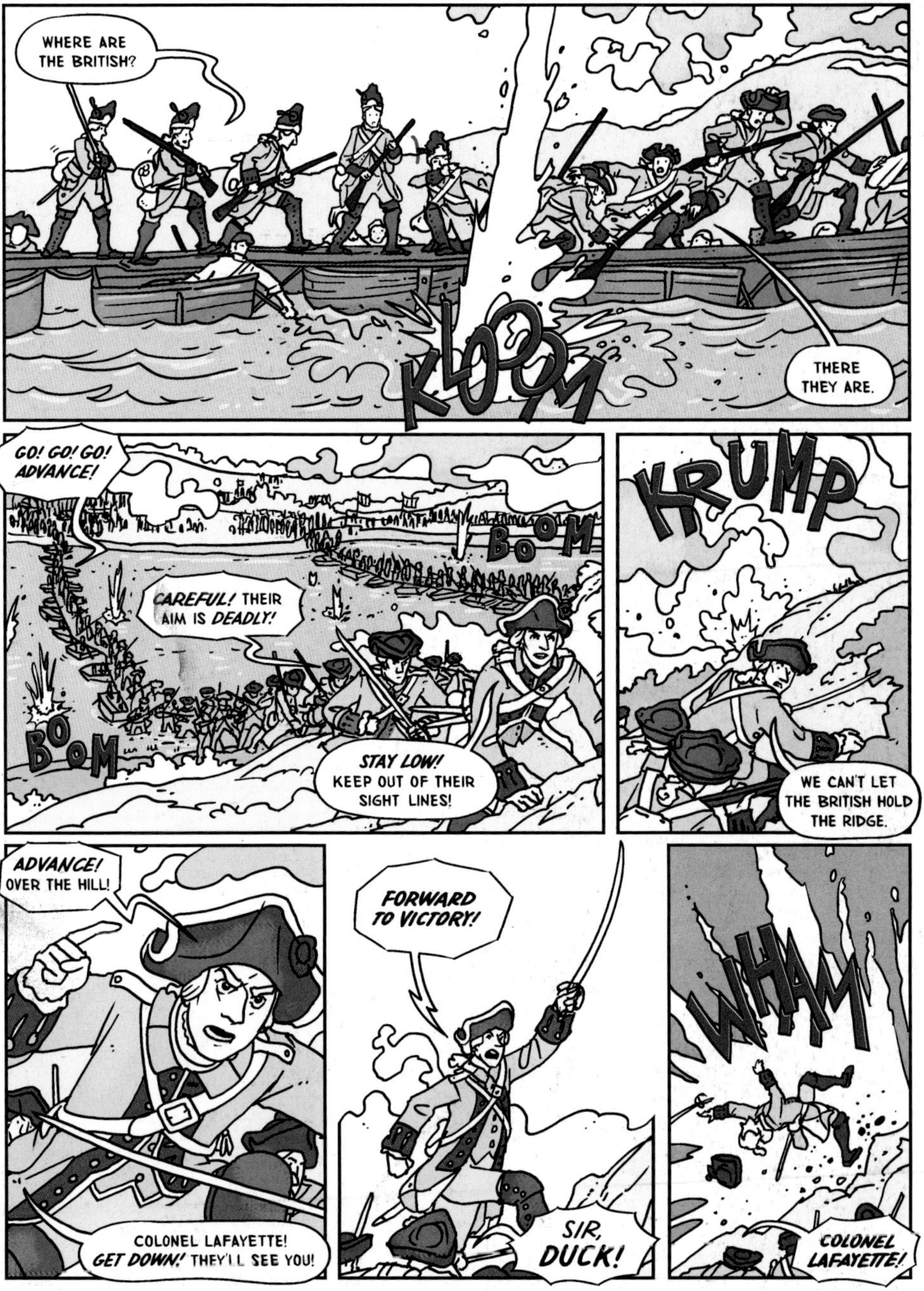
WHERE ARE THE BRITISH?
KLOOOM
THERE THEY ARE.
GO! GO! GO! ADVANCE!
BOOM
CAREFUL! THEIR AIM IS DEADLY!
BOOM
STAY LOW! KEEP OUT OF THEIR SIGHT LINES!
KRUMP
WE CAN'T LET THE BRITISH HOLD THE RIDGE.
ADVANCE! OVER THE HILL!
COLONEL LAFAYETTE! GET DOWN! THEY'LL SEE YOU!
FORWARD TO VICTORY!
SIR, DUCK!
WHAM
COLONEL LAFAYETTE!

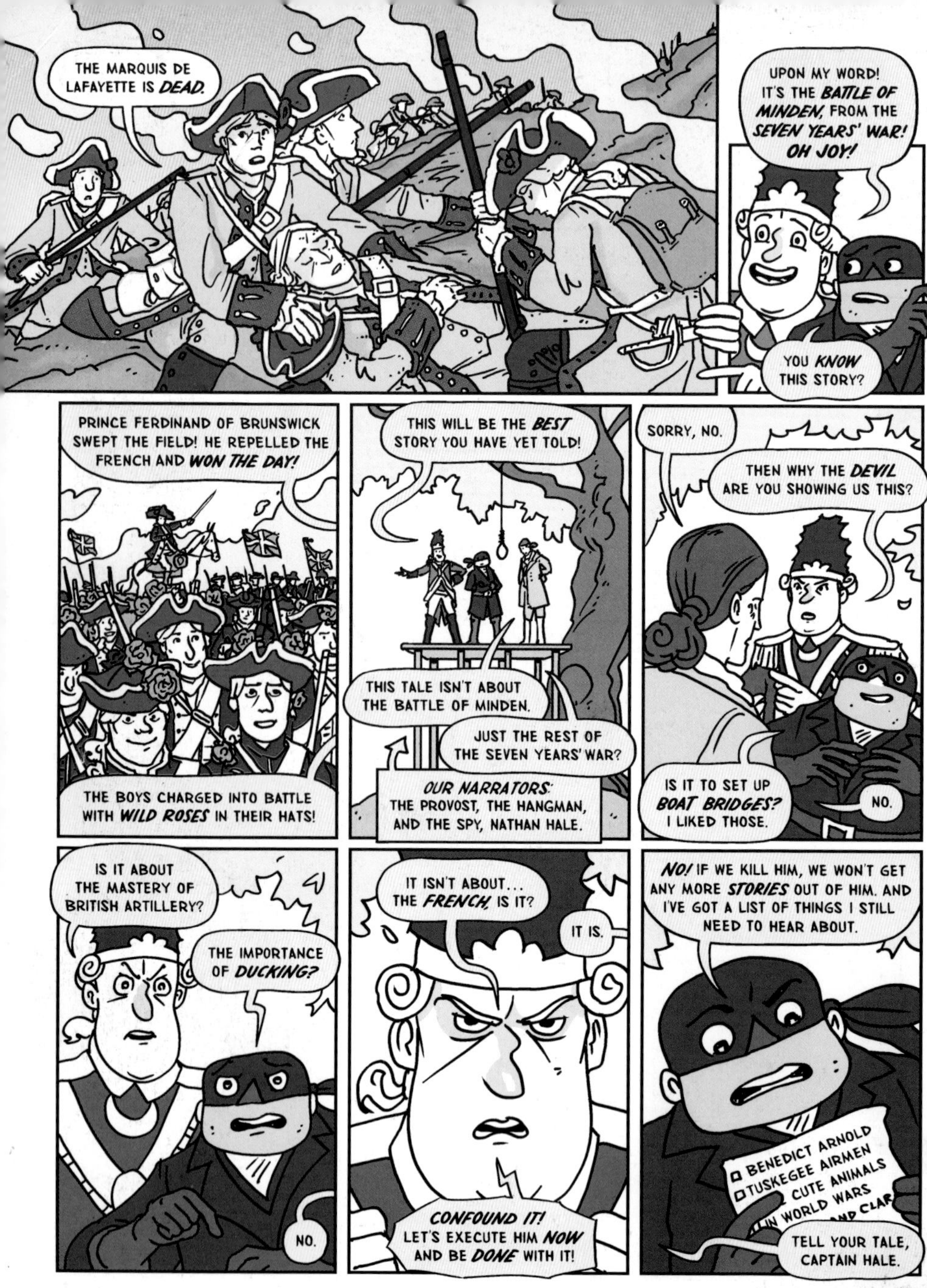
THE MARQUIS DE LAFAYETTE IS *DEAD.*
UPON MY WORD! IT'S THE *BATTLE OF MINDEN,* FROM THE *SEVEN YEARS' WAR! OH JOY!*
YOU *KNOW* THIS STORY?
PRINCE FERDINAND OF BRUNSWICK SWEPT THE FIELD! HE REPELLED THE FRENCH AND *WON THE DAY!*
THE BOYS CHARGED INTO BATTLE WITH *WILD ROSES* IN THEIR HATS!
THIS WILL BE THE *BEST* STORY YOU HAVE YET TOLD!
THIS TALE ISN'T ABOUT THE BATTLE OF MINDEN.
JUST THE REST OF THE SEVEN YEARS' WAR?
OUR NARRATORS: THE PROVOST, THE HANGMAN, AND THE SPY, NATHAN HALE.
SORRY, NO.
THEN WHY THE *DEVIL* ARE YOU SHOWING US THIS?
IS IT TO SET UP *BOAT BRIDGES?* I LIKED THOSE.
NO.
IS IT ABOUT THE MASTERY OF BRITISH ARTILLERY?
THE IMPORTANCE OF *DUCKING?*
NO.
IT ISN'T ABOUT... THE *FRENCH,* IS IT?
IT IS.
CONFOUND IT! LET'S EXECUTE HIM *NOW* AND BE *DONE* WITH IT!
NO! IF WE KILL HIM, WE WON'T GET ANY MORE *STORIES* OUT OF HIM. AND I'VE GOT A LIST OF THINGS I STILL NEED TO HEAR ABOUT.
BENEDICT ARNOLD
TUSKEGEE AIRMEN
CUTE ANIMALS
IN WORLD WARS
TELL YOUR TALE, CAPTAIN HALE.

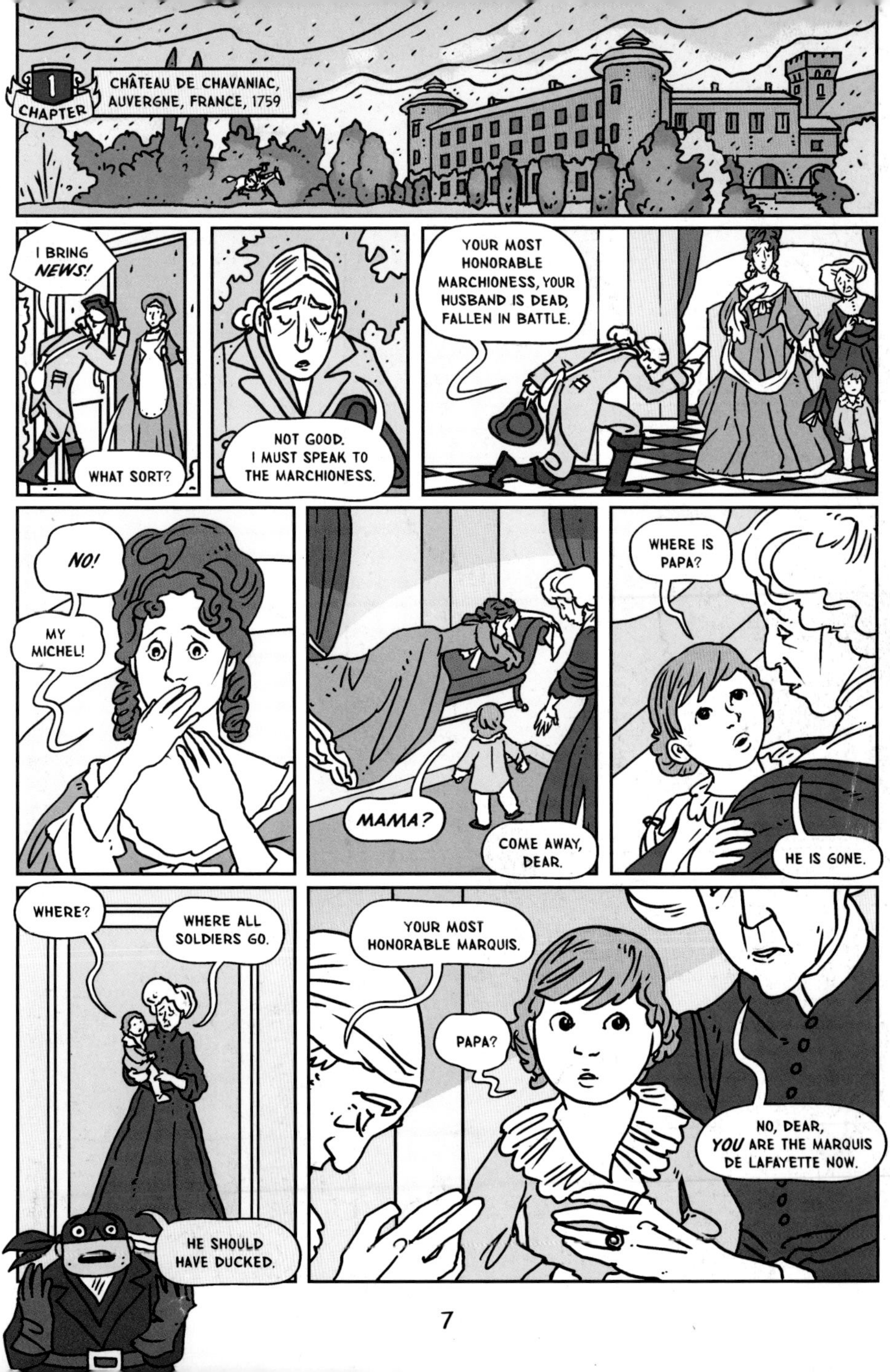
CHAPTER 1
CHÂTEAU DE CHAVANIAC, AUVERGNE, FRANCE, 1759
I BRING *NEWS!*
WHAT SORT?
NOT GOOD. I MUST SPEAK TO THE MARCHIONESS.
YOUR MOST HONORABLE MARCHIONESS, YOUR HUSBAND IS DEAD, FALLEN IN BATTLE.
NO!
MY MICHEL!
MAMA?
COME AWAY, DEAR.
WHERE IS PAPA?
HE IS GONE.
WHERE?
WHERE ALL SOLDIERS GO.
HE SHOULD HAVE DUCKED.
YOUR MOST HONORABLE MARQUIS.
PAPA?
NO, DEAR, *YOU* ARE THE MARQUIS DE LAFAYETTE NOW.

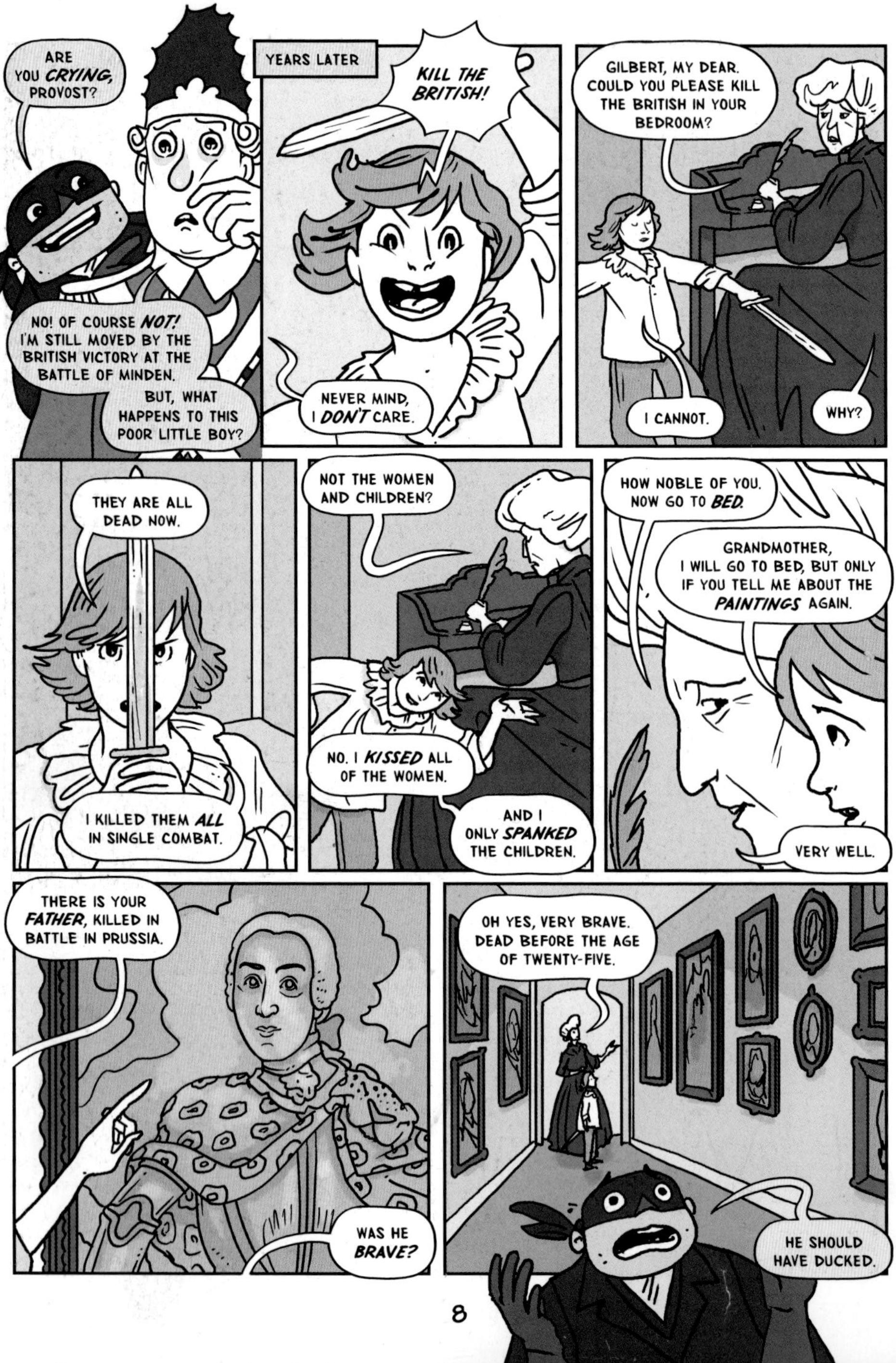
ARE YOU CRYING, PROVOST?
NO! OF COURSE NOT! I'M STILL MOVED BY THE BRITISH VICTORY AT THE BATTLE OF MINDEN.
BUT, WHAT HAPPENS TO THIS POOR LITTLE BOY?
YEARS LATER
KILL THE BRITISH!
NEVER MIND, I DON'T CARE.
GILBERT, MY DEAR. COULD YOU PLEASE KILL THE BRITISH IN YOUR BEDROOM?
I CANNOT.
WHY?
THEY ARE ALL DEAD NOW.
I KILLED THEM ALL IN SINGLE COMBAT.
NOT THE WOMEN AND CHILDREN?
NO. I KISSED ALL OF THE WOMEN.
AND I ONLY SPANKED THE CHILDREN.
HOW NOBLE OF YOU. NOW GO TO BED.
GRANDMOTHER, I WILL GO TO BED, BUT ONLY IF YOU TELL ME ABOUT THE PAINTINGS AGAIN.
VERY WELL.
THERE IS YOUR FATHER, KILLED IN BATTLE IN PRUSSIA.
WAS HE BRAVE?
OH YES, VERY BRAVE. DEAD BEFORE THE AGE OF TWENTY-FIVE.
HE SHOULD HAVE DUCKED.

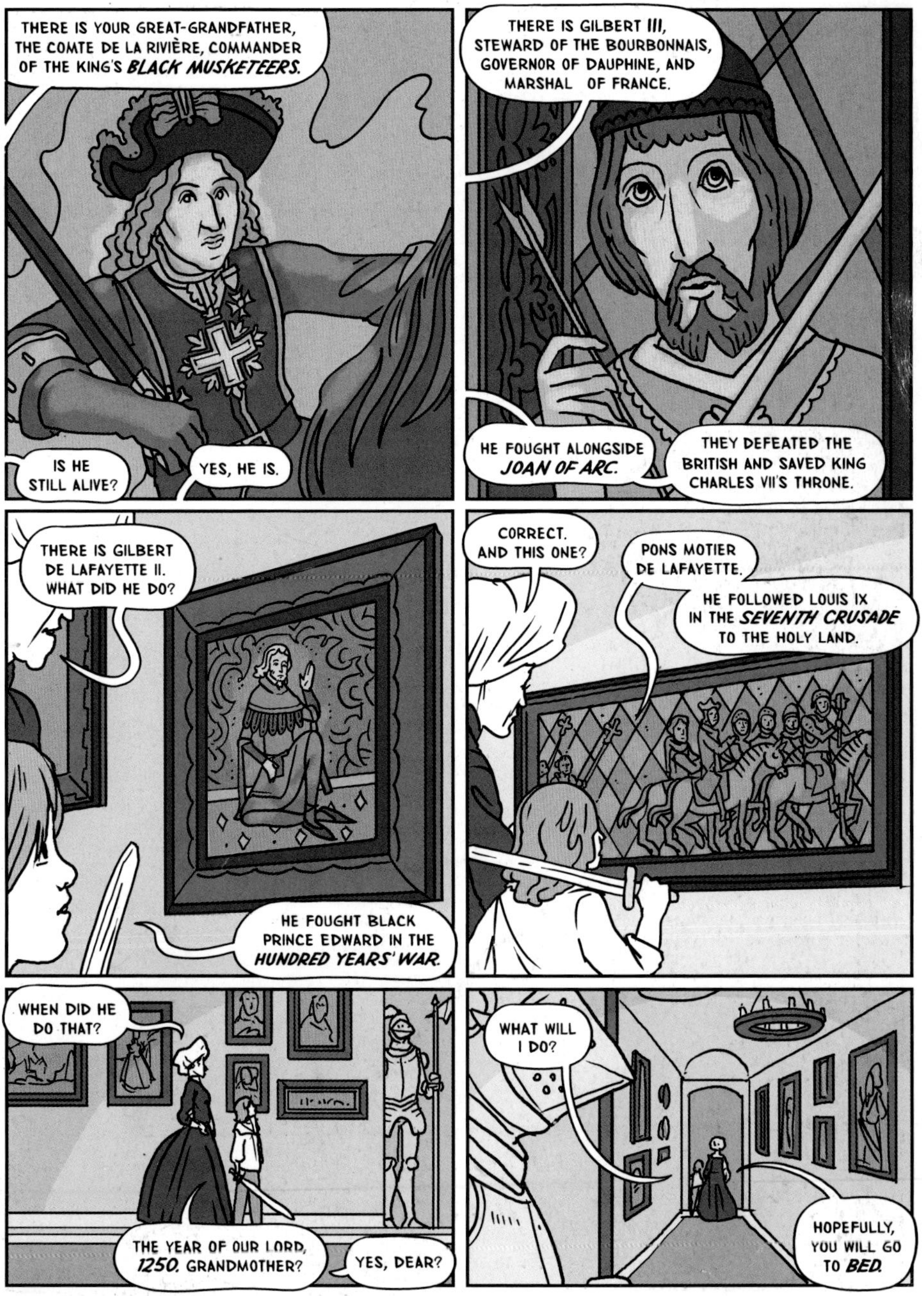
THERE IS YOUR GREAT-GRANDFATHER, THE COMTE DE LA RIVIÈRE, COMMANDER OF THE KING'S BLACK MUSKETEERS.
IS HE STILL ALIVE?
YES, HE IS.
THERE IS GILBERT III, STEWARD OF THE BOURBONNAIS, GOVERNOR OF DAUPHINE, AND MARSHAL OF FRANCE.
HE FOUGHT ALONGSIDE JOAN OF ARC.
THEY DEFEATED THE BRITISH AND SAVED KING CHARLES VII'S THRONE.
THERE IS GILBERT DE LAFAYETTE II. WHAT DID HE DO?
HE FOUGHT BLACK PRINCE EDWARD IN THE HUNDRED YEARS' WAR.
CORRECT. AND THIS ONE?
PONS MOTIER DE LAFAYETTE.
HE FOLLOWED LOUIS IX IN THE SEVENTH CRUSADE TO THE HOLY LAND.
WHEN DID HE DO THAT?
THE YEAR OF OUR LORD, 1250. GRANDMOTHER?
YES, DEAR?
WHAT WILL I DO?
HOPEFULLY, YOU WILL GO TO BED.

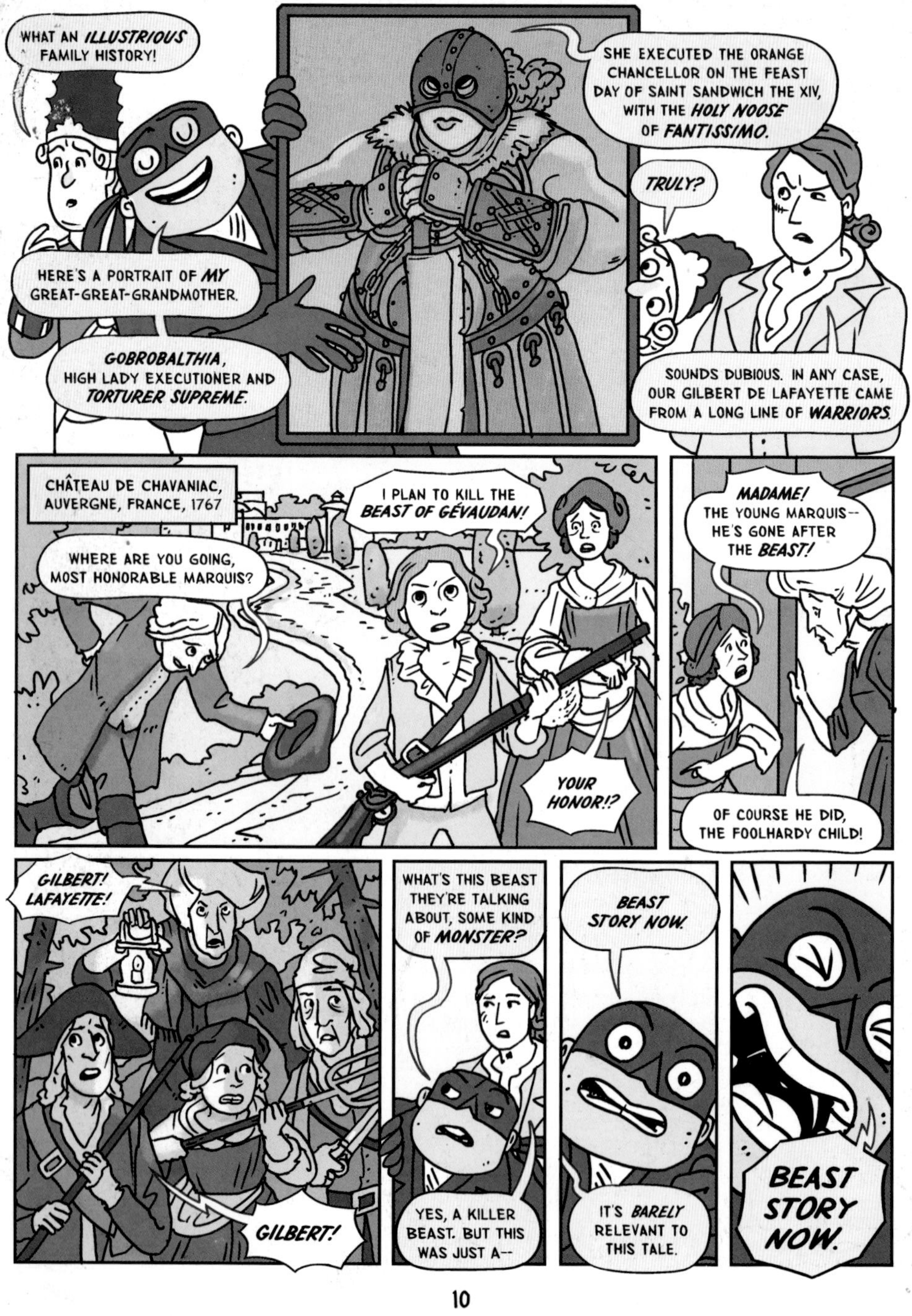

WHAT AN *ILLUSTRIOUS* FAMILY HISTORY!
HERE'S A PORTRAIT OF *MY* GREAT-GREAT-GRANDMOTHER.
GOBROBALTHIA, HIGH LADY EXECUTIONER AND *TORTURER SUPREME.*
SHE EXECUTED THE ORANGE CHANCELLOR ON THE FEAST DAY OF SAINT SANDWICH THE XIV, WITH THE *HOLY NOOSE* OF *FANTISSIMO.*
TRULY?
SOUNDS DUBIOUS. IN ANY CASE, OUR GILBERT DE LAFAYETTE CAME FROM A LONG LINE OF *WARRIORS.*
CHÂTEAU DE CHAVANIAC, AUVERGNE, FRANCE, 1767
WHERE ARE YOU GOING, MOST HONORABLE MARQUIS?
I PLAN TO KILL THE *BEAST OF GÉVAUDAN!*
YOUR HONOR!?
MADAME! THE YOUNG MARQUIS-- HE'S GONE AFTER THE *BEAST!*
OF COURSE HE DID, THE FOOLHARDY CHILD!
GILBERT! LAFAYETTE!
GILBERT!
WHAT'S THIS BEAST THEY'RE TALKING ABOUT, SOME KIND OF *MONSTER?*
YES, A KILLER BEAST. BUT THIS WAS JUST A--
BEAST STORY NOW.
IT'S *BARELY* RELEVANT TO THIS TALE.
BEAST STORY NOW.

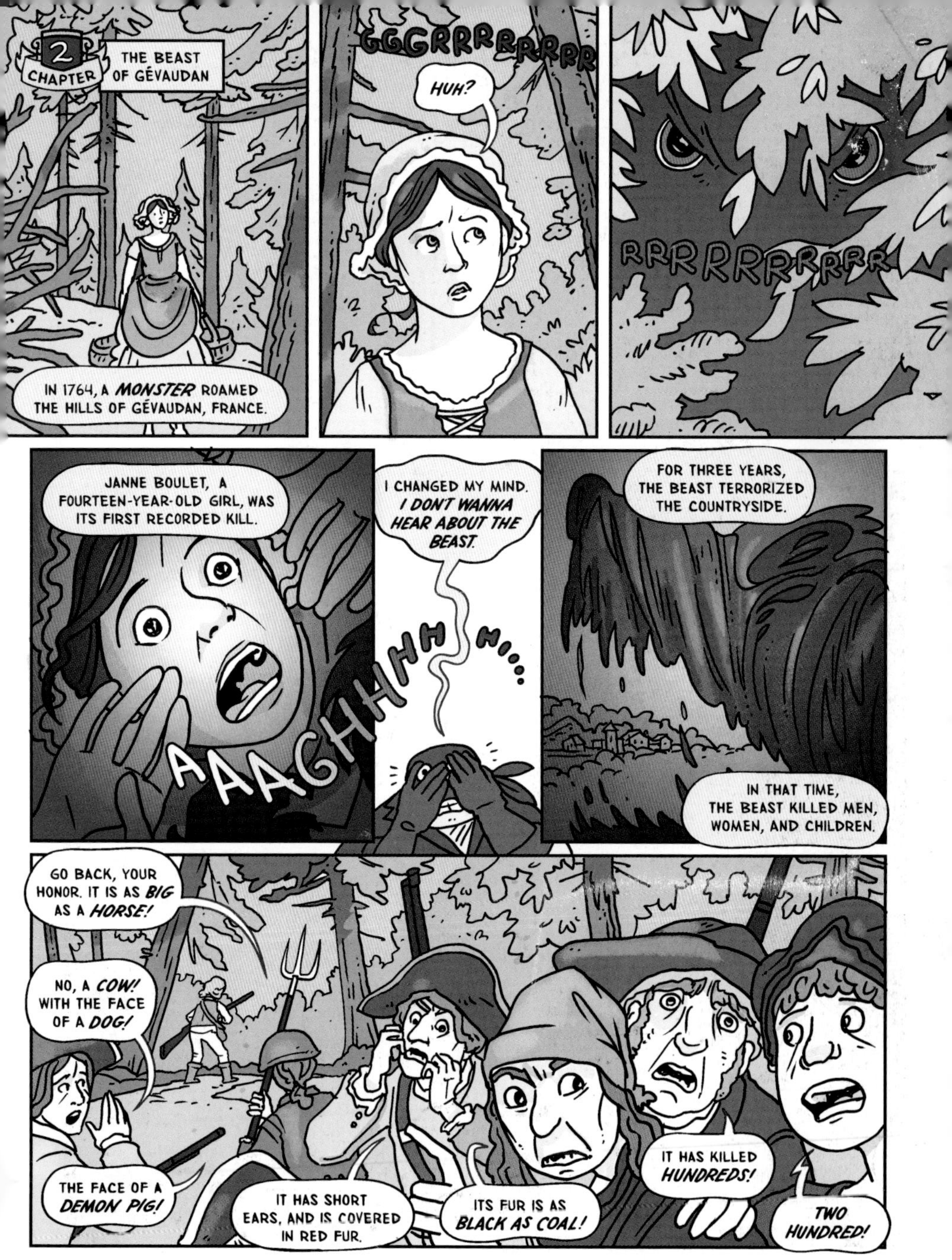
2 CHAPTER
THE BEAST OF GÉVAUDAN
IN 1764, A MONSTER ROAMED THE HILLS OF GÉVAUDAN, FRANCE.
GGGRRRRRRRRR
HUH?
RRRRRRRRRRRR
JANNE BOULET, A FOURTEEN-YEAR-OLD GIRL, WAS ITS FIRST RECORDED KILL.
AAAGHHHHH
I CHANGED MY MIND. I DON'T WANNA HEAR ABOUT THE BEAST.
Hiii...
FOR THREE YEARS, THE BEAST TERRORIZED THE COUNTRYSIDE.
IN THAT TIME, THE BEAST KILLED MEN, WOMEN, AND CHILDREN.
GO BACK, YOUR HONOR. IT IS AS BIG AS A HORSE!
NO, A COW! WITH THE FACE OF A DOG!
THE FACE OF A DEMON PIG!
IT HAS SHORT EARS, AND IS COVERED IN RED FUR.
ITS FUR IS AS BLACK AS COAL!
IT HAS KILLED HUNDREDS!
TWO HUNDRED!

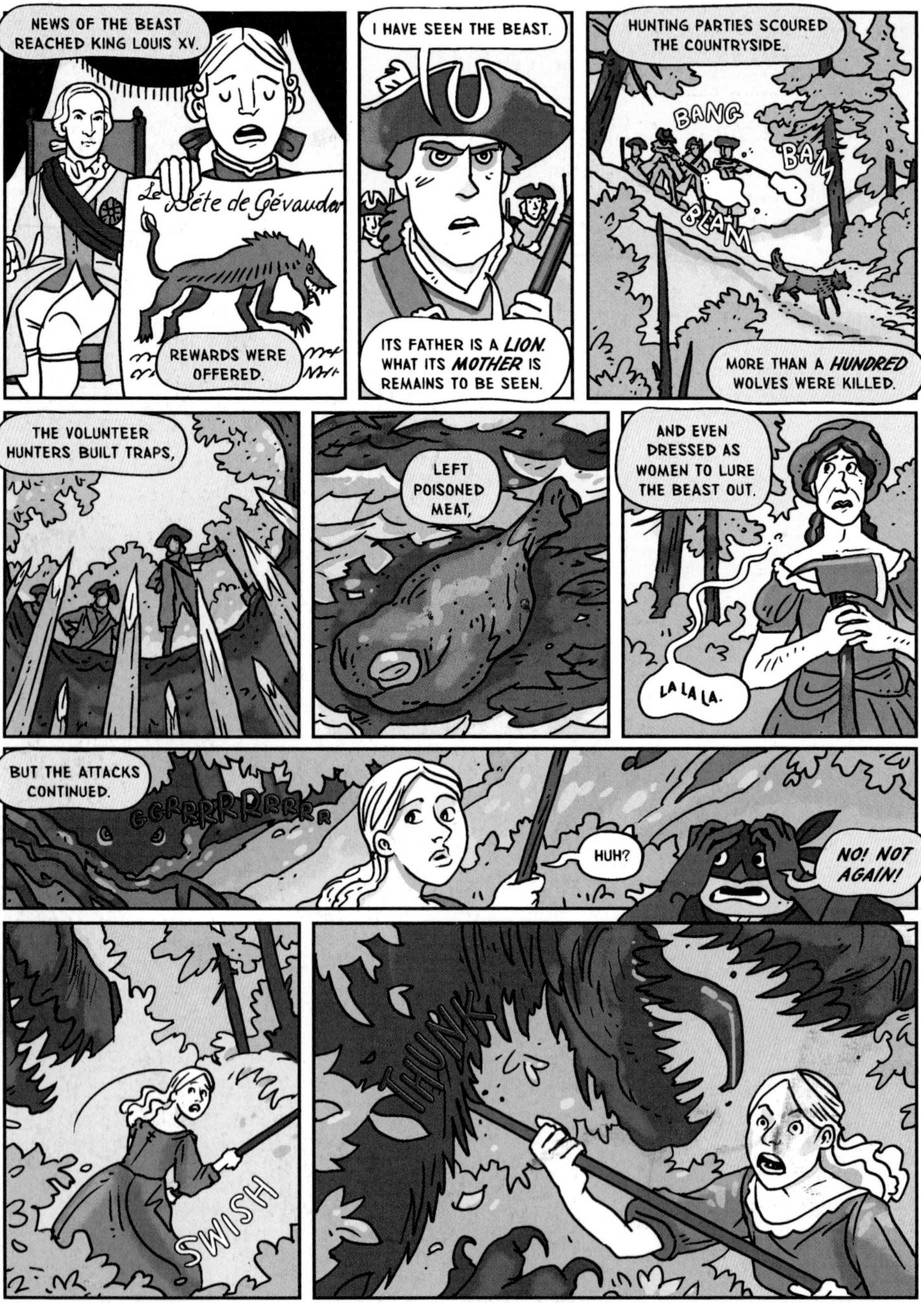
NEWS OF THE BEAST REACHED KING LOUIS XV.
Le Bête de Gévaudan
REWARDS WERE OFFERED.
I HAVE SEEN THE BEAST.
ITS FATHER IS A *LION*. WHAT ITS *MOTHER* IS REMAINS TO BE SEEN.
HUNTING PARTIES SCOURED THE COUNTRYSIDE.
BANG
BAM
BLAM
MORE THAN A *HUNDRED* WOLVES WERE KILLED.
THE VOLUNTEER HUNTERS BUILT TRAPS,
LEFT POISONED MEAT,
AND EVEN DRESSED AS WOMEN TO LURE THE BEAST OUT.
LA LA LA.
BUT THE ATTACKS CONTINUED.
GGRRRRRRRRRRR
HUH?
NO! NOT AGAIN!
SWISH
THUNK

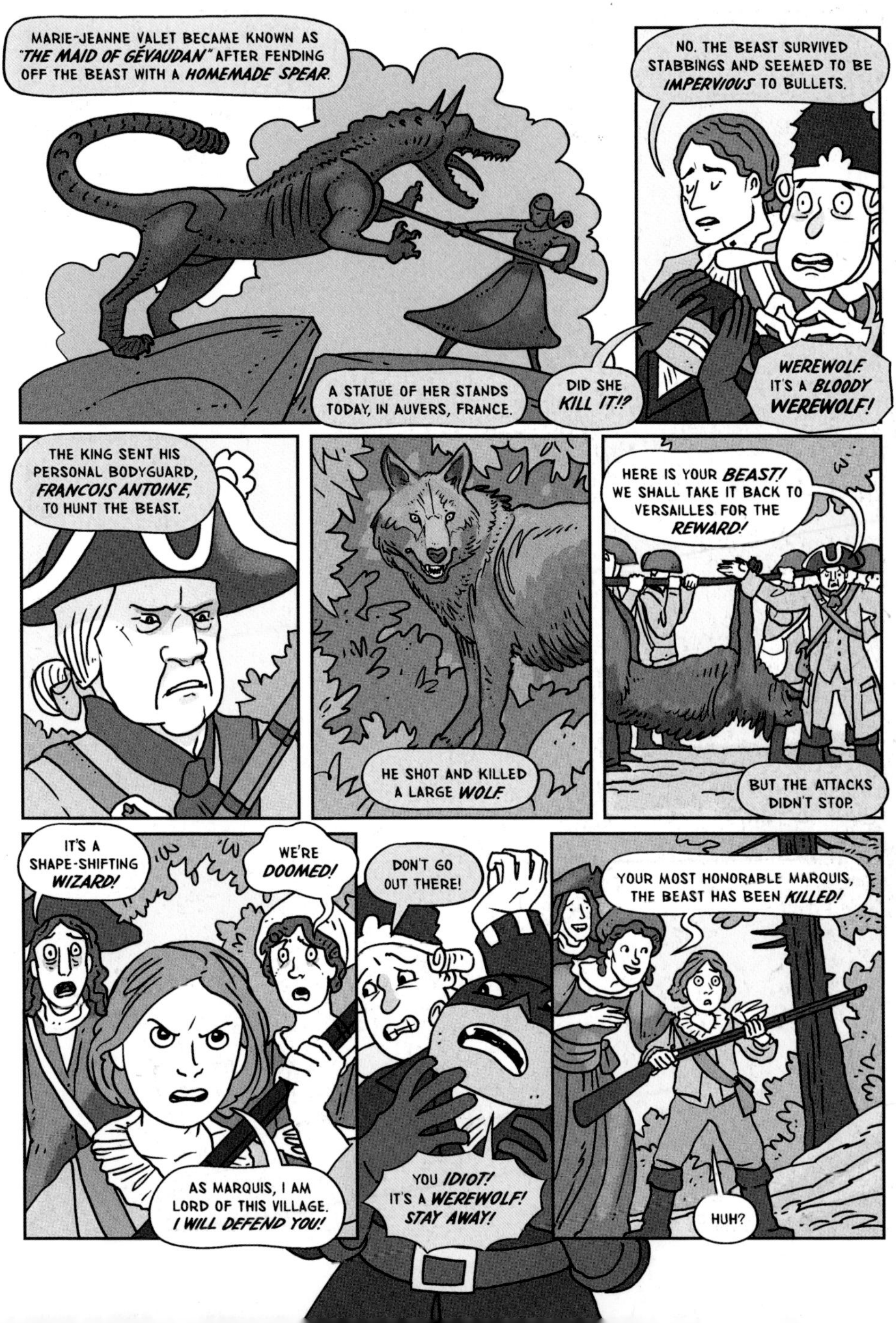

MARIE-JEANNE VALET BECAME KNOWN AS "THE MAID OF GÉVAUDAN" AFTER FENDING OFF THE BEAST WITH A HOMEMADE SPEAR.
A STATUE OF HER STANDS TODAY, IN AUVERS, FRANCE.
DID SHE KILL IT!?
NO. THE BEAST SURVIVED STABBINGS AND SEEMED TO BE IMPERVIOUS TO BULLETS.
WEREWOLF. IT'S A BLOODY WEREWOLF!
THE KING SENT HIS PERSONAL BODYGUARD, FRANCOIS ANTOINE, TO HUNT THE BEAST.
HE SHOT AND KILLED A LARGE WOLF.
HERE IS YOUR BEAST! WE SHALL TAKE IT BACK TO VERSAILLES FOR THE REWARD!
BUT THE ATTACKS DIDN'T STOP.
IT'S A SHAPE-SHIFTING WIZARD!
WE'RE DOOMED!
AS MARQUIS, I AM LORD OF THIS VILLAGE. I WILL DEFEND YOU!
DON'T GO OUT THERE!
YOU IDIOT! IT'S A WEREWOLF! STAY AWAY!
YOUR MOST HONORABLE MARQUIS, THE BEAST HAS BEEN KILLED!
HUH?

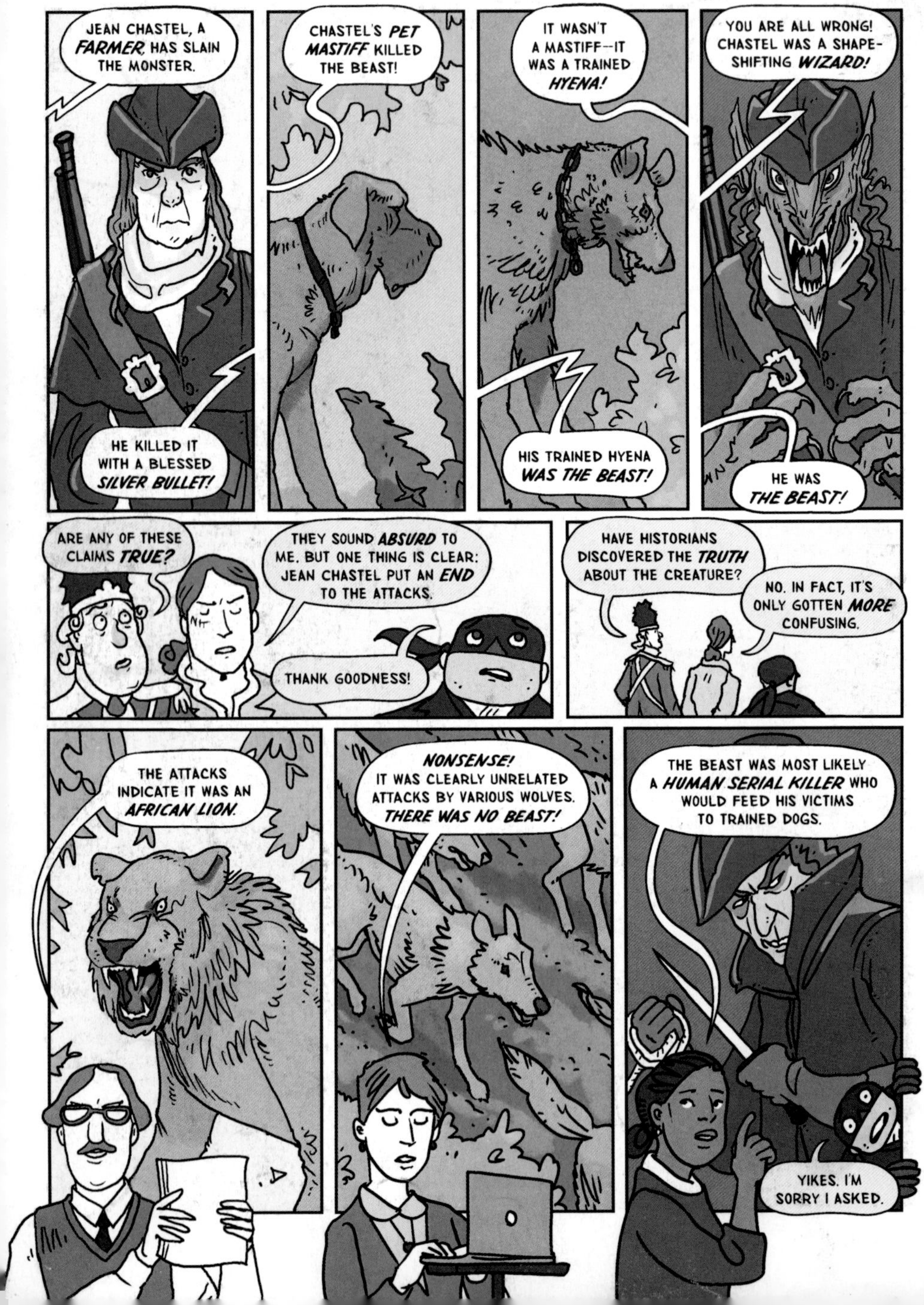
JEAN CHASTEL, A *FARMER*, HAS SLAIN THE MONSTER.
HE KILLED IT WITH A BLESSED *SILVER BULLET!*
CHASTEL'S *PET MASTIFF* KILLED THE BEAST!
IT WASN'T A MASTIFF--IT WAS A TRAINED *HYENA!*
HIS TRAINED HYENA *WAS THE BEAST!*
YOU ARE ALL WRONG! CHASTEL WAS A SHAPE-SHIFTING *WIZARD!*
HE WAS *THE BEAST!*
ARE ANY OF THESE CLAIMS *TRUE?*
THEY SOUND *ABSURD* TO ME. BUT ONE THING IS CLEAR: JEAN CHASTEL PUT AN *END* TO THE ATTACKS.
THANK GOODNESS!
HAVE HISTORIANS DISCOVERED THE *TRUTH* ABOUT THE CREATURE?
NO. IN FACT, IT'S ONLY GOTTEN *MORE* CONFUSING.
THE ATTACKS INDICATE IT WAS AN *AFRICAN LION.*
NONSENSE! IT WAS CLEARLY UNRELATED ATTACKS BY VARIOUS WOLVES. *THERE WAS NO BEAST!*
THE BEAST WAS MOST LIKELY A *HUMAN SERIAL KILLER* WHO WOULD FEED HIS VICTIMS TO TRAINED DOGS.
YIKES. I'M SORRY I ASKED.

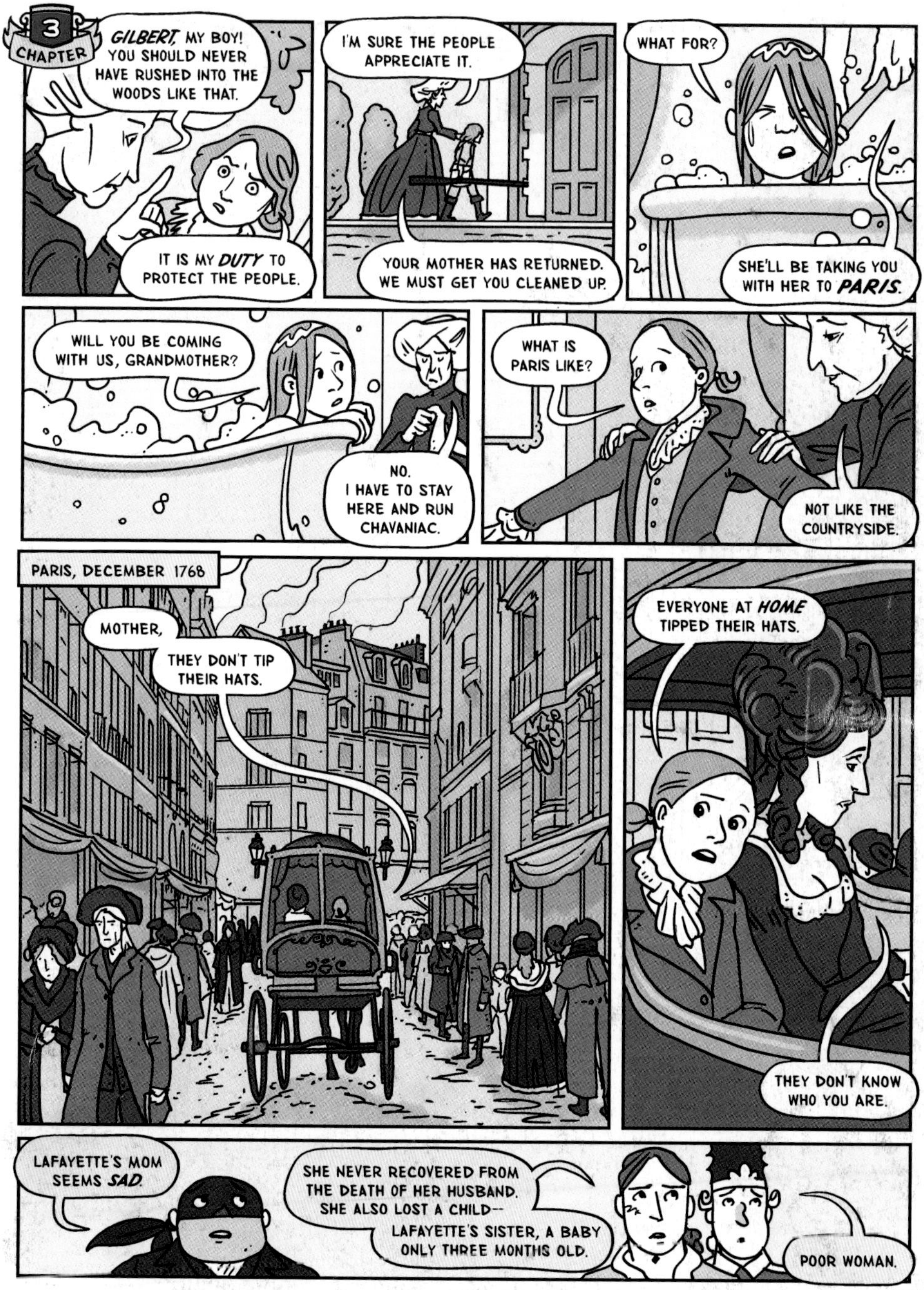
3
CHAPTER
GILBERT, MY BOY! YOU SHOULD NEVER HAVE RUSHED INTO THE WOODS LIKE THAT.
IT IS MY DUTY TO PROTECT THE PEOPLE.
I'M SURE THE PEOPLE APPRECIATE IT.
YOUR MOTHER HAS RETURNED. WE MUST GET YOU CLEANED UP.
WHAT FOR?
SHE'LL BE TAKING YOU WITH HER TO PARIS.
WILL YOU BE COMING WITH US, GRANDMOTHER?
NO. I HAVE TO STAY HERE AND RUN CHAVANIAC.
WHAT IS PARIS LIKE?
NOT LIKE THE COUNTRYSIDE.
PARIS, DECEMBER 1768
MOTHER,
THEY DON'T TIP THEIR HATS.
EVERYONE AT HOME TIPPED THEIR HATS.
THEY DON'T KNOW WHO YOU ARE.
LAFAYETTE'S MOM SEEMS SAD.
SHE NEVER RECOVERED FROM THE DEATH OF HER HUSBAND. SHE ALSO LOST A CHILD--
LAFAYETTE'S SISTER, A BABY ONLY THREE MONTHS OLD.
POOR WOMAN.

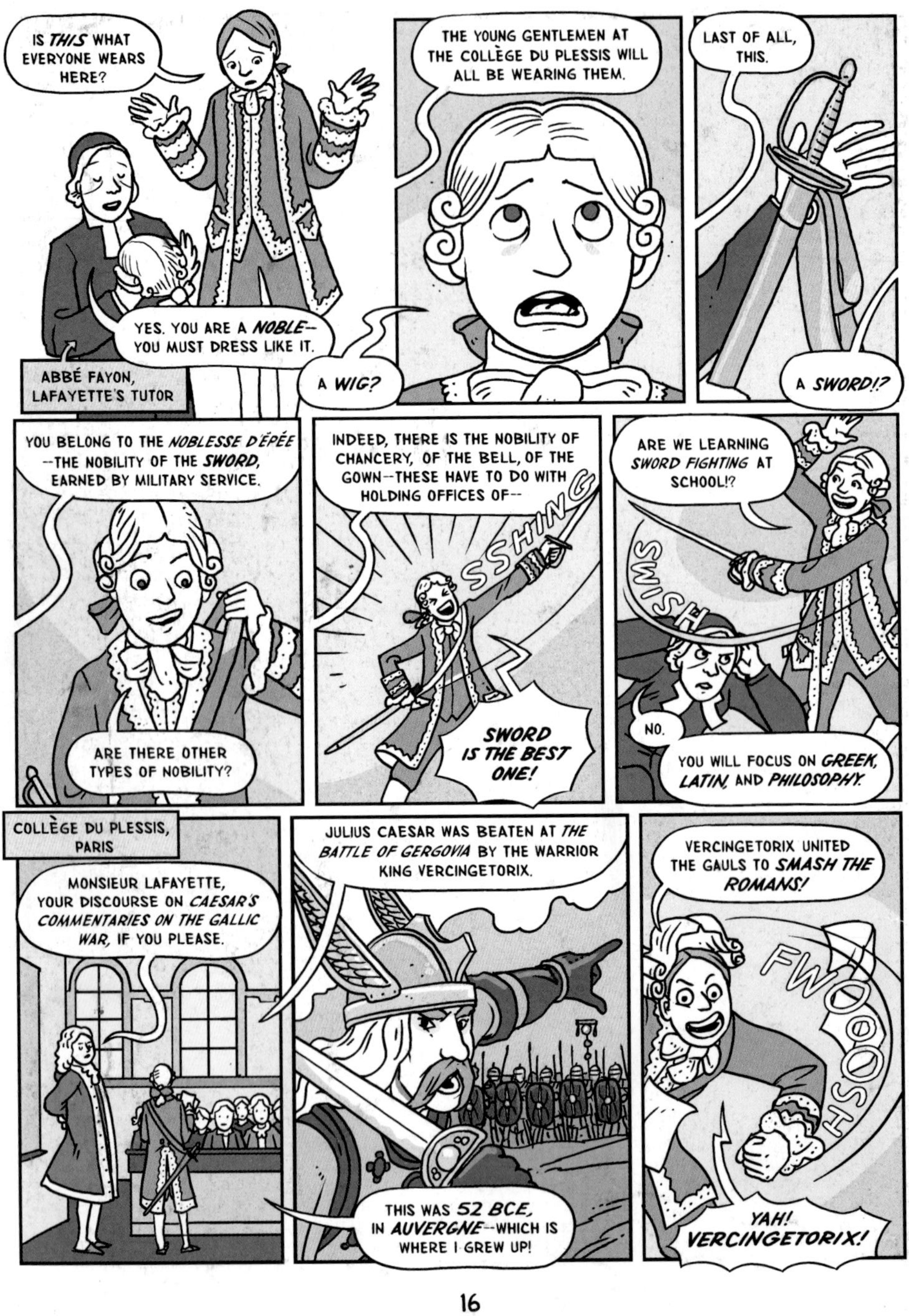
IS THIS WHAT EVERYONE WEARS HERE?
YES. YOU ARE A NOBLE--YOU MUST DRESS LIKE IT.
ABBÉ FAYON, LAFAYETTE'S TUTOR
THE YOUNG GENTLEMEN AT THE COLLÈGE DU PLESSIS WILL ALL BE WEARING THEM.
A WIG?
LAST OF ALL, THIS.
A SWORD!?
YOU BELONG TO THE NOBLESSE D'ÉPÉE--THE NOBILITY OF THE SWORD, EARNED BY MILITARY SERVICE.
ARE THERE OTHER TYPES OF NOBILITY?
INDEED, THERE IS THE NOBILITY OF CHANCERY, OF THE BELL, OF THE GOWN--THESE HAVE TO DO WITH HOLDING OFFICES OF--
SSHING
SWORD IS THE BEST ONE!
ARE WE LEARNING SWORD FIGHTING AT SCHOOL!?
SWISH
NO.
YOU WILL FOCUS ON GREEK, LATIN, AND PHILOSOPHY.
COLLÈGE DU PLESSIS, PARIS
MONSIEUR LAFAYETTE, YOUR DISCOURSE ON CAESAR'S COMMENTARIES ON THE GALLIC WAR, IF YOU PLEASE.
JULIUS CAESAR WAS BEATEN AT THE BATTLE OF GERGOVIA BY THE WARRIOR KING VERCINGETORIX.
THIS WAS 52 BCE, IN AUVERGNE--WHICH IS WHERE I GREW UP!
VERCINGETORIX UNITED THE GAULS TO SMASH THE ROMANS!
FWOOOOSH
YAH! VERCINGETORIX!

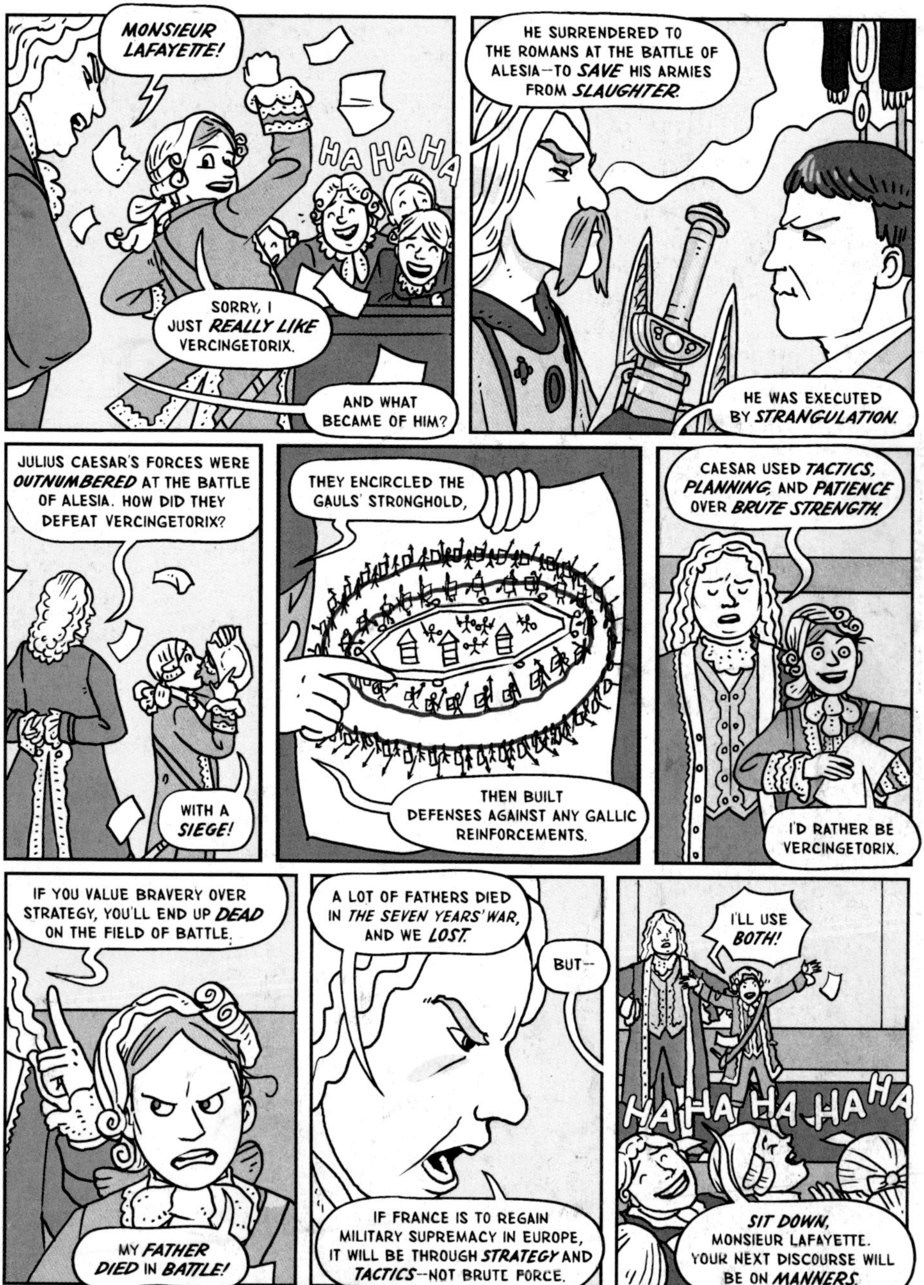
MONSIEUR LAFAYETTE!
HA HA HA
SORRY, I JUST REALLY LIKE VERCINGETORIX.
AND WHAT BECAME OF HIM?
HE SURRENDERED TO THE ROMANS AT THE BATTLE OF ALESIA--TO SAVE HIS ARMIES FROM SLAUGHTER.
HE WAS EXECUTED BY STRANGULATION.
JULIUS CAESAR'S FORCES WERE OUTNUMBERED AT THE BATTLE OF ALESIA. HOW DID THEY DEFEAT VERCINGETORIX?
WITH A SIEGE!
THEY ENCIRCLED THE GAULS' STRONGHOLD,
THEN BUILT DEFENSES AGAINST ANY GALLIC REINFORCEMENTS.
CAESAR USED TACTICS, PLANNING, AND PATIENCE OVER BRUTE STRENGTH.
I'D RATHER BE VERCINGETORIX.
IF YOU VALUE BRAVERY OVER STRATEGY, YOU'LL END UP DEAD ON THE FIELD OF BATTLE.
MY FATHER DIED IN BATTLE!
A LOT OF FATHERS DIED IN THE SEVEN YEARS' WAR, AND WE LOST.
BUT--
IF FRANCE IS TO REGAIN MILITARY SUPREMACY IN EUROPE, IT WILL BE THROUGH STRATEGY AND TACTICS--NOT BRUTE FORCE.
I'LL USE BOTH!
HA HA HA HA HA HA HA
SIT DOWN, MONSIEUR LAFAYETTE. YOUR NEXT DISCOURSE WILL BE ON MANNERS.

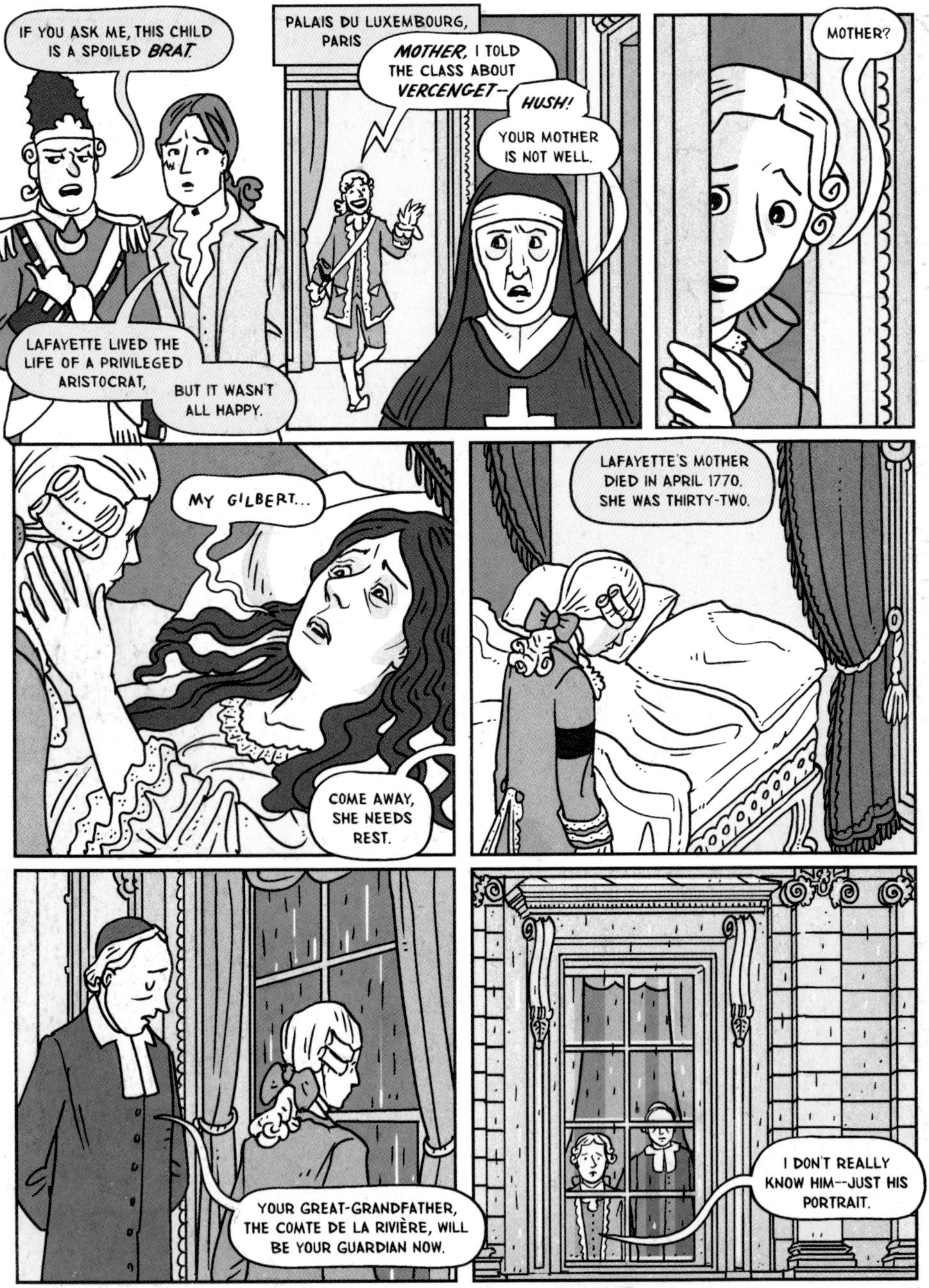
IF YOU ASK ME, THIS CHILD IS A SPOILED BRAT.
LAFAYETTE LIVED THE LIFE OF A PRIVILEGED ARISTOCRAT,
BUT IT WASN'T ALL HAPPY.
PALAIS DU LUXEMBOURG, PARIS
MOTHER, I TOLD THE CLASS ABOUT VERCENGET--
HUSH!
YOUR MOTHER IS NOT WELL.
MOTHER?
MY GILBERT...
COME AWAY, SHE NEEDS REST.
LAFAYETTE'S MOTHER DIED IN APRIL 1770. SHE WAS THIRTY-TWO.
YOUR GREAT-GRANDFATHER, THE COMTE DE LA RIVIÈRE, WILL BE YOUR GUARDIAN NOW.
I DON'T REALLY KNOW HIM--JUST HIS PORTRAIT.

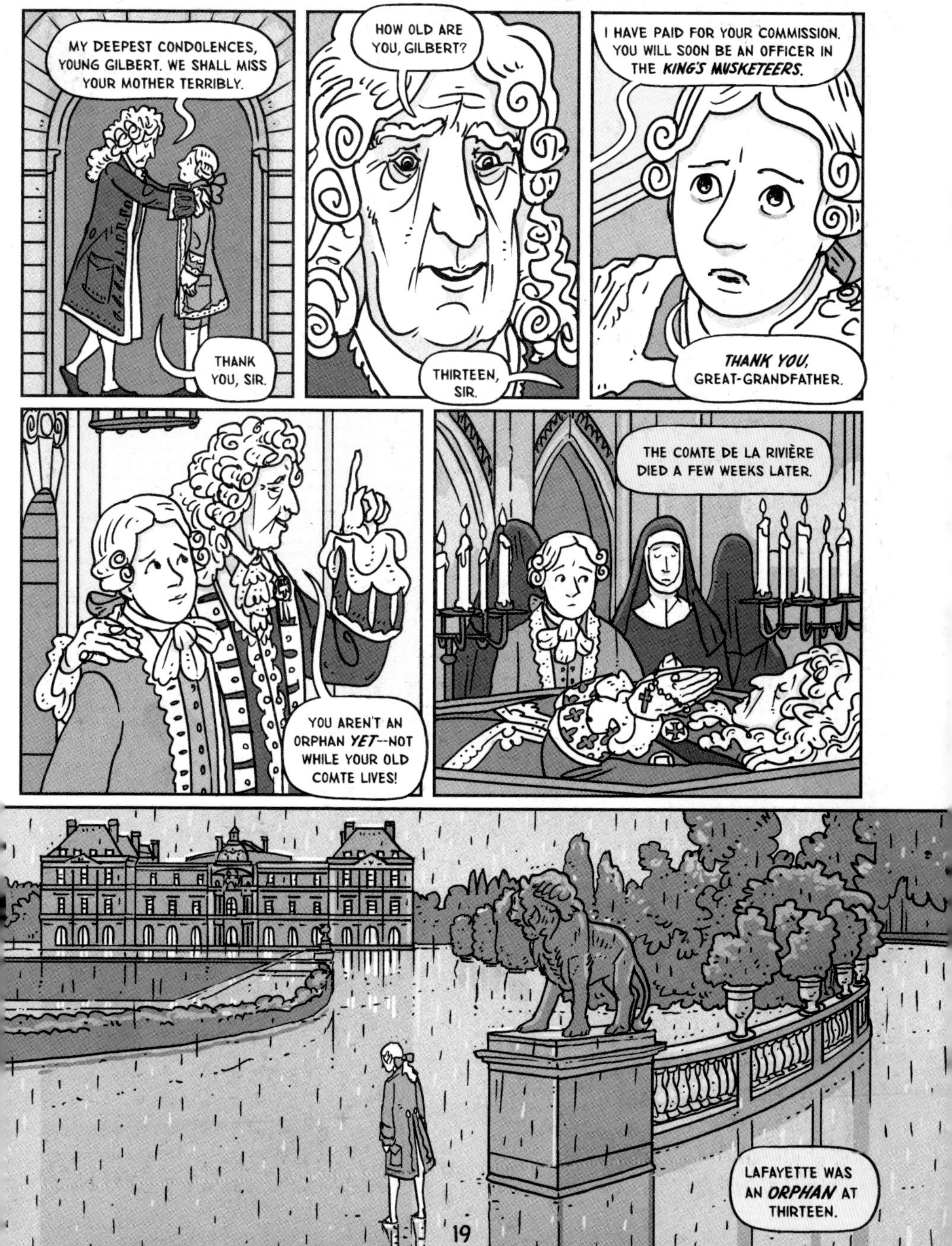
MY DEEPEST CONDOLENCES, YOUNG GILBERT. WE SHALL MISS YOUR MOTHER TERRIBLY.
THANK YOU, SIR.
HOW OLD ARE YOU, GILBERT?
THIRTEEN, SIR.
I HAVE PAID FOR YOUR COMMISSION. YOU WILL SOON BE AN OFFICER IN THE *KING'S MUSKETEERS.*
THANK YOU, GREAT-GRANDFATHER.
YOU AREN'T AN ORPHAN *YET*--NOT WHILE YOUR OLD COMTE LIVES!
THE COMTE DE LA RIVIÈRE DIED A FEW WEEKS LATER.
LAFAYETTE WAS AN *ORPHAN* AT THIRTEEN.

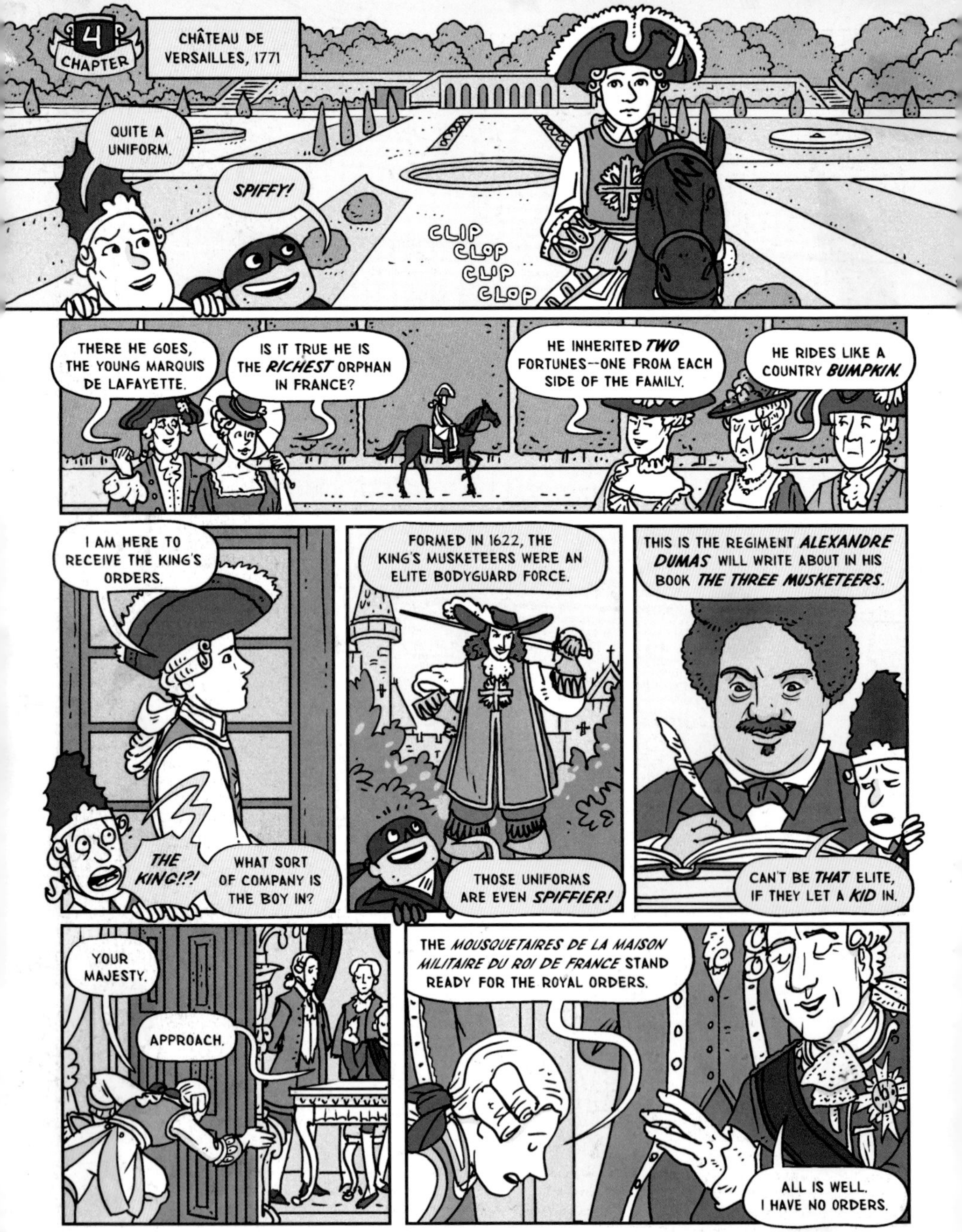
4
CHAPTER
CHÂTEAU DE VERSAILLES, 1771
QUITE A UNIFORM.
SPIFFY!
CLIP CLOP CLIP CLOP
THERE HE GOES, THE YOUNG MARQUIS DE LAFAYETTE.
IS IT TRUE HE IS THE RICHEST ORPHAN IN FRANCE?
HE INHERITED TWO FORTUNES--ONE FROM EACH SIDE OF THE FAMILY.
HE RIDES LIKE A COUNTRY BUMPKIN.
I AM HERE TO RECEIVE THE KING'S ORDERS.
THE KING!?!
WHAT SORT OF COMPANY IS THE BOY IN?
FORMED IN 1622, THE KING'S MUSKETEERS WERE AN ELITE BODYGUARD FORCE.
THOSE UNIFORMS ARE EVEN SPIFFIER!
THIS IS THE REGIMENT ALEXANDRE DUMAS WILL WRITE ABOUT IN HIS BOOK THE THREE MUSKETEERS.
CAN'T BE THAT ELITE, IF THEY LET A KID IN.
YOUR MAJESTY.
APPROACH.
THE MOUSQUETAIRES DE LA MAISON MILITAIRE DU ROI DE FRANCE STAND READY FOR THE ROYAL ORDERS.
ALL IS WELL. I HAVE NO ORDERS.

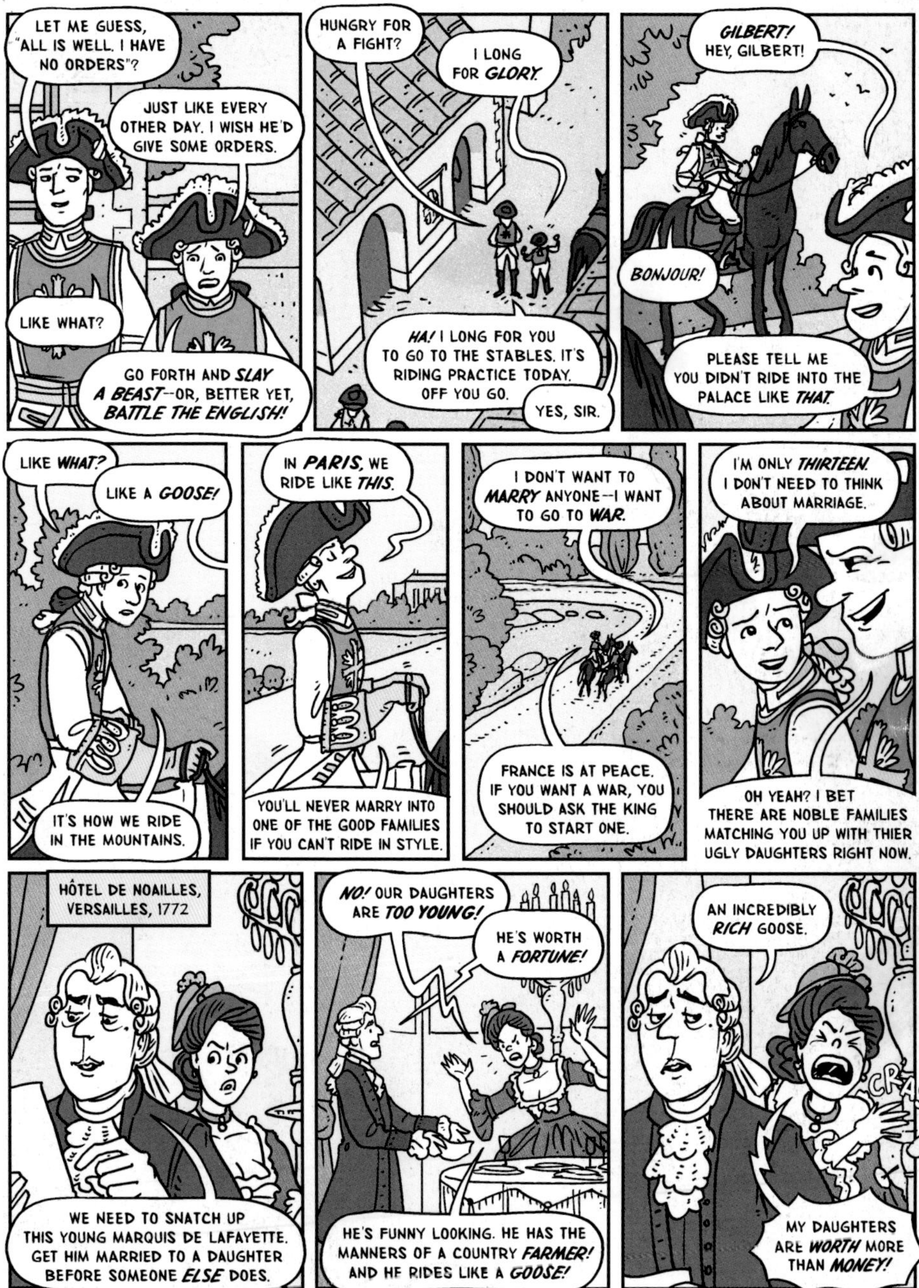
LET ME GUESS, "ALL IS WELL. I HAVE NO ORDERS"?
JUST LIKE EVERY OTHER DAY. I WISH HE'D GIVE SOME ORDERS.
LIKE WHAT?
GO FORTH AND SLAY A BEAST--OR, BETTER YET, BATTLE THE ENGLISH!
HUNGRY FOR A FIGHT?
I LONG FOR GLORY.
HA! I LONG FOR YOU TO GO TO THE STABLES. IT'S RIDING PRACTICE TODAY. OFF YOU GO.
YES, SIR.
GILBERT! HEY, GILBERT!
BONJOUR!
PLEASE TELL ME YOU DIDN'T RIDE INTO THE PALACE LIKE THAT.
LIKE WHAT?
LIKE A GOOSE!
IT'S HOW WE RIDE IN THE MOUNTAINS.
IN PARIS, WE RIDE LIKE THIS.
YOU'LL NEVER MARRY INTO ONE OF THE GOOD FAMILIES IF YOU CAN'T RIDE IN STYLE.
I DON'T WANT TO MARRY ANYONE--I WANT TO GO TO WAR.
FRANCE IS AT PEACE. IF YOU WANT A WAR, YOU SHOULD ASK THE KING TO START ONE.
I'M ONLY THIRTEEN. I DON'T NEED TO THINK ABOUT MARRIAGE.
OH YEAH? I BET THERE ARE NOBLE FAMILIES MATCHING YOU UP WITH THIER UGLY DAUGHTERS RIGHT NOW.
HÔTEL DE NOAILLES, VERSAILLES, 1772
WE NEED TO SNATCH UP THIS YOUNG MARQUIS DE LAFAYETTE. GET HIM MARRIED TO A DAUGHTER BEFORE SOMEONE ELSE DOES.
NO! OUR DAUGHTERS ARE TOO YOUNG!
HE'S WORTH A FORTUNE!
HE'S FUNNY LOOKING. HE HAS THE MANNERS OF A COUNTRY FARMER! AND HE RIDES LIKE A GOOSE!
AN INCREDIBLY RICH GOOSE.
MY DAUGHTERS ARE WORTH MORE THAN MONEY!
CRASH!

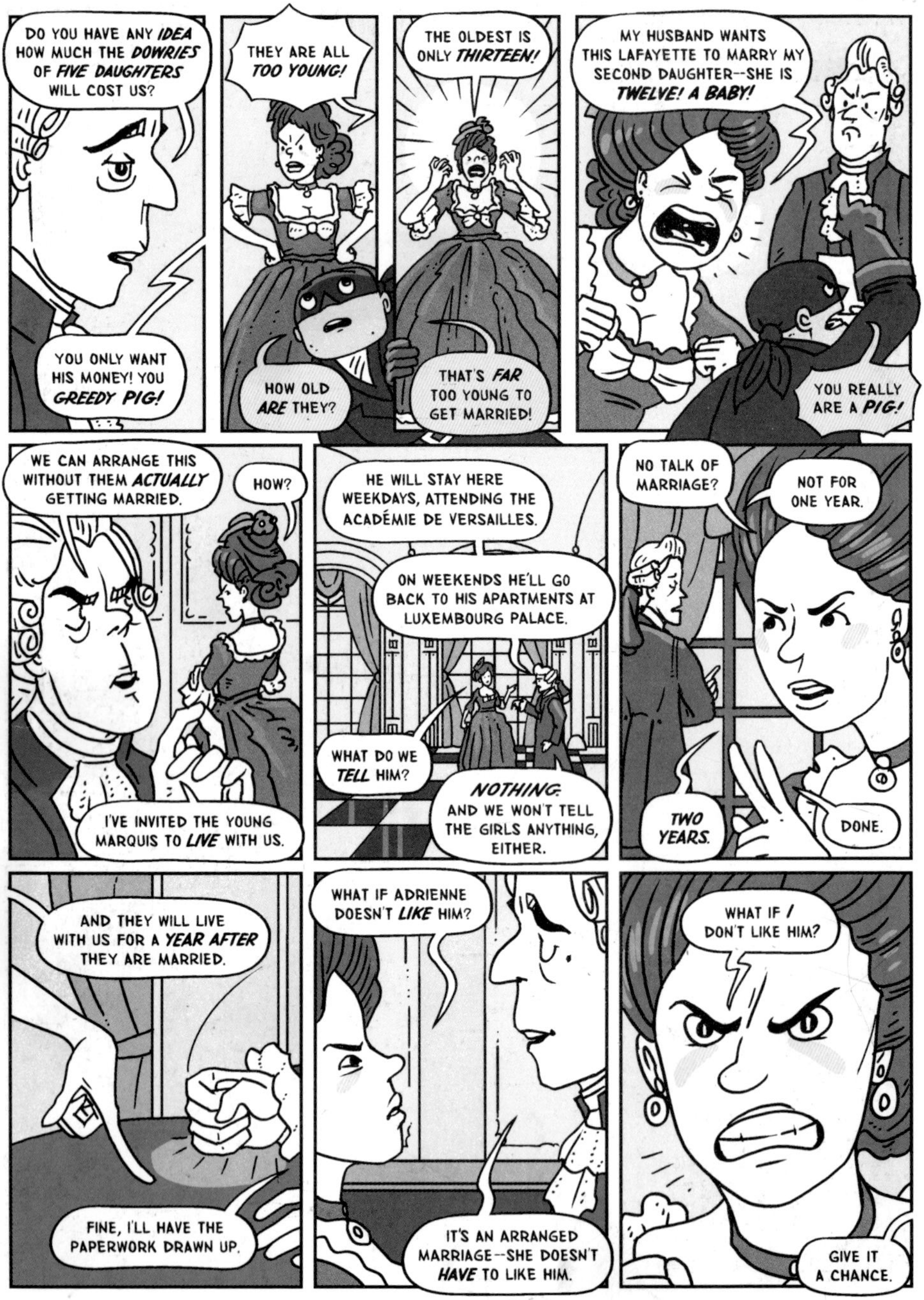
DO YOU HAVE ANY *IDEA* HOW MUCH THE *DOWRIES* OF *FIVE DAUGHTERS* WILL COST US?
YOU ONLY WANT HIS MONEY! YOU *GREEDY PIG!*
THEY ARE ALL *TOO YOUNG!*
HOW OLD *ARE* THEY?
THE OLDEST IS ONLY *THIRTEEN!*
THAT'S *FAR* TOO YOUNG TO GET MARRIED!
MY HUSBAND WANTS THIS LAFAYETTE TO MARRY MY SECOND DAUGHTER--SHE IS *TWELVE! A BABY!*
YOU REALLY ARE A *PIG!*
WE CAN ARRANGE THIS WITHOUT THEM *ACTUALLY* GETTING MARRIED.
HOW?
I'VE INVITED THE YOUNG MARQUIS TO *LIVE* WITH US.
HE WILL STAY HERE WEEKDAYS, ATTENDING THE ACADÉMIE DE VERSAILLES.
ON WEEKENDS HE'LL GO BACK TO HIS APARTMENTS AT LUXEMBOURG PALACE.
WHAT DO WE *TELL* HIM?
NOTHING. AND WE WON'T TELL THE GIRLS ANYTHING, EITHER.
NO TALK OF MARRIAGE?
NOT FOR ONE YEAR.
TWO YEARS.
DONE.
AND THEY WILL LIVE WITH US FOR A *YEAR AFTER* THEY ARE MARRIED.
FINE, I'LL HAVE THE PAPERWORK DRAWN UP.
WHAT IF ADRIENNE DOESN'T *LIKE* HIM?
IT'S AN ARRANGED MARRIAGE--SHE DOESN'T *HAVE* TO LIKE HIM.
WHAT IF *I* DON'T LIKE HIM?
GIVE IT A CHANCE.

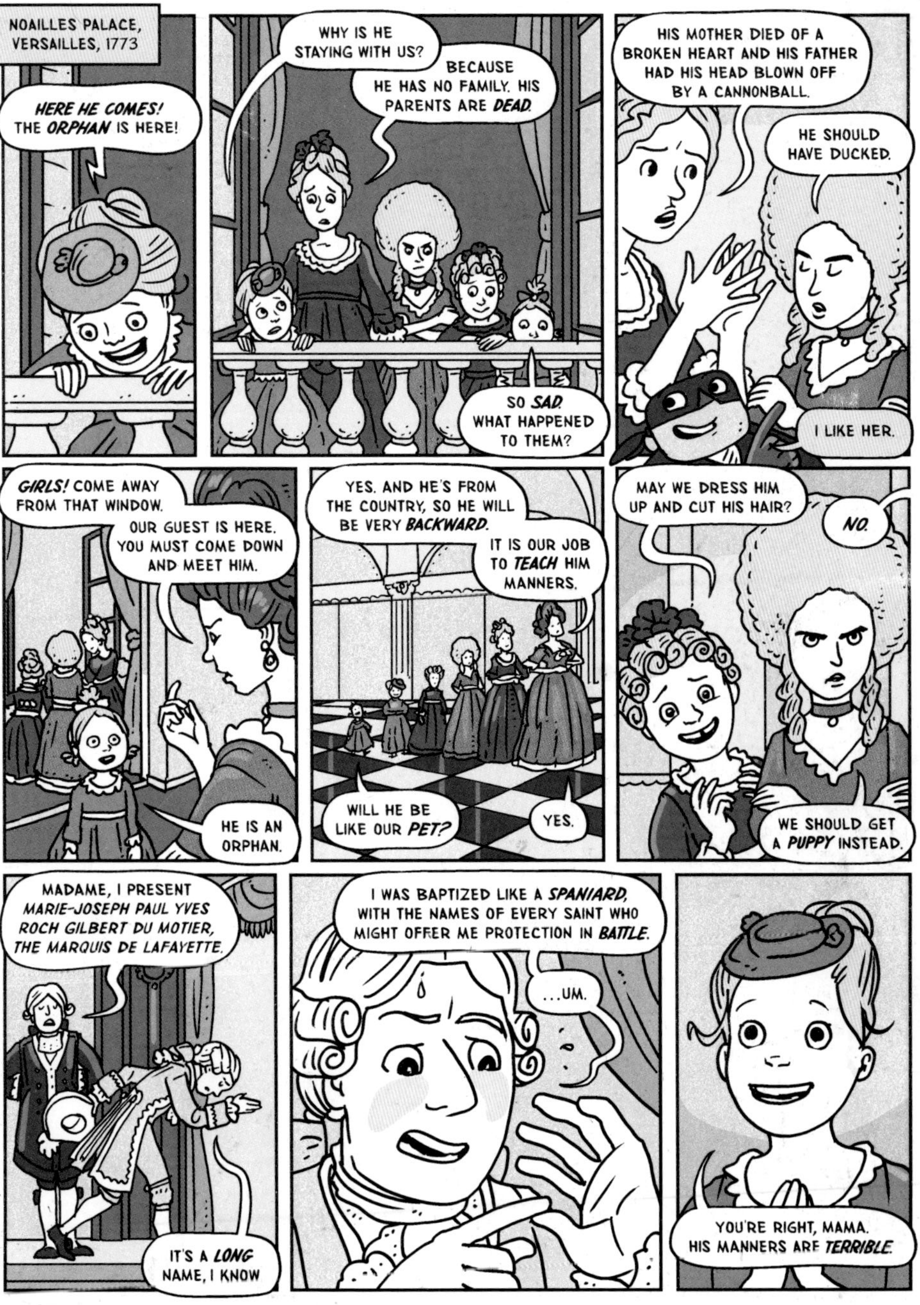
NOAILLES PALACE, VERSAILLES, 1773
HERE HE COMES! THE ORPHAN IS HERE!
WHY IS HE STAYING WITH US?
BECAUSE HE HAS NO FAMILY. HIS PARENTS ARE DEAD.
SO SAD. WHAT HAPPENED TO THEM?
HIS MOTHER DIED OF A BROKEN HEART AND HIS FATHER HAD HIS HEAD BLOWN OFF BY A CANNONBALL.
HE SHOULD HAVE DUCKED.
I LIKE HER.
GIRLS! COME AWAY FROM THAT WINDOW.
OUR GUEST IS HERE. YOU MUST COME DOWN AND MEET HIM.
HE IS AN ORPHAN.
YES. AND HE'S FROM THE COUNTRY, SO HE WILL BE VERY BACKWARD.
IT IS OUR JOB TO TEACH HIM MANNERS.
WILL HE BE LIKE OUR PET?
YES.
MAY WE DRESS HIM UP AND CUT HIS HAIR?
NO.
WE SHOULD GET A PUPPY INSTEAD.
MADAME, I PRESENT MARIE-JOSEPH PAUL YVES ROCH GILBERT DU MOTIER, THE MARQUIS DE LAFAYETTE.
IT'S A LONG NAME, I KNOW
I WAS BAPTIZED LIKE A SPANIARD, WITH THE NAMES OF EVERY SAINT WHO MIGHT OFFER ME PROTECTION IN BATTLE.
...UM.
YOU'RE RIGHT, MAMA. HIS MANNERS ARE TERRIBLE.

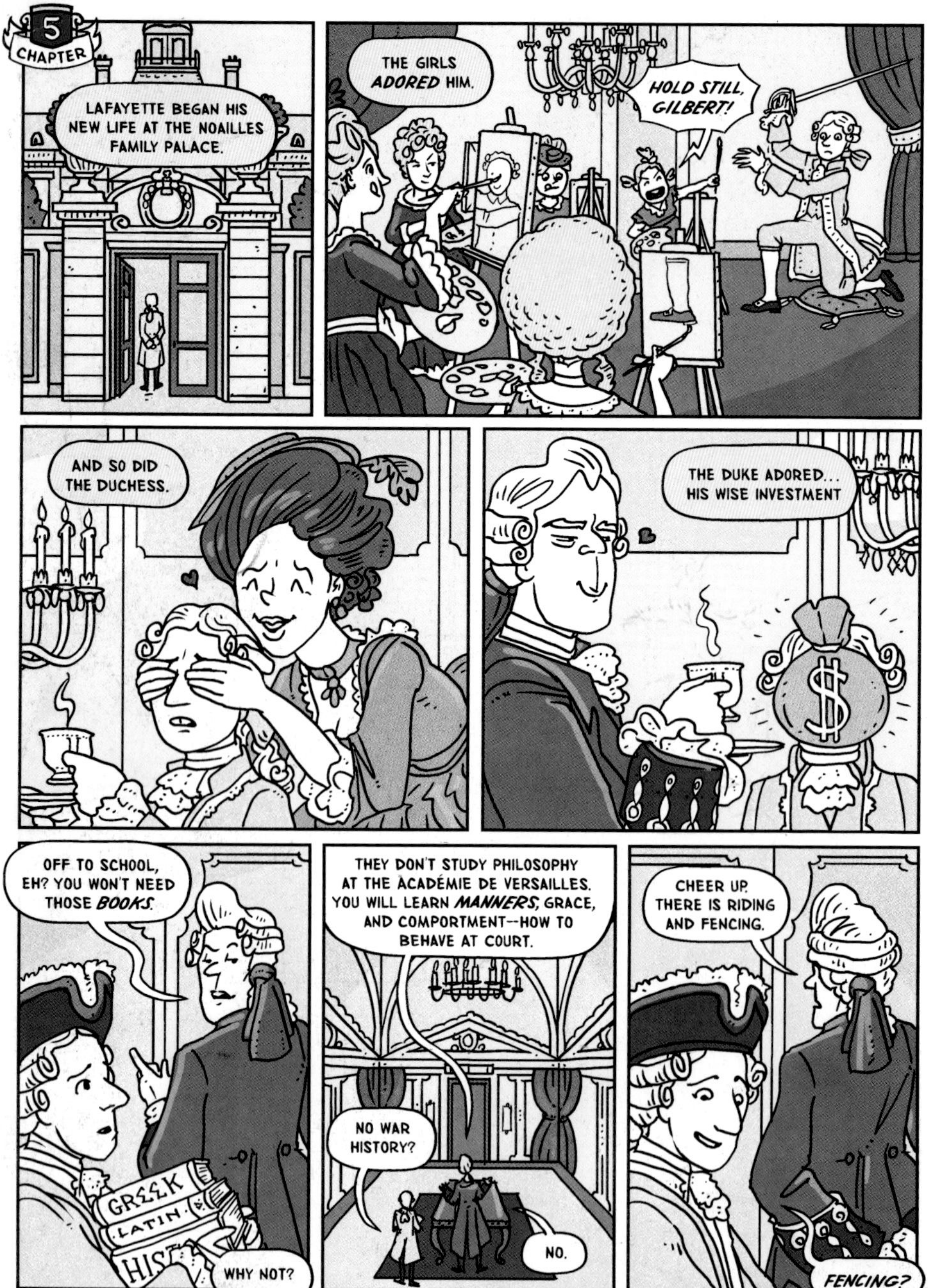
5 CHAPTER
LAFAYETTE BEGAN HIS NEW LIFE AT THE NOAILLES FAMILY PALACE.
THE GIRLS ADORED HIM.
HOLD STILL, GILBERT!
AND SO DID THE DUCHESS.
THE DUKE ADORED... HIS WISE INVESTMENT
$
OFF TO SCHOOL, EH? YOU WON'T NEED THOSE BOOKS.
GREEK
LATIN
HIST
WHY NOT?
THEY DON'T STUDY PHILOSOPHY AT THE ACADÉMIE DE VERSAILLES. YOU WILL LEARN MANNERS, GRACE, AND COMPORTMENT--HOW TO BEHAVE AT COURT.
NO WAR HISTORY?
NO.
CHEER UP. THERE IS RIDING AND FENCING.
FENCING?

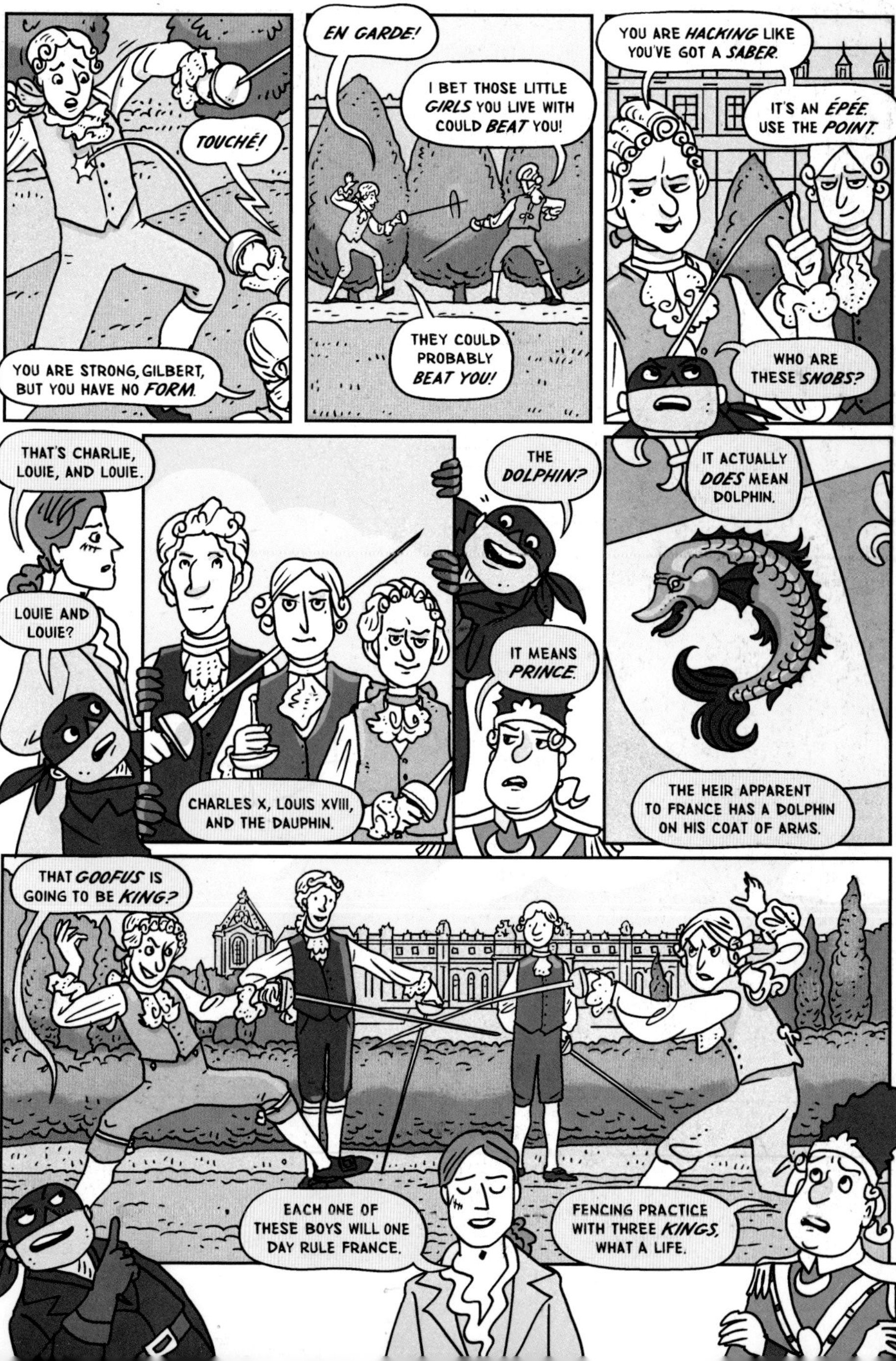
TOUCHÉ!
YOU ARE STRONG, GILBERT, BUT YOU HAVE NO *FORM*.
EN GARDE!
I BET THOSE LITTLE *GIRLS* YOU LIVE WITH COULD *BEAT* YOU!
THEY COULD PROBABLY *BEAT YOU!*
YOU ARE *HACKING* LIKE YOU'VE GOT A *SABER*.
IT'S AN *ÉPÉE*. USE THE *POINT*.
WHO ARE THESE *SNOBS?*
THAT'S CHARLIE, LOUIE, AND LOUIE.
LOUIE AND LOUIE?
CHARLES X, LOUIS XVIII, AND THE DAUPHIN.
THE *DOLPHIN?*
IT MEANS *PRINCE*.
IT ACTUALLY *DOES* MEAN DOLPHIN.
THE HEIR APPARENT TO FRANCE HAS A DOLPHIN ON HIS COAT OF ARMS.
THAT *GOOFUS* IS GOING TO BE *KING?*
EACH ONE OF THESE BOYS WILL ONE DAY RULE FRANCE.
FENCING PRACTICE WITH THREE *KINGS*, WHAT A LIFE.

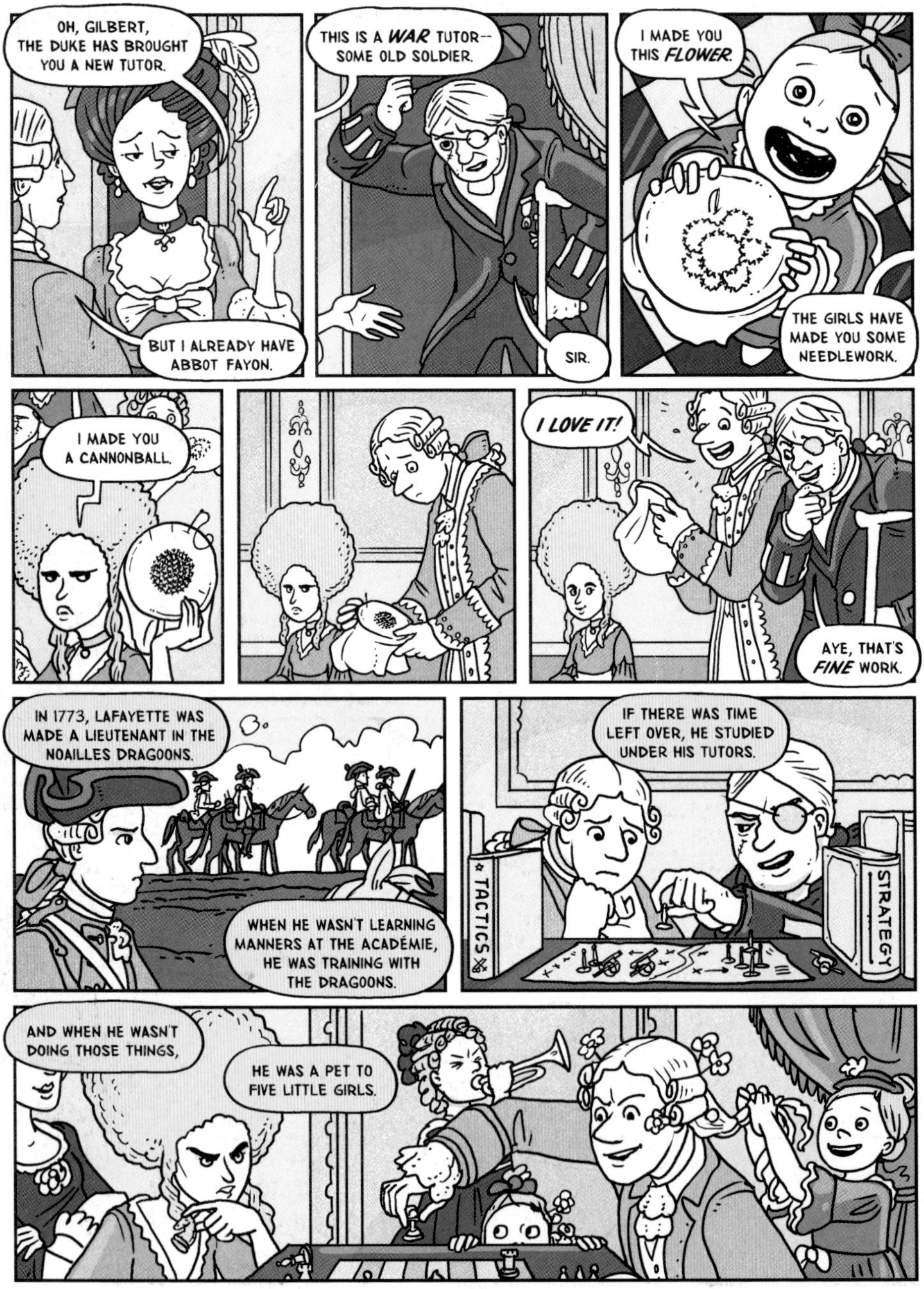
OH, GILBERT, THE DUKE HAS BROUGHT YOU A NEW TUTOR.
BUT I ALREADY HAVE ABBOT FAYON.
THIS IS A WAR TUTOR-- SOME OLD SOLDIER.
SIR.
I MADE YOU THIS FLOWER.
THE GIRLS HAVE MADE YOU SOME NEEDLEWORK.
I MADE YOU A CANNONBALL.
I LOVE IT!
AYE, THAT'S FINE WORK.
IN 1773, LAFAYETTE WAS MADE A LIEUTENANT IN THE NOAILLES DRAGOONS.
WHEN HE WASN'T LEARNING MANNERS AT THE ACADÉMIE, HE WAS TRAINING WITH THE DRAGOONS.
IF THERE WAS TIME LEFT OVER, HE STUDIED UNDER HIS TUTORS.
TACTICS
STRATEGY
AND WHEN HE WASN'T DOING THOSE THINGS,
HE WAS A PET TO FIVE LITTLE GIRLS.

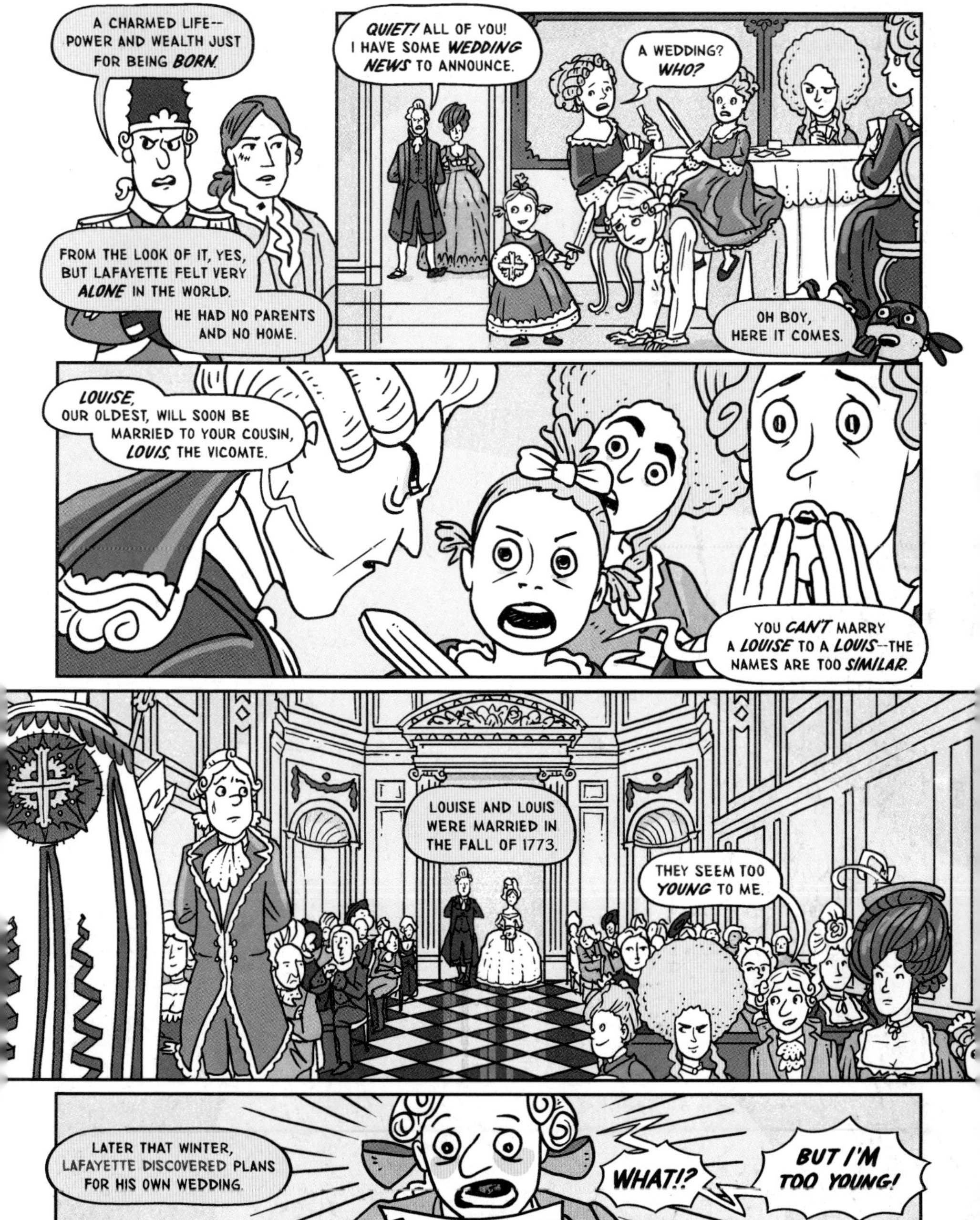
A CHARMED LIFE--POWER AND WEALTH JUST FOR BEING BORN.
FROM THE LOOK OF IT, YES, BUT LAFAYETTE FELT VERY ALONE IN THE WORLD.
HE HAD NO PARENTS AND NO HOME.
QUIET! ALL OF YOU! I HAVE SOME WEDDING NEWS TO ANNOUNCE.
A WEDDING? WHO?
OH BOY, HERE IT COMES.
LOUISE, OUR OLDEST, WILL SOON BE MARRIED TO YOUR COUSIN, LOUIS, THE VICOMTE.
YOU CAN'T MARRY A LOUISE TO A LOUIS--THE NAMES ARE TOO SIMILAR.
LOUISE AND LOUIS WERE MARRIED IN THE FALL OF 1773.
THEY SEEM TOO YOUNG TO ME.
LATER THAT WINTER, LAFAYETTE DISCOVERED PLANS FOR HIS OWN WEDDING.
WHAT!?
BUT I'M TOO YOUNG!

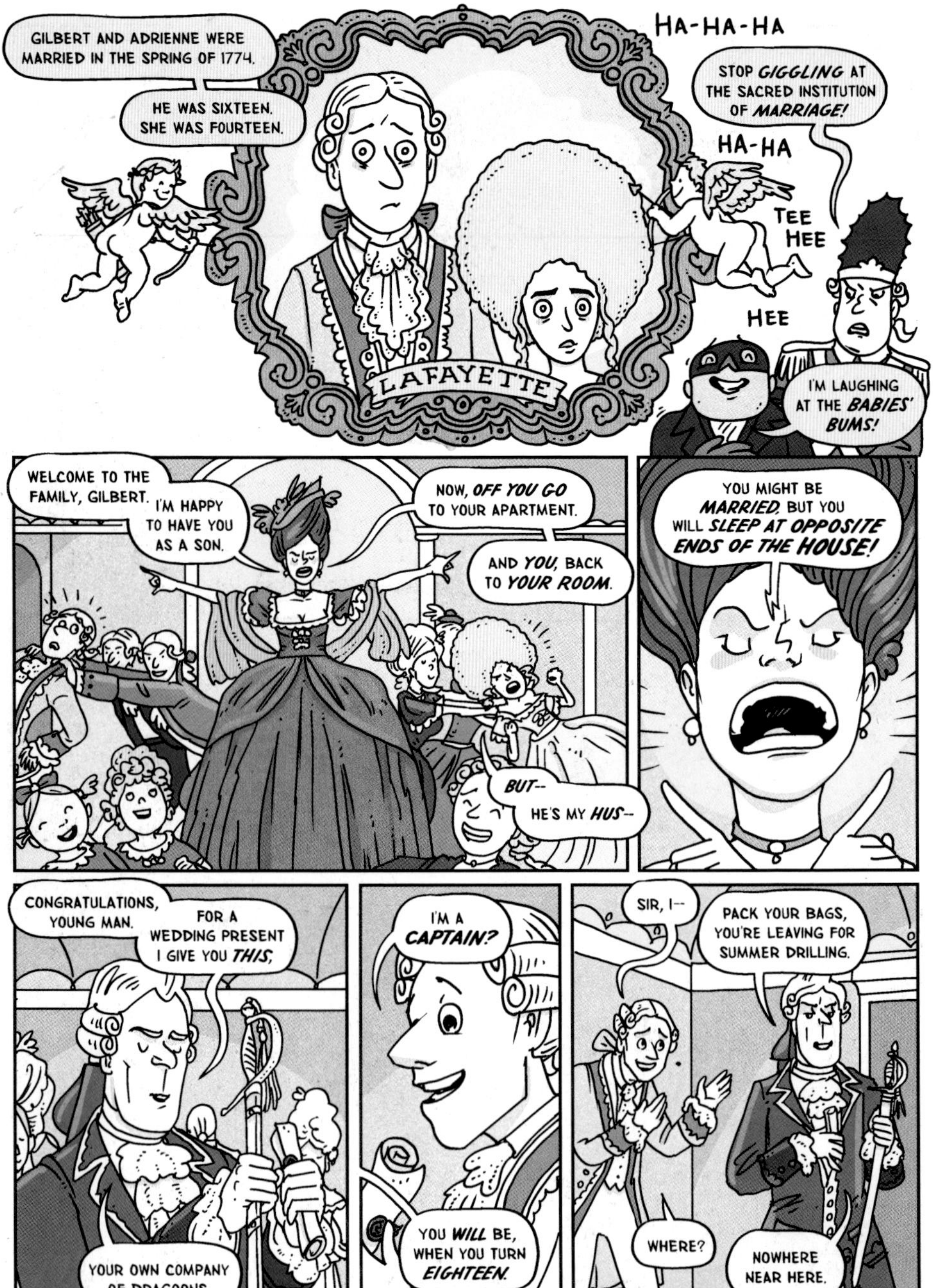

GILBERT AND ADRIENNE WERE MARRIED IN THE SPRING OF 1774.
HE WAS SIXTEEN. SHE WAS FOURTEEN.
LAFAYETTE
HA-HA-HA
STOP GIGGLING AT THE SACRED INSTITUTION OF MARRIAGE!
HA-HA
TEE HEE
HEE
I'M LAUGHING AT THE BABIES' BUMS!
WELCOME TO THE FAMILY, GILBERT.
I'M HAPPY TO HAVE YOU AS A SON.
NOW, OFF YOU GO TO YOUR APARTMENT.
AND YOU, BACK TO YOUR ROOM.
BUT--
HE'S MY HUS--
YOU MIGHT BE MARRIED, BUT YOU WILL SLEEP AT OPPOSITE ENDS OF THE HOUSE!
CONGRATULATIONS, YOUNG MAN.
FOR A WEDDING PRESENT I GIVE YOU THIS,
YOUR OWN COMPANY OF DRAGOONS.
I'M A CAPTAIN?
YOU WILL BE, WHEN YOU TURN EIGHTEEN.
SIR, I--
PACK YOUR BAGS, YOU'RE LEAVING FOR SUMMER DRILLING.
WHERE?
NOWHERE NEAR HERE.

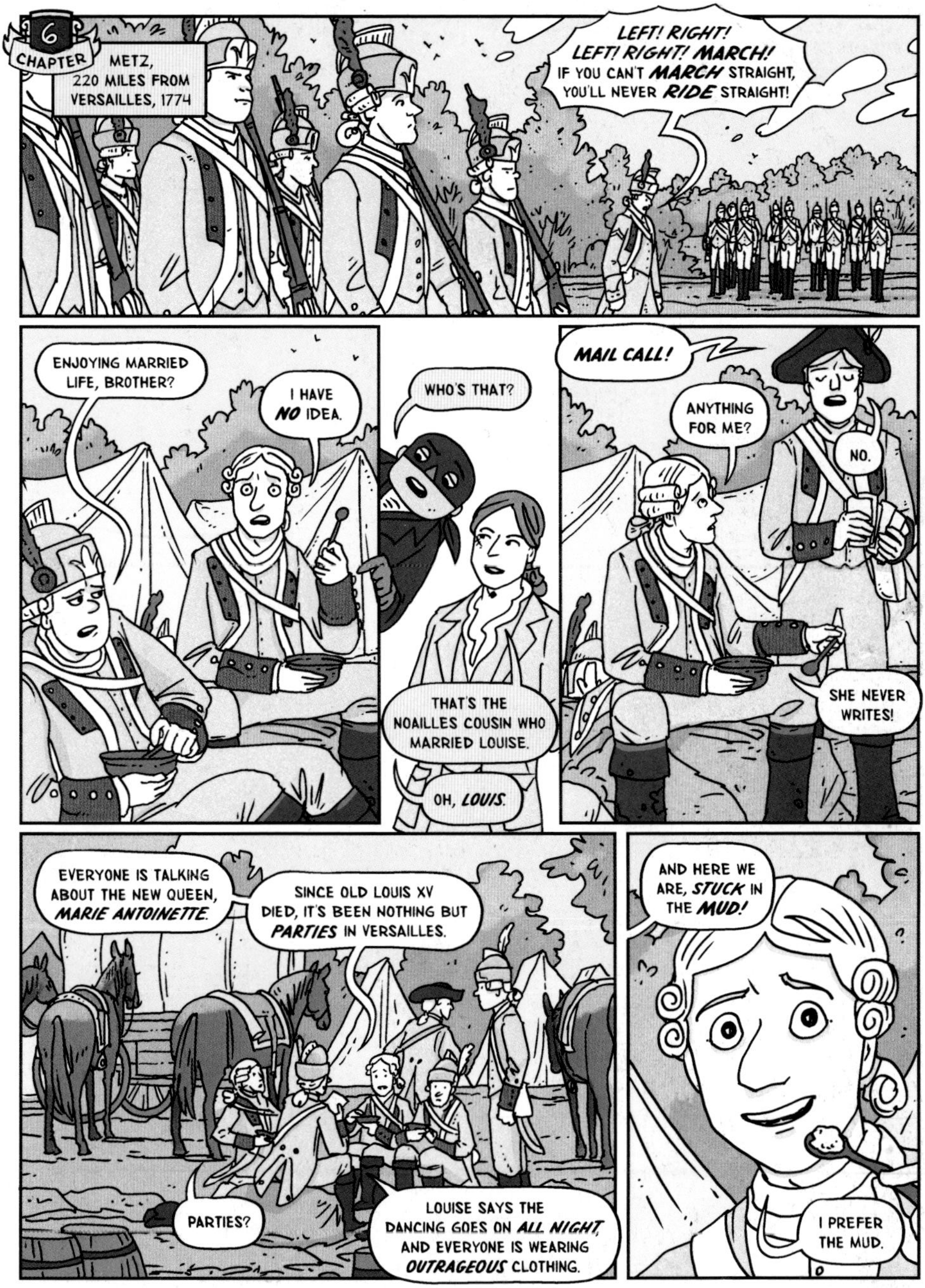
6 CHAPTER
METZ, 220 MILES FROM VERSAILLES, 1774
LEFT! RIGHT! LEFT! RIGHT! MARCH! IF YOU CAN'T MARCH STRAIGHT, YOU'LL NEVER RIDE STRAIGHT!
ENJOYING MARRIED LIFE, BROTHER?
I HAVE NO IDEA.
WHO'S THAT?
THAT'S THE NOAILLES COUSIN WHO MARRIED LOUISE.
OH, LOUIS.
MAIL CALL!
ANYTHING FOR ME?
NO.
SHE NEVER WRITES!
EVERYONE IS TALKING ABOUT THE NEW QUEEN, MARIE ANTOINETTE.
SINCE OLD LOUIS XV DIED, IT'S BEEN NOTHING BUT PARTIES IN VERSAILLES.
PARTIES?
LOUISE SAYS THE DANCING GOES ON ALL NIGHT, AND EVERYONE IS WEARING OUTRAGEOUS CLOTHING.
AND HERE WE ARE, STUCK IN THE MUD!
I PREFER THE MUD.

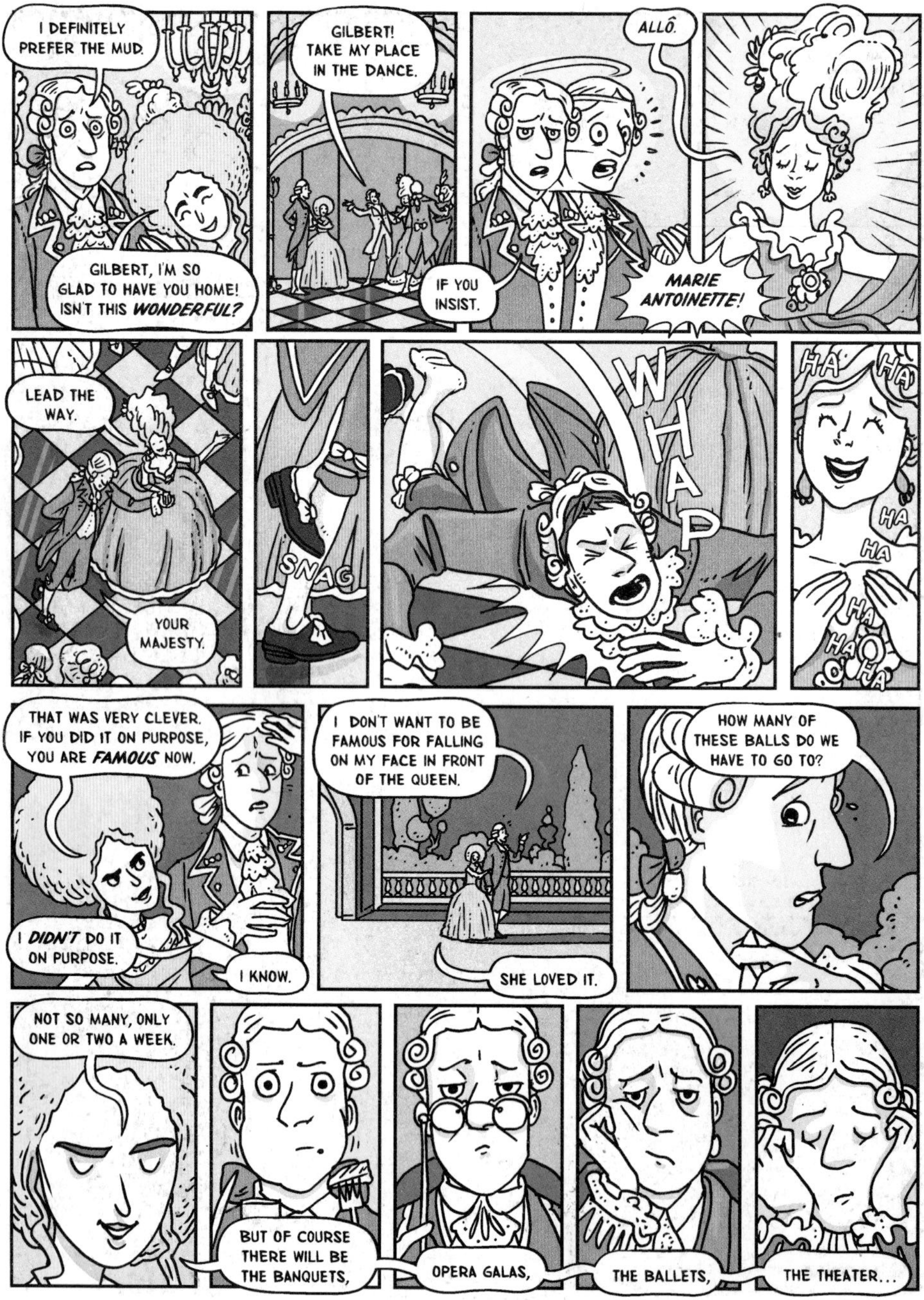
I DEFINITELY PREFER THE MUD.
GILBERT, I'M SO GLAD TO HAVE YOU HOME! ISN'T THIS *WONDERFUL?*
GILBERT! TAKE MY PLACE IN THE DANCE.
IF YOU INSIST.
ALLÔ.
MARIE ANTOINETTE!
LEAD THE WAY.
YOUR MAJESTY.
SNAG
WHAP
HA HA HA HA HA HA HA
THAT WAS VERY CLEVER. IF YOU DID IT ON PURPOSE, YOU ARE *FAMOUS* NOW.
I *DIDN'T* DO IT ON PURPOSE.
I KNOW.
I DON'T WANT TO BE FAMOUS FOR FALLING ON MY FACE IN FRONT OF THE QUEEN.
SHE LOVED IT.
HOW MANY OF THESE BALLS DO WE HAVE TO GO TO?
NOT SO MANY, ONLY ONE OR TWO A WEEK.
BUT OF COURSE THERE WILL BE THE BANQUETS,
OPERA GALAS,
THE BALLETS,
THE THEATER...

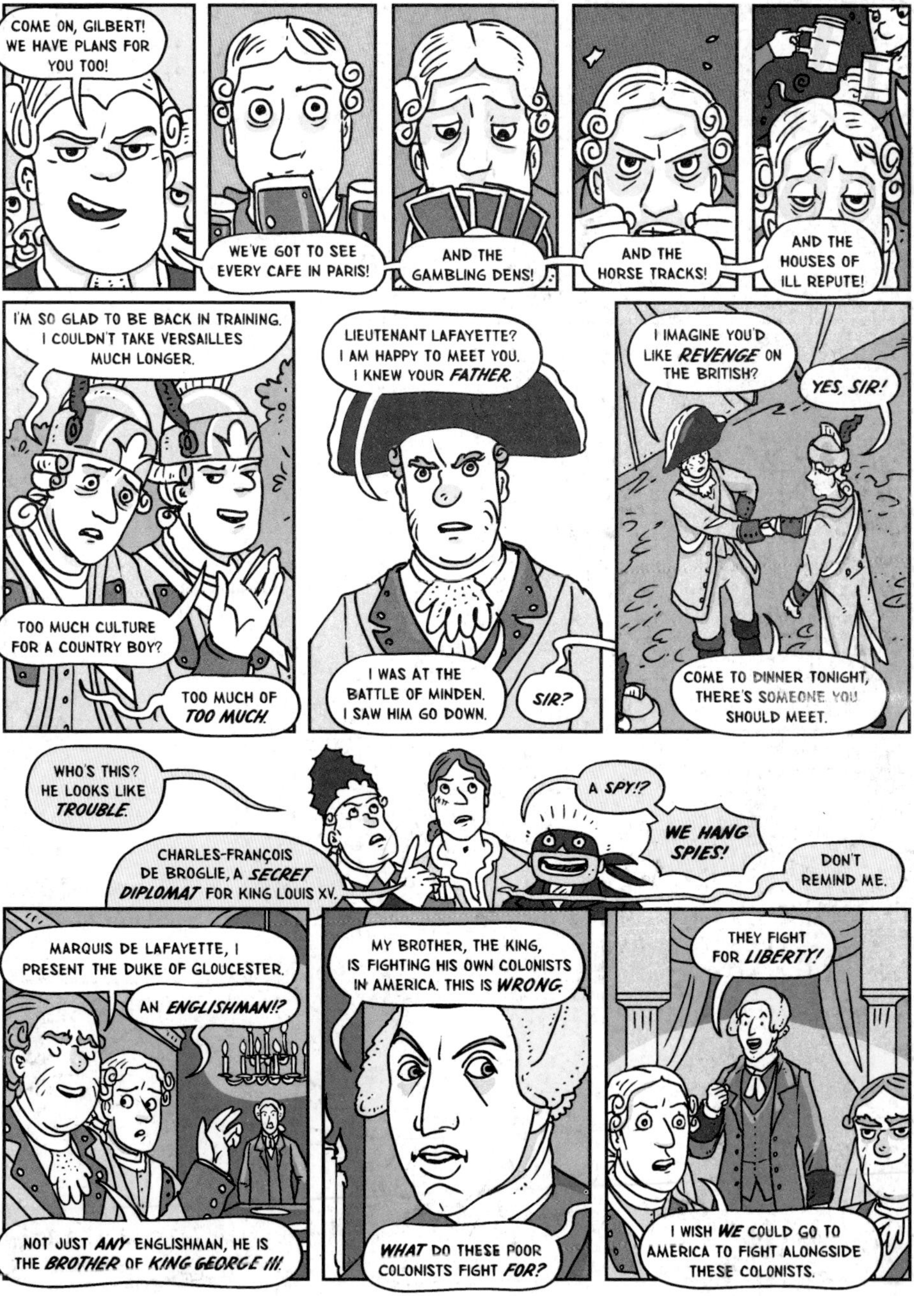

COME ON, GILBERT! WE HAVE PLANS FOR YOU TOO!
WE'VE GOT TO SEE EVERY CAFE IN PARIS!
AND THE GAMBLING DENS!
AND THE HORSE TRACKS!
AND THE HOUSES OF ILL REPUTE!
I'M SO GLAD TO BE BACK IN TRAINING. I COULDN'T TAKE VERSAILLES MUCH LONGER.
TOO MUCH CULTURE FOR A COUNTRY BOY?
TOO MUCH OF *TOO MUCH.*
LIEUTENANT LAFAYETTE? I AM HAPPY TO MEET YOU. I KNEW YOUR *FATHER.*
I WAS AT THE BATTLE OF MINDEN. I SAW HIM GO DOWN.
SIR?
I IMAGINE YOU'D LIKE *REVENGE* ON THE BRITISH?
YES, SIR!
COME TO DINNER TONIGHT, THERE'S SOMEONE YOU SHOULD MEET.
WHO'S THIS? HE LOOKS LIKE *TROUBLE.*
CHARLES-FRANÇOIS DE BROGLIE, A *SECRET DIPLOMAT* FOR KING LOUIS XV.
A *SPY!?*
WE HANG SPIES!
DON'T REMIND ME.
MARQUIS DE LAFAYETTE, I PRESENT THE DUKE OF GLOUCESTER.
AN *ENGLISHMAN!?*
NOT JUST *ANY* ENGLISHMAN, HE IS THE *BROTHER* OF *KING GEORGE III.*
MY BROTHER, THE KING, IS FIGHTING HIS OWN COLONISTS IN AMERICA. THIS IS *WRONG.*
WHAT DO THESE POOR COLONISTS FIGHT *FOR?*
THEY FIGHT FOR *LIBERTY!*
I WISH *WE* COULD GO TO AMERICA TO FIGHT ALONGSIDE THESE COLONISTS.

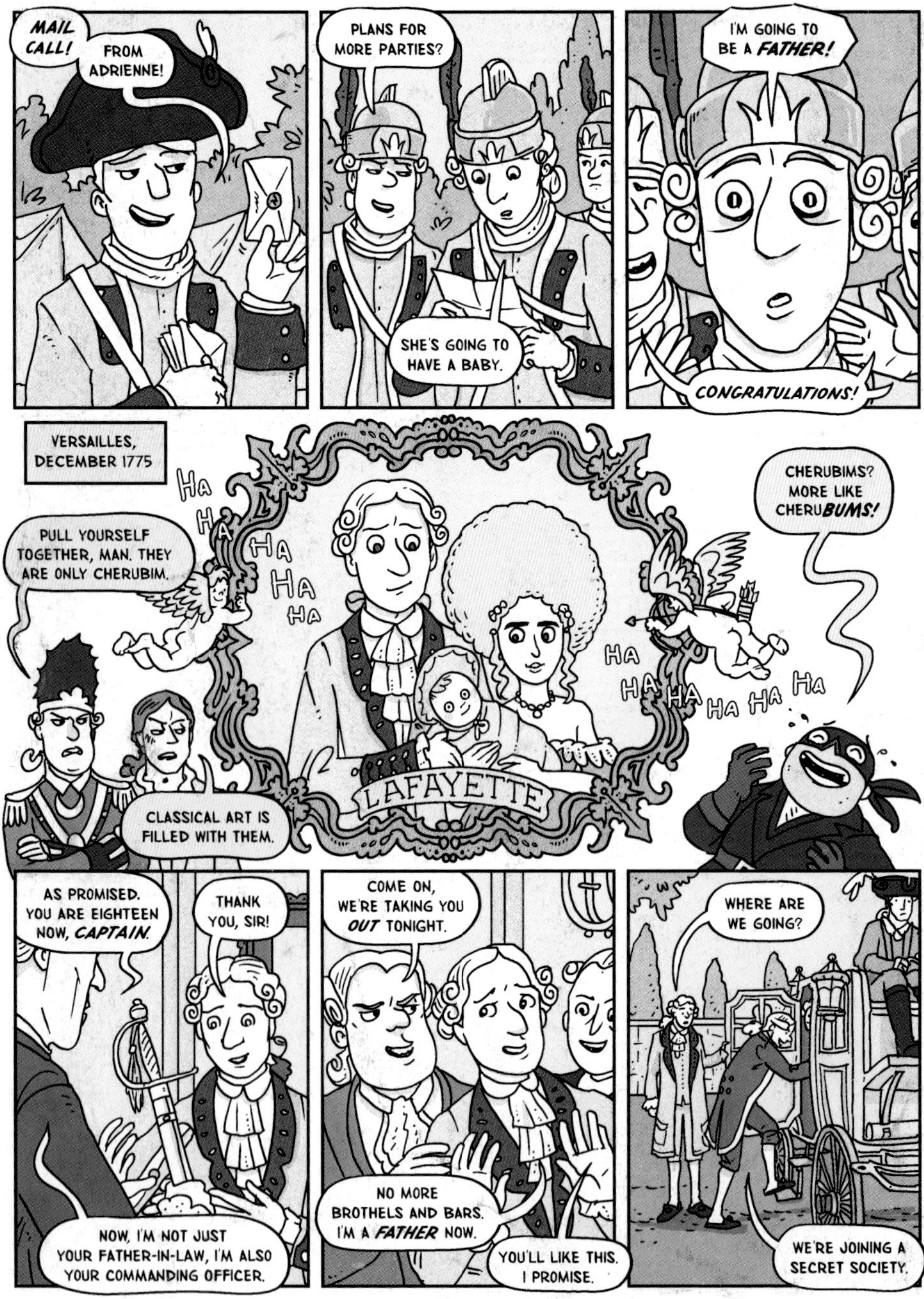
MAIL CALL!
FROM ADRIENNE!
PLANS FOR MORE PARTIES?
SHE'S GOING TO HAVE A BABY.
I'M GOING TO BE A FATHER!
CONGRATULATIONS!
VERSAILLES, DECEMBER 1775
PULL YOURSELF TOGETHER, MAN. THEY ARE ONLY CHERUBIM.
HA HA HA HA HA HA
LAFAYETTE
CLASSICAL ART IS FILLED WITH THEM.
CHERUBIMS? MORE LIKE CHERUBUMS!
HA HA HA HA HA HA HA
AS PROMISED. YOU ARE EIGHTEEN NOW, CAPTAIN.
THANK YOU, SIR!
NOW, I'M NOT JUST YOUR FATHER-IN-LAW, I'M ALSO YOUR COMMANDING OFFICER.
COME ON, WE'RE TAKING YOU OUT TONIGHT.
NO MORE BROTHELS AND BARS. I'M A FATHER NOW.
YOU'LL LIKE THIS. I PROMISE.
WHERE ARE WE GOING?
WE'RE JOINING A SECRET SOCIETY.

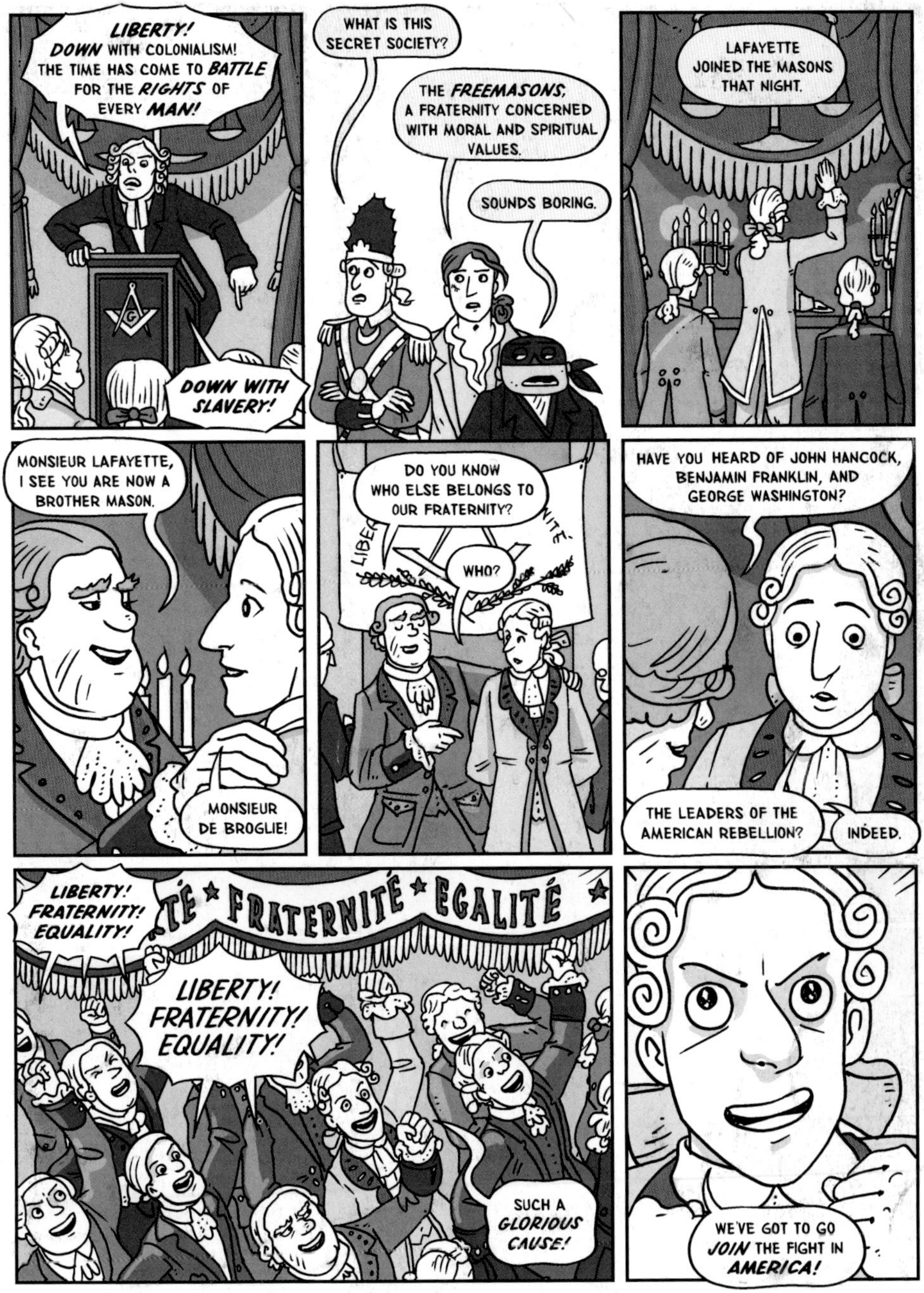
LIBERTY! DOWN WITH COLONIALISM! THE TIME HAS COME TO BATTLE FOR THE RIGHTS OF EVERY MAN!
DOWN WITH SLAVERY!
WHAT IS THIS SECRET SOCIETY?
THE FREEMASONS, A FRATERNITY CONCERNED WITH MORAL AND SPIRITUAL VALUES.
SOUNDS BORING.
LAFAYETTE JOINED THE MASONS THAT NIGHT.
MONSIEUR LAFAYETTE, I SEE YOU ARE NOW A BROTHER MASON.
MONSIEUR DE BROGLIE!
DO YOU KNOW WHO ELSE BELONGS TO OUR FRATERNITY?
WHO?
HAVE YOU HEARD OF JOHN HANCOCK, BENJAMIN FRANKLIN, AND GEORGE WASHINGTON?
THE LEADERS OF THE AMERICAN REBELLION?
INDEED.
TÉ ★ FRATERNITÉ ★ EGALITÉ ★
LIBERTY! FRATERNITY! EQUALITY!
LIBERTY! FRATERNITY! EQUALITY!
SUCH A GLORIOUS CAUSE!
WE'VE GOT TO GO JOIN THE FIGHT IN AMERICA!

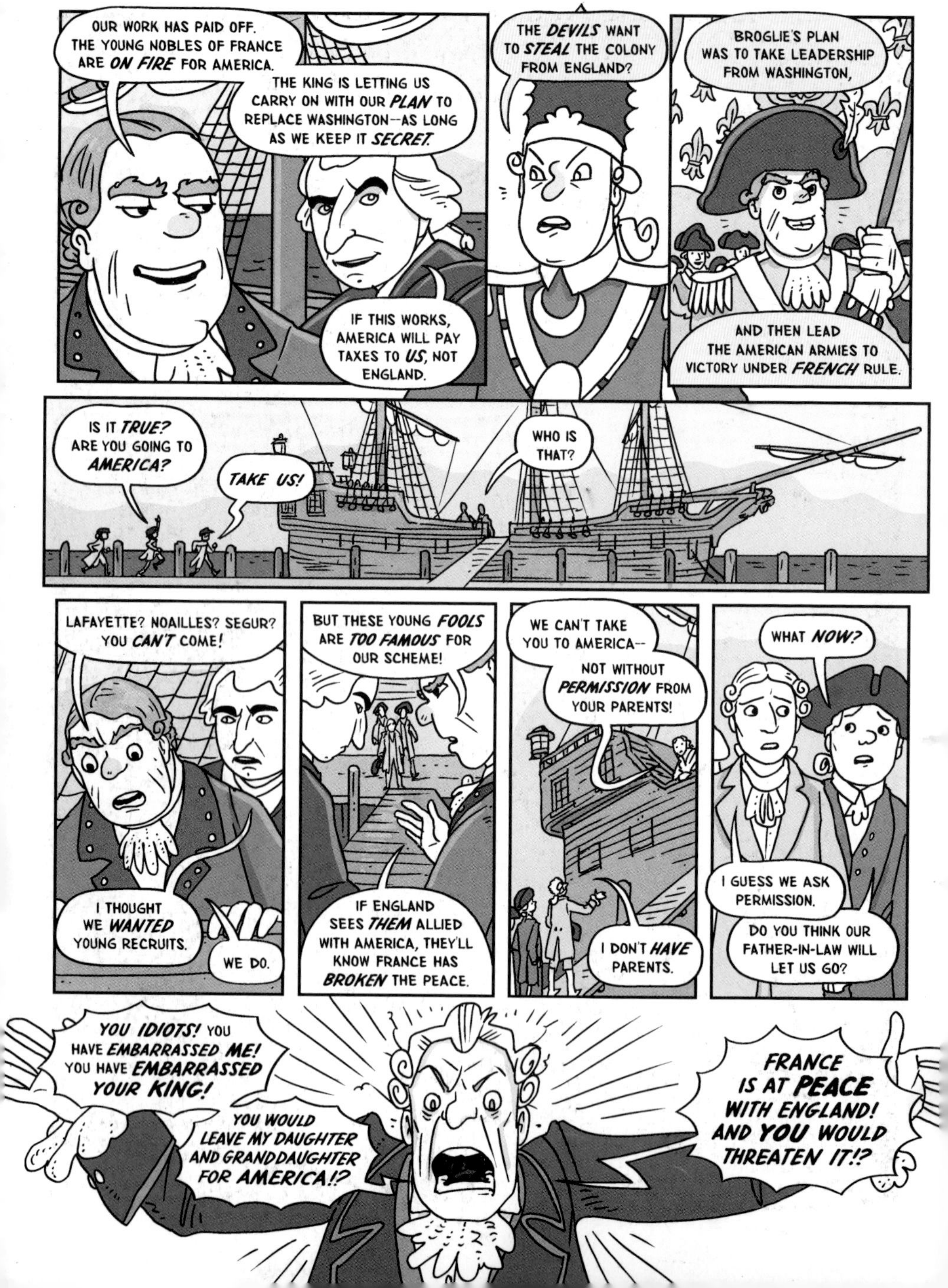

OUR WORK HAS PAID OFF. THE YOUNG NOBLES OF FRANCE ARE ON FIRE FOR AMERICA.
THE KING IS LETTING US CARRY ON WITH OUR PLAN TO REPLACE WASHINGTON--AS LONG AS WE KEEP IT SECRET.
IF THIS WORKS, AMERICA WILL PAY TAXES TO US, NOT ENGLAND.
THE DEVILS WANT TO STEAL THE COLONY FROM ENGLAND?
BROGLIE'S PLAN WAS TO TAKE LEADERSHIP FROM WASHINGTON,
AND THEN LEAD THE AMERICAN ARMIES TO VICTORY UNDER FRENCH RULE.
IS IT TRUE? ARE YOU GOING TO AMERICA?
TAKE US!
WHO IS THAT?
LAFAYETTE? NOAILLES? SEGUR? YOU CAN'T COME!
I THOUGHT WE WANTED YOUNG RECRUITS.
WE DO.
BUT THESE YOUNG FOOLS ARE TOO FAMOUS FOR OUR SCHEME!
IF ENGLAND SEES THEM ALLIED WITH AMERICA, THEY'LL KNOW FRANCE HAS BROKEN THE PEACE.
WE CAN'T TAKE YOU TO AMERICA--
NOT WITHOUT PERMISSION FROM YOUR PARENTS!
I DON'T HAVE PARENTS.
WHAT NOW?
I GUESS WE ASK PERMISSION.
DO YOU THINK OUR FATHER-IN-LAW WILL LET US GO?
YOU IDIOTS! YOU HAVE EMBARRASSED ME! YOU HAVE EMBARRASSED YOUR KING!
YOU WOULD LEAVE MY DAUGHTER AND GRANDDAUGHTER FOR AMERICA!?
FRANCE IS AT PEACE WITH ENGLAND! AND YOU WOULD THREATEN IT!?

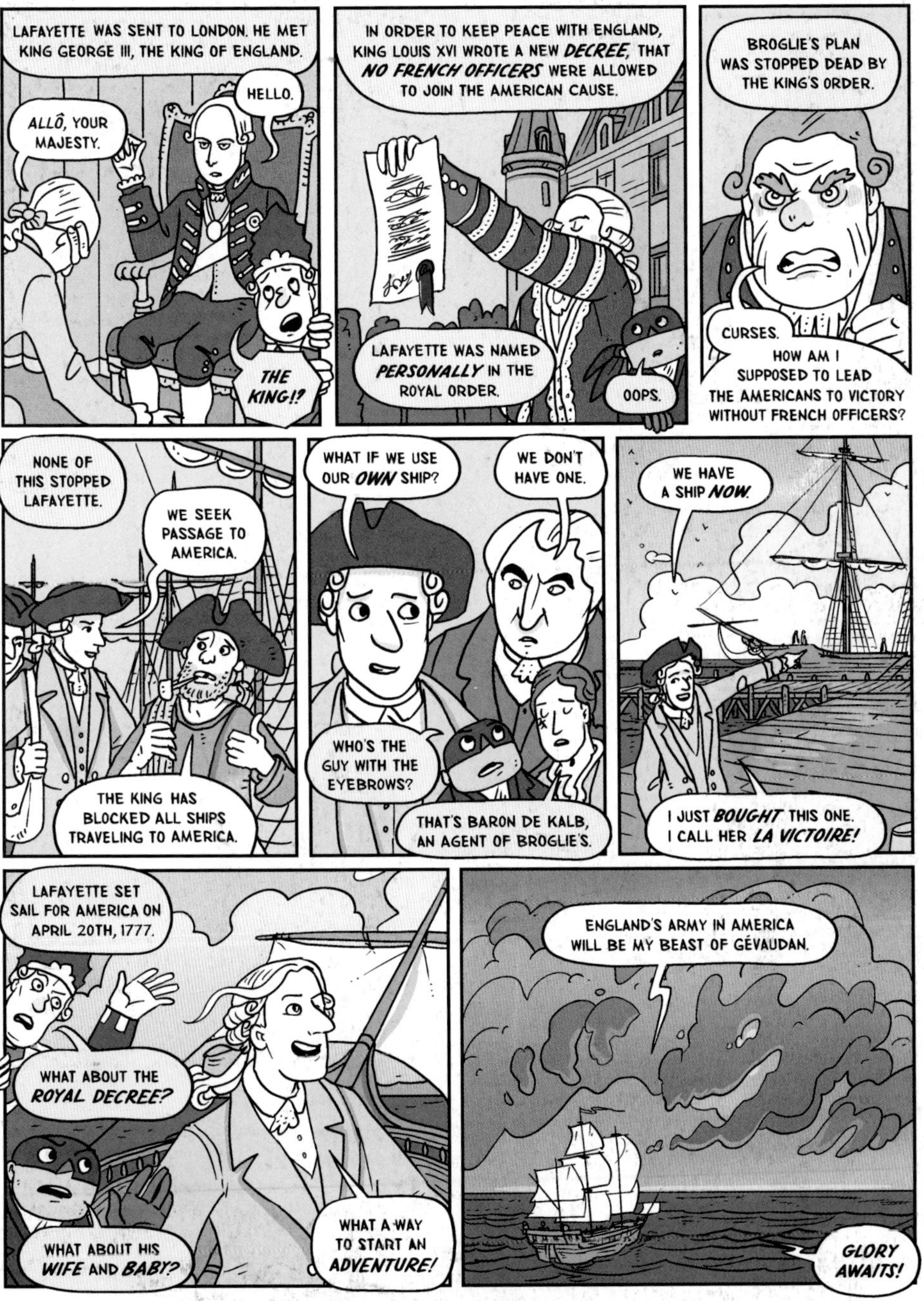
LAFAYETTE WAS SENT TO LONDON. HE MET KING GEORGE III, THE KING OF ENGLAND.
ALLÔ, YOUR MAJESTY.
HELLO.
THE KING!?
IN ORDER TO KEEP PEACE WITH ENGLAND, KING LOUIS XVI WROTE A NEW DECREE, THAT NO FRENCH OFFICERS WERE ALLOWED TO JOIN THE AMERICAN CAUSE.
LAFAYETTE WAS NAMED PERSONALLY IN THE ROYAL ORDER.
OOPS.
BROGLIE'S PLAN WAS STOPPED DEAD BY THE KING'S ORDER.
CURSES.
HOW AM I SUPPOSED TO LEAD THE AMERICANS TO VICTORY WITHOUT FRENCH OFFICERS?
NONE OF THIS STOPPED LAFAYETTE.
WE SEEK PASSAGE TO AMERICA.
THE KING HAS BLOCKED ALL SHIPS TRAVELING TO AMERICA.
WHAT IF WE USE OUR OWN SHIP?
WE DON'T HAVE ONE.
WHO'S THE GUY WITH THE EYEBROWS?
THAT'S BARON DE KALB, AN AGENT OF BROGLIE'S.
WE HAVE A SHIP NOW.
I JUST BOUGHT THIS ONE. I CALL HER LA VICTOIRE!
LAFAYETTE SET SAIL FOR AMERICA ON APRIL 20TH, 1777.
WHAT ABOUT THE ROYAL DECREE?
WHAT ABOUT HIS WIFE AND BABY?
WHAT A WAY TO START AN ADVENTURE!
ENGLAND'S ARMY IN AMERICA WILL BE MY BEAST OF GÉVAUDAN.
GLORY AWAITS!

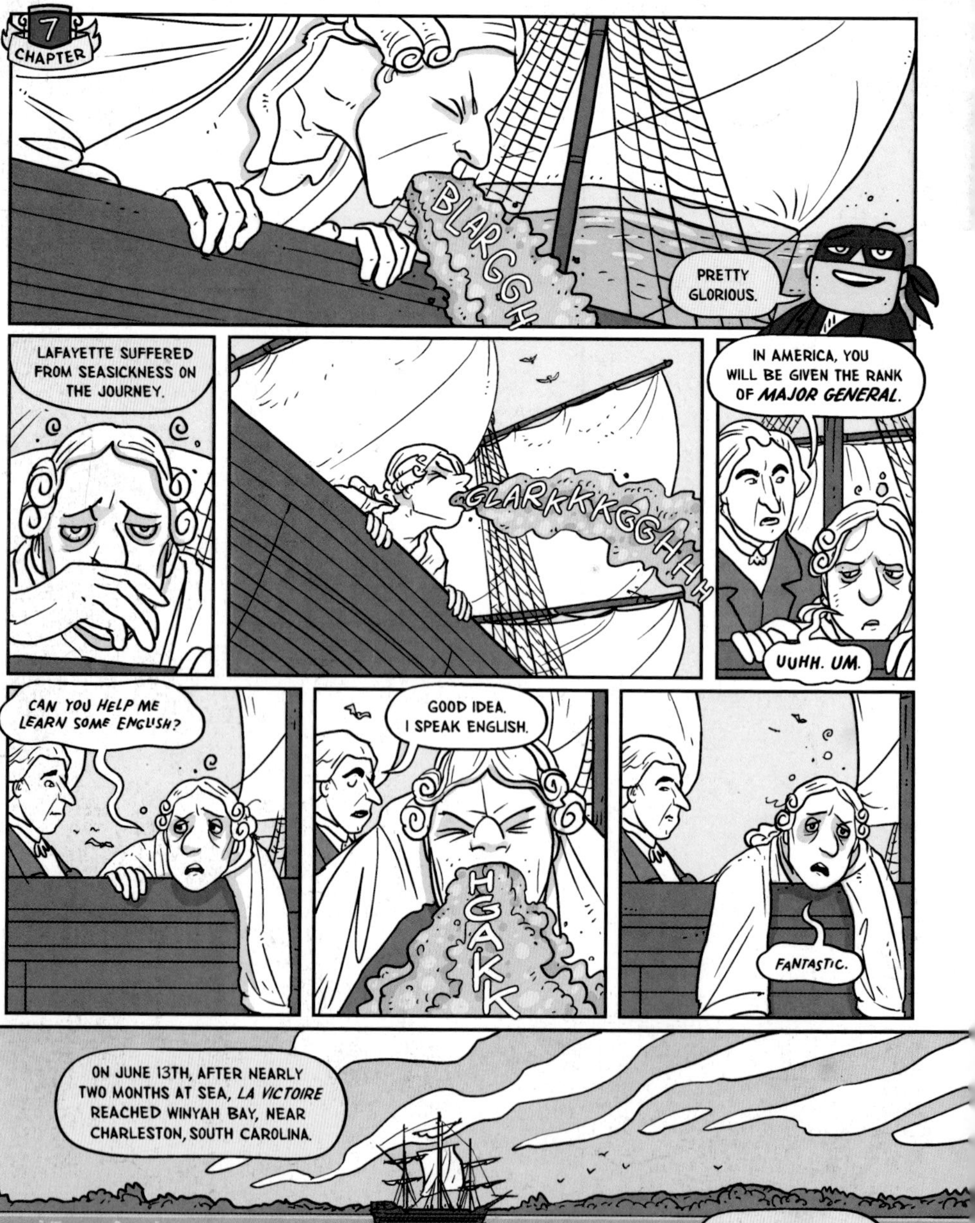

7
CHAPTER
BLARGGH
PRETTY GLORIOUS.
LAFAYETTE SUFFERED FROM SEASICKNESS ON THE JOURNEY.
GLARKKKGGHHH
IN AMERICA, YOU WILL BE GIVEN THE RANK OF ***MAJOR GENERAL***.
UUHH. UM.
CAN YOU HELP ME LEARN SOME ENGLISH?
GOOD IDEA. I SPEAK ENGLISH.
HGAKK
FANTASTIC.
ON JUNE 13TH, AFTER NEARLY TWO MONTHS AT SEA, *LA VICTOIRE* REACHED WINYAH BAY, NEAR CHARLESTON, SOUTH CAROLINA.
LAFAYETTE HAD ARRIVED IN AMERICA.

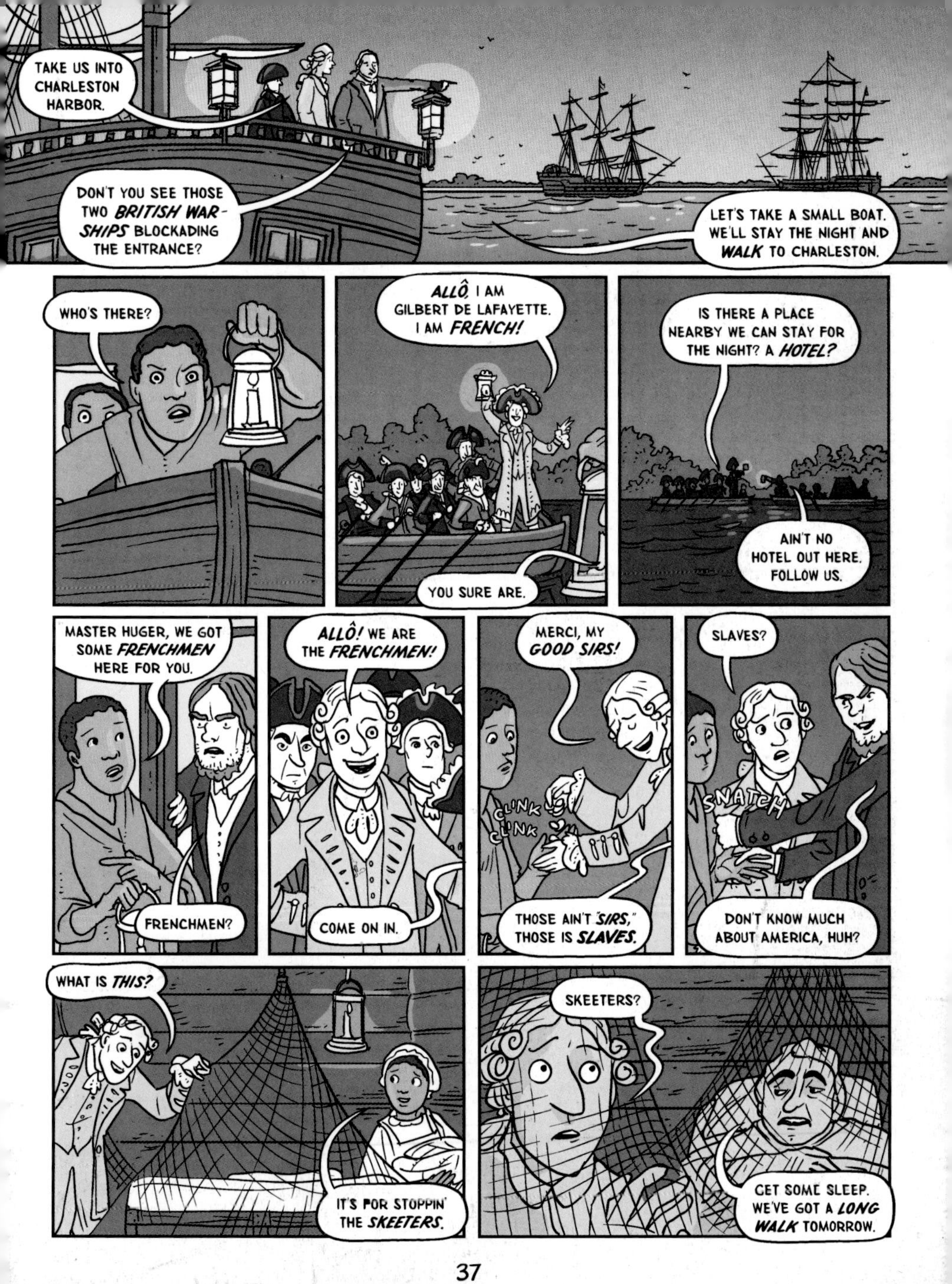
TAKE US INTO CHARLESTON HARBOR.
DON'T YOU SEE THOSE TWO BRITISH WARSHIPS BLOCKADING THE ENTRANCE?
LET'S TAKE A SMALL BOAT. WE'LL STAY THE NIGHT AND WALK TO CHARLESTON.
WHO'S THERE?
ALLÔ, I AM GILBERT DE LAFAYETTE. I AM FRENCH!
YOU SURE ARE.
IS THERE A PLACE NEARBY WE CAN STAY FOR THE NIGHT? A HOTEL?
AIN'T NO HOTEL OUT HERE. FOLLOW US.
MASTER HUGER, WE GOT SOME FRENCHMEN HERE FOR YOU.
FRENCHMEN?
ALLÔ! WE ARE THE FRENCHMEN!
COME ON IN.
MERCI, MY GOOD SIRS!
CLINK
CLINK
THOSE AIN'T "SIRS," THOSE IS SLAVES.
SLAVES?
SNATCH
DON'T KNOW MUCH ABOUT AMERICA, HUH?
WHAT IS THIS?
IT'S FOR STOPPIN' THE SKEETERS.
SKEETERS?
GET SOME SLEEP. WE'VE GOT A LONG WALK TOMORROW.

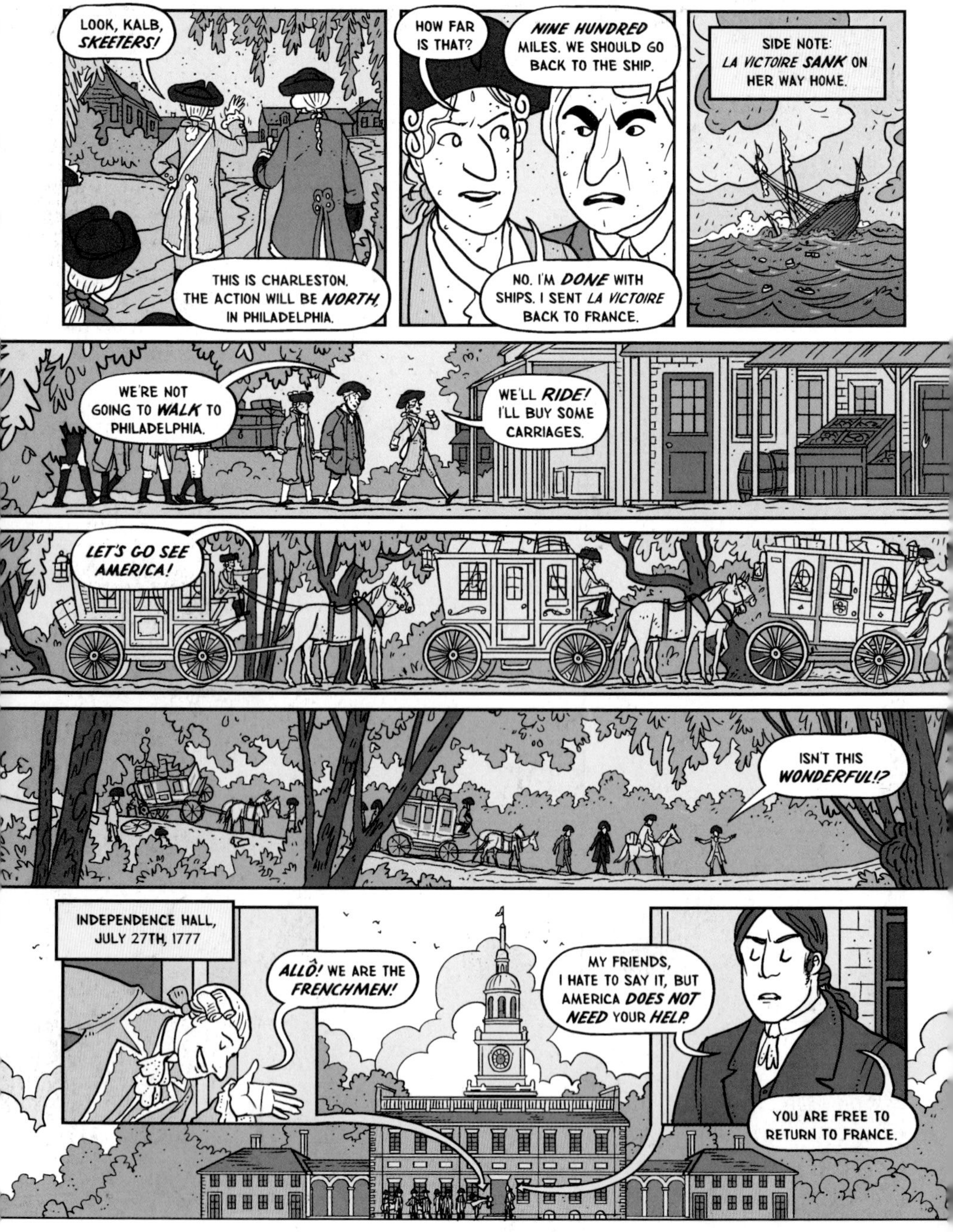
LOOK, KALB, SKEETERS!
THIS IS CHARLESTON. THE ACTION WILL BE NORTH, IN PHILADELPHIA.
HOW FAR IS THAT?
NINE HUNDRED MILES. WE SHOULD GO BACK TO THE SHIP.
NO. I'M DONE WITH SHIPS. I SENT LA VICTOIRE BACK TO FRANCE.
SIDE NOTE: LA VICTOIRE SANK ON HER WAY HOME.
WE'RE NOT GOING TO WALK TO PHILADELPHIA.
WE'LL RIDE! I'LL BUY SOME CARRIAGES.
LET'S GO SEE AMERICA!
ISN'T THIS WONDERFUL!?
INDEPENDENCE HALL, JULY 27TH, 1777
ALLÔ! WE ARE THE FRENCHMEN!
MY FRIENDS, I HATE TO SAY IT, BUT AMERICA DOES NOT NEED YOUR HELP.
YOU ARE FREE TO RETURN TO FRANCE.

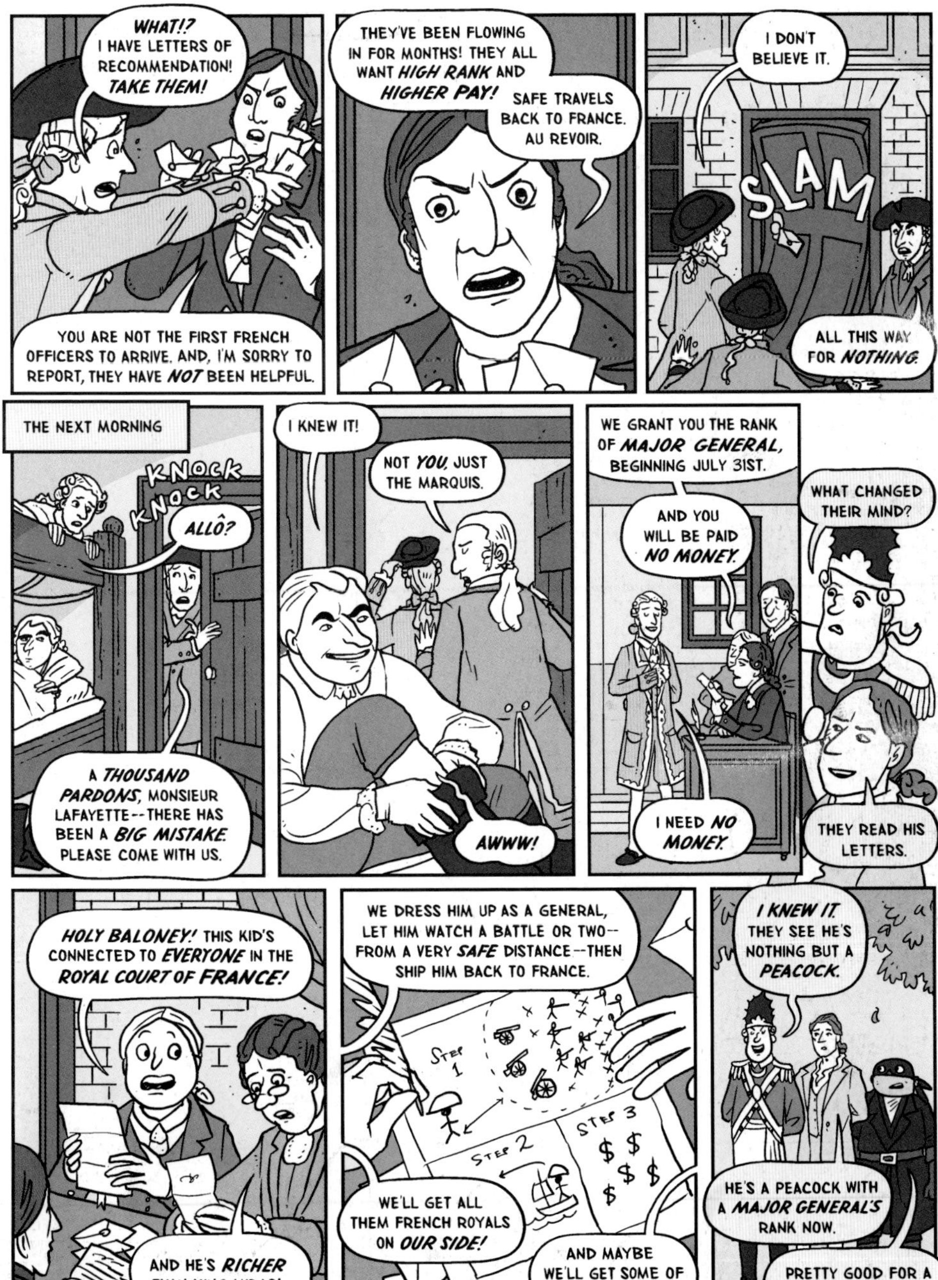
WHAT!? I HAVE LETTERS OF RECOMMENDATION! TAKE THEM!
YOU ARE NOT THE FIRST FRENCH OFFICERS TO ARRIVE. AND, I'M SORRY TO REPORT, THEY HAVE NOT BEEN HELPFUL.
THEY'VE BEEN FLOWING IN FOR MONTHS! THEY ALL WANT HIGH RANK AND HIGHER PAY!
SAFE TRAVELS BACK TO FRANCE. AU REVOIR.
I DON'T BELIEVE IT.
SLAM
ALL THIS WAY FOR NOTHING.
THE NEXT MORNING
KNOCK KNOCK
ALLÔ?
A THOUSAND PARDONS, MONSIEUR LAFAYETTE--THERE HAS BEEN A BIG MISTAKE. PLEASE COME WITH US.
I KNEW IT!
NOT YOU, JUST THE MARQUIS.
AWWW!
WE GRANT YOU THE RANK OF MAJOR GENERAL, BEGINNING JULY 31ST.
AND YOU WILL BE PAID NO MONEY.
I NEED NO MONEY.
WHAT CHANGED THEIR MIND?
THEY READ HIS LETTERS.
HOLY BALONEY! THIS KID'S CONNECTED TO EVERYONE IN THE ROYAL COURT OF FRANCE!
AND HE'S RICHER THAN KING MIDAS!
WE DRESS HIM UP AS A GENERAL, LET HIM WATCH A BATTLE OR TWO--FROM A VERY SAFE DISTANCE--THEN SHIP HIM BACK TO FRANCE.
STEP 1
STEP 2
STEP 3
$ $ $ $ $
WE'LL GET ALL THEM FRENCH ROYALS ON OUR SIDE!
AND MAYBE WE'LL GET SOME OF HIS MONEY.
I KNEW IT. THEY SEE HE'S NOTHING BUT A PEACOCK.
HE'S A PEACOCK WITH A MAJOR GENERAL'S RANK NOW.
PRETTY GOOD FOR A NINETEEN-YEAR-OLD.

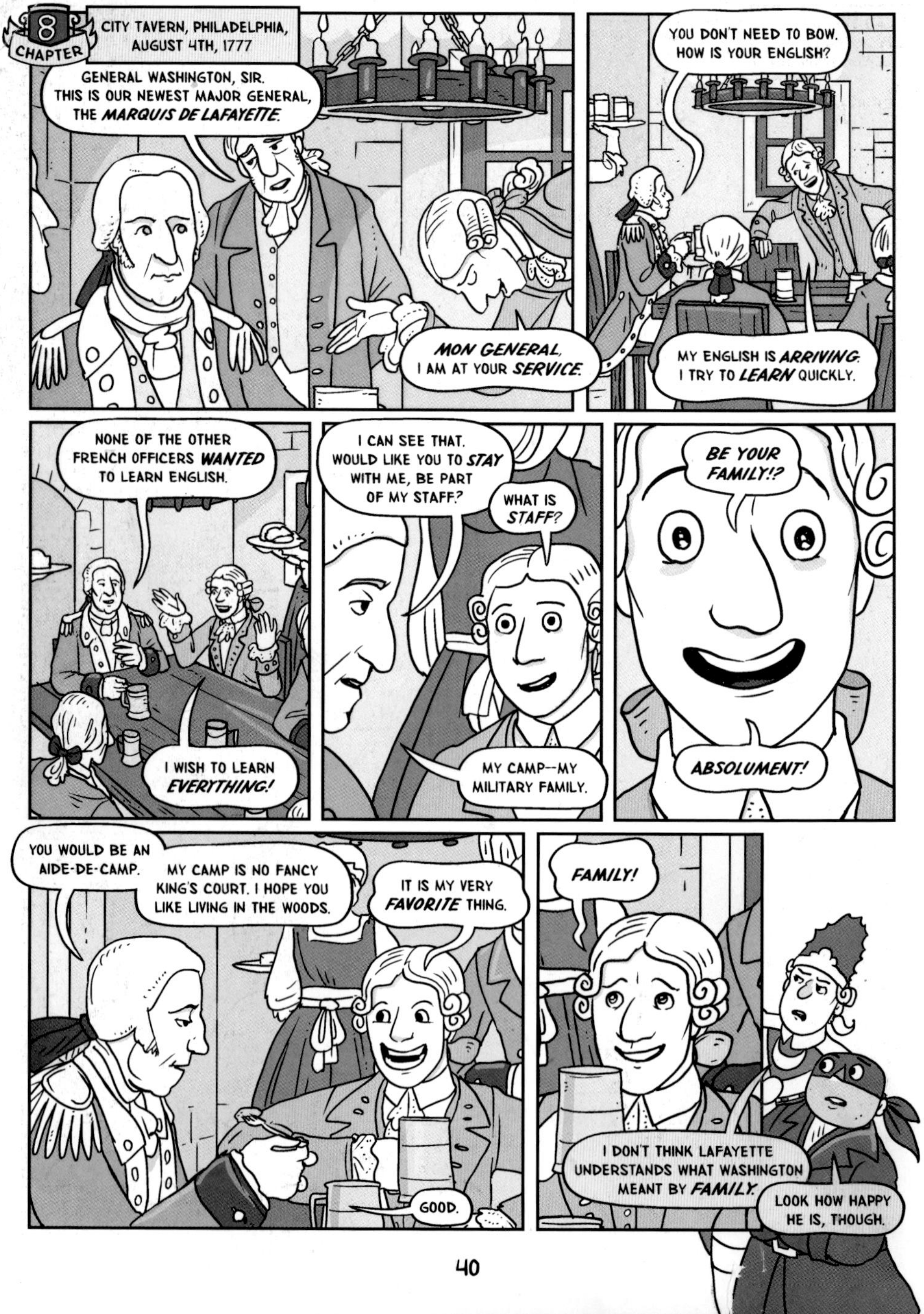
8 CHAPTER
CITY TAVERN, PHILADELPHIA, AUGUST 4TH, 1777
GENERAL WASHINGTON, SIR. THIS IS OUR NEWEST MAJOR GENERAL, THE MARQUIS DE LAFAYETTE.
MON GENERAL, I AM AT YOUR SERVICE.
YOU DON'T NEED TO BOW. HOW IS YOUR ENGLISH?
MY ENGLISH IS ARRIVING. I TRY TO LEARN QUICKLY.
NONE OF THE OTHER FRENCH OFFICERS WANTED TO LEARN ENGLISH.
I WISH TO LEARN EVERYTHING!
I CAN SEE THAT. WOULD LIKE YOU TO STAY WITH ME, BE PART OF MY STAFF?
WHAT IS STAFF?
MY CAMP--MY MILITARY FAMILY.
BE YOUR FAMILY!?
ABSOLUMENT!
YOU WOULD BE AN AIDE-DE-CAMP.
MY CAMP IS NO FANCY KING'S COURT. I HOPE YOU LIKE LIVING IN THE WOODS.
IT IS MY VERY FAVORITE THING.
GOOD.
FAMILY!
I DON'T THINK LAFAYETTE UNDERSTANDS WHAT WASHINGTON MEANT BY FAMILY.
LOOK HOW HAPPY HE IS, THOUGH.

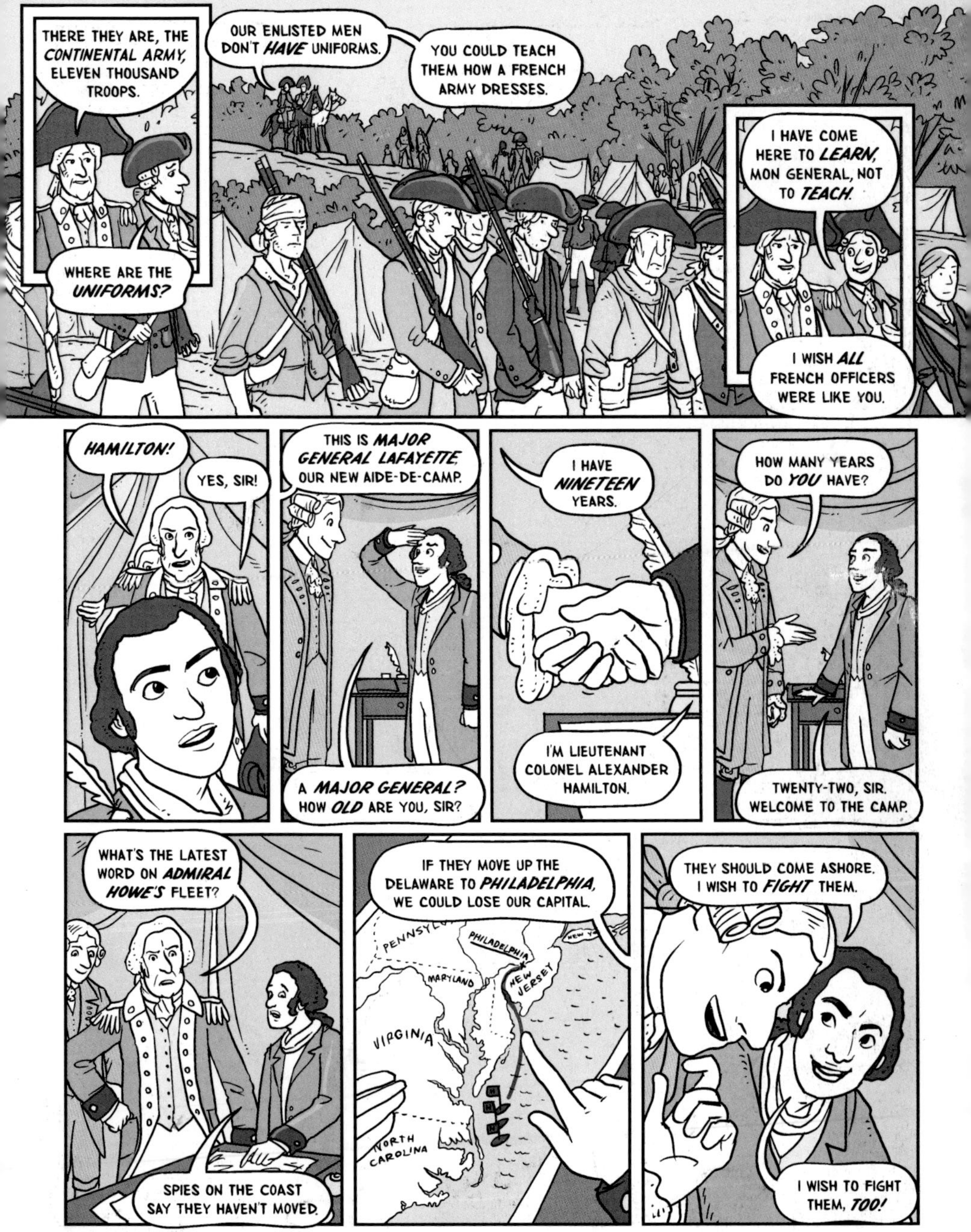

THERE THEY ARE, THE *CONTINENTAL ARMY*, ELEVEN THOUSAND TROOPS.
WHERE ARE THE *UNIFORMS?*
OUR ENLISTED MEN DON'T *HAVE* UNIFORMS.
YOU COULD TEACH THEM HOW A FRENCH ARMY DRESSES.
I HAVE COME HERE TO *LEARN*, MON GENERAL, NOT TO *TEACH*.
I WISH *ALL* FRENCH OFFICERS WERE LIKE YOU.
HAMILTON!
YES, SIR!
THIS IS *MAJOR GENERAL LAFAYETTE*, OUR NEW AIDE-DE-CAMP.
A *MAJOR GENERAL?* HOW *OLD* ARE YOU, SIR?
I HAVE *NINETEEN* YEARS.
I'M LIEUTENANT COLONEL ALEXANDER HAMILTON.
HOW MANY YEARS DO *YOU* HAVE?
TWENTY-TWO, SIR. WELCOME TO THE CAMP.
WHAT'S THE LATEST WORD ON *ADMIRAL HOWE'S* FLEET?
SPIES ON THE COAST SAY THEY HAVEN'T MOVED.
IF THEY MOVE UP THE DELAWARE TO *PHILADELPHIA*, WE COULD LOSE OUR CAPITAL.
PHILADELPHIA
MARYLAND
NEW JERSEY
VIRGINIA
NORTH CAROLINA
THEY SHOULD COME ASHORE. I WISH TO *FIGHT* THEM.
I WISH TO FIGHT THEM, *TOO!*

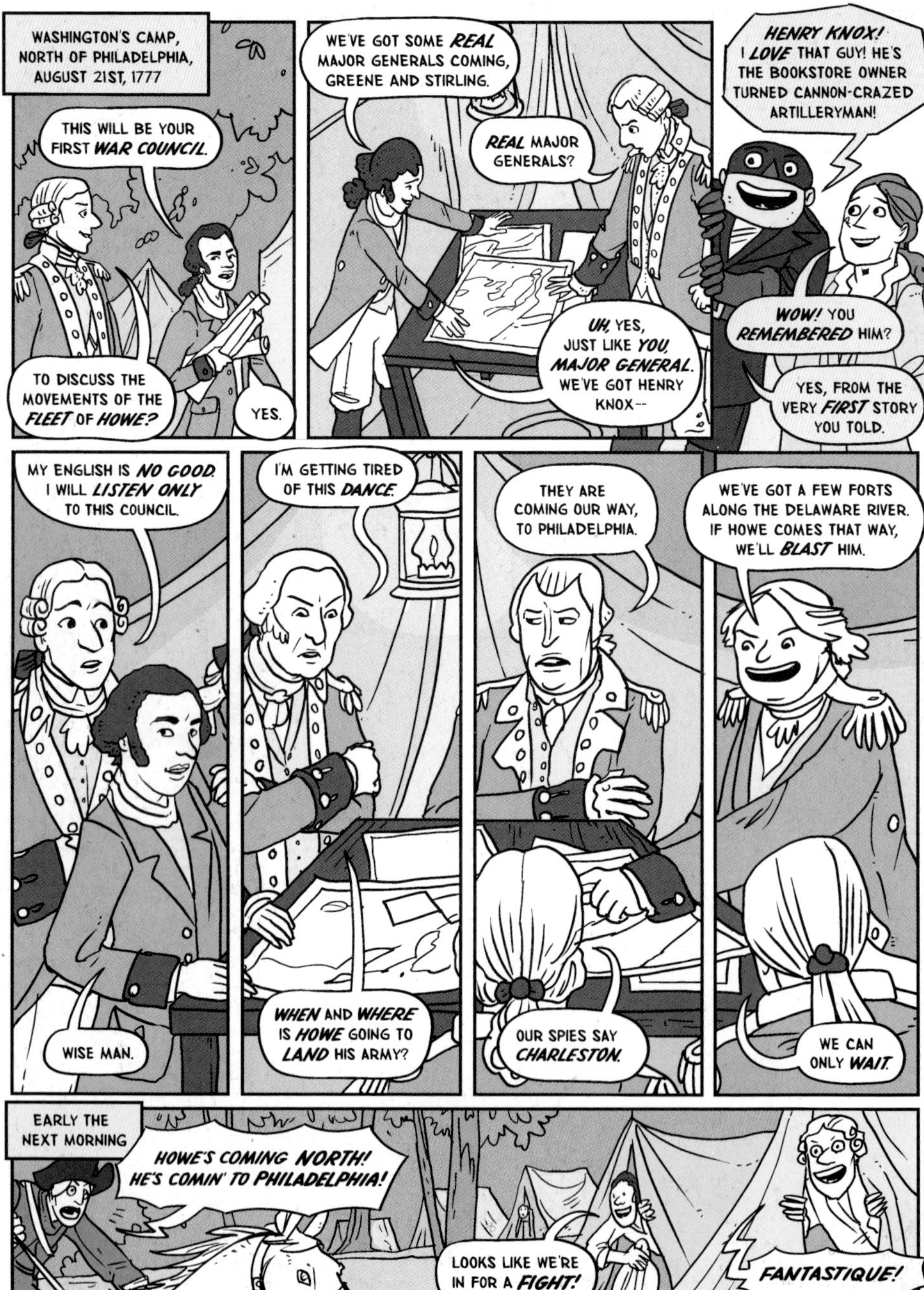

WASHINGTON'S CAMP, NORTH OF PHILADELPHIA, AUGUST 21ST, 1777
THIS WILL BE YOUR FIRST WAR COUNCIL.
TO DISCUSS THE MOVEMENTS OF THE FLEET OF HOWE?
YES.
WE'VE GOT SOME REAL MAJOR GENERALS COMING, GREENE AND STIRLING.
REAL MAJOR GENERALS?
UH, YES, JUST LIKE YOU, MAJOR GENERAL. WE'VE GOT HENRY KNOX--
HENRY KNOX! I LOVE THAT GUY! HE'S THE BOOKSTORE OWNER TURNED CANNON-CRAZED ARTILLERYMAN!
WOW! YOU REMEMBERED HIM?
YES, FROM THE VERY FIRST STORY YOU TOLD.
MY ENGLISH IS NO GOOD. I WILL LISTEN ONLY TO THIS COUNCIL.
WISE MAN.
I'M GETTING TIRED OF THIS DANCE.
WHEN AND WHERE IS HOWE GOING TO LAND HIS ARMY?
THEY ARE COMING OUR WAY, TO PHILADELPHIA.
OUR SPIES SAY CHARLESTON.
WE'VE GOT A FEW FORTS ALONG THE DELAWARE RIVER. IF HOWE COMES THAT WAY, WE'LL BLAST HIM.
WE CAN ONLY WAIT.
EARLY THE NEXT MORNING
HOWE'S COMING NORTH! HE'S COMIN' TO PHILADELPHIA!
LOOKS LIKE WE'RE IN FOR A FIGHT!
FANTASTIQUE!

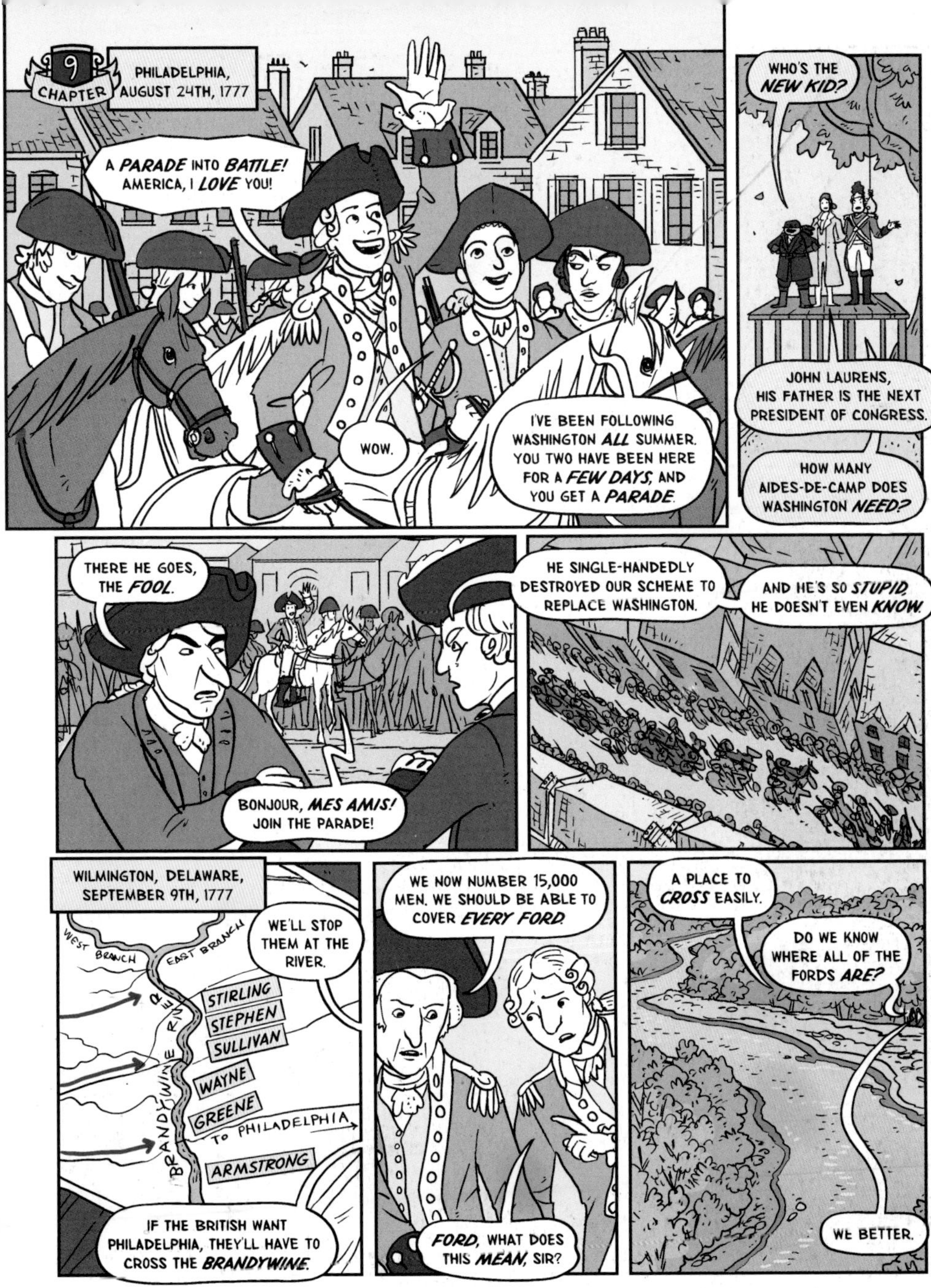
9
CHAPTER
PHILADELPHIA, AUGUST 24TH, 1777
A PARADE INTO BATTLE! AMERICA, I LOVE YOU!
WOW.
I'VE BEEN FOLLOWING WASHINGTON ALL SUMMER. YOU TWO HAVE BEEN HERE FOR A FEW DAYS, AND YOU GET A PARADE.
WHO'S THE NEW KID?
JOHN LAURENS, HIS FATHER IS THE NEXT PRESIDENT OF CONGRESS.
HOW MANY AIDES-DE-CAMP DOES WASHINGTON NEED?
THERE HE GOES, THE FOOL.
BONJOUR, MES AMIS! JOIN THE PARADE!
HE SINGLE-HANDEDLY DESTROYED OUR SCHEME TO REPLACE WASHINGTON.
AND HE'S SO STUPID, HE DOESN'T EVEN KNOW.
WILMINGTON, DELAWARE, SEPTEMBER 9TH, 1777
WEST BRANCH
EAST BRANCH
BRANDYWINE RIVER
STIRLING
STEPHEN
SULLIVAN
WAYNE
GREENE
TO PHILADELPHIA
ARMSTRONG
WE'LL STOP THEM AT THE RIVER.
IF THE BRITISH WANT PHILADELPHIA, THEY'LL HAVE TO CROSS THE BRANDYWINE.
WE NOW NUMBER 15,000 MEN. WE SHOULD BE ABLE TO COVER EVERY FORD.
FORD, WHAT DOES THIS MEAN, SIR?
A PLACE TO CROSS EASILY.
DO WE KNOW WHERE ALL OF THE FORDS ARE?
WE BETTER.

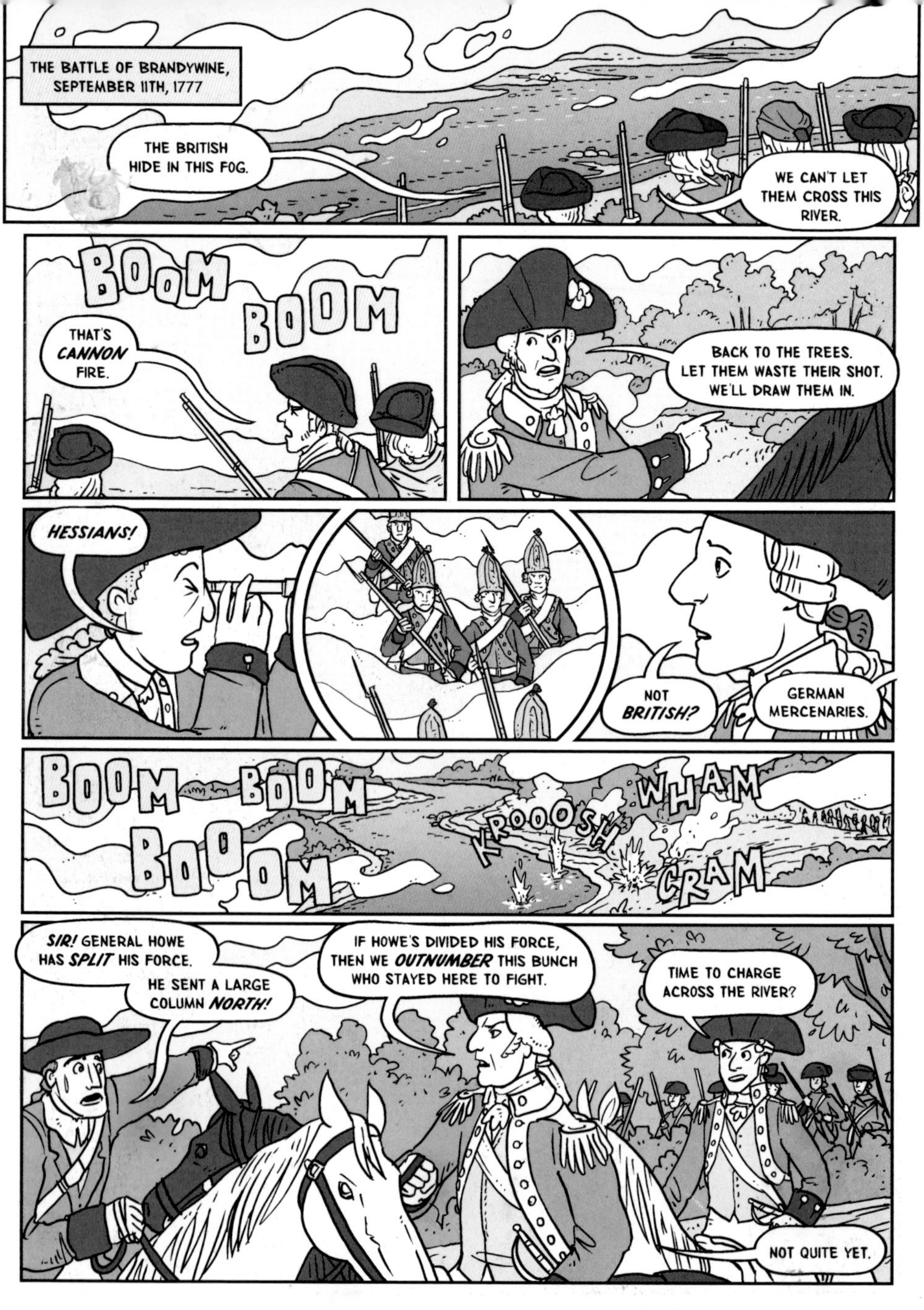
THE BATTLE OF BRANDYWINE, SEPTEMBER 11TH, 1777
THE BRITISH HIDE IN THIS FOG.
WE CAN'T LET THEM CROSS THIS RIVER.
BOOM
BOOM
THAT'S *CANNON* FIRE.
BACK TO THE TREES. LET THEM WASTE THEIR SHOT. WE'LL DRAW THEM IN.
HESSIANS!
NOT *BRITISH?*
GERMAN MERCENARIES.
BOOM BOOM
BOOOM
KROOOSH
WHAM
CRAM
SIR! GENERAL HOWE HAS *SPLIT* HIS FORCE.
HE SENT A LARGE COLUMN *NORTH!*
IF HOWE'S DIVIDED HIS FORCE, THEN WE *OUTNUMBER* THIS BUNCH WHO STAYED HERE TO FIGHT.
TIME TO CHARGE ACROSS THE RIVER?
NOT QUITE YET.

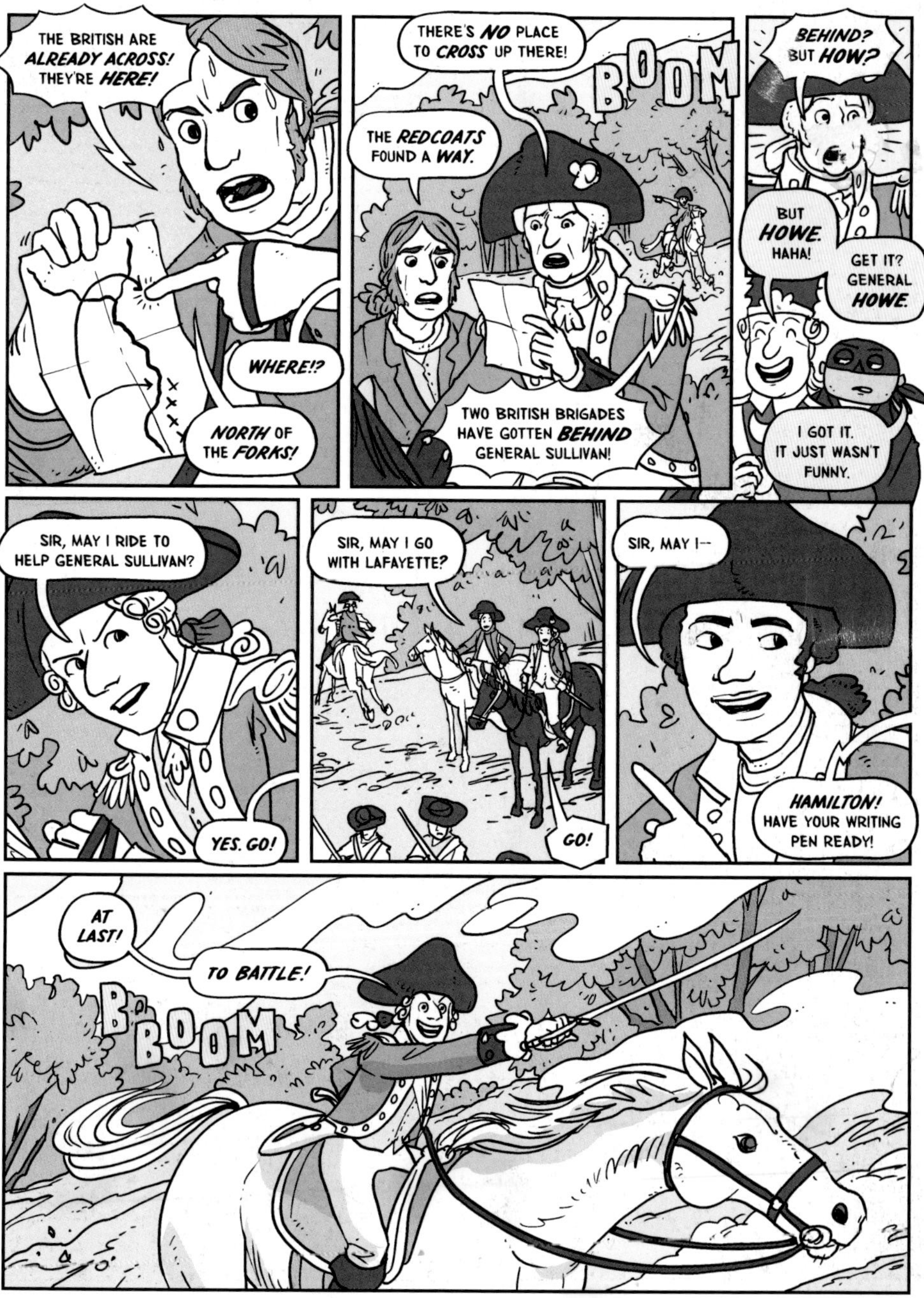
THE BRITISH ARE ALREADY ACROSS! THEY'RE HERE!
WHERE!?
NORTH OF THE FORKS!
THERE'S NO PLACE TO CROSS UP THERE!
BOOM
THE REDCOATS FOUND A WAY.
TWO BRITISH BRIGADES HAVE GOTTEN BEHIND GENERAL SULLIVAN!
BEHIND? BUT HOW?
BUT HOWE. HAHA!
GET IT? GENERAL HOWE.
I GOT IT. IT JUST WASN'T FUNNY.
SIR, MAY I RIDE TO HELP GENERAL SULLIVAN?
YES. GO!
SIR, MAY I GO WITH LAFAYETTE?
GO!
SIR, MAY I--
HAMILTON! HAVE YOUR WRITING PEN READY!
AT LAST!
TO BATTLE!
BBOOM

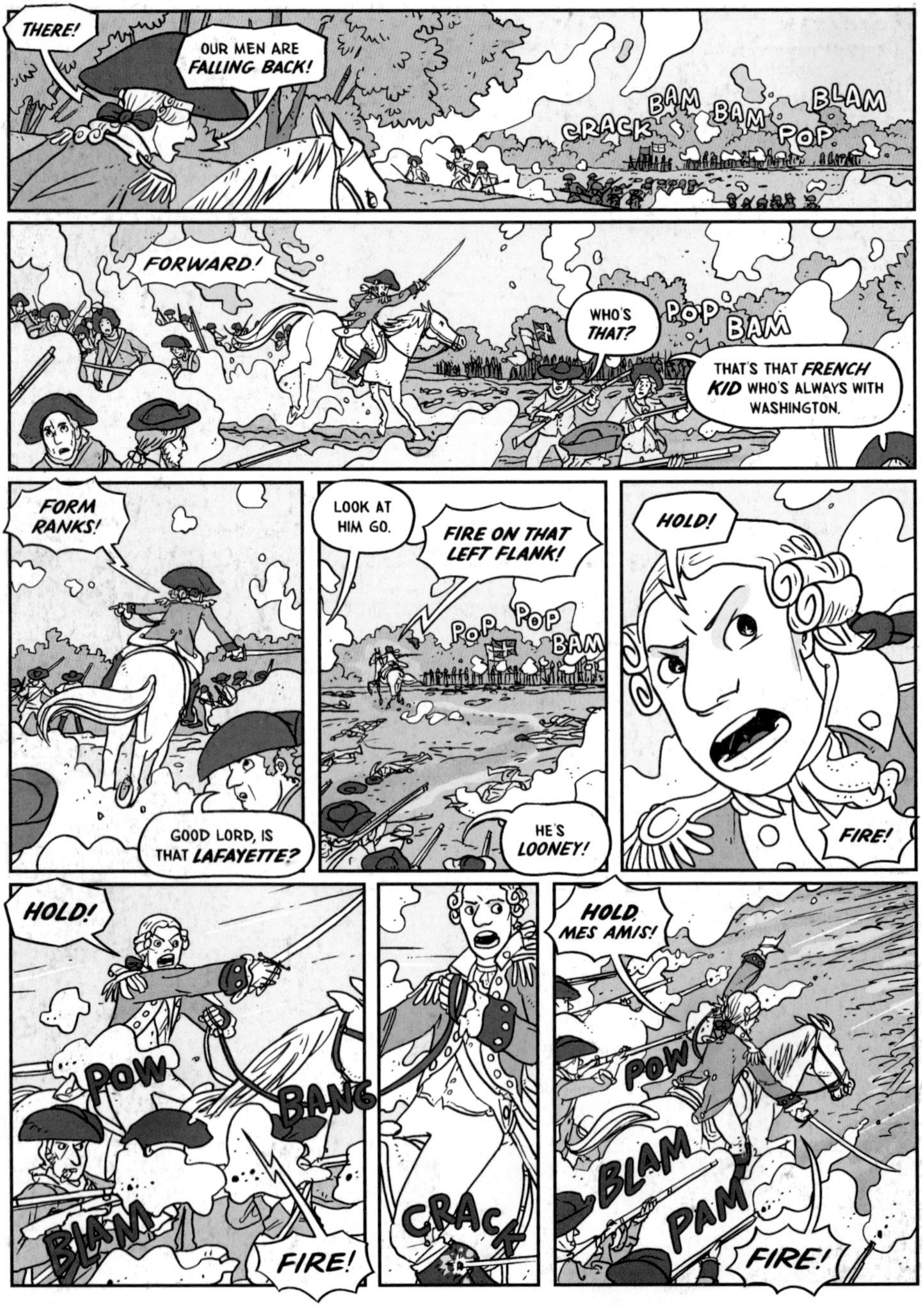
THERE!
OUR MEN ARE FALLING BACK!
CRACK BAM BAM POP BLAM
FORWARD!
WHO'S THAT?
POP BAM
THAT'S THAT FRENCH KID WHO'S ALWAYS WITH WASHINGTON.
FORM RANKS!
GOOD LORD, IS THAT LAFAYETTE?
LOOK AT HIM GO.
FIRE ON THAT LEFT FLANK!
POP POP BAM
HE'S LOONEY!
HOLD!
FIRE!
HOLD!
POW
BANG
BLAM
FIRE!
CRACK
HOLD, MES AMIS!
POW
BLAM
PAM
FIRE!

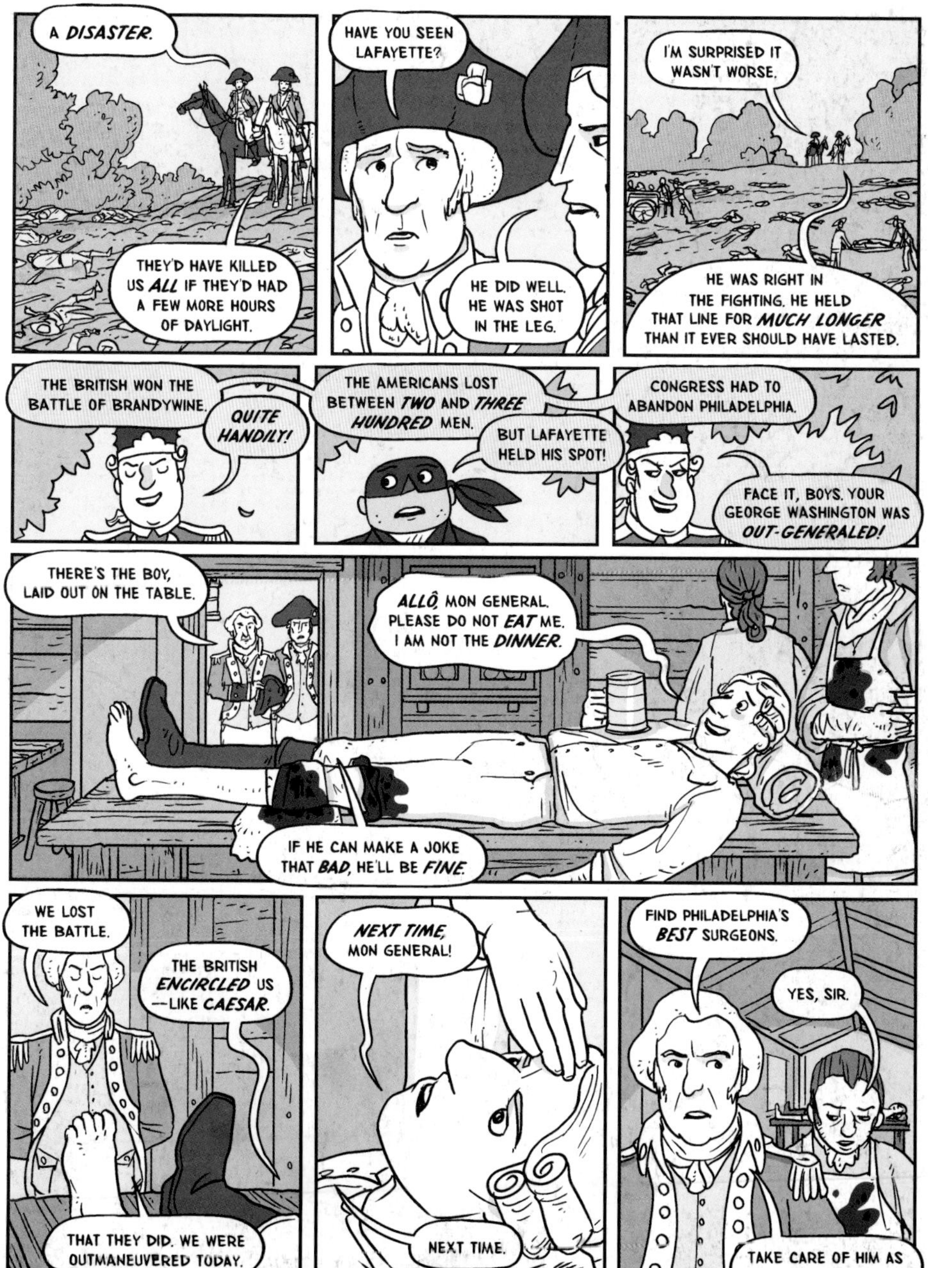
A DISASTER.
THEY'D HAVE KILLED US ALL IF THEY'D HAD A FEW MORE HOURS OF DAYLIGHT.
HAVE YOU SEEN LAFAYETTE?
HE DID WELL. HE WAS SHOT IN THE LEG.
I'M SURPRISED IT WASN'T WORSE.
HE WAS RIGHT IN THE FIGHTING. HE HELD THAT LINE FOR MUCH LONGER THAN IT EVER SHOULD HAVE LASTED.
THE BRITISH WON THE BATTLE OF BRANDYWINE.
QUITE HANDILY!
THE AMERICANS LOST BETWEEN TWO AND THREE HUNDRED MEN.
BUT LAFAYETTE HELD HIS SPOT!
CONGRESS HAD TO ABANDON PHILADELPHIA.
FACE IT, BOYS. YOUR GEORGE WASHINGTON WAS OUT-GENERALED!
THERE'S THE BOY, LAID OUT ON THE TABLE.
ALLÔ, MON GENERAL. PLEASE DO NOT EAT ME. I AM NOT THE DINNER.
IF HE CAN MAKE A JOKE THAT BAD, HE'LL BE FINE.
WE LOST THE BATTLE.
THE BRITISH ENCIRCLED US —LIKE CAESAR.
THAT THEY DID. WE WERE OUTMANEUVERED TODAY.
NEXT TIME, MON GENERAL!
NEXT TIME.
FIND PHILADELPHIA'S BEST SURGEONS.
YES, SIR.
TAKE CARE OF HIM AS IF HE WERE MY SON.

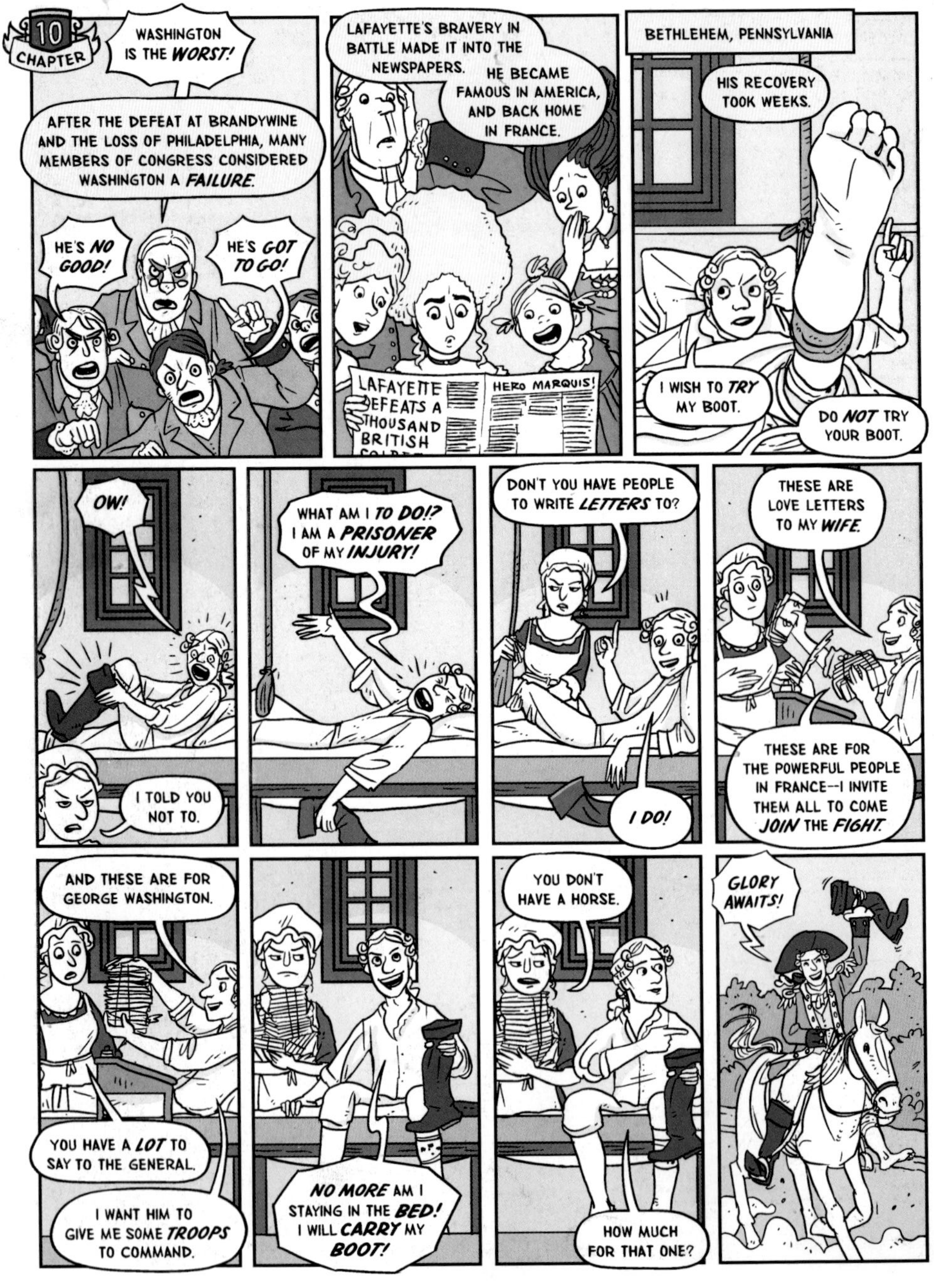
10
CHAPTER
WASHINGTON IS THE WORST!
AFTER THE DEFEAT AT BRANDYWINE AND THE LOSS OF PHILADELPHIA, MANY MEMBERS OF CONGRESS CONSIDERED WASHINGTON A FAILURE.
HE'S NO GOOD!
HE'S GOT TO GO!
LAFAYETTE'S BRAVERY IN BATTLE MADE IT INTO THE NEWSPAPERS.
HE BECAME FAMOUS IN AMERICA, AND BACK HOME IN FRANCE.
LAFAYETTE DEFEATS A THOUSAND BRITISH
HERO MARQUIS!
BETHLEHEM, PENNSYLVANIA
HIS RECOVERY TOOK WEEKS.
I WISH TO TRY MY BOOT.
DO NOT TRY YOUR BOOT.
OW!
I TOLD YOU NOT TO.
WHAT AM I TO DO!? I AM A PRISONER OF MY INJURY!
DON'T YOU HAVE PEOPLE TO WRITE LETTERS TO?
I DO!
THESE ARE LOVE LETTERS TO MY WIFE.
THESE ARE FOR THE POWERFUL PEOPLE IN FRANCE--I INVITE THEM ALL TO COME JOIN THE FIGHT.
AND THESE ARE FOR GEORGE WASHINGTON.
YOU HAVE A LOT TO SAY TO THE GENERAL.
I WANT HIM TO GIVE ME SOME TROOPS TO COMMAND.
NO MORE AM I STAYING IN THE BED! I WILL CARRY MY BOOT!
YOU DON'T HAVE A HORSE.
HOW MUCH FOR THAT ONE?
GLORY AWAITS!

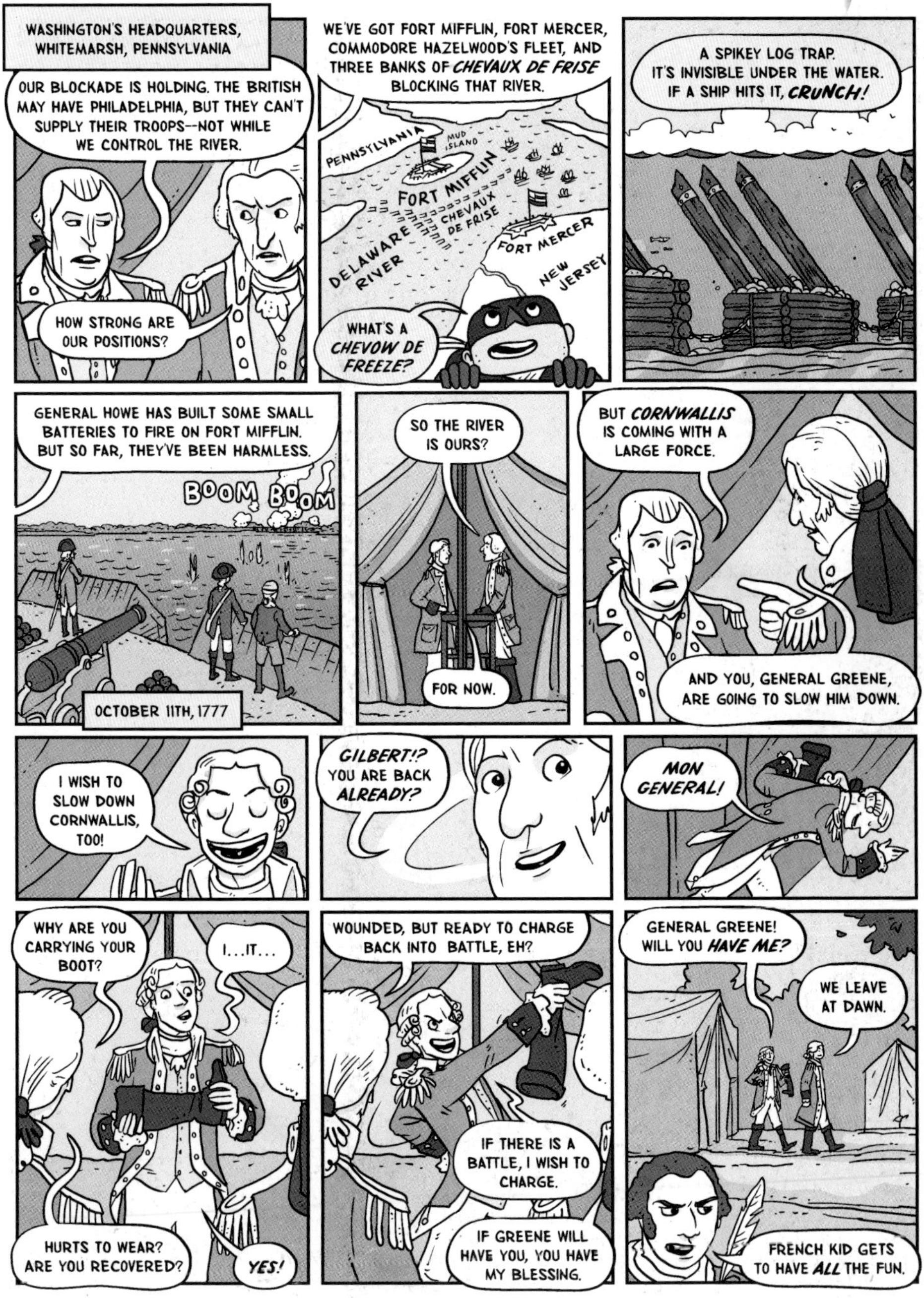

WASHINGTON'S HEADQUARTERS, WHITEMARSH, PENNSYLVANIA
OUR BLOCKADE IS HOLDING. THE BRITISH MAY HAVE PHILADELPHIA, BUT THEY CAN'T SUPPLY THEIR TROOPS--NOT WHILE WE CONTROL THE RIVER.
HOW STRONG ARE OUR POSITIONS?
WE'VE GOT FORT MIFFLIN, FORT MERCER, COMMODORE HAZELWOOD'S FLEET, AND THREE BANKS OF *CHEVAUX DE FRISE* BLOCKING THAT RIVER.
PENNSYLVANIA
MUD ISLAND
FORT MIFFLIN
CHEVAUX DE FRISE
DELAWARE RIVER
FORT MERCER
NEW JERSEY
WHAT'S A *CHEVOW DE FREEZE?*
A SPIKEY LOG TRAP. IT'S INVISIBLE UNDER THE WATER. IF A SHIP HITS IT, *CRUNCH!*
GENERAL HOWE HAS BUILT SOME SMALL BATTERIES TO FIRE ON FORT MIFFLIN. BUT SO FAR, THEY'VE BEEN HARMLESS.
BOOM BOOM
OCTOBER 11TH, 1777
SO THE RIVER IS OURS?
FOR NOW.
BUT *CORNWALLIS* IS COMING WITH A LARGE FORCE.
AND YOU, GENERAL GREENE, ARE GOING TO SLOW HIM DOWN.
I WISH TO SLOW DOWN CORNWALLIS, TOO!
GILBERT!? YOU ARE BACK *ALREADY?*
MON GENERAL!
WHY ARE YOU CARRYING YOUR BOOT?
I...IT...
HURTS TO WEAR? ARE YOU RECOVERED?
YES!
WOUNDED, BUT READY TO CHARGE BACK INTO BATTLE, EH?
IF THERE IS A BATTLE, I WISH TO CHARGE.
IF GREENE WILL HAVE YOU, YOU HAVE MY BLESSING.
GENERAL GREENE! WILL YOU *HAVE ME?*
WE LEAVE AT DAWN.
FRENCH KID GETS TO HAVE *ALL* THE FUN.

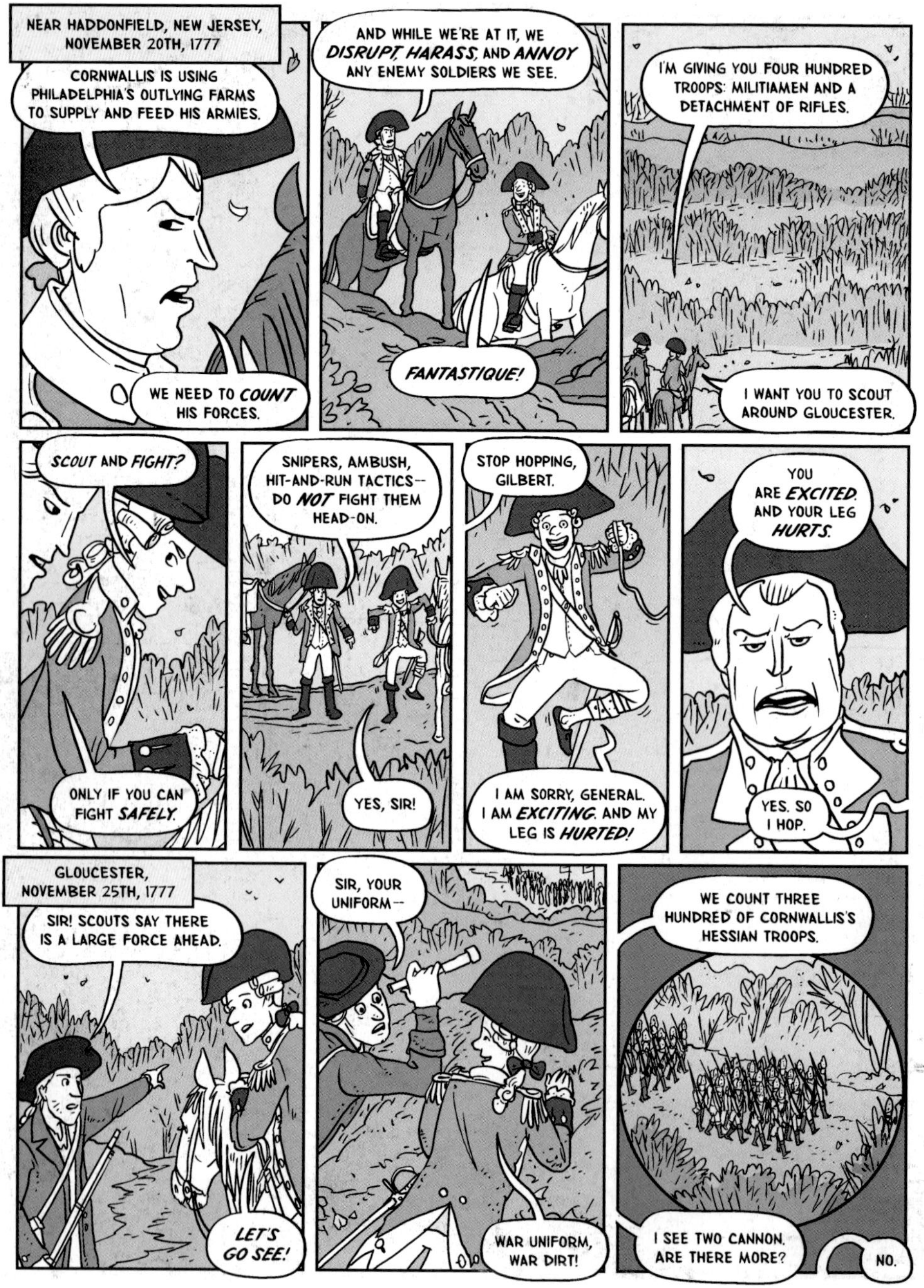
NEAR HADDONFIELD, NEW JERSEY, NOVEMBER 20TH, 1777
CORNWALLIS IS USING PHILADELPHIA'S OUTLYING FARMS TO SUPPLY AND FEED HIS ARMIES.
WE NEED TO *COUNT* HIS FORCES.
AND WHILE WE'RE AT IT, WE *DISRUPT, HARASS,* AND *ANNOY* ANY ENEMY SOLDIERS WE SEE.
FANTASTIQUE!
I'M GIVING YOU FOUR HUNDRED TROOPS: MILITIAMEN AND A DETACHMENT OF RIFLES.
I WANT YOU TO SCOUT AROUND GLOUCESTER.
SCOUT AND *FIGHT?*
ONLY IF YOU CAN FIGHT *SAFELY.*
SNIPERS, AMBUSH, HIT-AND-RUN TACTICS-- DO *NOT* FIGHT THEM HEAD-ON.
YES, SIR!
STOP HOPPING, GILBERT.
I AM SORRY, GENERAL. I AM *EXCITING.* AND MY LEG IS *HURTED!*
YOU ARE *EXCITED.* AND YOUR LEG *HURTS.*
YES. SO I HOP.
GLOUCESTER, NOVEMBER 25TH, 1777
SIR! SCOUTS SAY THERE IS A LARGE FORCE AHEAD.
LET'S GO SEE!
SIR, YOUR UNIFORM--
WAR UNIFORM, WAR DIRT!
WE COUNT THREE HUNDRED OF CORNWALLIS'S HESSIAN TROOPS.
I SEE TWO CANNON. ARE THERE MORE?
NO.

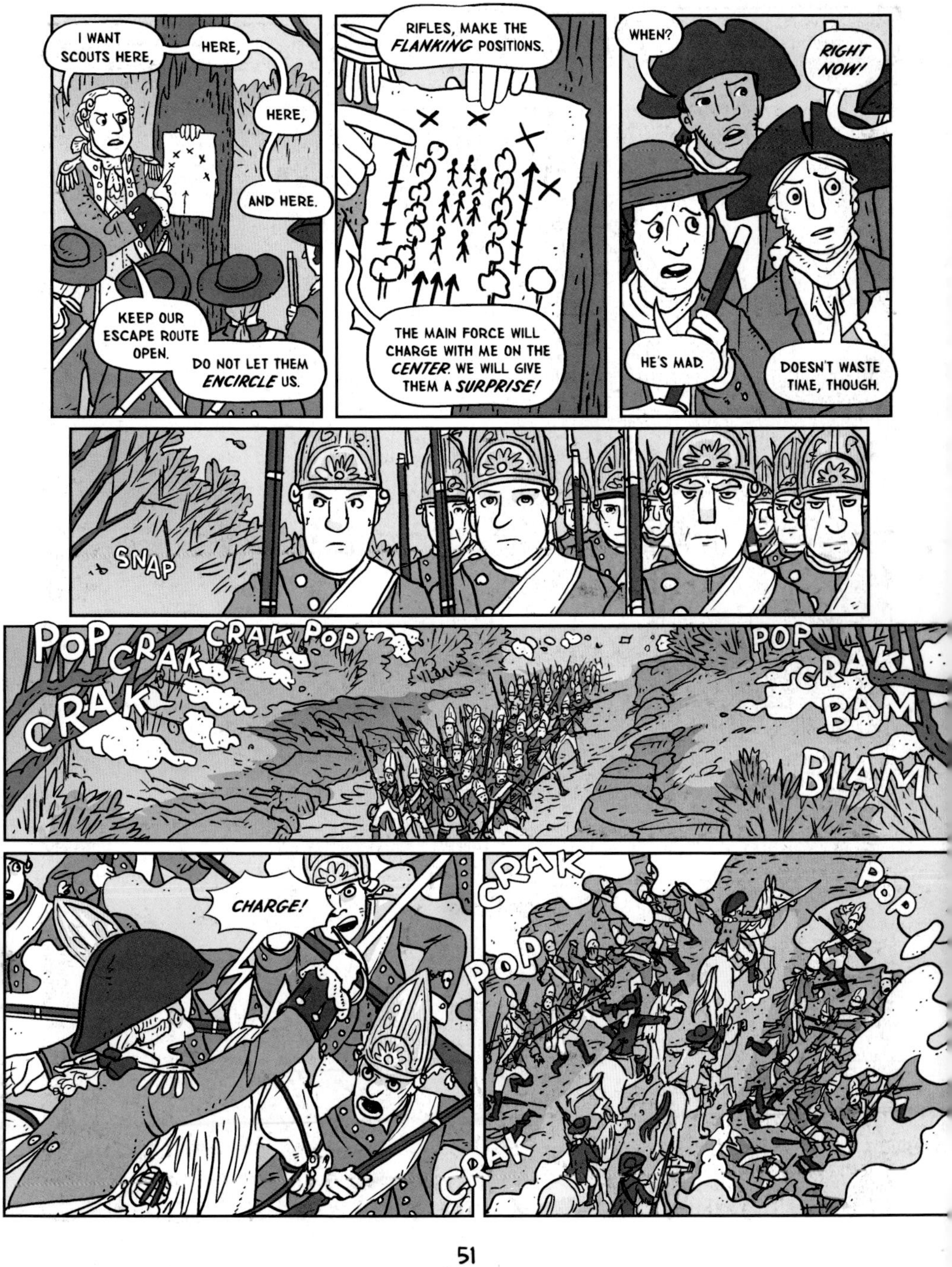

I WANT SCOUTS HERE,
HERE,
HERE,
AND HERE.
KEEP OUR ESCAPE ROUTE OPEN.
DO NOT LET THEM *ENCIRCLE* US.
RIFLES, MAKE THE *FLANKING* POSITIONS.
THE MAIN FORCE WILL CHARGE WITH ME ON THE *CENTER*. WE WILL GIVE THEM A *SURPRISE*!
WHEN?
RIGHT NOW!
HE'S MAD.
DOESN'T WASTE TIME, THOUGH.
SNAP
POP
CRAK
CRAK
CRAK
POP
POP
CRAK
BAM
BLAM
CHARGE!
CRAK
POP
POP
CRAK

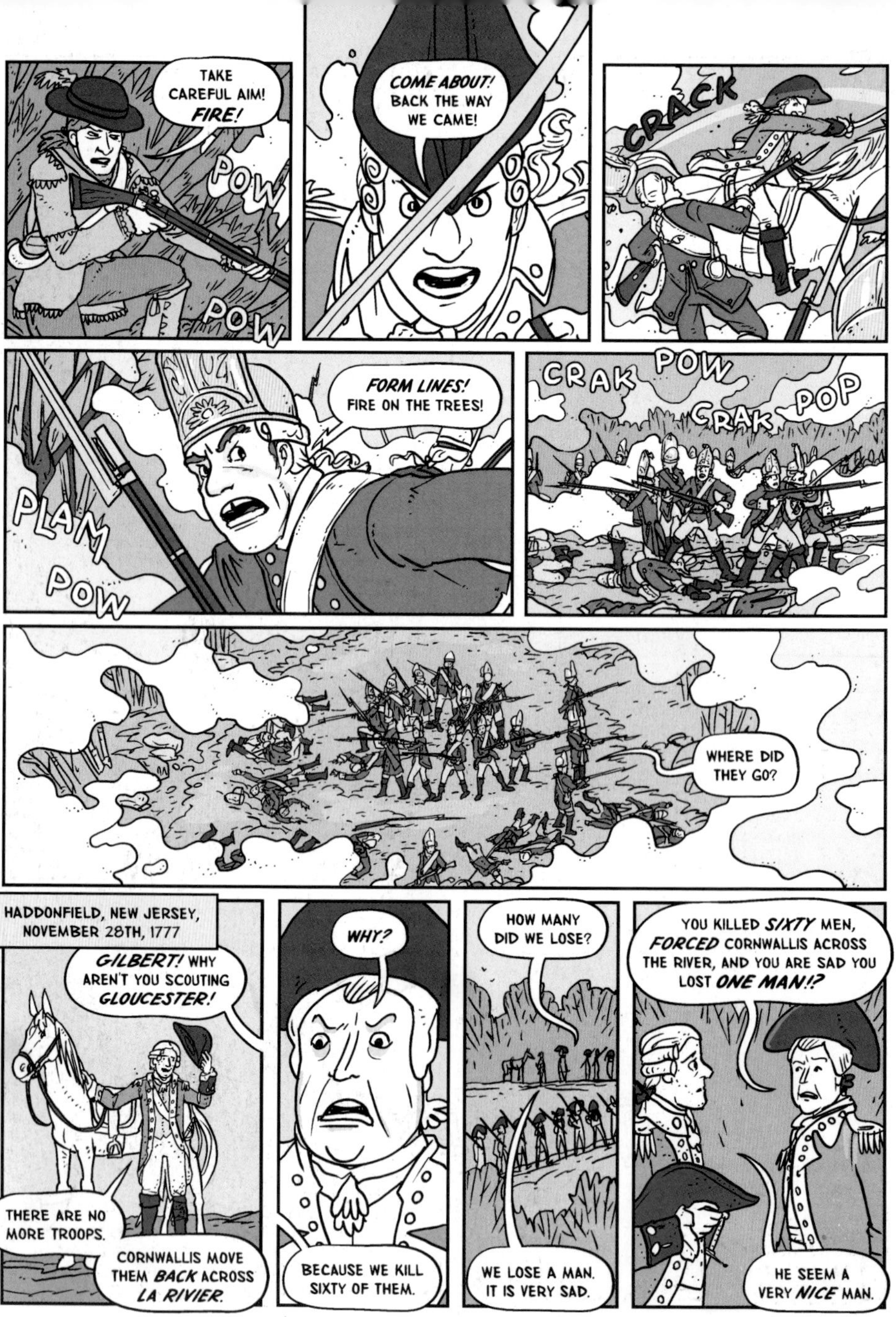
TAKE CAREFUL AIM! FIRE!
POW
POW
COME ABOUT! BACK THE WAY WE CAME!
CRACK
FORM LINES! FIRE ON THE TREES!
PLAM
POW
CRAK POW
CRAK POP
WHERE DID THEY GO?
HADDONFIELD, NEW JERSEY, NOVEMBER 28TH, 1777
GILBERT! WHY AREN'T YOU SCOUTING GLOUCESTER!
THERE ARE NO MORE TROOPS.
CORNWALLIS MOVE THEM BACK ACROSS LA RIVIER.
WHY?
BECAUSE WE KILL SIXTY OF THEM.
HOW MANY DID WE LOSE?
WE LOSE A MAN. IT IS VERY SAD.
YOU KILLED SIXTY MEN, FORCED CORNWALLIS ACROSS THE RIVER, AND YOU ARE SAD YOU LOST ONE MAN!?
HE SEEM A VERY NICE MAN.

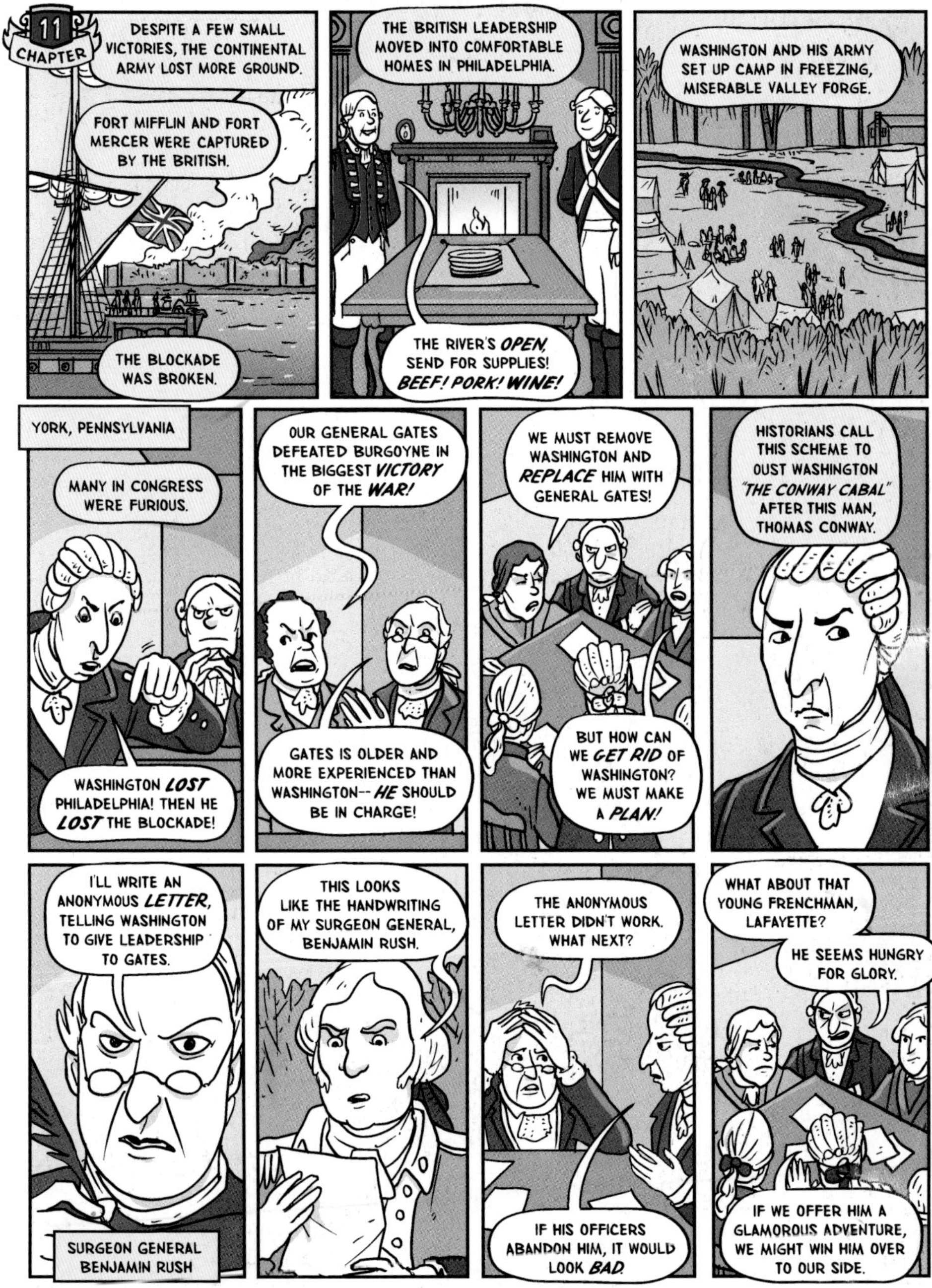
11 CHAPTER
DESPITE A FEW SMALL VICTORIES, THE CONTINENTAL ARMY LOST MORE GROUND.
FORT MIFFLIN AND FORT MERCER WERE CAPTURED BY THE BRITISH.
THE BLOCKADE WAS BROKEN.
THE BRITISH LEADERSHIP MOVED INTO COMFORTABLE HOMES IN PHILADELPHIA.
THE RIVER'S *OPEN*, SEND FOR SUPPLIES! ***BEEF! PORK! WINE!***
WASHINGTON AND HIS ARMY SET UP CAMP IN FREEZING, MISERABLE VALLEY FORGE.
YORK, PENNSYLVANIA
MANY IN CONGRESS WERE FURIOUS.
WASHINGTON ***LOST*** PHILADELPHIA! THEN HE ***LOST*** THE BLOCKADE!
OUR GENERAL GATES DEFEATED BURGOYNE IN THE BIGGEST ***VICTORY*** OF THE ***WAR!***
GATES IS OLDER AND MORE EXPERIENCED THAN WASHINGTON-- ***HE*** SHOULD BE IN CHARGE!
WE MUST REMOVE WASHINGTON AND ***REPLACE*** HIM WITH GENERAL GATES!
BUT HOW CAN WE ***GET RID*** OF WASHINGTON? WE MUST MAKE A ***PLAN!***
HISTORIANS CALL THIS SCHEME TO OUST WASHINGTON ***"THE CONWAY CABAL"*** AFTER THIS MAN, THOMAS CONWAY.
I'LL WRITE AN ANONYMOUS ***LETTER***, TELLING WASHINGTON TO GIVE LEADERSHIP TO GATES.
SURGEON GENERAL BENJAMIN RUSH
THIS LOOKS LIKE THE HANDWRITING OF MY SURGEON GENERAL, BENJAMIN RUSH.
THE ANONYMOUS LETTER DIDN'T WORK. WHAT NEXT?
IF HIS OFFICERS ABANDON HIM, IT WOULD LOOK ***BAD***.
WHAT ABOUT THAT YOUNG FRENCHMAN, LAFAYETTE?
HE SEEMS HUNGRY FOR GLORY.
IF WE OFFER HIM A GLAMOROUS ADVENTURE, WE MIGHT WIN HIM OVER TO OUR SIDE.

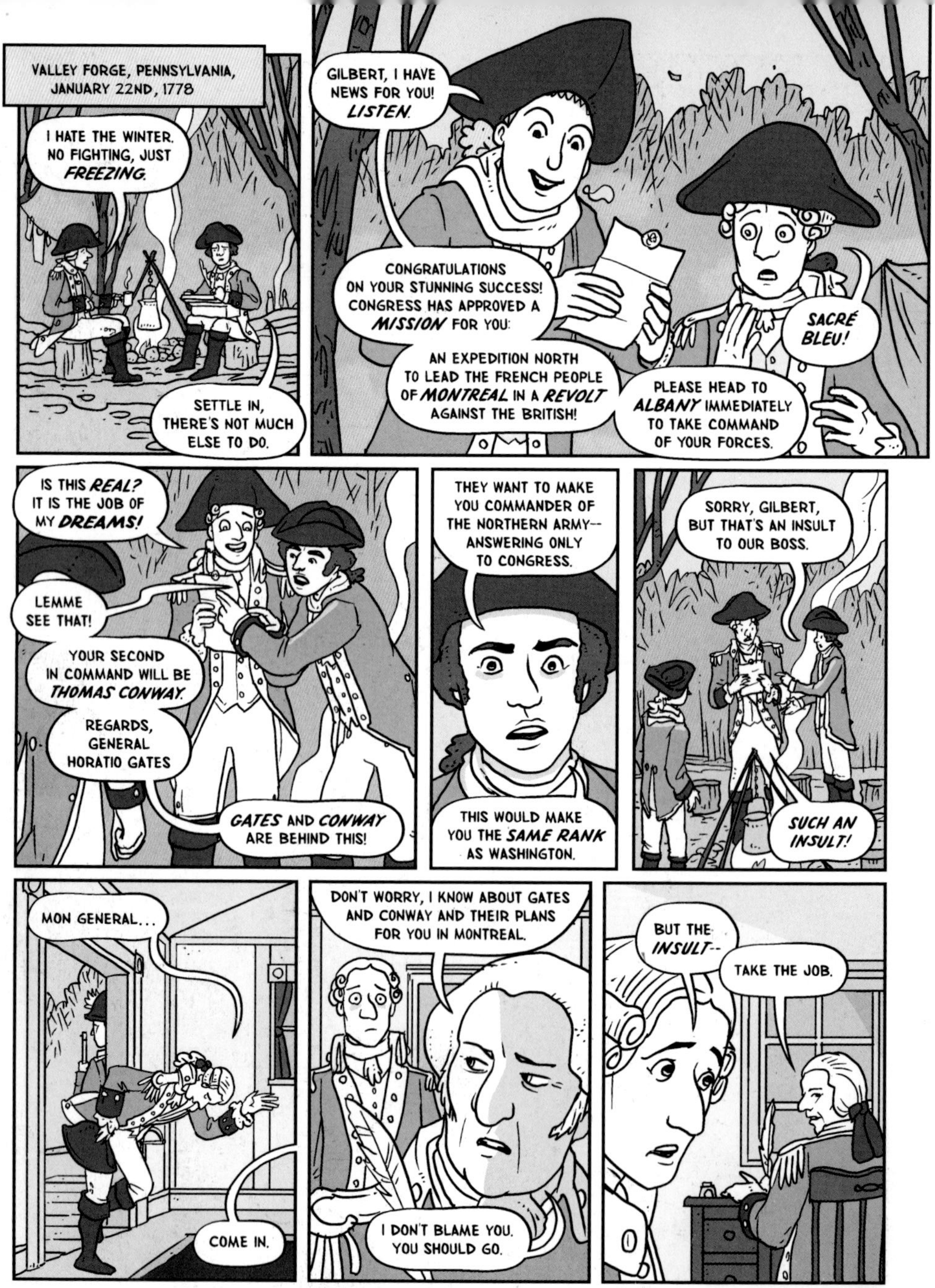
VALLEY FORGE, PENNSYLVANIA, JANUARY 22ND, 1778
I HATE THE WINTER. NO FIGHTING, JUST FREEZING.
SETTLE IN, THERE'S NOT MUCH ELSE TO DO.
GILBERT, I HAVE NEWS FOR YOU! LISTEN.
CONGRATULATIONS ON YOUR STUNNING SUCCESS! CONGRESS HAS APPROVED A MISSION FOR YOU:
AN EXPEDITION NORTH TO LEAD THE FRENCH PEOPLE OF MONTREAL IN A REVOLT AGAINST THE BRITISH!
SACRÉ BLEU!
PLEASE HEAD TO ALBANY IMMEDIATELY TO TAKE COMMAND OF YOUR FORCES.
IS THIS REAL? IT IS THE JOB OF MY DREAMS!
LEMME SEE THAT!
YOUR SECOND IN COMMAND WILL BE THOMAS CONWAY.
REGARDS, GENERAL HORATIO GATES
GATES AND CONWAY ARE BEHIND THIS!
THEY WANT TO MAKE YOU COMMANDER OF THE NORTHERN ARMY-- ANSWERING ONLY TO CONGRESS.
THIS WOULD MAKE YOU THE SAME RANK AS WASHINGTON.
SORRY, GILBERT, BUT THAT'S AN INSULT TO OUR BOSS.
SUCH AN INSULT!
MON GENERAL...
COME IN.
DON'T WORRY, I KNOW ABOUT GATES AND CONWAY AND THEIR PLANS FOR YOU IN MONTREAL.
I DON'T BLAME YOU. YOU SHOULD GO.
BUT THE INSULT--
TAKE THE JOB.

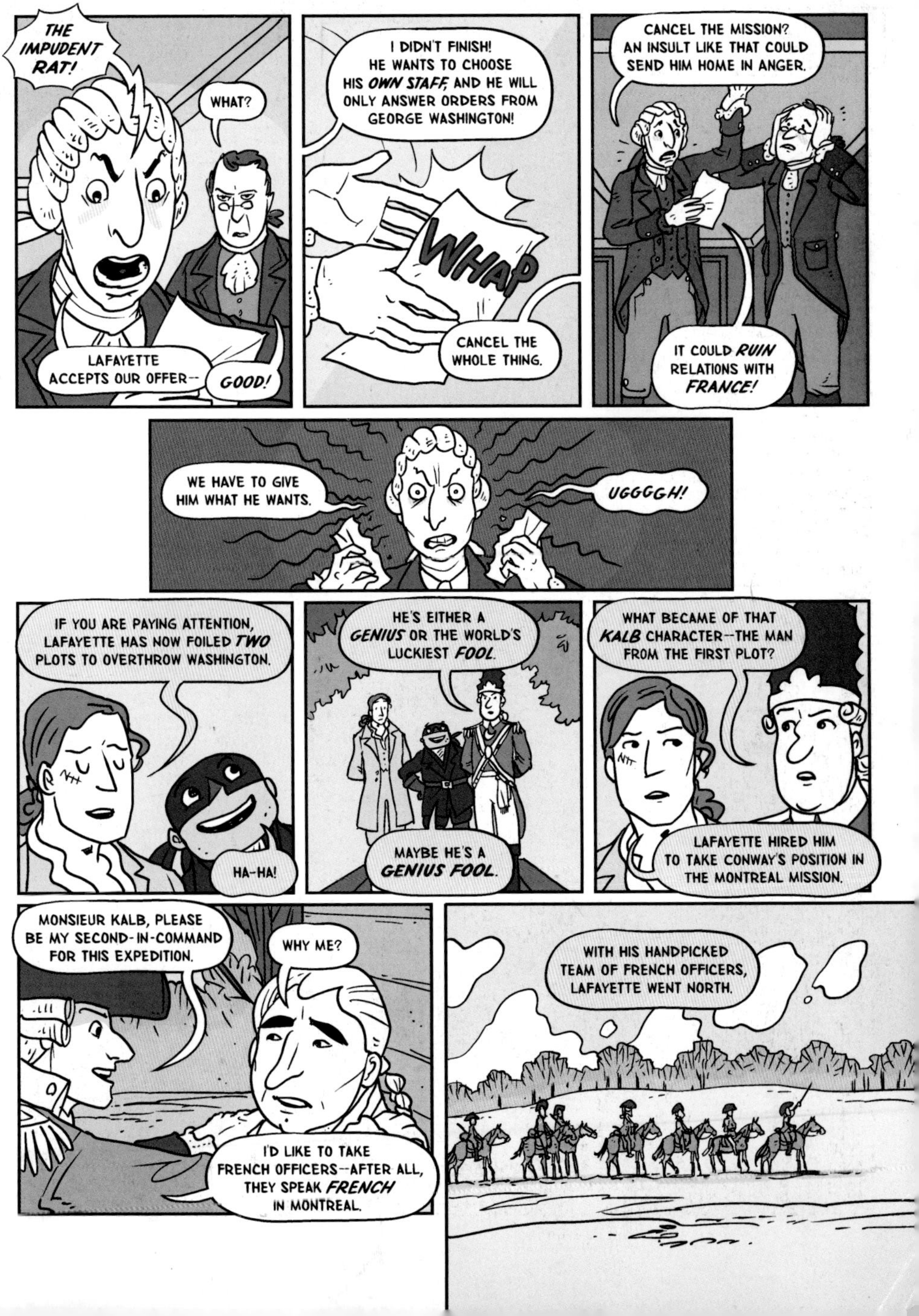
THE IMPUDENT RAT!
WHAT?
LAFAYETTE ACCEPTS OUR OFFER--
GOOD!
I DIDN'T FINISH! HE WANTS TO CHOOSE HIS OWN STAFF, AND HE WILL ONLY ANSWER ORDERS FROM GEORGE WASHINGTON!
WHAP
CANCEL THE WHOLE THING.
CANCEL THE MISSION? AN INSULT LIKE THAT COULD SEND HIM HOME IN ANGER.
IT COULD RUIN RELATIONS WITH FRANCE!
WE HAVE TO GIVE HIM WHAT HE WANTS.
UGGGGH!
IF YOU ARE PAYING ATTENTION, LAFAYETTE HAS NOW FOILED TWO PLOTS TO OVERTHROW WASHINGTON.
HA-HA!
HE'S EITHER A GENIUS OR THE WORLD'S LUCKIEST FOOL.
MAYBE HE'S A GENIUS FOOL.
WHAT BECAME OF THAT KALB CHARACTER--THE MAN FROM THE FIRST PLOT?
LAFAYETTE HIRED HIM TO TAKE CONWAY'S POSITION IN THE MONTREAL MISSION.
MONSIEUR KALB, PLEASE BE MY SECOND-IN-COMMAND FOR THIS EXPEDITION.
WHY ME?
I'D LIKE TO TAKE FRENCH OFFICERS--AFTER ALL, THEY SPEAK FRENCH IN MONTREAL.
WITH HIS HANDPICKED TEAM OF FRENCH OFFICERS, LAFAYETTE WENT NORTH.

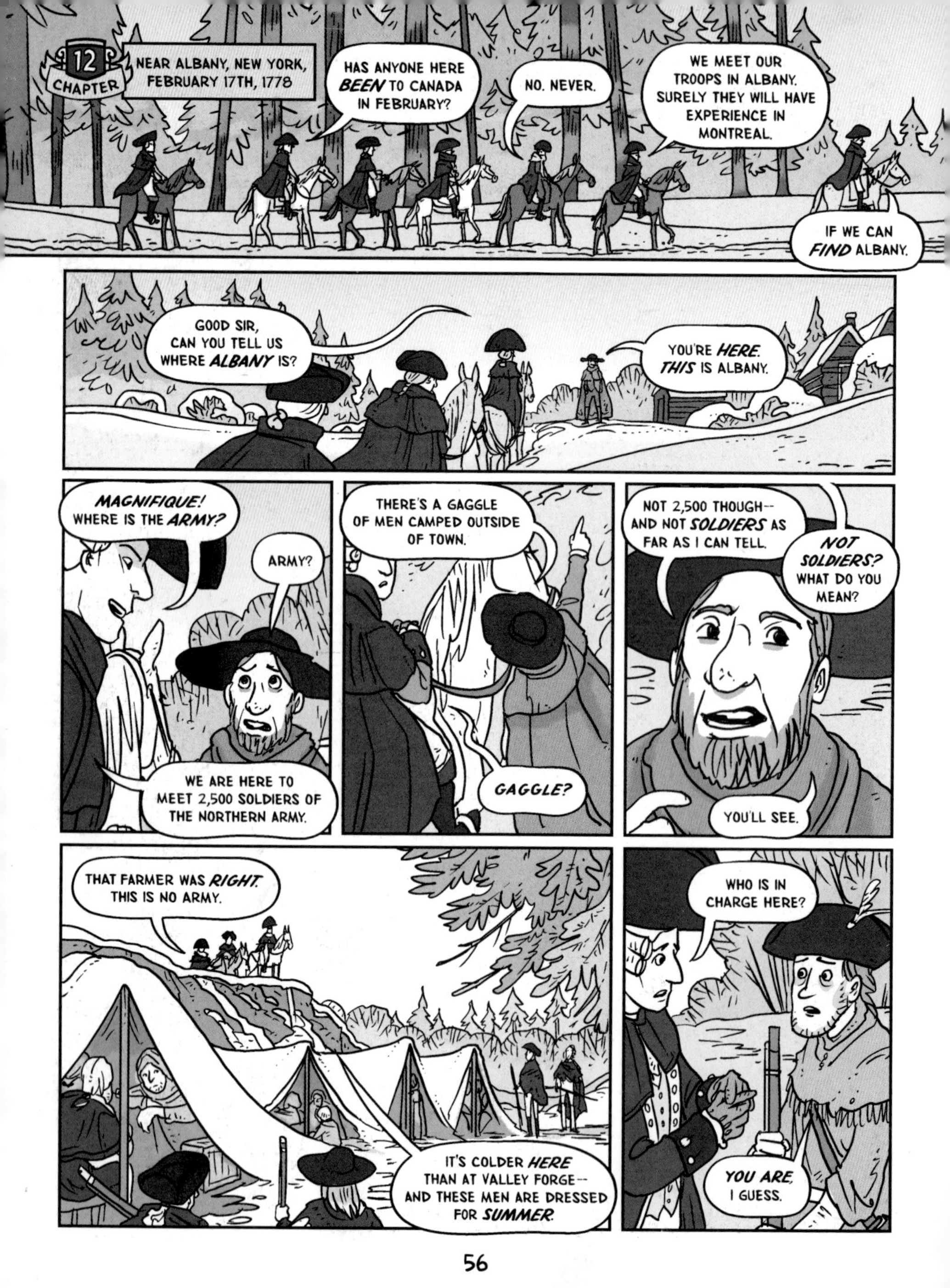
12 CHAPTER
NEAR ALBANY, NEW YORK, FEBRUARY 17TH, 1778
HAS ANYONE HERE BEEN TO CANADA IN FEBRUARY?
NO. NEVER.
WE MEET OUR TROOPS IN ALBANY. SURELY THEY WILL HAVE EXPERIENCE IN MONTREAL.
IF WE CAN FIND ALBANY.
GOOD SIR, CAN YOU TELL US WHERE ALBANY IS?
YOU'RE HERE. THIS IS ALBANY.
MAGNIFIQUE! WHERE IS THE ARMY?
ARMY?
WE ARE HERE TO MEET 2,500 SOLDIERS OF THE NORTHERN ARMY.
THERE'S A GAGGLE OF MEN CAMPED OUTSIDE OF TOWN.
GAGGLE?
NOT 2,500 THOUGH-- AND NOT SOLDIERS AS FAR AS I CAN TELL.
NOT SOLDIERS? WHAT DO YOU MEAN?
YOU'LL SEE.
THAT FARMER WAS RIGHT. THIS IS NO ARMY.
IT'S COLDER HERE THAN AT VALLEY FORGE-- AND THESE MEN ARE DRESSED FOR SUMMER.
WHO IS IN CHARGE HERE?
YOU ARE, I GUESS.

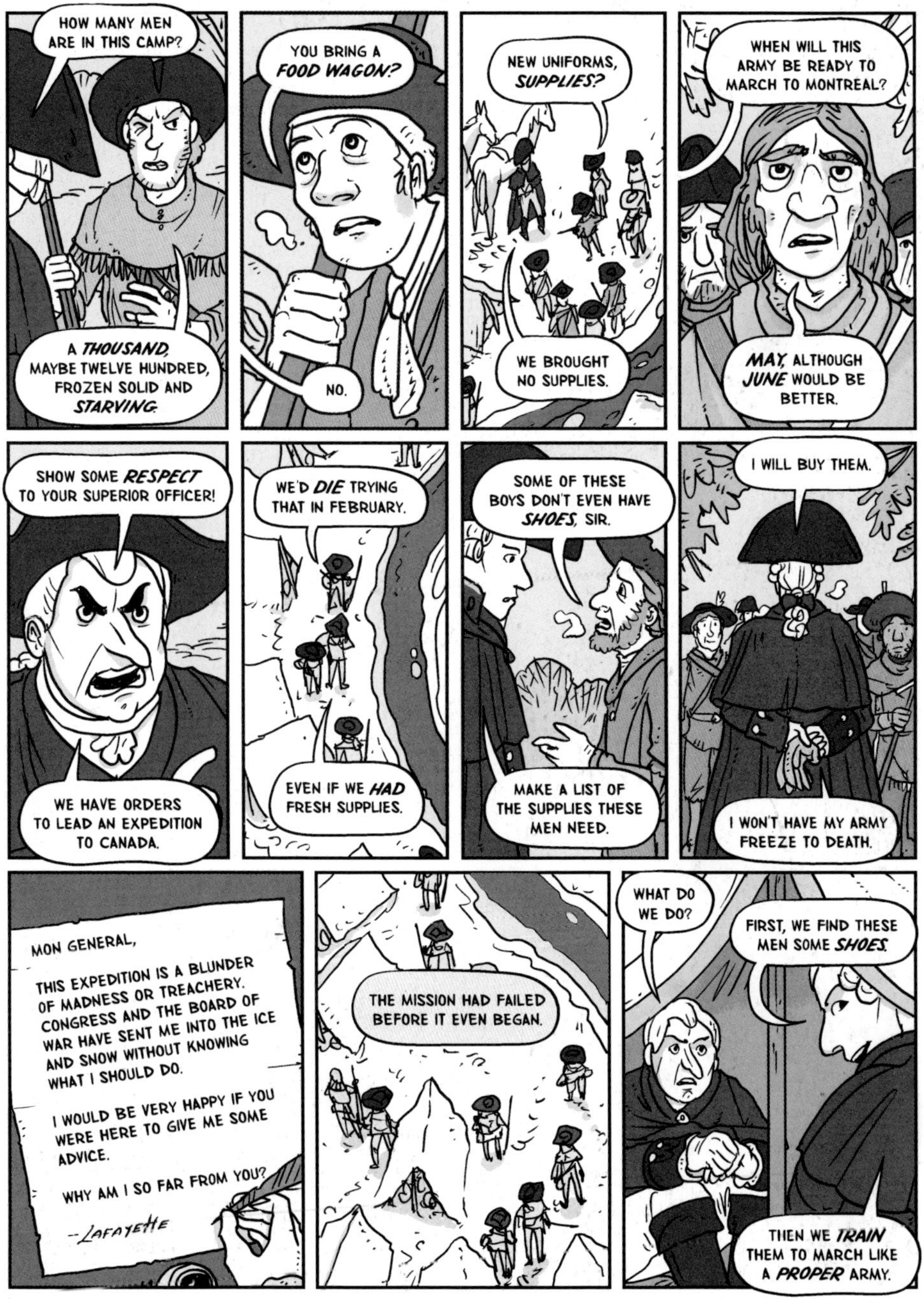
HOW MANY MEN ARE IN THIS CAMP?
A *THOUSAND,* MAYBE TWELVE HUNDRED, FROZEN SOLID AND *STARVING.*
YOU BRING A *FOOD WAGON?*
NO.
NEW UNIFORMS, *SUPPLIES?*
WE BROUGHT NO SUPPLIES.
WHEN WILL THIS ARMY BE READY TO MARCH TO MONTREAL?
MAY, ALTHOUGH *JUNE* WOULD BE BETTER.
SHOW SOME *RESPECT* TO YOUR SUPERIOR OFFICER!
WE HAVE ORDERS TO LEAD AN EXPEDITION TO CANADA.
WE'D *DIE* TRYING THAT IN FEBRUARY.
EVEN IF WE *HAD* FRESH SUPPLIES.
SOME OF THESE BOYS DON'T EVEN HAVE *SHOES,* SIR.
MAKE A LIST OF THE SUPPLIES THESE MEN NEED.
I WILL BUY THEM.
I WON'T HAVE MY ARMY FREEZE TO DEATH.
MON GENERAL,
THIS EXPEDITION IS A BLUNDER OF MADNESS OR TREACHERY. CONGRESS AND THE BOARD OF WAR HAVE SENT ME INTO THE ICE AND SNOW WITHOUT KNOWING WHAT I SHOULD DO.
I WOULD BE VERY HAPPY IF YOU WERE HERE TO GIVE ME SOME ADVICE.
WHY AM I SO FAR FROM YOU?
—LAFAYETTE
THE MISSION HAD FAILED BEFORE IT EVEN BEGAN.
WHAT DO WE DO?
FIRST, WE FIND THESE MEN SOME *SHOES.*
THEN WE *TRAIN* THEM TO MARCH LIKE A *PROPER* ARMY.

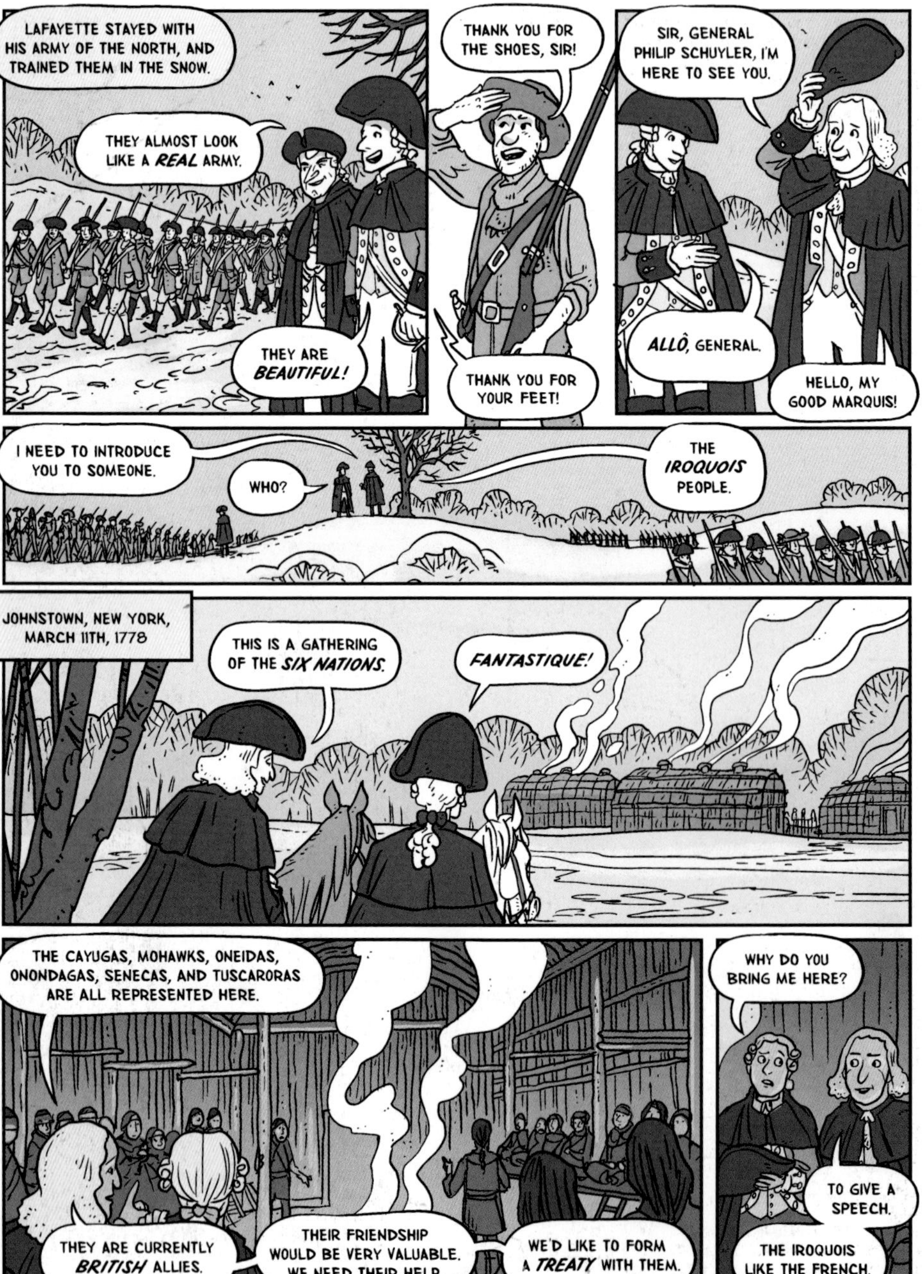
LAFAYETTE STAYED WITH HIS ARMY OF THE NORTH, AND TRAINED THEM IN THE SNOW.
THEY ALMOST LOOK LIKE A REAL ARMY.
THEY ARE BEAUTIFUL!
THANK YOU FOR THE SHOES, SIR!
THANK YOU FOR YOUR FEET!
SIR, GENERAL PHILIP SCHUYLER, I'M HERE TO SEE YOU.
ALLÔ, GENERAL.
HELLO, MY GOOD MARQUIS!
I NEED TO INTRODUCE YOU TO SOMEONE.
WHO?
THE IROQUOIS PEOPLE.
JOHNSTOWN, NEW YORK, MARCH 11TH, 1778
THIS IS A GATHERING OF THE SIX NATIONS.
FANTASTIQUE!
THE CAYUGAS, MOHAWKS, ONEIDAS, ONONDAGAS, SENECAS, AND TUSCARORAS ARE ALL REPRESENTED HERE.
THEY ARE CURRENTLY BRITISH ALLIES.
THEIR FRIENDSHIP WOULD BE VERY VALUABLE. WE NEED THEIR HELP.
WE'D LIKE TO FORM A TREATY WITH THEM.
WHY DO YOU BRING ME HERE?
TO GIVE A SPEECH.
THE IROQUOIS LIKE THE FRENCH.

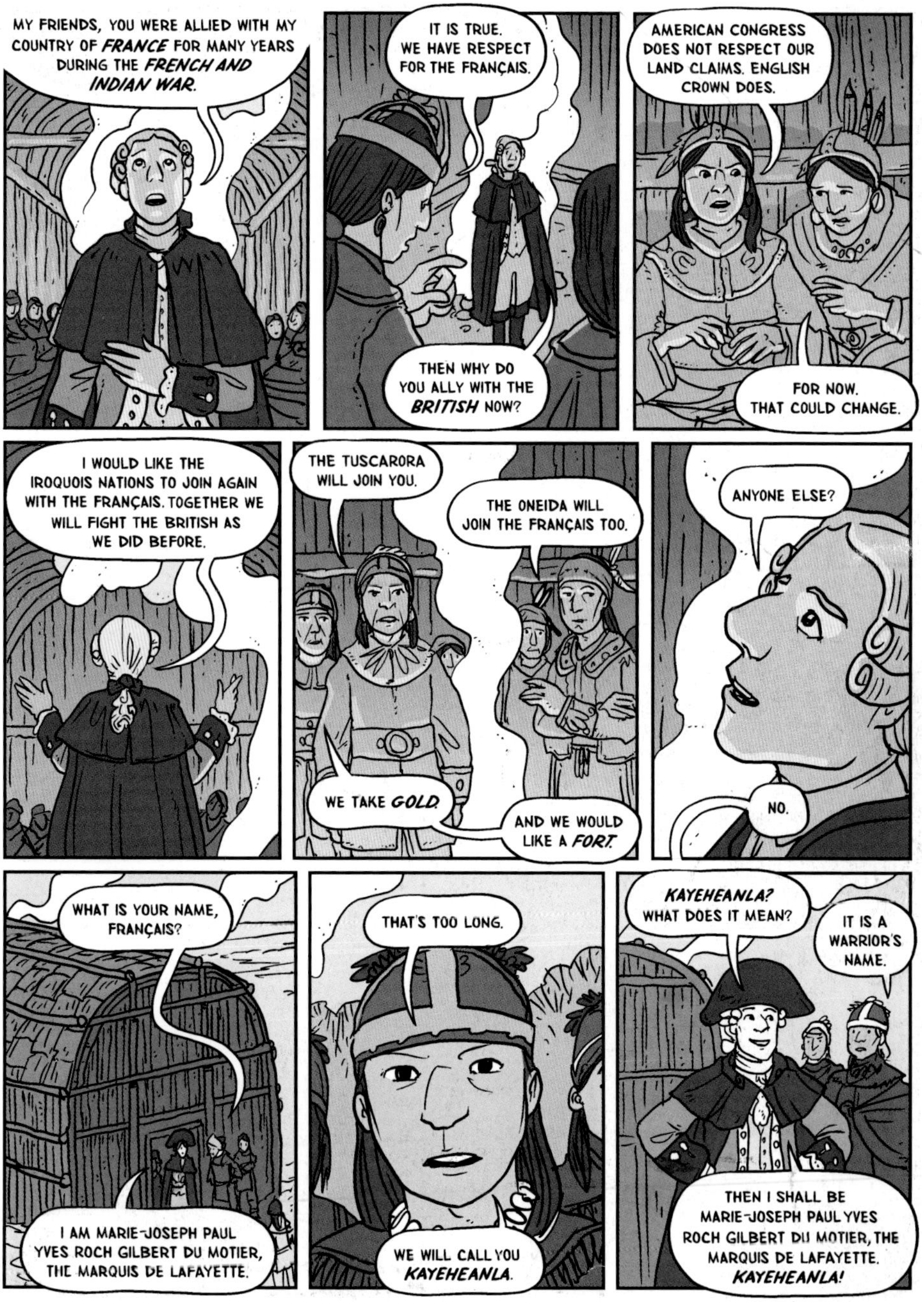
MY FRIENDS, YOU WERE ALLIED WITH MY COUNTRY OF *FRANCE* FOR MANY YEARS DURING THE *FRENCH AND INDIAN WAR*.
IT IS TRUE. WE HAVE RESPECT FOR THE FRANÇAIS.
THEN WHY DO YOU ALLY WITH THE *BRITISH* NOW?
AMERICAN CONGRESS DOES NOT RESPECT OUR LAND CLAIMS. ENGLISH CROWN DOES.
FOR NOW. THAT COULD CHANGE.
I WOULD LIKE THE IROQUOIS NATIONS TO JOIN AGAIN WITH THE FRANÇAIS. TOGETHER WE WILL FIGHT THE BRITISH AS WE DID BEFORE.
THE TUSCARORA WILL JOIN YOU.
THE ONEIDA WILL JOIN THE FRANÇAIS TOO.
WE TAKE *GOLD*.
AND WE WOULD LIKE A *FORT*.
ANYONE ELSE?
NO.
WHAT IS YOUR NAME, FRANÇAIS?
I AM MARIE-JOSEPH PAUL YVES ROCH GILBERT DU MOTIER, THE MARQUIS DE LAFAYETTE.
THAT'S TOO LONG.
WE WILL CALL YOU *KAYEHEANLA*.
KAYEHEANLA? WHAT DOES IT MEAN?
IT IS A WARRIOR'S NAME.
THEN I SHALL BE MARIE-JOSEPH PAUL YVES ROCH GILBERT DU MOTIER, THE MARQUIS DE LAFAYETTE. *KAYEHEANLA!*

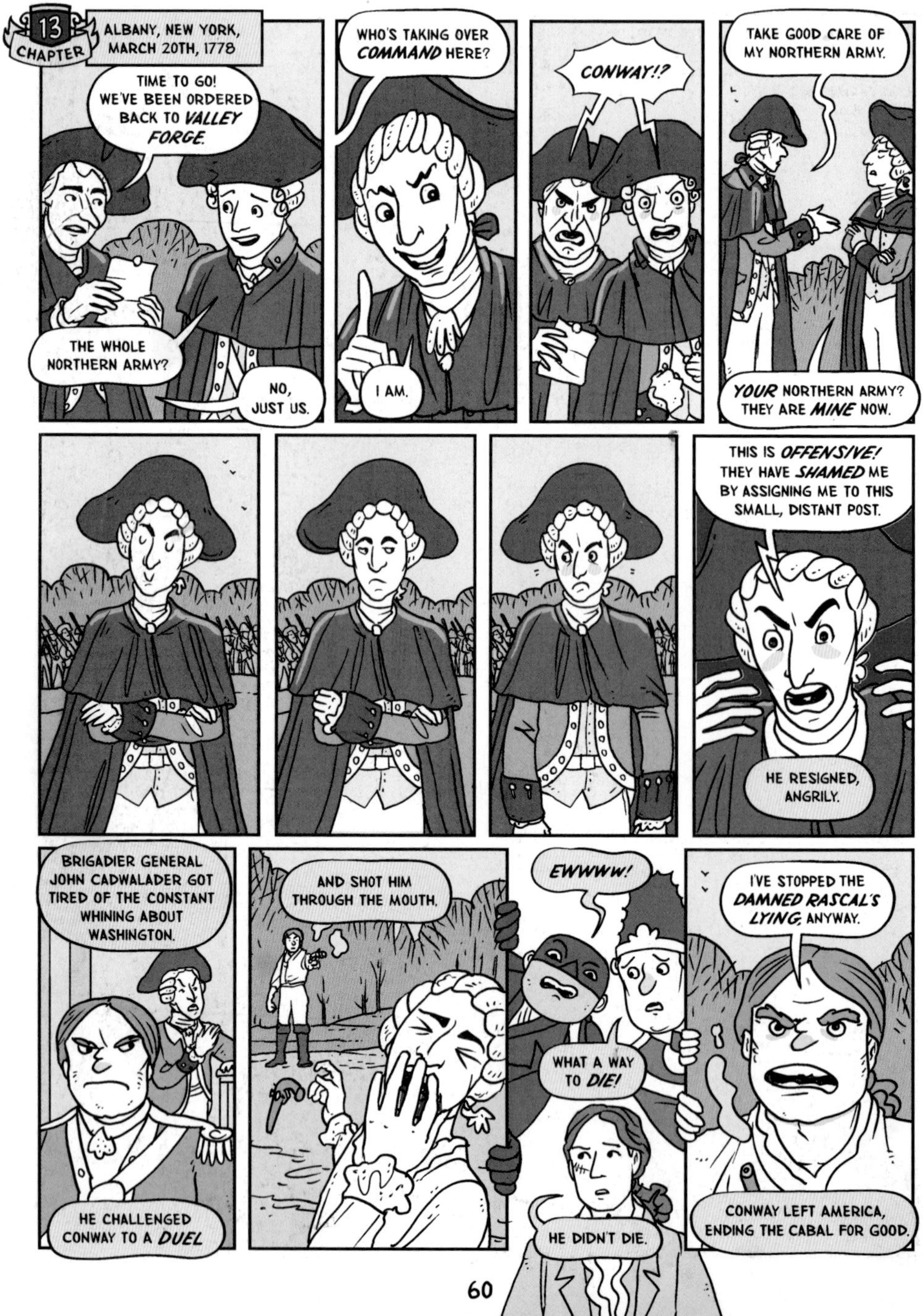
13 CHAPTER
ALBANY, NEW YORK, MARCH 20TH, 1778
TIME TO GO! WE'VE BEEN ORDERED BACK TO *VALLEY FORGE.*
THE WHOLE NORTHERN ARMY?
NO, JUST US.
WHO'S TAKING OVER *COMMAND* HERE?
I AM.
CONWAY!?
TAKE GOOD CARE OF MY NORTHERN ARMY.
YOUR NORTHERN ARMY? THEY ARE *MINE* NOW.
THIS IS *OFFENSIVE!* THEY HAVE *SHAMED* ME BY ASSIGNING ME TO THIS SMALL, DISTANT POST.
HE RESIGNED, ANGRILY.
BRIGADIER GENERAL JOHN CADWALADER GOT TIRED OF THE CONSTANT WHINING ABOUT WASHINGTON.
HE CHALLENGED CONWAY TO A *DUEL*
AND SHOT HIM THROUGH THE MOUTH.
EWWWW!
WHAT A WAY TO *DIE!*
HE DIDN'T DIE.
I'VE STOPPED THE *DAMNED RASCAL'S LYING,* ANYWAY.
CONWAY LEFT AMERICA, ENDING THE CABAL FOR GOOD.

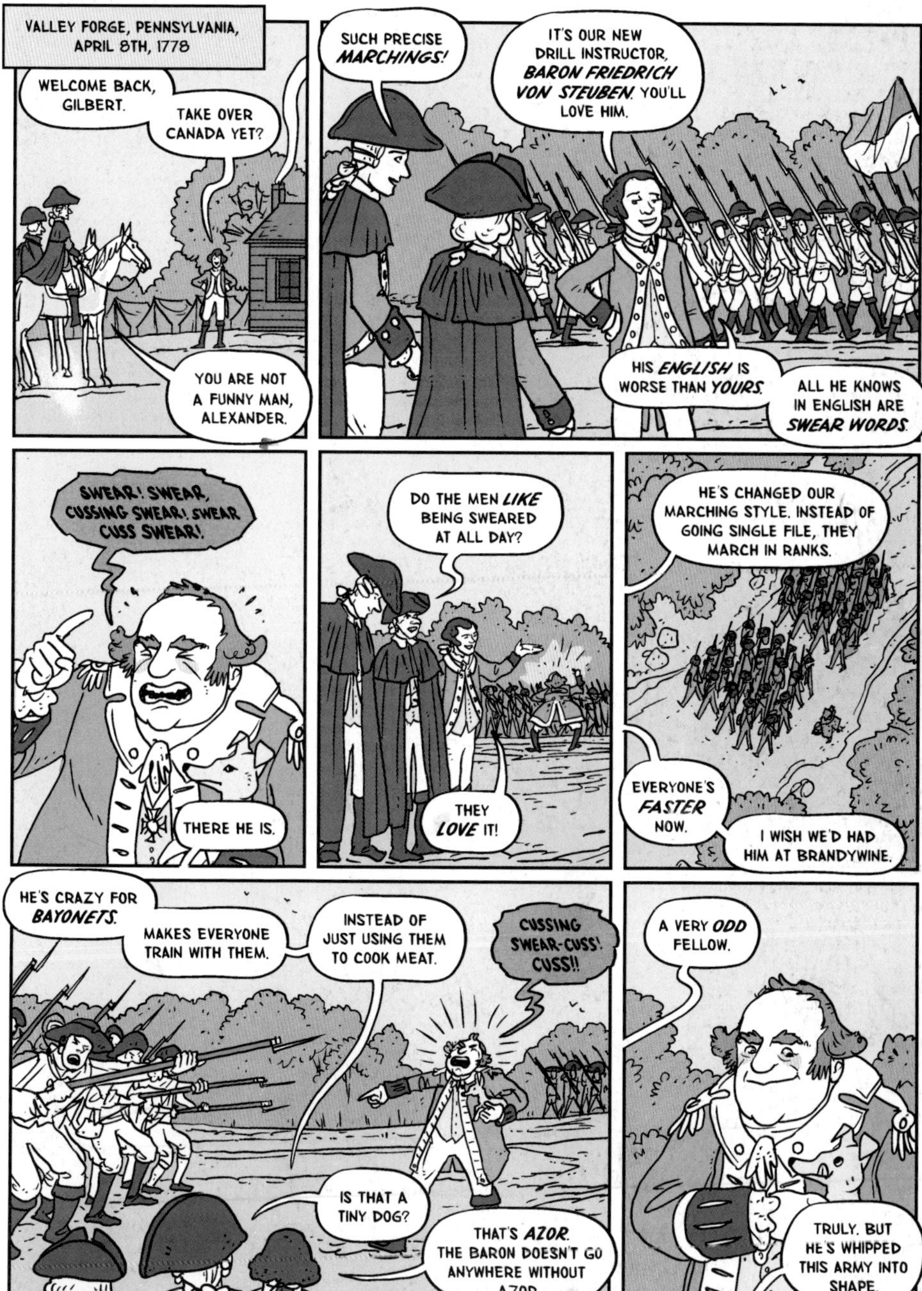
VALLEY FORGE, PENNSYLVANIA, APRIL 8TH, 1778
WELCOME BACK, GILBERT.
TAKE OVER CANADA YET?
YOU ARE NOT A FUNNY MAN, ALEXANDER.
SUCH PRECISE MARCHINGS!
IT'S OUR NEW DRILL INSTRUCTOR, BARON FRIEDRICH VON STEUBEN. YOU'LL LOVE HIM.
HIS ENGLISH IS WORSE THAN YOURS.
ALL HE KNOWS IN ENGLISH ARE SWEAR WORDS.
SWEAR! SWEAR, CUSSING SWEAR!, SWEAR CUSS SWEAR!
THERE HE IS.
DO THE MEN LIKE BEING SWEARED AT ALL DAY?
THEY LOVE IT!
HE'S CHANGED OUR MARCHING STYLE. INSTEAD OF GOING SINGLE FILE, THEY MARCH IN RANKS.
EVERYONE'S FASTER NOW.
I WISH WE'D HAD HIM AT BRANDYWINE.
HE'S CRAZY FOR BAYONETS.
MAKES EVERYONE TRAIN WITH THEM.
INSTEAD OF JUST USING THEM TO COOK MEAT.
CUSSING SWEAR-CUSS! CUSS!!
IS THAT A TINY DOG?
THAT'S AZOR. THE BARON DOESN'T GO ANYWHERE WITHOUT AZOR.
A VERY ODD FELLOW.
TRULY. BUT HE'S WHIPPED THIS ARMY INTO SHAPE.

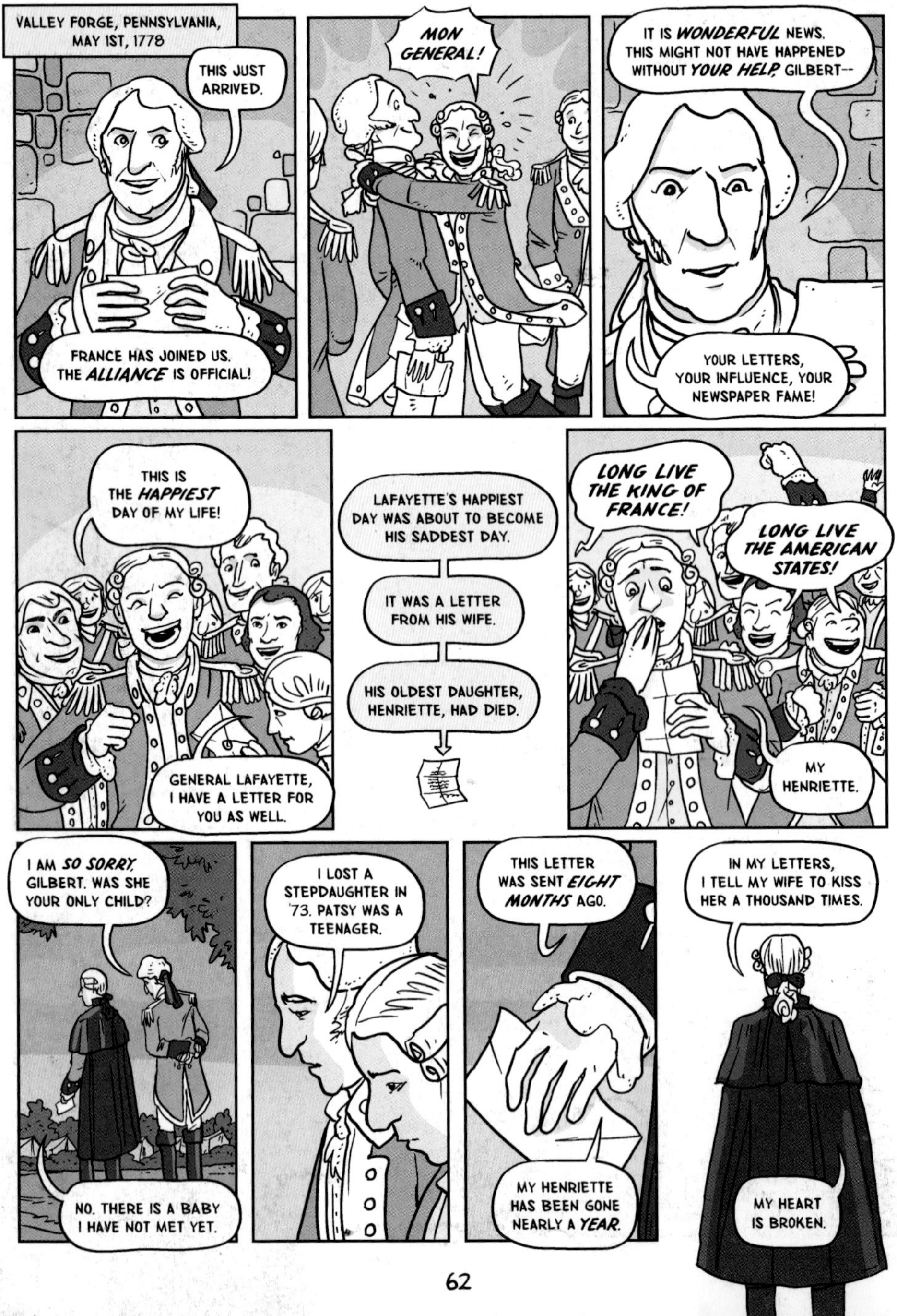
VALLEY FORGE, PENNSYLVANIA, MAY 1ST, 1778
THIS JUST ARRIVED.
FRANCE HAS JOINED US. THE ALLIANCE IS OFFICIAL!
MON GENERAL!
IT IS WONDERFUL NEWS. THIS MIGHT NOT HAVE HAPPENED WITHOUT YOUR HELP, GILBERT--
YOUR LETTERS, YOUR INFLUENCE, YOUR NEWSPAPER FAME!
THIS IS THE HAPPIEST DAY OF MY LIFE!
GENERAL LAFAYETTE, I HAVE A LETTER FOR YOU AS WELL.
LAFAYETTE'S HAPPIEST DAY WAS ABOUT TO BECOME HIS SADDEST DAY.
IT WAS A LETTER FROM HIS WIFE.
HIS OLDEST DAUGHTER, HENRIETTE, HAD DIED.
LONG LIVE THE KING OF FRANCE!
LONG LIVE THE AMERICAN STATES!
MY HENRIETTE.
I AM SO SORRY, GILBERT. WAS SHE YOUR ONLY CHILD?
NO. THERE IS A BABY I HAVE NOT MET YET.
I LOST A STEPDAUGHTER IN '73. PATSY WAS A TEENAGER.
THIS LETTER WAS SENT EIGHT MONTHS AGO.
MY HENRIETTE HAS BEEN GONE NEARLY A YEAR.
IN MY LETTERS, I TELL MY WIFE TO KISS HER A THOUSAND TIMES.
MY HEART IS BROKEN.

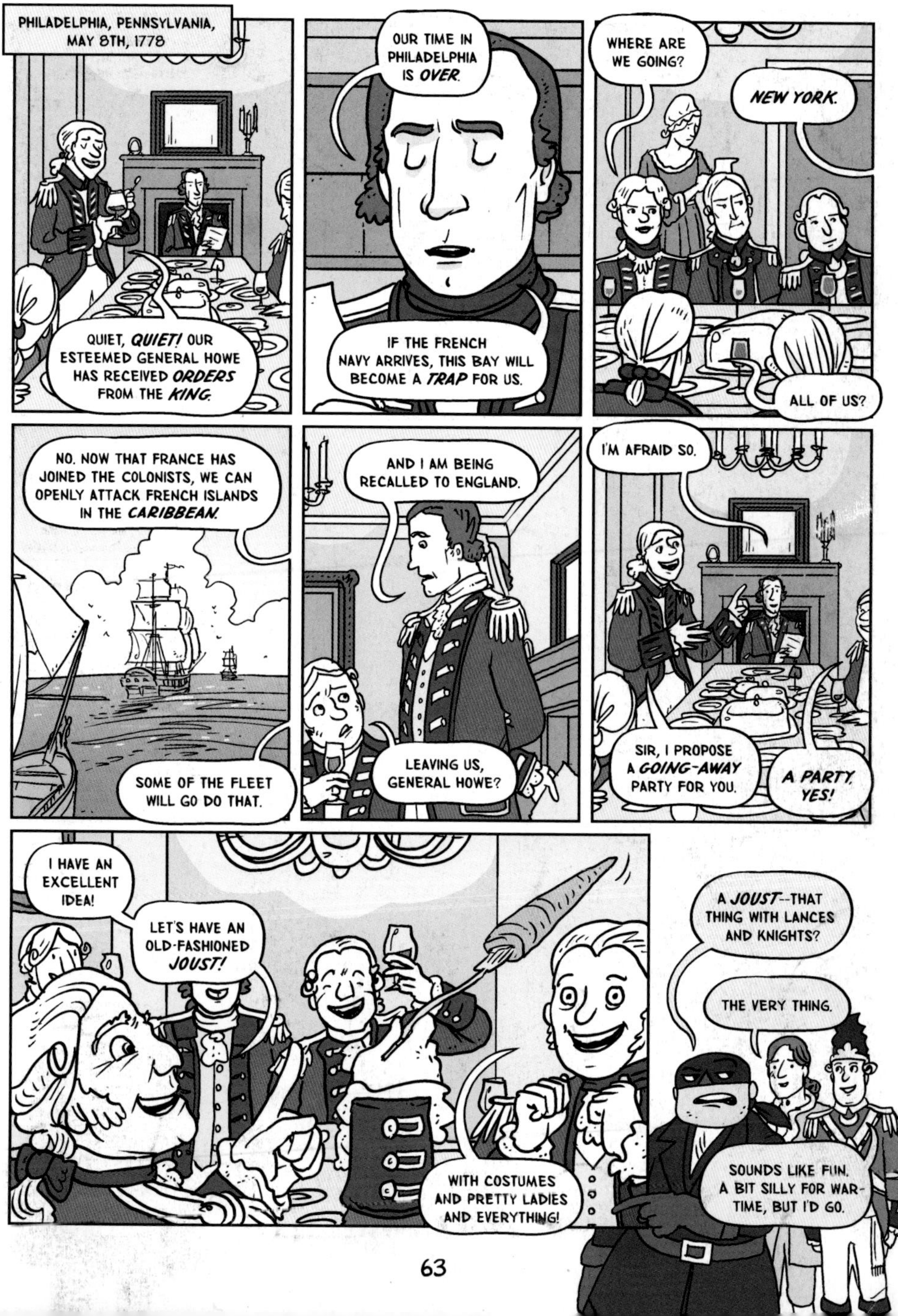
PHILADELPHIA, PENNSYLVANIA, MAY 8TH, 1778
QUIET, *QUIET!* OUR ESTEEMED GENERAL HOWE HAS RECEIVED *ORDERS* FROM THE *KING*.
OUR TIME IN PHILADELPHIA IS *OVER*.
IF THE FRENCH NAVY ARRIVES, THIS BAY WILL BECOME A *TRAP* FOR US.
WHERE ARE WE GOING?
NEW YORK.
ALL OF US?
NO. NOW THAT FRANCE HAS JOINED THE COLONISTS, WE CAN OPENLY ATTACK FRENCH ISLANDS IN THE *CARIBBEAN*.
SOME OF THE FLEET WILL GO DO THAT.
AND I AM BEING RECALLED TO ENGLAND.
LEAVING US, GENERAL HOWE?
I'M AFRAID SO.
SIR, I PROPOSE A *GOING-AWAY* PARTY FOR YOU.
A PARTY, YES!
I HAVE AN EXCELLENT IDEA!
LET'S HAVE AN OLD-FASHIONED *JOUST!*
WITH COSTUMES AND PRETTY LADIES AND EVERYTHING!
A *JOUST*--THAT THING WITH LANCES AND KNIGHTS?
THE VERY THING.
SOUNDS LIKE FUN. A BIT SILLY FOR WAR-TIME, BUT I'D GO.

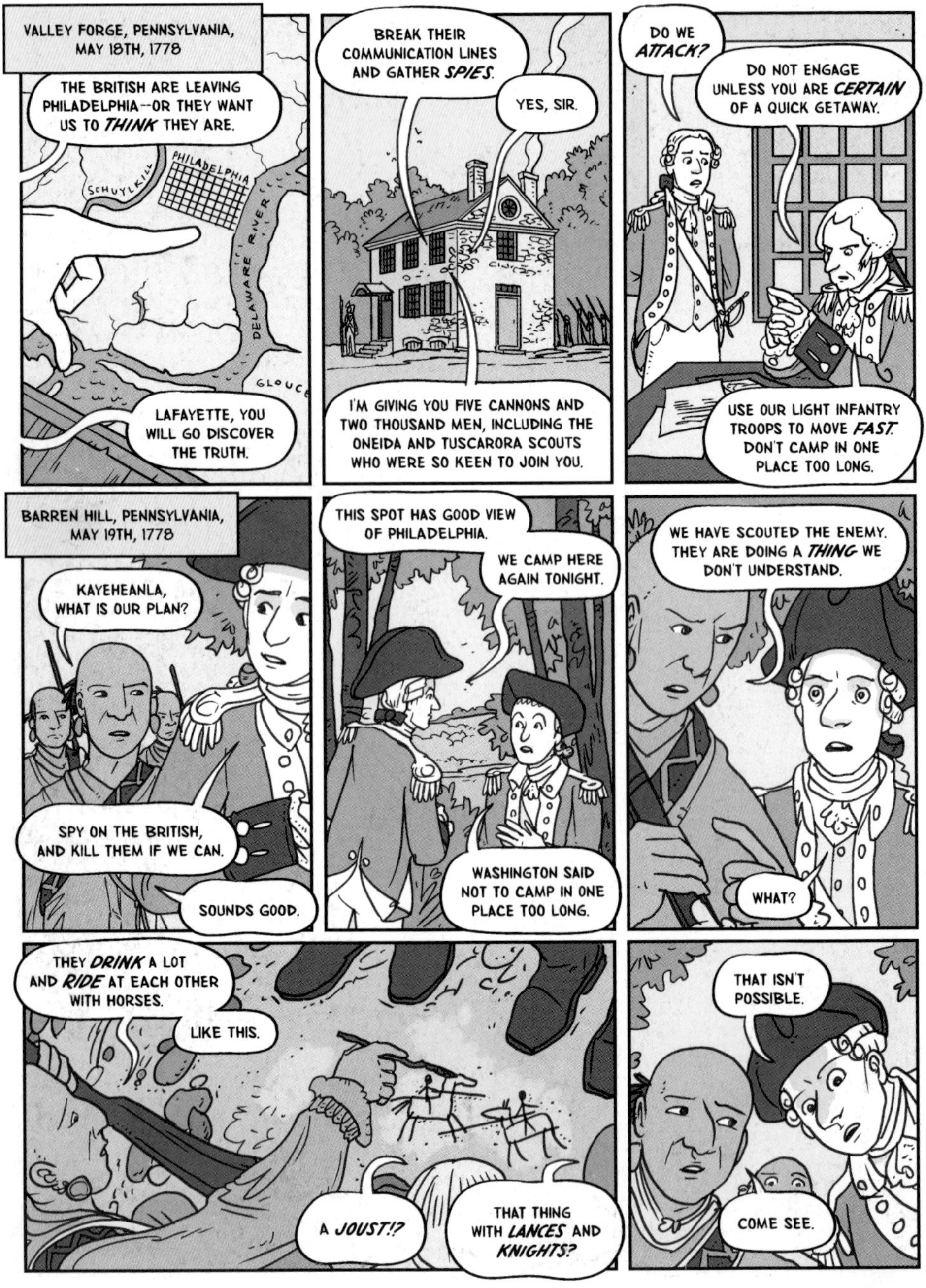

VALLEY FORGE, PENNSYLVANIA, MAY 18TH, 1778
THE BRITISH ARE LEAVING PHILADELPHIA--OR THEY WANT US TO THINK THEY ARE.
SCHUYLKILL
PHILADELPHIA
DELAWARE RIVER
GLOUC
LAFAYETTE, YOU WILL GO DISCOVER THE TRUTH.
BREAK THEIR COMMUNICATION LINES AND GATHER SPIES.
YES, SIR.
I'M GIVING YOU FIVE CANNONS AND TWO THOUSAND MEN, INCLUDING THE ONEIDA AND TUSCARORA SCOUTS WHO WERE SO KEEN TO JOIN YOU.
DO WE ATTACK?
DO NOT ENGAGE UNLESS YOU ARE CERTAIN OF A QUICK GETAWAY.
USE OUR LIGHT INFANTRY TROOPS TO MOVE FAST. DON'T CAMP IN ONE PLACE TOO LONG.
BARREN HILL, PENNSYLVANIA, MAY 19TH, 1778
KAYEHEANLA, WHAT IS OUR PLAN?
SPY ON THE BRITISH, AND KILL THEM IF WE CAN.
SOUNDS GOOD.
THIS SPOT HAS GOOD VIEW OF PHILADELPHIA.
WE CAMP HERE AGAIN TONIGHT.
WASHINGTON SAID NOT TO CAMP IN ONE PLACE TOO LONG.
WE HAVE SCOUTED THE ENEMY. THEY ARE DOING A THING WE DON'T UNDERSTAND.
WHAT?
THEY DRINK A LOT AND RIDE AT EACH OTHER WITH HORSES.
LIKE THIS.
A JOUST!?
THAT THING WITH LANCES AND KNIGHTS?
THAT ISN'T POSSIBLE.
COME SEE.

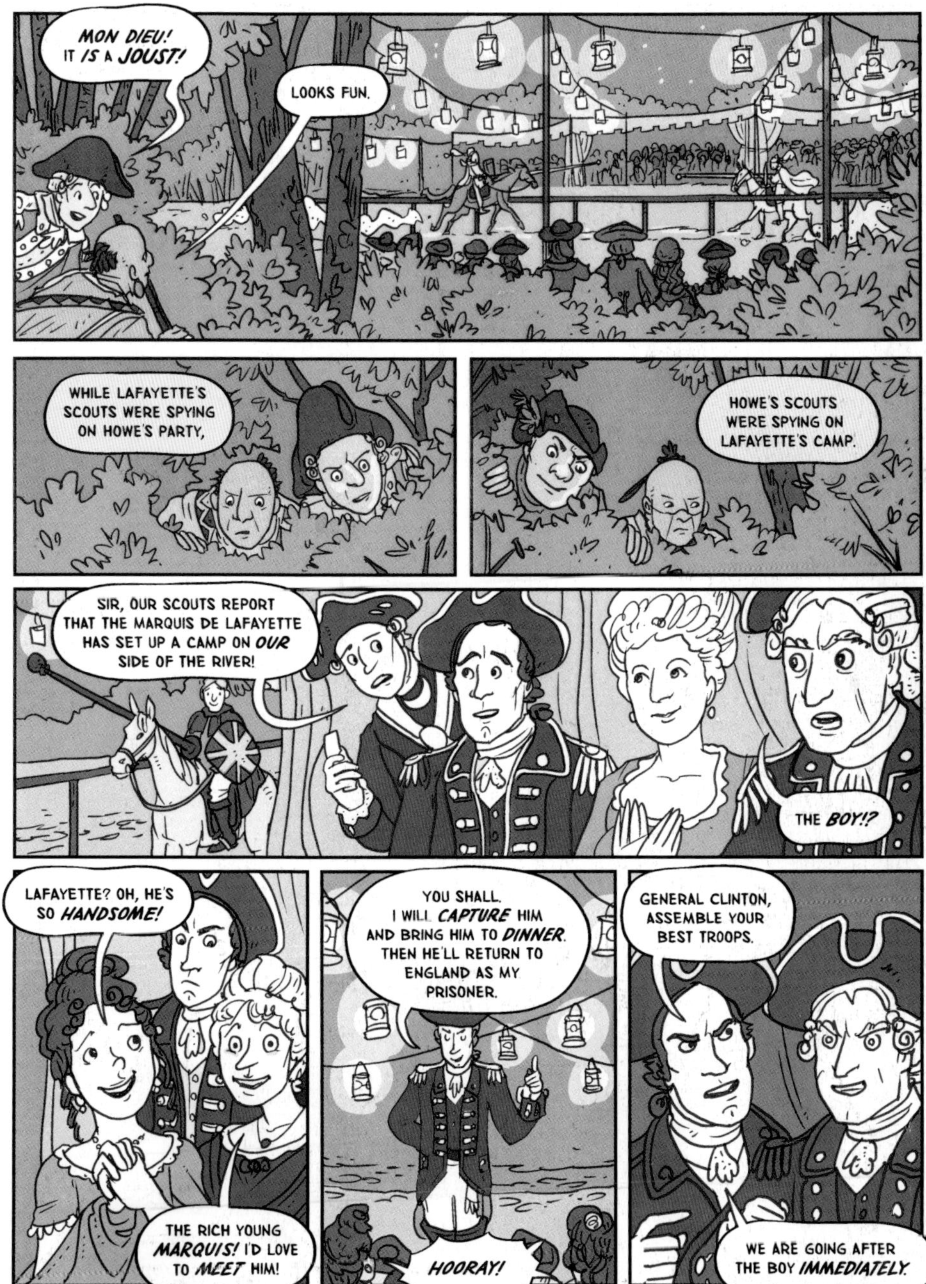
MON DIEU! IT IS A JOUST!
LOOKS FUN.
WHILE LAFAYETTE'S SCOUTS WERE SPYING ON HOWE'S PARTY,
HOWE'S SCOUTS WERE SPYING ON LAFAYETTE'S CAMP.
SIR, OUR SCOUTS REPORT THAT THE MARQUIS DE LAFAYETTE HAS SET UP A CAMP ON OUR SIDE OF THE RIVER!
THE BOY!?
LAFAYETTE? OH, HE'S SO HANDSOME!
THE RICH YOUNG MARQUIS! I'D LOVE TO MEET HIM!
YOU SHALL. I WILL CAPTURE HIM AND BRING HIM TO DINNER. THEN HE'LL RETURN TO ENGLAND AS MY PRISONER.
HOORAY!
GENERAL CLINTON, ASSEMBLE YOUR BEST TROOPS.
WE ARE GOING AFTER THE BOY IMMEDIATELY.

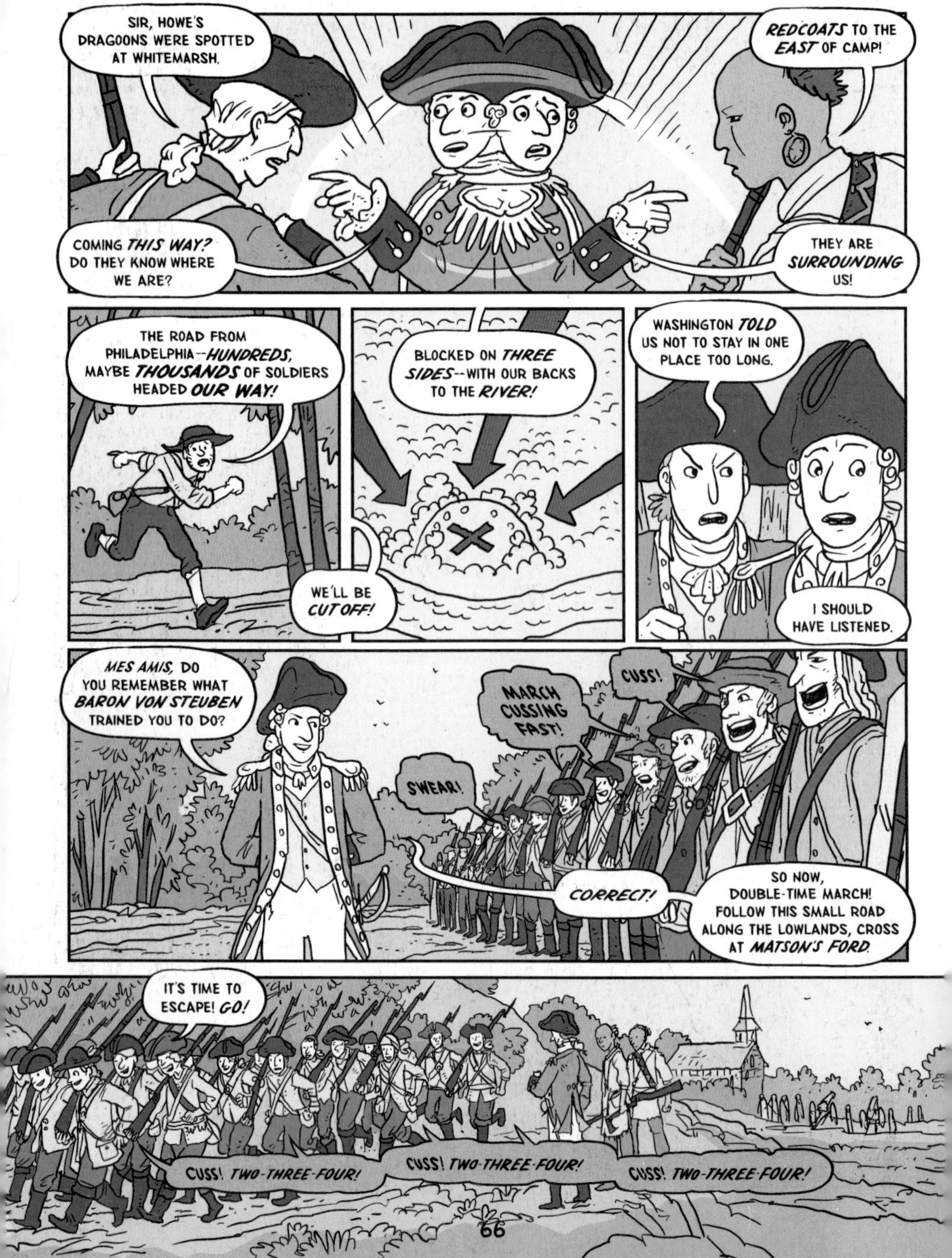
SIR, HOWE'S DRAGOONS WERE SPOTTED AT WHITEMARSH.
REDCOATS TO THE EAST OF CAMP!
COMING THIS WAY? DO THEY KNOW WHERE WE ARE?
THEY ARE SURROUNDING US!
THE ROAD FROM PHILADELPHIA--HUNDREDS, MAYBE THOUSANDS OF SOLDIERS HEADED OUR WAY!
BLOCKED ON THREE SIDES--WITH OUR BACKS TO THE RIVER!
WE'LL BE CUT OFF!
WASHINGTON TOLD US NOT TO STAY IN ONE PLACE TOO LONG.
I SHOULD HAVE LISTENED.
MES AMIS, DO YOU REMEMBER WHAT BARON VON STEUBEN TRAINED YOU TO DO?
CUSS!
MARCH CUSSING FAST!
SWEAR!
CORRECT!
SO NOW, DOUBLE-TIME MARCH! FOLLOW THIS SMALL ROAD ALONG THE LOWLANDS, CROSS AT MATSON'S FORD.
IT'S TIME TO ESCAPE! GO!
CUSS! TWO-THREE-FOUR!
CUSS! TWO-THREE-FOUR!
CUSS! TWO-THREE-FOUR!

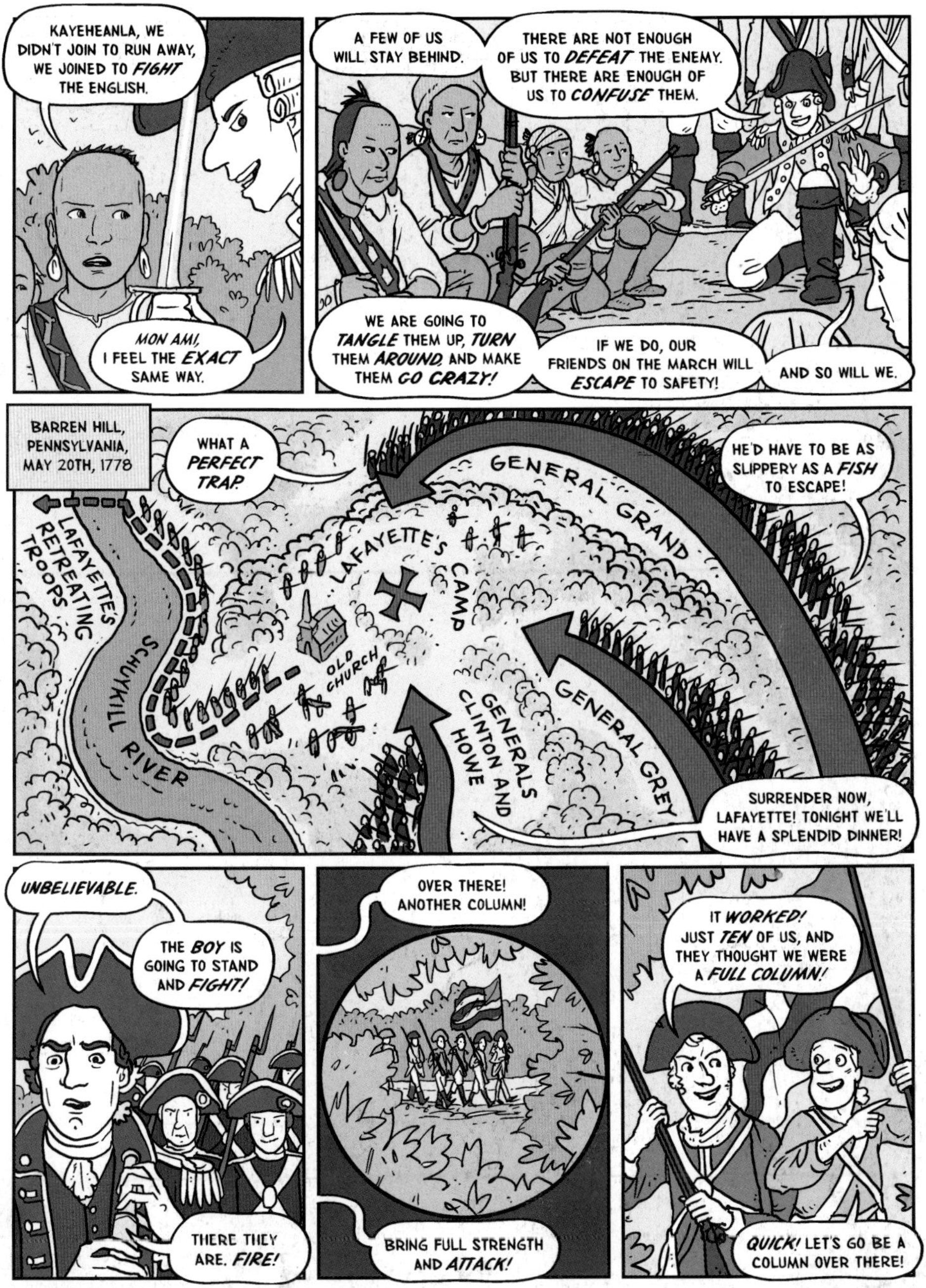
KAYEHEANLA, WE DIDN'T JOIN TO RUN AWAY, WE JOINED TO *FIGHT* THE ENGLISH.
MON AMI, I FEEL THE *EXACT* SAME WAY.
A FEW OF US WILL STAY BEHIND.
THERE ARE NOT ENOUGH OF US TO *DEFEAT* THE ENEMY. BUT THERE ARE ENOUGH OF US TO *CONFUSE* THEM.
WE ARE GOING TO *TANGLE* THEM UP, *TURN* THEM *AROUND,* AND MAKE THEM *GO CRAZY!*
IF WE DO, OUR FRIENDS ON THE MARCH WILL *ESCAPE* TO SAFETY!
AND SO WILL WE.
BARREN HILL, PENNSYLVANIA, MAY 20TH, 1778
WHAT A *PERFECT TRAP.*
HE'D HAVE TO BE AS SLIPPERY AS A *FISH* TO ESCAPE!
GENERAL GRAND
LAFAYETTE'S RETREATING TROOPS
LAFAYETTE'S CAMP
OLD CHURCH
SCHUYKILL RIVER
GENERALS CLINTON AND HOWE
GENERAL GREY
SURRENDER NOW, LAFAYETTE! TONIGHT WE'LL HAVE A SPLENDID DINNER!
UNBELIEVABLE.
THE *BOY* IS GOING TO STAND AND *FIGHT!*
THERE THEY ARE. *FIRE!*
OVER THERE! ANOTHER COLUMN!
BRING FULL STRENGTH AND *ATTACK!*
IT *WORKED!* JUST *TEN* OF US, AND THEY THOUGHT WE WERE A *FULL COLUMN!*
QUICK! LET'S GO BE A COLUMN OVER THERE!

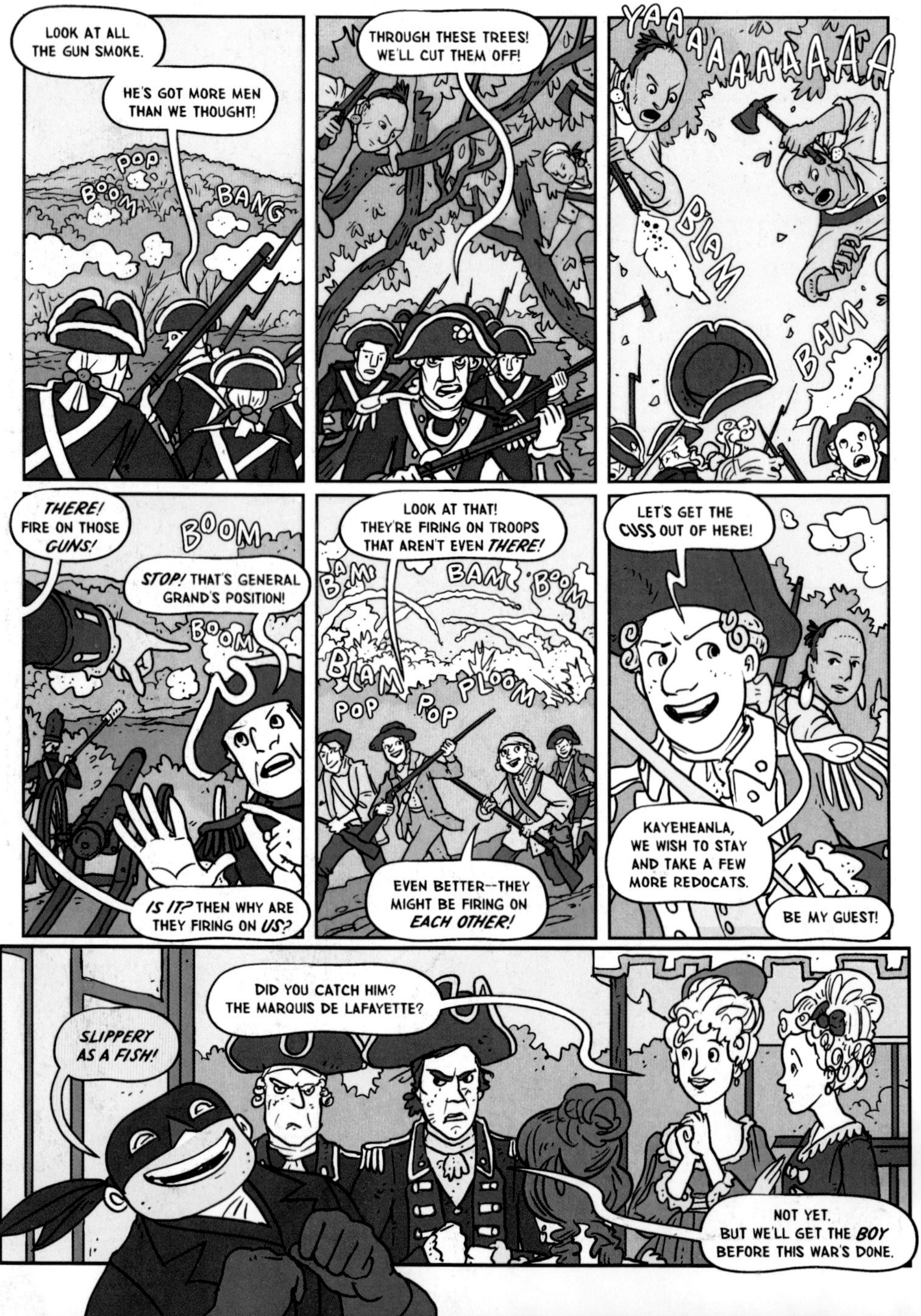
LOOK AT ALL THE GUN SMOKE.
HE'S GOT MORE MEN THAN WE THOUGHT!
POP
BOOM
BANG
THROUGH THESE TREES! WE'LL CUT THEM OFF!
YAAAAAAAAAAA
BLAM
BAM
THERE! FIRE ON THOSE GUNS!
BOOM
STOP! THAT'S GENERAL GRAND'S POSITION!
BOOM
IS IT? THEN WHY ARE THEY FIRING ON US?
LOOK AT THAT! THEY'RE FIRING ON TROOPS THAT AREN'T EVEN THERE!
BAM
BAM
BOOM
BLAM
POP
POP
PLOOM
EVEN BETTER--THEY MIGHT BE FIRING ON EACH OTHER!
LET'S GET THE CUSS OUT OF HERE!
KAYEHEANLA, WE WISH TO STAY AND TAKE A FEW MORE REDOCATS.
BE MY GUEST!
DID YOU CATCH HIM? THE MARQUIS DE LAFAYETTE?
SLIPPERY AS A FISH!
NOT YET. BUT WE'LL GET THE BOY BEFORE THIS WAR'S DONE.

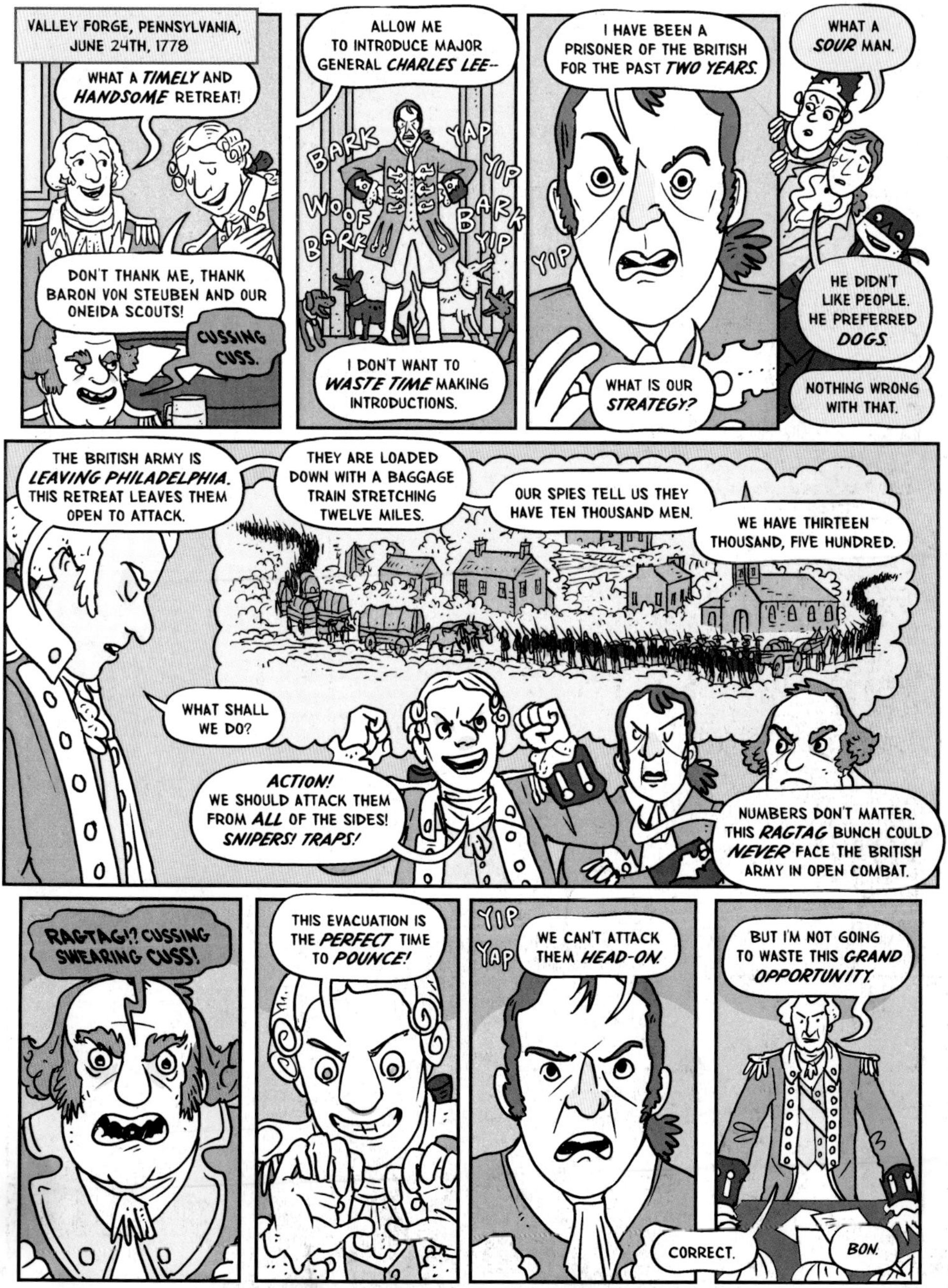
VALLEY FORGE, PENNSYLVANIA, JUNE 24TH, 1778
WHAT A TIMELY AND HANDSOME RETREAT!
DON'T THANK ME, THANK BARON VON STEUBEN AND OUR ONEIDA SCOUTS!
CUSSING CUSS.
ALLOW ME TO INTRODUCE MAJOR GENERAL CHARLES LEE--
BARK YAP YIP WOOF BARK BARK BARK YIP
I DON'T WANT TO WASTE TIME MAKING INTRODUCTIONS.
I HAVE BEEN A PRISONER OF THE BRITISH FOR THE PAST TWO YEARS.
YIP
WHAT IS OUR STRATEGY?
WHAT A SOUR MAN.
HE DIDN'T LIKE PEOPLE. HE PREFERRED DOGS.
NOTHING WRONG WITH THAT.
THE BRITISH ARMY IS LEAVING PHILADELPHIA. THIS RETREAT LEAVES THEM OPEN TO ATTACK.
THEY ARE LOADED DOWN WITH A BAGGAGE TRAIN STRETCHING TWELVE MILES.
OUR SPIES TELL US THEY HAVE TEN THOUSAND MEN.
WE HAVE THIRTEEN THOUSAND, FIVE HUNDRED.
WHAT SHALL WE DO?
ACTION! WE SHOULD ATTACK THEM FROM ALL OF THE SIDES! SNIPERS! TRAPS!
NUMBERS DON'T MATTER. THIS RAGTAG BUNCH COULD NEVER FACE THE BRITISH ARMY IN OPEN COMBAT.
RAGTAG!? CUSSING SWEARING CUSS!
THIS EVACUATION IS THE PERFECT TIME TO POUNCE!
YIP YAP
WE CAN'T ATTACK THEM HEAD-ON.
CORRECT.
BUT I'M NOT GOING TO WASTE THIS GRAND OPPORTUNITY.
BON.

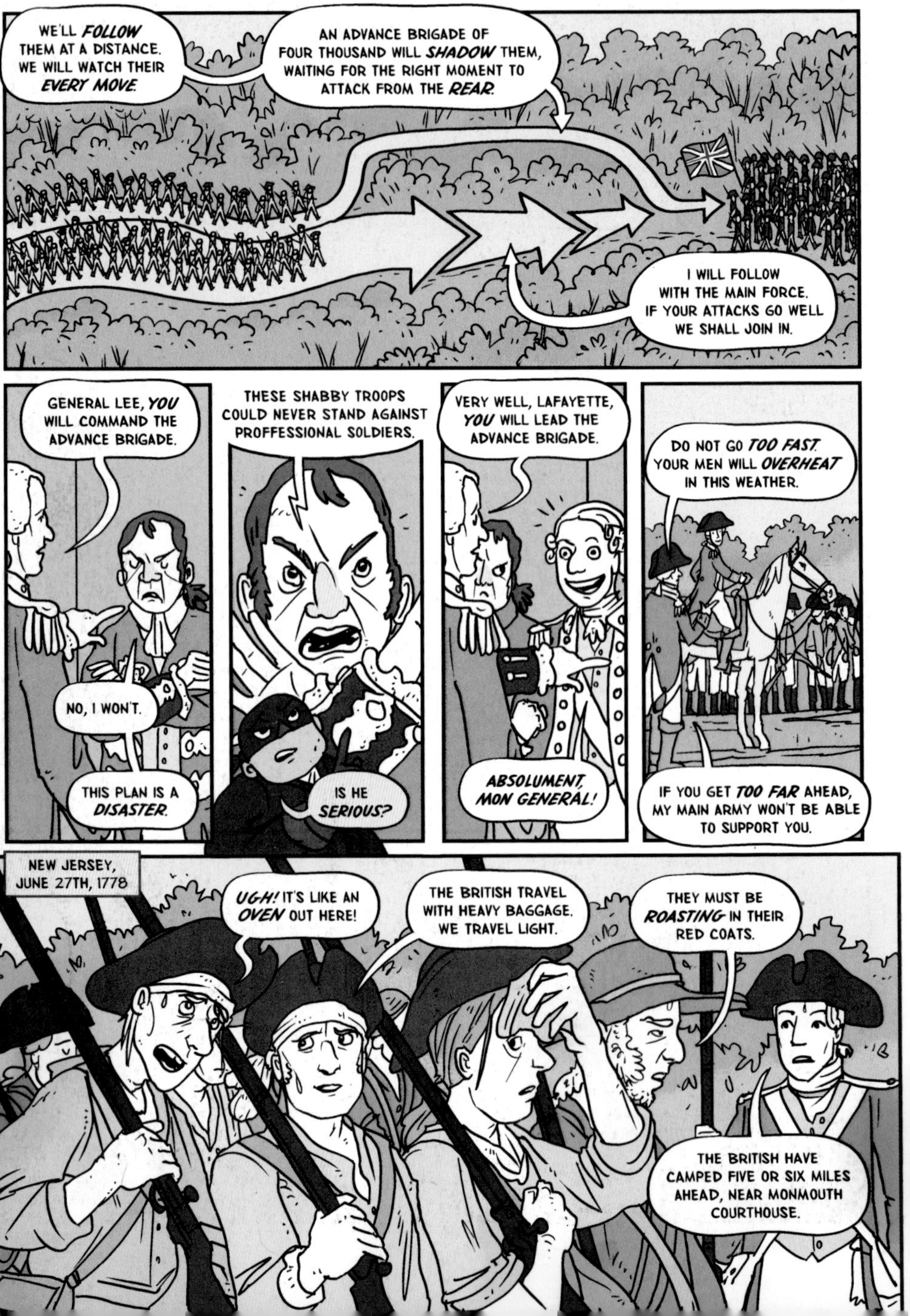
WE'LL FOLLOW THEM AT A DISTANCE. WE WILL WATCH THEIR EVERY MOVE.
AN ADVANCE BRIGADE OF FOUR THOUSAND WILL SHADOW THEM, WAITING FOR THE RIGHT MOMENT TO ATTACK FROM THE REAR.
I WILL FOLLOW WITH THE MAIN FORCE. IF YOUR ATTACKS GO WELL WE SHALL JOIN IN.
GENERAL LEE, YOU WILL COMMAND THE ADVANCE BRIGADE.
NO, I WON'T.
THIS PLAN IS A DISASTER.
THESE SHABBY TROOPS COULD NEVER STAND AGAINST PROFFESSIONAL SOLDIERS.
IS HE SERIOUS?
VERY WELL, LAFAYETTE, YOU WILL LEAD THE ADVANCE BRIGADE.
ABSOLUMENT, MON GENERAL!
DO NOT GO TOO FAST. YOUR MEN WILL OVERHEAT IN THIS WEATHER.
IF YOU GET TOO FAR AHEAD, MY MAIN ARMY WON'T BE ABLE TO SUPPORT YOU.
NEW JERSEY, JUNE 27TH, 1778
UGH! IT'S LIKE AN OVEN OUT HERE!
THE BRITISH TRAVEL WITH HEAVY BAGGAGE. WE TRAVEL LIGHT.
THEY MUST BE ROASTING IN THEIR RED COATS.
THE BRITISH HAVE CAMPED FIVE OR SIX MILES AHEAD, NEAR MONMOUTH COURTHOUSE.

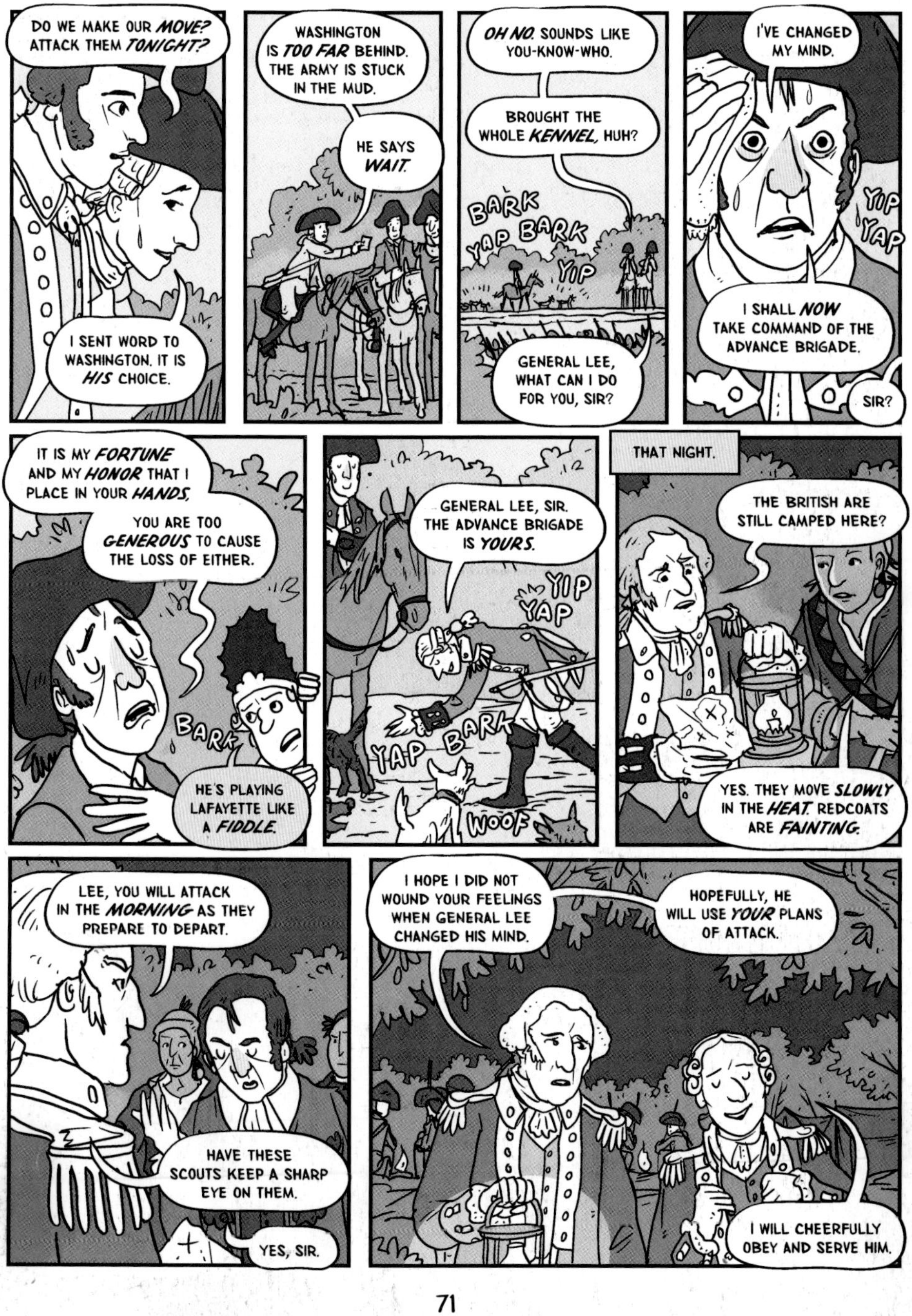
DO WE MAKE OUR MOVE? ATTACK THEM TONIGHT?
I SENT WORD TO WASHINGTON. IT IS HIS CHOICE.
WASHINGTON IS TOO FAR BEHIND. THE ARMY IS STUCK IN THE MUD.
HE SAYS WAIT.
OH NO. SOUNDS LIKE YOU-KNOW-WHO.
BROUGHT THE WHOLE KENNEL, HUH?
BARK
YAP BARK
YIP
GENERAL LEE, WHAT CAN I DO FOR YOU, SIR?
I'VE CHANGED MY MIND.
YIP
YAP
I SHALL NOW TAKE COMMAND OF THE ADVANCE BRIGADE.
SIR?
IT IS MY FORTUNE AND MY HONOR THAT I PLACE IN YOUR HANDS,
YOU ARE TOO GENEROUS TO CAUSE THE LOSS OF EITHER.
BARK
HE'S PLAYING LAFAYETTE LIKE A FIDDLE.
GENERAL LEE, SIR. THE ADVANCE BRIGADE IS YOURS.
YIP
YAP
YAP
BARK
WOOF
THAT NIGHT.
THE BRITISH ARE STILL CAMPED HERE?
YES. THEY MOVE SLOWLY IN THE HEAT. REDCOATS ARE FAINTING.
LEE, YOU WILL ATTACK IN THE MORNING AS THEY PREPARE TO DEPART.
HAVE THESE SCOUTS KEEP A SHARP EYE ON THEM.
YES, SIR.
I HOPE I DID NOT WOUND YOUR FEELINGS WHEN GENERAL LEE CHANGED HIS MIND.
HOPEFULLY, HE WILL USE YOUR PLANS OF ATTACK.
I WILL CHEERFULLY OBEY AND SERVE HIM.

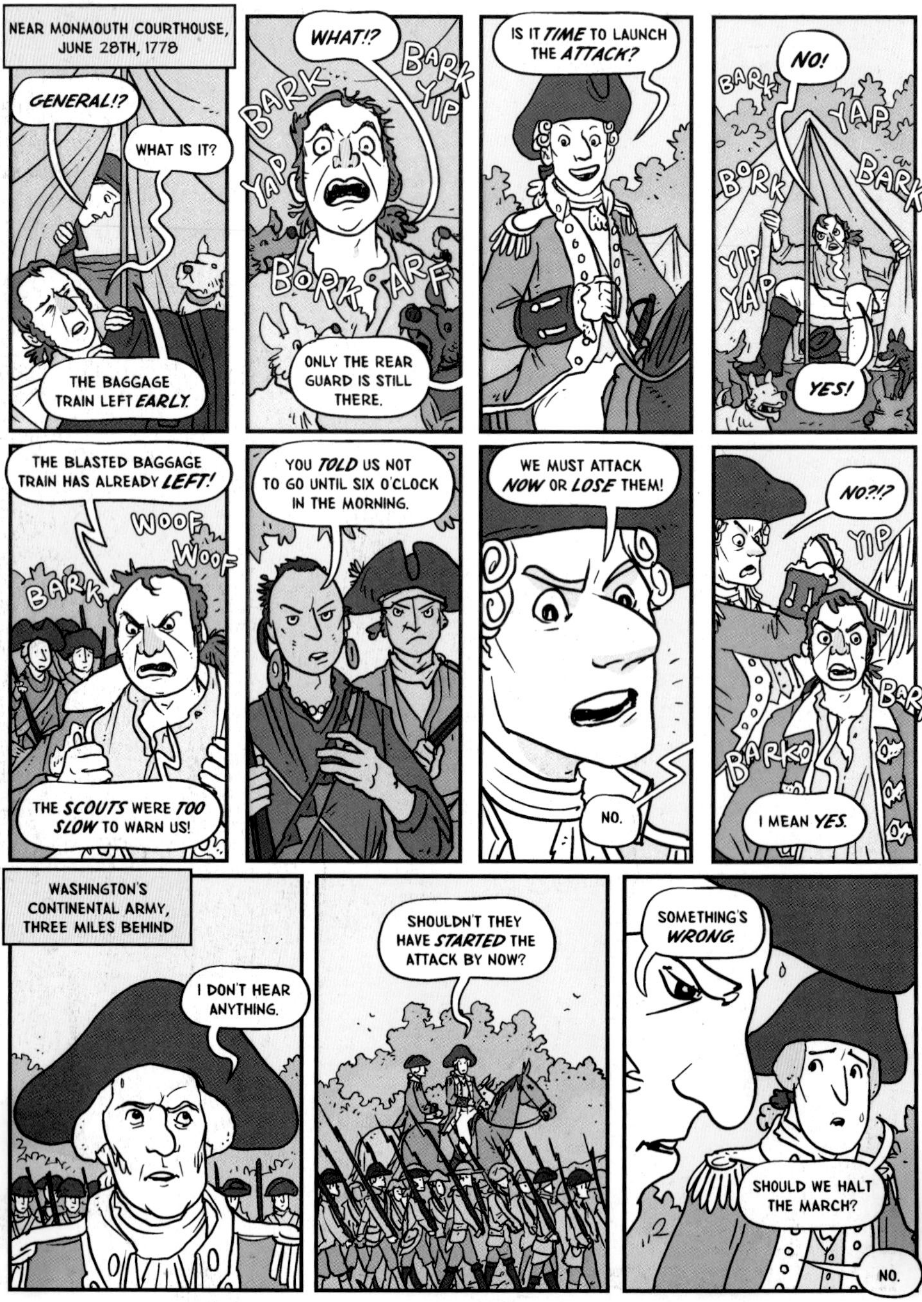
NEAR MONMOUTH COURTHOUSE, JUNE 28TH, 1778
GENERAL!?
WHAT IS IT?
THE BAGGAGE TRAIN LEFT EARLY.
WHAT!?
BARK
BARK YIP
BARK
YAP
BORK
ARF
ONLY THE REAR GUARD IS STILL THERE.
IS IT TIME TO LAUNCH THE ATTACK?
NO!
BARK
YAP
BORK
BARK
YIP
YAP
YES!
THE BLASTED BAGGAGE TRAIN HAS ALREADY LEFT!
WOOF
WOOF
BARK
THE SCOUTS WERE TOO SLOW TO WARN US!
YOU TOLD US NOT TO GO UNTIL SIX O'CLOCK IN THE MORNING.
WE MUST ATTACK NOW OR LOSE THEM!
NO.
NO?!?
YIP
BARK
BARKO
I MEAN YES.
WASHINGTON'S CONTINENTAL ARMY, THREE MILES BEHIND
I DON'T HEAR ANYTHING.
SHOULDN'T THEY HAVE STARTED THE ATTACK BY NOW?
SOMETHING'S WRONG.
SHOULD WE HALT THE MARCH?
NO.

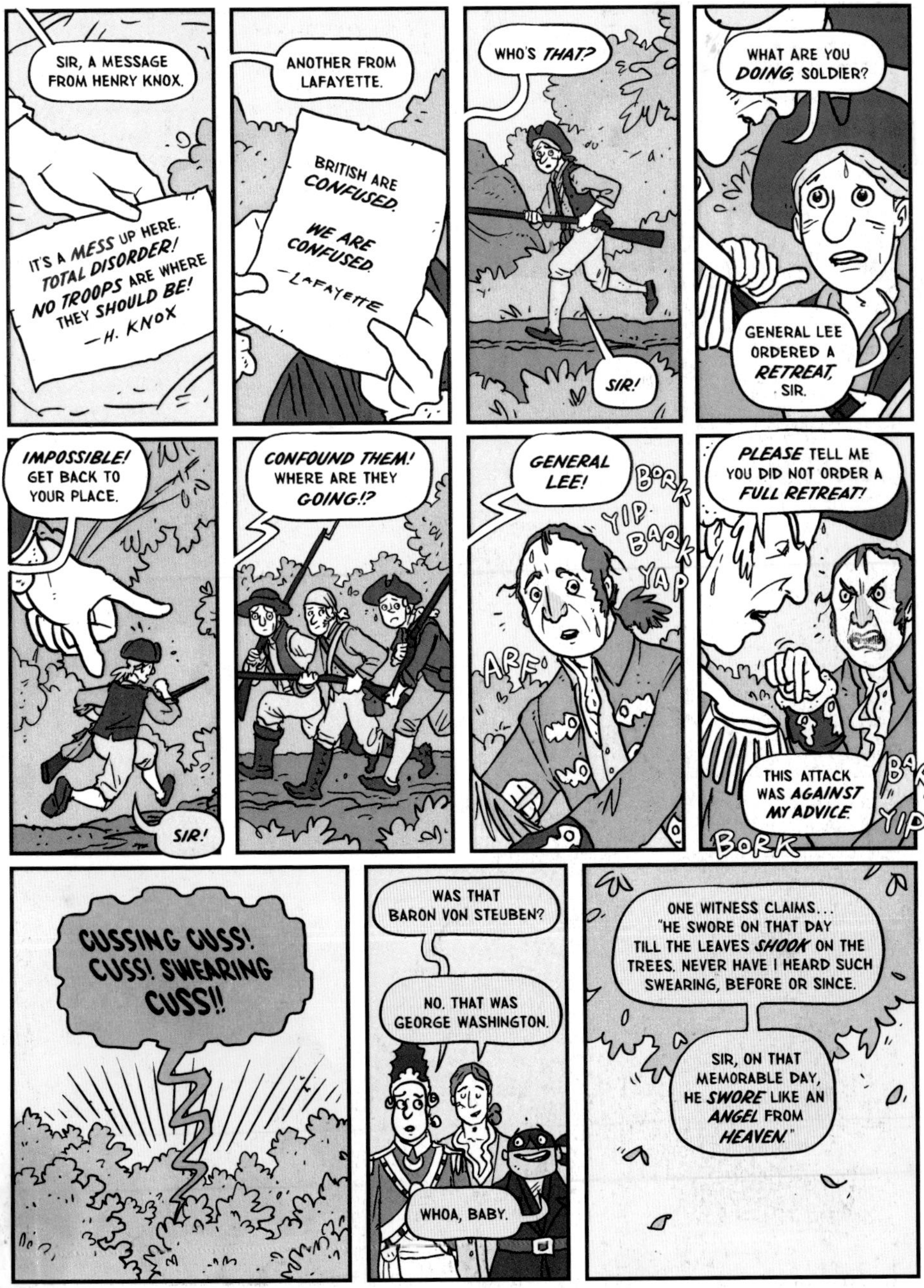
SIR, A MESSAGE FROM HENRY KNOX.
IT'S A MESS UP HERE. TOTAL DISORDER! NO TROOPS ARE WHERE THEY SHOULD BE! —H. KNOX
ANOTHER FROM LAFAYETTE.
BRITISH ARE CONFUSED. WE ARE CONFUSED. —LAFAYETTE
WHO'S THAT?
SIR!
WHAT ARE YOU DOING, SOLDIER?
GENERAL LEE ORDERED A RETREAT, SIR.
IMPOSSIBLE! GET BACK TO YOUR PLACE.
SIR!
CONFOUND THEM! WHERE ARE THEY GOING!?
GENERAL LEE!
BORK
YIP
BARK
YAP
ARF
PLEASE TELL ME YOU DID NOT ORDER A FULL RETREAT!
THIS ATTACK WAS AGAINST MY ADVICE.
BARK
YIP
BORK
CUSSING CUSS! CUSS! SWEARING CUSS!!
WAS THAT BARON VON STEUBEN?
NO. THAT WAS GEORGE WASHINGTON.
WHOA, BABY.
ONE WITNESS CLAIMS... "HE SWORE ON THAT DAY TILL THE LEAVES SHOOK ON THE TREES. NEVER HAVE I HEARD SUCH SWEARING, BEFORE OR SINCE.
SIR, ON THAT MEMORABLE DAY, HE SWORE LIKE AN ANGEL FROM HEAVEN."

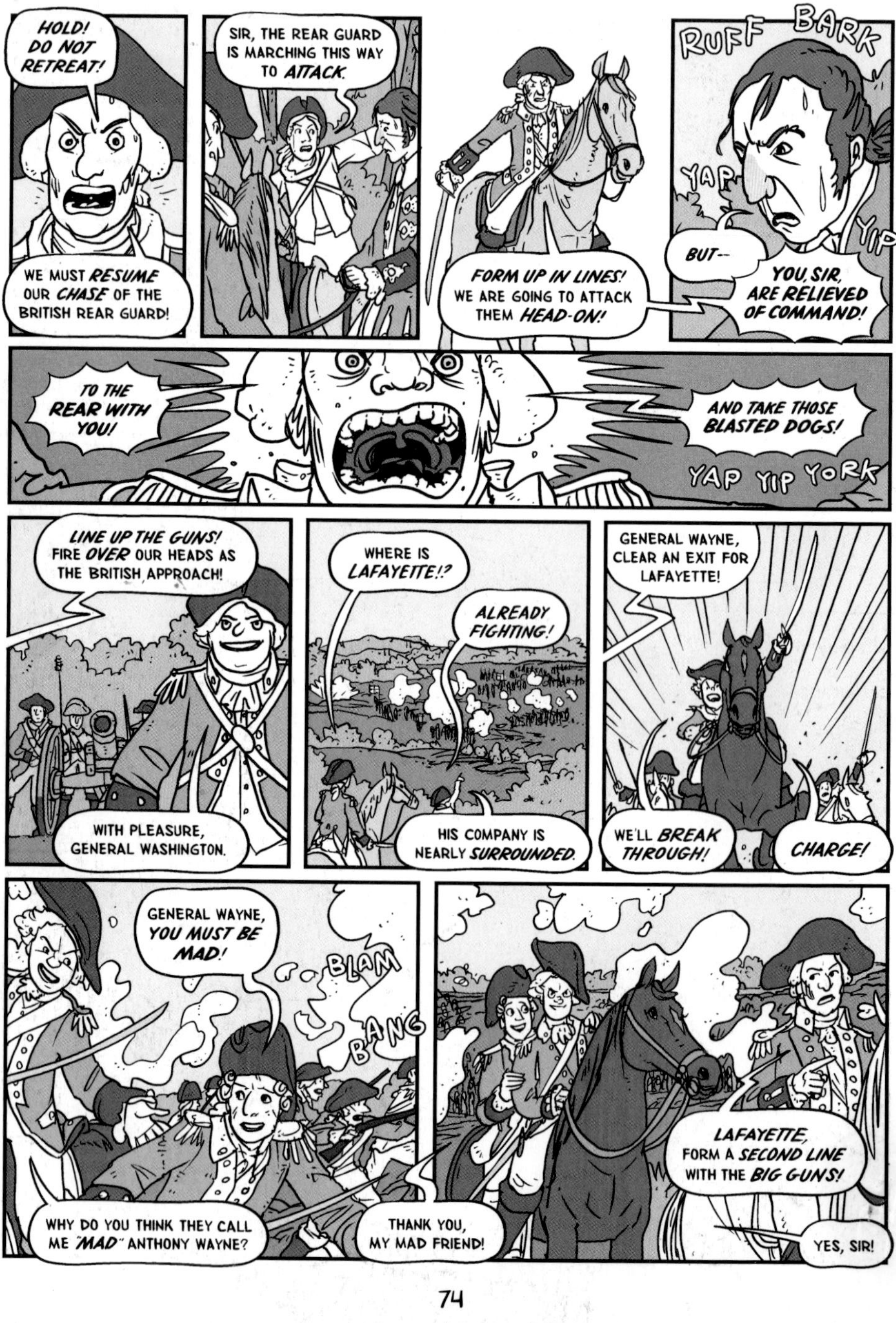
HOLD! DO NOT RETREAT!
WE MUST RESUME OUR CHASE OF THE BRITISH REAR GUARD!
SIR, THE REAR GUARD IS MARCHING THIS WAY TO ATTACK.
FORM UP IN LINES! WE ARE GOING TO ATTACK THEM HEAD-ON!
RUFF BARK
YAP
YIP
BUT--
YOU, SIR, ARE RELIEVED OF COMMAND!
TO THE REAR WITH YOU!
AND TAKE THOSE BLASTED DOGS!
YAP YIP YORK
LINE UP THE GUNS! FIRE OVER OUR HEADS AS THE BRITISH APPROACH!
WITH PLEASURE, GENERAL WASHINGTON.
WHERE IS LAFAYETTE!?
ALREADY FIGHTING!
HIS COMPANY IS NEARLY SURROUNDED.
GENERAL WAYNE, CLEAR AN EXIT FOR LAFAYETTE!
WE'LL BREAK THROUGH!
CHARGE!
GENERAL WAYNE, YOU MUST BE MAD!
BLAM
BANG
WHY DO YOU THINK THEY CALL ME "MAD" ANTHONY WAYNE?
THANK YOU, MY MAD FRIEND!
LAFAYETTE, FORM A SECOND LINE WITH THE BIG GUNS!
YES, SIR!

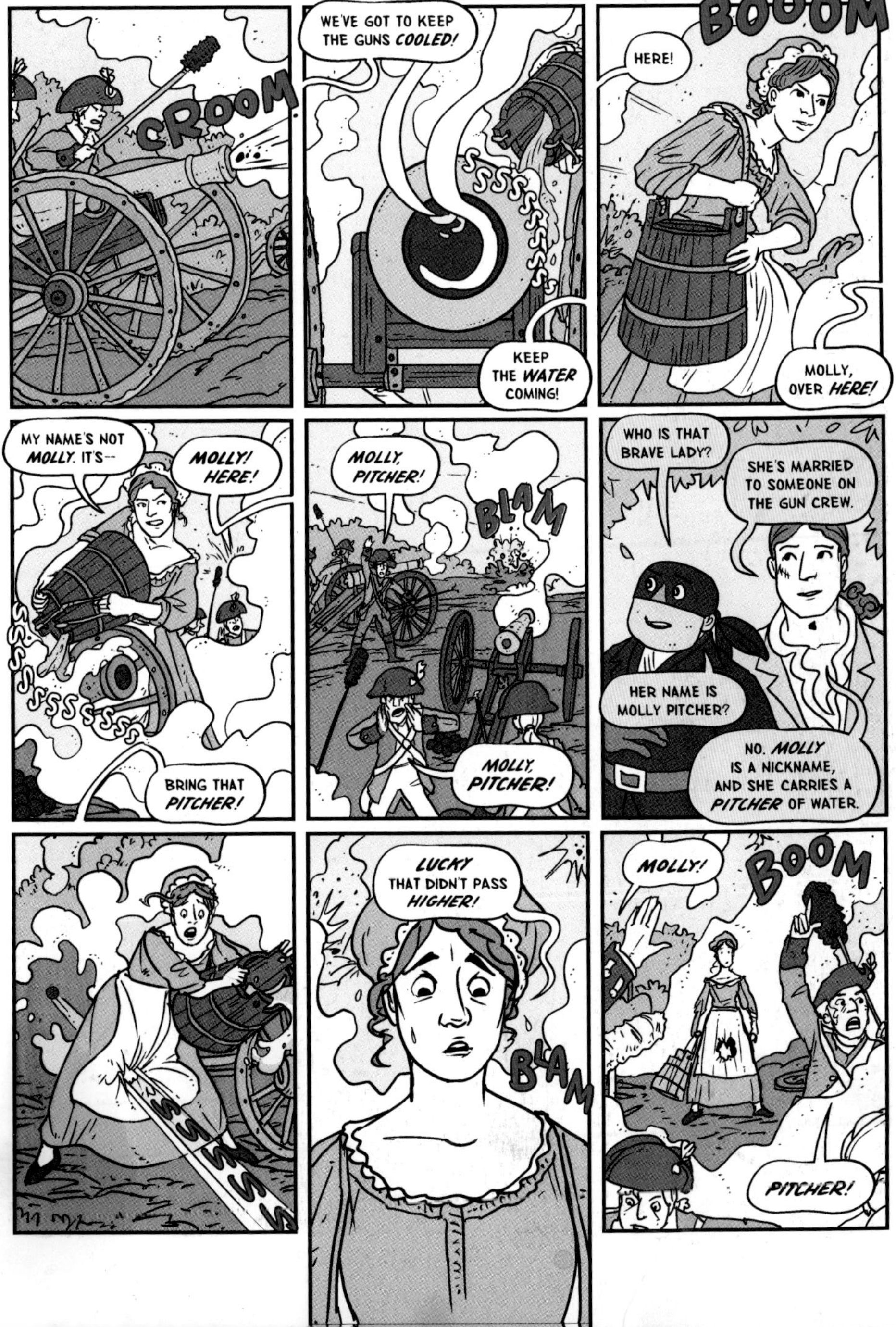
CROOM
WE'VE GOT TO KEEP THE GUNS COOLED!
SSSSSSSSS
KEEP THE WATER COMING!
BOOOM
HERE!
MOLLY, OVER HERE!
MY NAME'S NOT MOLLY. IT'S--
MOLLY! HERE!
SSSSSSSSSSS
BRING THAT PITCHER!
MOLLY, PITCHER!
BLAM
MOLLY, PITCHER!
WHO IS THAT BRAVE LADY?
SHE'S MARRIED TO SOMEONE ON THE GUN CREW.
HER NAME IS MOLLY PITCHER?
NO. MOLLY IS A NICKNAME, AND SHE CARRIES A PITCHER OF WATER.
SSSSS
LUCKY THAT DIDN'T PASS HIGHER!
BLAM
MOLLY!
BOOM
PITCHER!

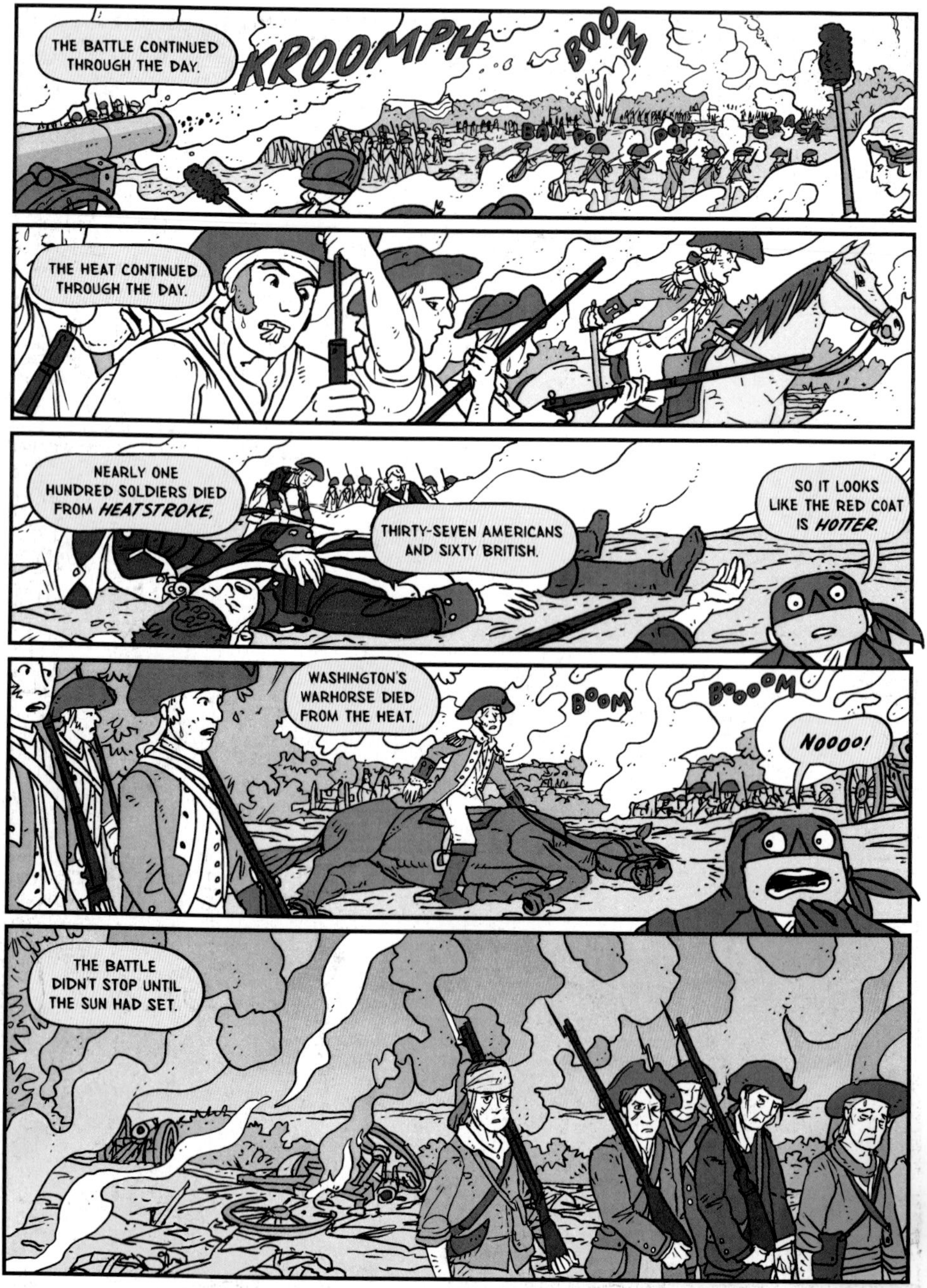
THE BATTLE CONTINUED THROUGH THE DAY.
KROOMPH
BOOM
BAM POP
POP
CRACK
THE HEAT CONTINUED THROUGH THE DAY.
NEARLY ONE HUNDRED SOLDIERS DIED FROM *HEATSTROKE*.
THIRTY-SEVEN AMERICANS AND SIXTY BRITISH.
SO IT LOOKS LIKE THE RED COAT IS *HOTTER*.
WASHINGTON'S WARHORSE DIED FROM THE HEAT.
BOOM
BOOOOM
NOOOO!
THE BATTLE DIDN'T STOP UNTIL THE SUN HAD SET.

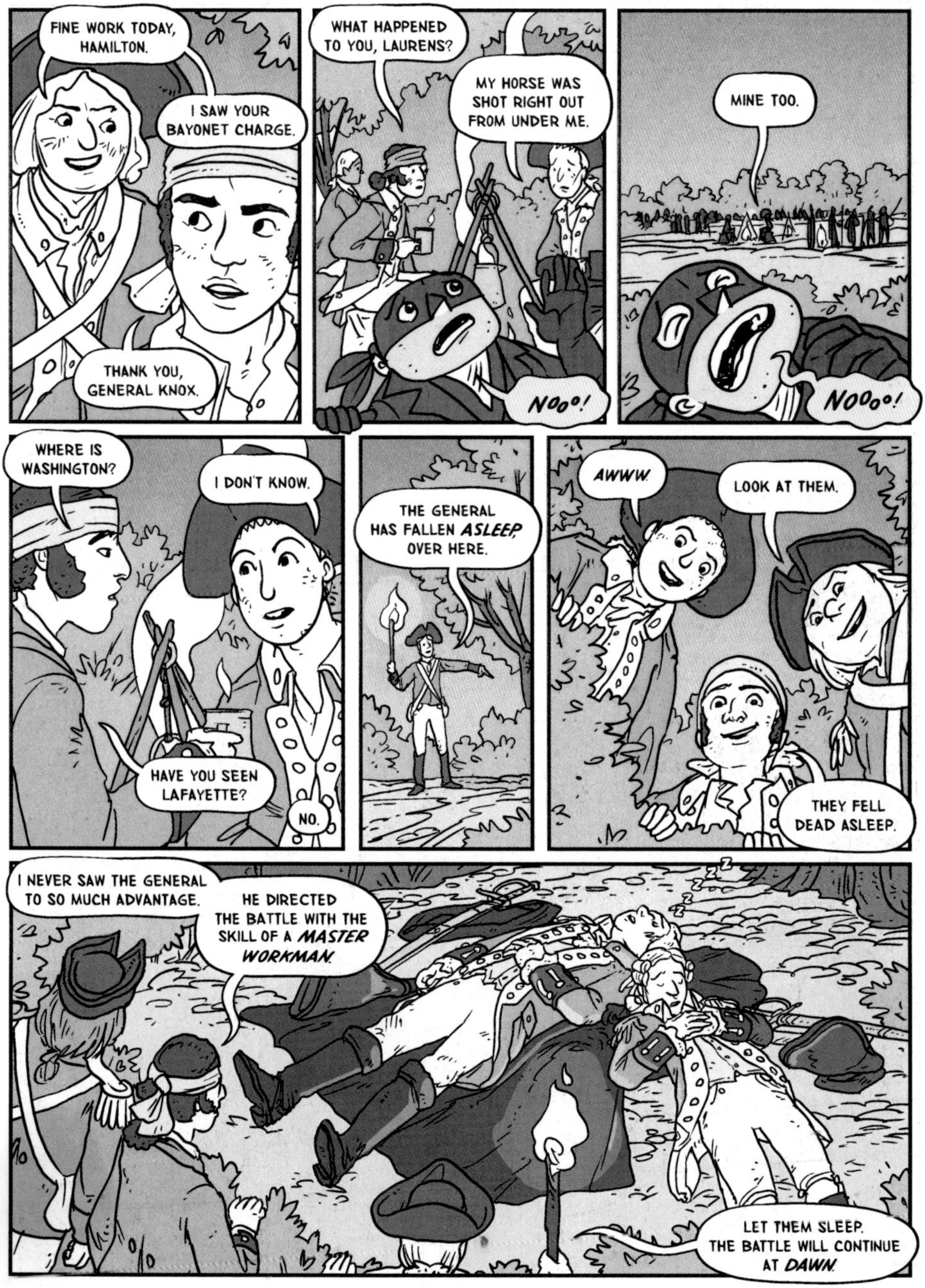
FINE WORK TODAY, HAMILTON.
I SAW YOUR BAYONET CHARGE.
THANK YOU, GENERAL KNOX.
WHAT HAPPENED TO YOU, LAURENS?
MY HORSE WAS SHOT RIGHT OUT FROM UNDER ME.
NOoo!
MINE TOO.
NOooo!
WHERE IS WASHINGTON?
I DON'T KNOW.
HAVE YOU SEEN LAFAYETTE?
NO.
THE GENERAL HAS FALLEN ASLEEP, OVER HERE.
AWWW.
LOOK AT THEM.
THEY FELL DEAD ASLEEP.
I NEVER SAW THE GENERAL TO SO MUCH ADVANTAGE.
HE DIRECTED THE BATTLE WITH THE SKILL OF A MASTER WORKMAN.
Z Z Z
LET THEM SLEEP. THE BATTLE WILL CONTINUE AT DAWN.

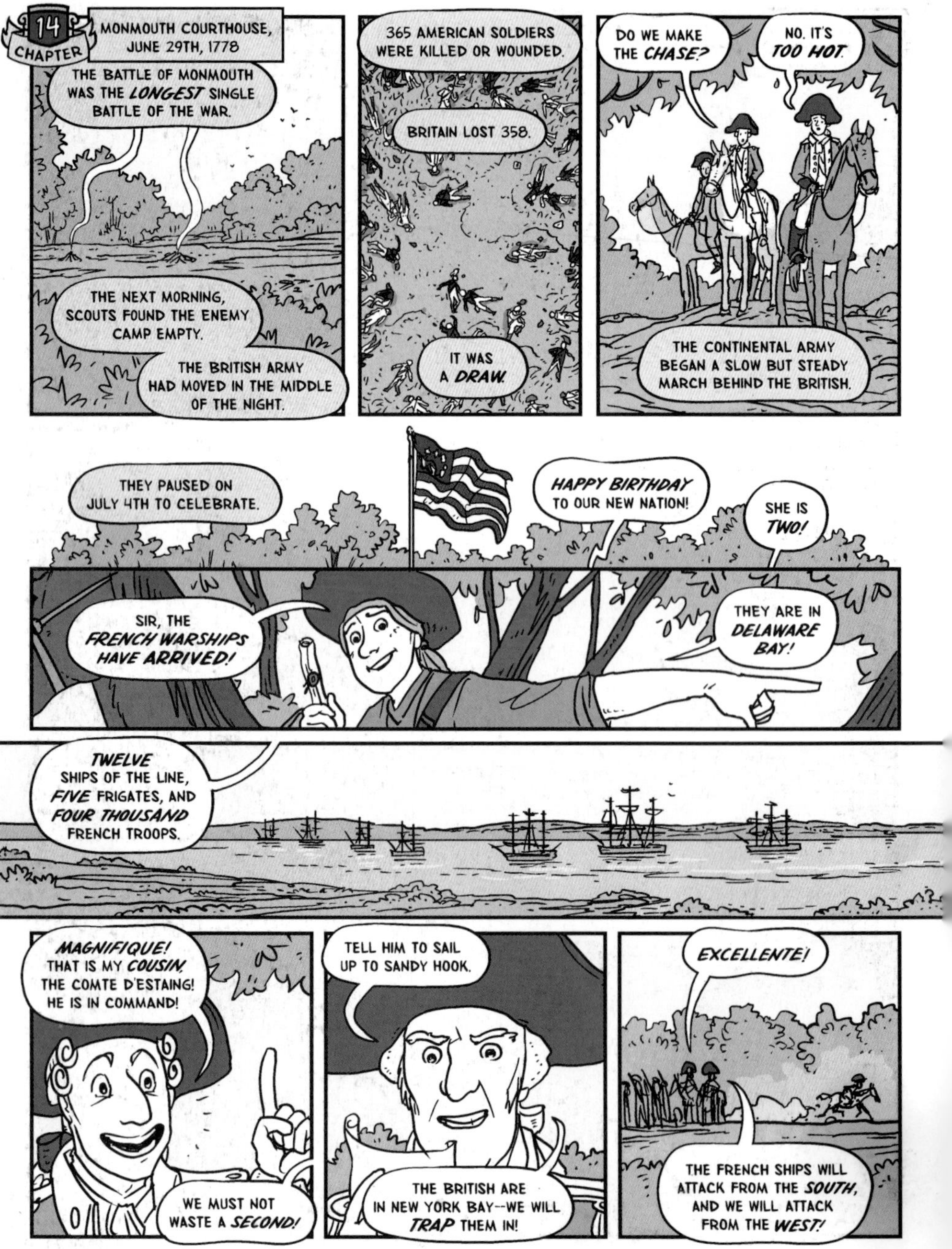
14
CHAPTER
MONMOUTH COURTHOUSE, JUNE 29TH, 1778
THE BATTLE OF MONMOUTH WAS THE LONGEST SINGLE BATTLE OF THE WAR.
THE NEXT MORNING, SCOUTS FOUND THE ENEMY CAMP EMPTY.
THE BRITISH ARMY HAD MOVED IN THE MIDDLE OF THE NIGHT.
365 AMERICAN SOLDIERS WERE KILLED OR WOUNDED.
BRITAIN LOST 358.
IT WAS A DRAW.
DO WE MAKE THE CHASE?
NO. IT'S TOO HOT.
THE CONTINENTAL ARMY BEGAN A SLOW BUT STEADY MARCH BEHIND THE BRITISH.
THEY PAUSED ON JULY 4TH TO CELEBRATE.
HAPPY BIRTHDAY TO OUR NEW NATION!
SHE IS TWO!
SIR, THE FRENCH WARSHIPS HAVE ARRIVED!
THEY ARE IN DELAWARE BAY!
TWELVE SHIPS OF THE LINE, FIVE FRIGATES, AND FOUR THOUSAND FRENCH TROOPS.
MAGNIFIQUE! THAT IS MY COUSIN, THE COMTE D'ESTAING! HE IS IN COMMAND!
WE MUST NOT WASTE A SECOND!
TELL HIM TO SAIL UP TO SANDY HOOK.
THE BRITISH ARE IN NEW YORK BAY--WE WILL TRAP THEM IN!
EXCELLENTE!
THE FRENCH SHIPS WILL ATTACK FROM THE SOUTH, AND WE WILL ATTACK FROM THE WEST!

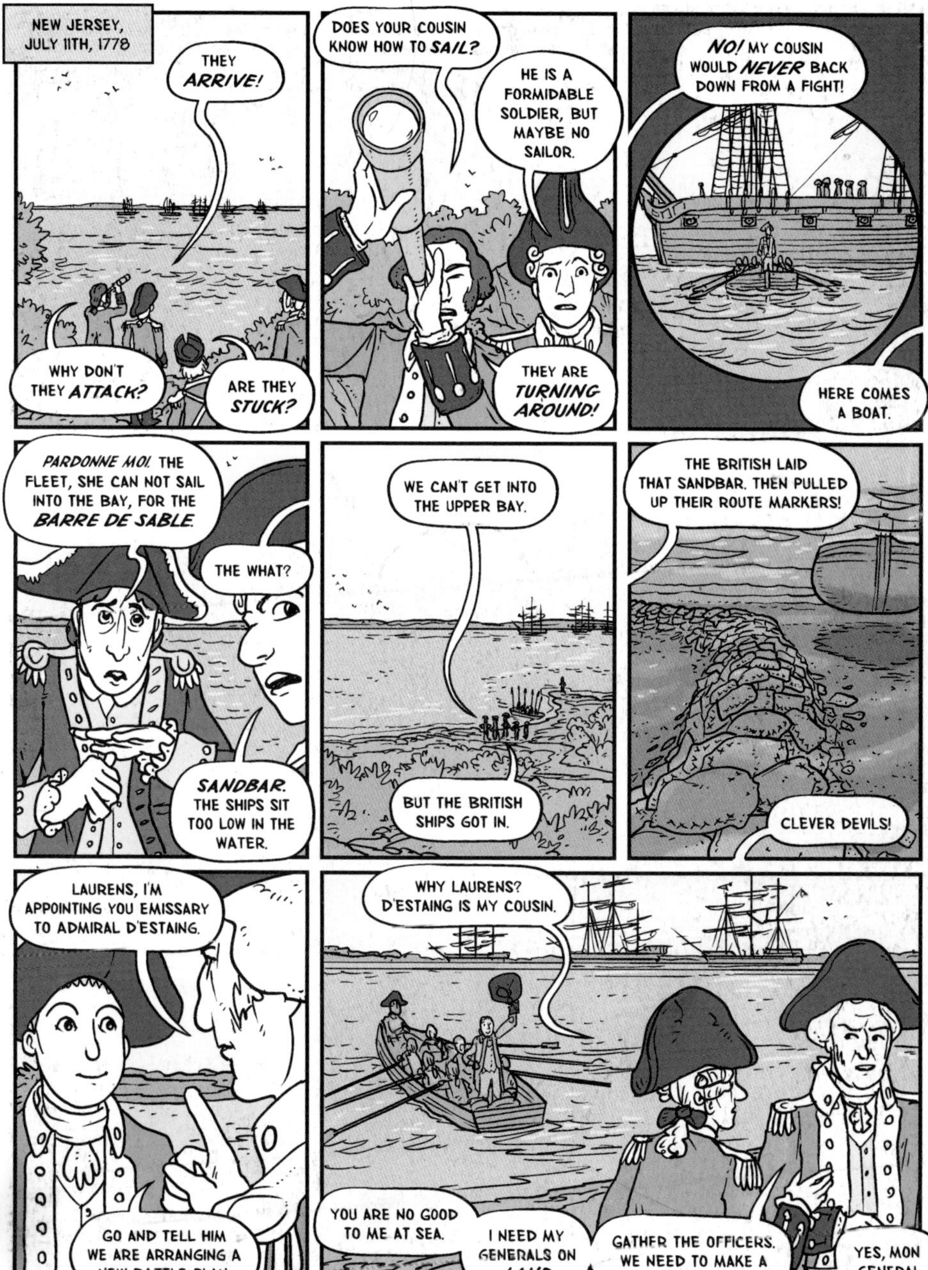

NEW JERSEY, JULY 11TH, 1778
THEY ARRIVE!
WHY DON'T THEY ATTACK?
ARE THEY STUCK?
DOES YOUR COUSIN KNOW HOW TO SAIL?
HE IS A FORMIDABLE SOLDIER, BUT MAYBE NO SAILOR.
THEY ARE TURNING AROUND!
NO! MY COUSIN WOULD NEVER BACK DOWN FROM A FIGHT!
HERE COMES A BOAT.
PARDONNE MOI. THE FLEET, SHE CAN NOT SAIL INTO THE BAY, FOR THE BARRE DE SABLE.
THE WHAT?
SANDBAR. THE SHIPS SIT TOO LOW IN THE WATER.
WE CAN'T GET INTO THE UPPER BAY.
BUT THE BRITISH SHIPS GOT IN.
THE BRITISH LAID THAT SANDBAR. THEN PULLED UP THEIR ROUTE MARKERS!
CLEVER DEVILS!
LAURENS, I'M APPOINTING YOU EMISSARY TO ADMIRAL D'ESTAING.
GO AND TELL HIM WE ARE ARRANGING A NEW BATTLE PLAN.
WHY LAURENS? D'ESTAING IS MY COUSIN.
YOU ARE NO GOOD TO ME AT SEA.
I NEED MY GENERALS ON LAND.
GATHER THE OFFICERS. WE NEED TO MAKE A NEW BATTLE PLAN.
YES, MON GENERAL.

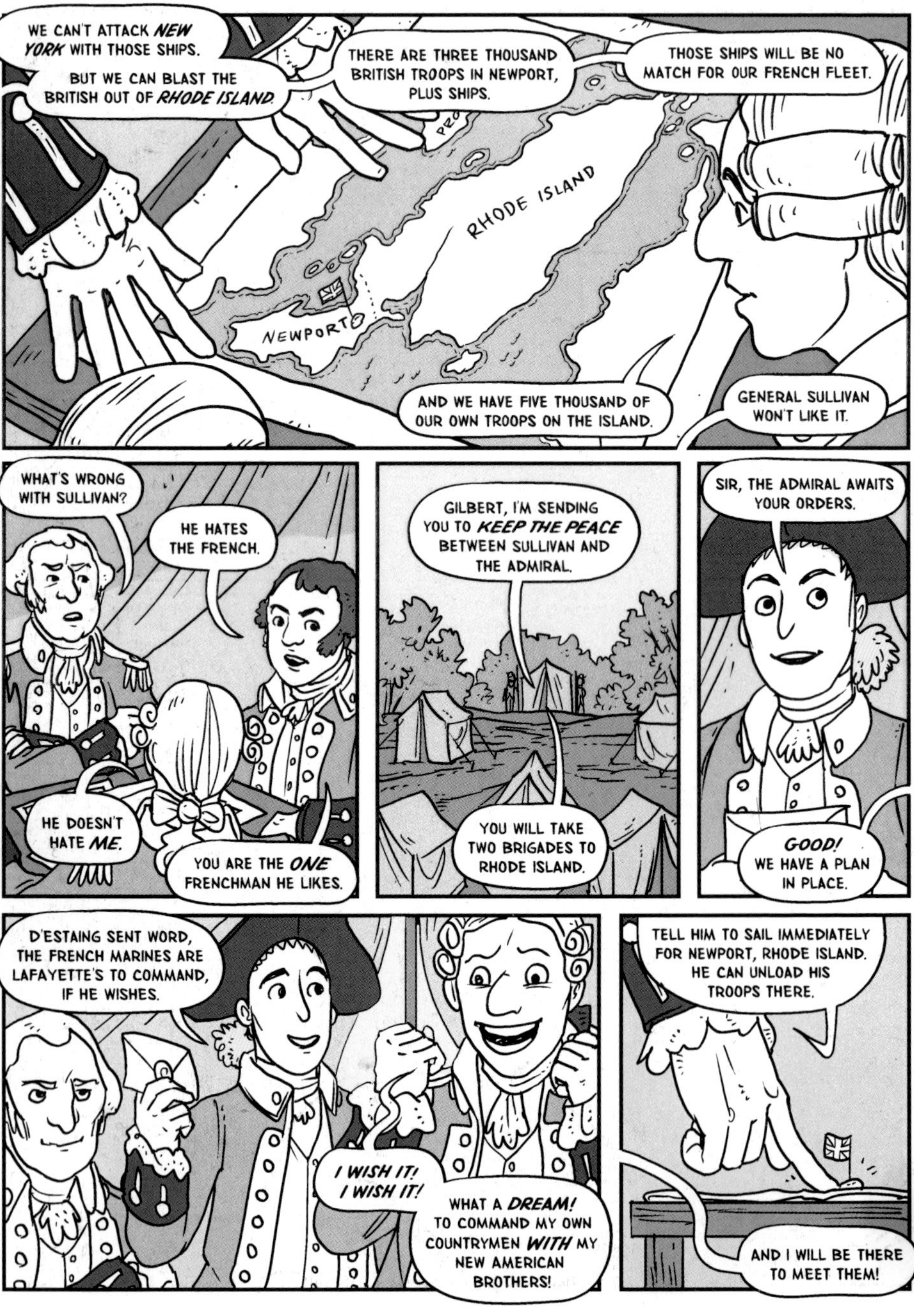
WE CAN'T ATTACK *NEW YORK* WITH THOSE SHIPS.
BUT WE CAN BLAST THE BRITISH OUT OF *RHODE ISLAND.*
THERE ARE THREE THOUSAND BRITISH TROOPS IN NEWPORT, PLUS SHIPS.
THOSE SHIPS WILL BE NO MATCH FOR OUR FRENCH FLEET.
RHODE ISLAND
NEWPORT
AND WE HAVE FIVE THOUSAND OF OUR OWN TROOPS ON THE ISLAND.
GENERAL SULLIVAN WON'T LIKE IT.
WHAT'S WRONG WITH SULLIVAN?
HE HATES THE FRENCH.
HE DOESN'T HATE *ME.*
YOU ARE THE *ONE* FRENCHMAN HE LIKES.
GILBERT, I'M SENDING YOU TO *KEEP THE PEACE* BETWEEN SULLIVAN AND THE ADMIRAL.
YOU WILL TAKE TWO BRIGADES TO RHODE ISLAND.
SIR, THE ADMIRAL AWAITS YOUR ORDERS.
GOOD! WE HAVE A PLAN IN PLACE.
D'ESTAING SENT WORD, THE FRENCH MARINES ARE LAFAYETTE'S TO COMMAND, IF HE WISHES.
I WISH IT! I WISH IT!
WHAT A *DREAM!* TO COMMAND MY OWN COUNTRYMEN *WITH* MY NEW AMERICAN BROTHERS!
TELL HIM TO SAIL IMMEDIATELY FOR NEWPORT, RHODE ISLAND. HE CAN UNLOAD HIS TROOPS THERE.
AND I WILL BE THERE TO MEET THEM!

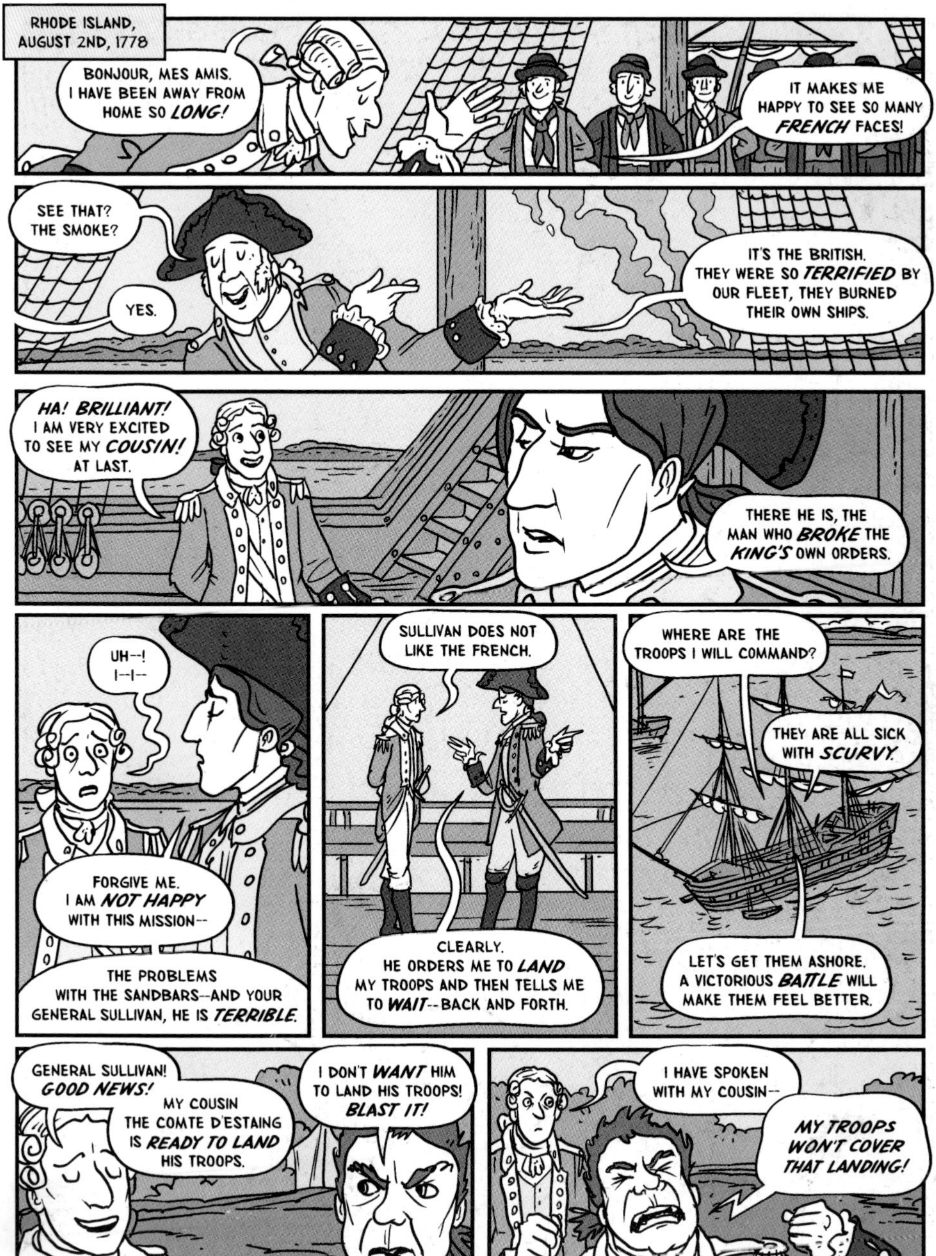
RHODE ISLAND, AUGUST 2ND, 1778
BONJOUR, MES AMIS. I HAVE BEEN AWAY FROM HOME SO *LONG!*
IT MAKES ME HAPPY TO SEE SO MANY *FRENCH* FACES!
SEE THAT? THE SMOKE?
YES.
IT'S THE BRITISH. THEY WERE SO *TERRIFIED* BY OUR FLEET, THEY BURNED THEIR OWN SHIPS.
HA! BRILLIANT! I AM VERY EXCITED TO SEE MY *COUSIN!* AT LAST.
THERE HE IS, THE MAN WHO *BROKE* THE *KING'S* OWN ORDERS.
UH--! I--I--
FORGIVE ME. I AM *NOT HAPPY* WITH THIS MISSION--
THE PROBLEMS WITH THE SANDBARS--AND YOUR GENERAL SULLIVAN, HE IS *TERRIBLE.*
SULLIVAN DOES NOT LIKE THE FRENCH.
CLEARLY. HE ORDERS ME TO *LAND* MY TROOPS AND THEN TELLS ME TO *WAIT*--BACK AND FORTH.
WHERE ARE THE TROOPS I WILL COMMAND?
THEY ARE ALL SICK WITH *SCURVY.*
LET'S GET THEM ASHORE. A VICTORIOUS *BATTLE* WILL MAKE THEM FEEL BETTER.
GENERAL SULLIVAN! *GOOD NEWS!*
MY COUSIN THE COMTE D'ESTAING IS *READY TO LAND* HIS TROOPS.
I DON'T *WANT* HIM TO LAND HIS TROOPS! *BLAST IT!*
I HAVE SPOKEN WITH MY COUSIN--
MY TROOPS WON'T COVER THAT LANDING!

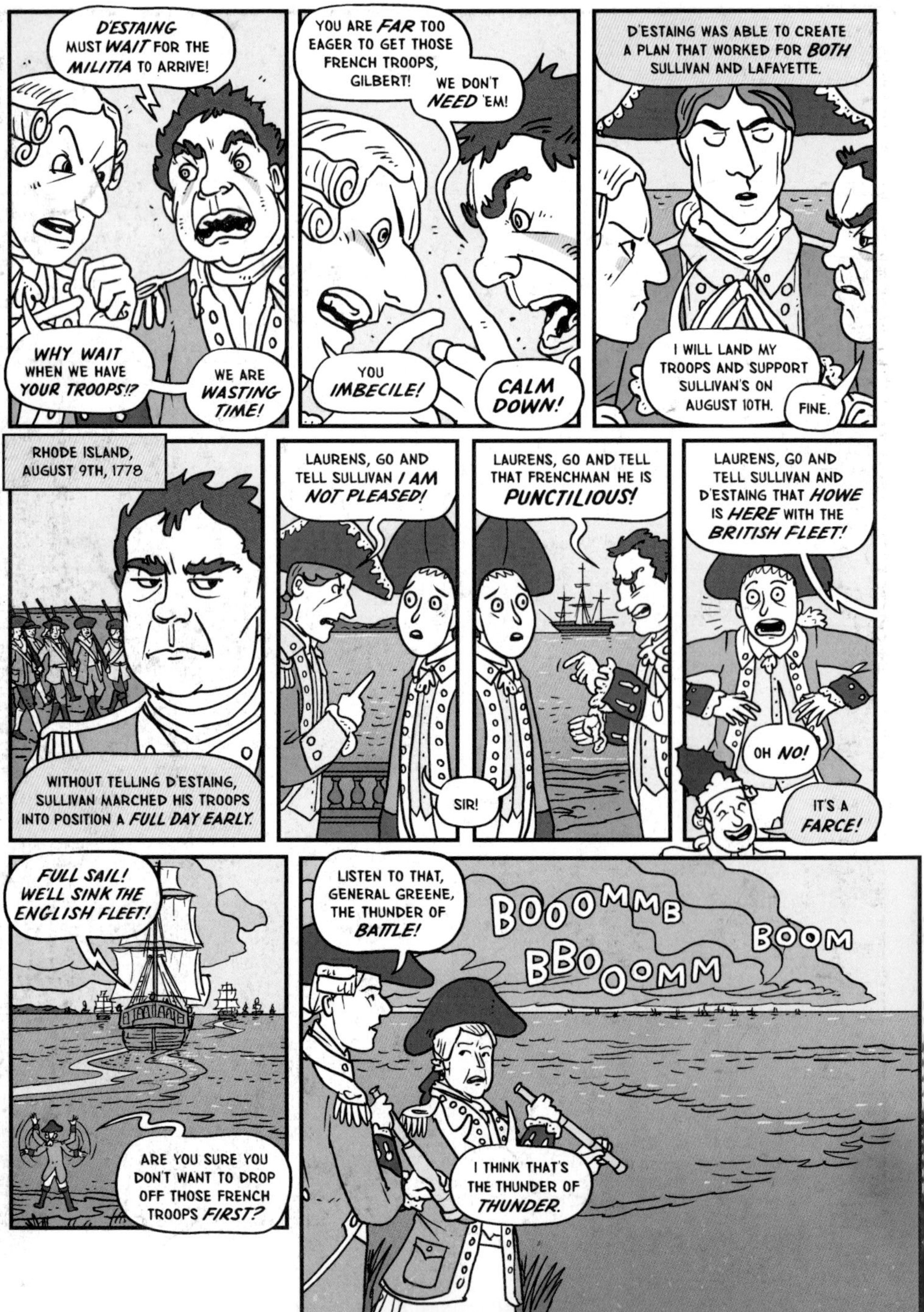
D'ESTAING MUST WAIT FOR THE MILITIA TO ARRIVE!
WHY WAIT WHEN WE HAVE YOUR TROOPS!?
WE ARE WASTING TIME!
YOU ARE FAR TOO EAGER TO GET THOSE FRENCH TROOPS, GILBERT!
WE DON'T NEED 'EM!
YOU IMBECILE!
CALM DOWN!
D'ESTAING WAS ABLE TO CREATE A PLAN THAT WORKED FOR BOTH SULLIVAN AND LAFAYETTE.
I WILL LAND MY TROOPS AND SUPPORT SULLIVAN'S ON AUGUST 10TH.
FINE.
RHODE ISLAND, AUGUST 9TH, 1778
WITHOUT TELLING D'ESTAING, SULLIVAN MARCHED HIS TROOPS INTO POSITION A FULL DAY EARLY.
LAURENS, GO AND TELL SULLIVAN I AM NOT PLEASED!
SIR!
LAURENS, GO AND TELL THAT FRENCHMAN HE IS PUNCTILIOUS!
LAURENS, GO AND TELL SULLIVAN AND D'ESTAING THAT HOWE IS HERE WITH THE BRITISH FLEET!
OH NO!
IT'S A FARCE!
FULL SAIL! WE'LL SINK THE ENGLISH FLEET!
ARE YOU SURE YOU DON'T WANT TO DROP OFF THOSE FRENCH TROOPS FIRST?
LISTEN TO THAT, GENERAL GREENE, THE THUNDER OF BATTLE!
BOOOMMMB
BOOM
BBOOOMM
I THINK THAT'S THE THUNDER OF THUNDER.

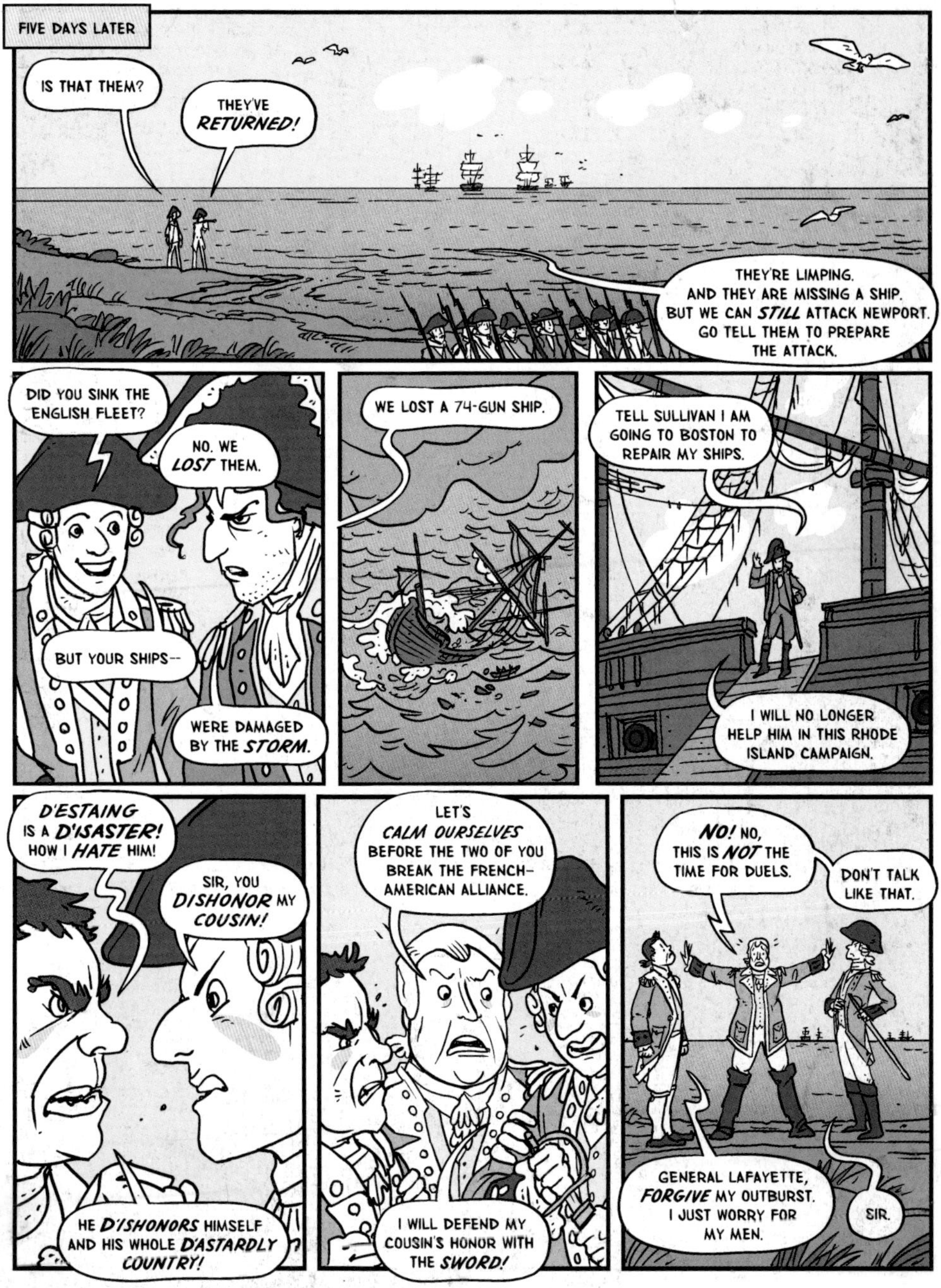
FIVE DAYS LATER
IS THAT THEM?
THEY'VE RETURNED!
THEY'RE LIMPING. AND THEY ARE MISSING A SHIP. BUT WE CAN STILL ATTACK NEWPORT. GO TELL THEM TO PREPARE THE ATTACK.
DID YOU SINK THE ENGLISH FLEET?
NO. WE LOST THEM.
BUT YOUR SHIPS--
WERE DAMAGED BY THE STORM.
WE LOST A 74-GUN SHIP.
TELL SULLIVAN I AM GOING TO BOSTON TO REPAIR MY SHIPS.
I WILL NO LONGER HELP HIM IN THIS RHODE ISLAND CAMPAIGN.
D'ESTAING IS A D'ISASTER! HOW I HATE HIM!
SIR, YOU DISHONOR MY COUSIN!
HE D'ISHONORS HIMSELF AND HIS WHOLE D'ASTARDLY COUNTRY!
LET'S CALM OURSELVES BEFORE THE TWO OF YOU BREAK THE FRENCH-AMERICAN ALLIANCE.
I WILL DEFEND MY COUSIN'S HONOR WITH THE SWORD!
NO! NO, THIS IS NOT THE TIME FOR DUELS.
DON'T TALK LIKE THAT.
GENERAL LAFAYETTE, FORGIVE MY OUTBURST. I JUST WORRY FOR MY MEN.
SIR.

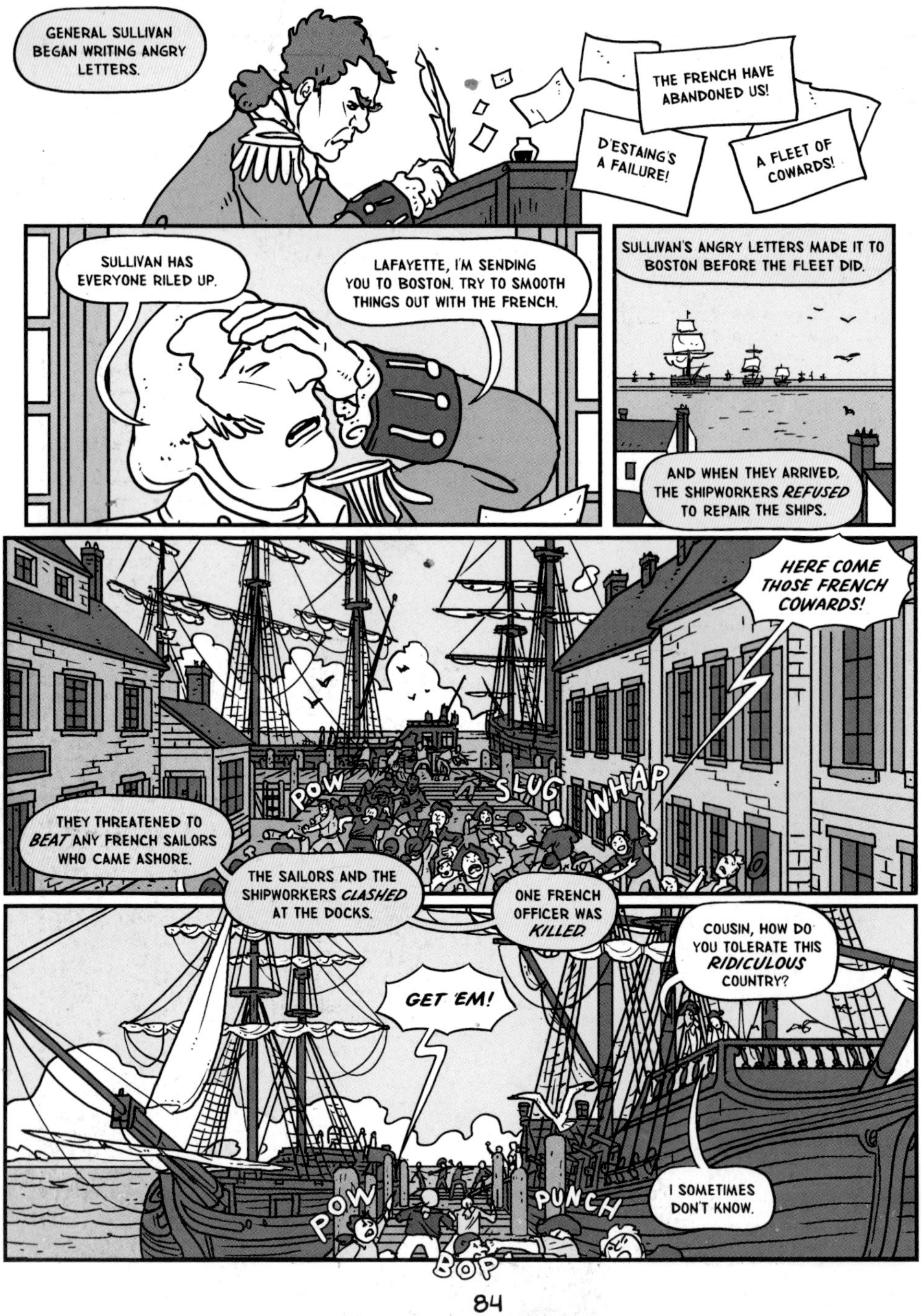
GENERAL SULLIVAN BEGAN WRITING ANGRY LETTERS.
THE FRENCH HAVE ABANDONED US!
D'ESTAING'S A FAILURE!
A FLEET OF COWARDS!
SULLIVAN HAS EVERYONE RILED UP.
LAFAYETTE, I'M SENDING YOU TO BOSTON. TRY TO SMOOTH THINGS OUT WITH THE FRENCH.
SULLIVAN'S ANGRY LETTERS MADE IT TO BOSTON BEFORE THE FLEET DID.
AND WHEN THEY ARRIVED, THE SHIPWORKERS *REFUSED* TO REPAIR THE SHIPS.
HERE COME THOSE FRENCH COWARDS!
POW
SLUG
WHAP
THEY THREATENED TO *BEAT* ANY FRENCH SAILORS WHO CAME ASHORE.
THE SAILORS AND THE SHIPWORKERS *CLASHED* AT THE DOCKS.
ONE FRENCH OFFICER WAS *KILLED.*
COUSIN, HOW DO YOU TOLERATE THIS *RIDICULOUS* COUNTRY?
GET 'EM!
I SOMETIMES DON'T KNOW.
POW
PUNCH
BOP

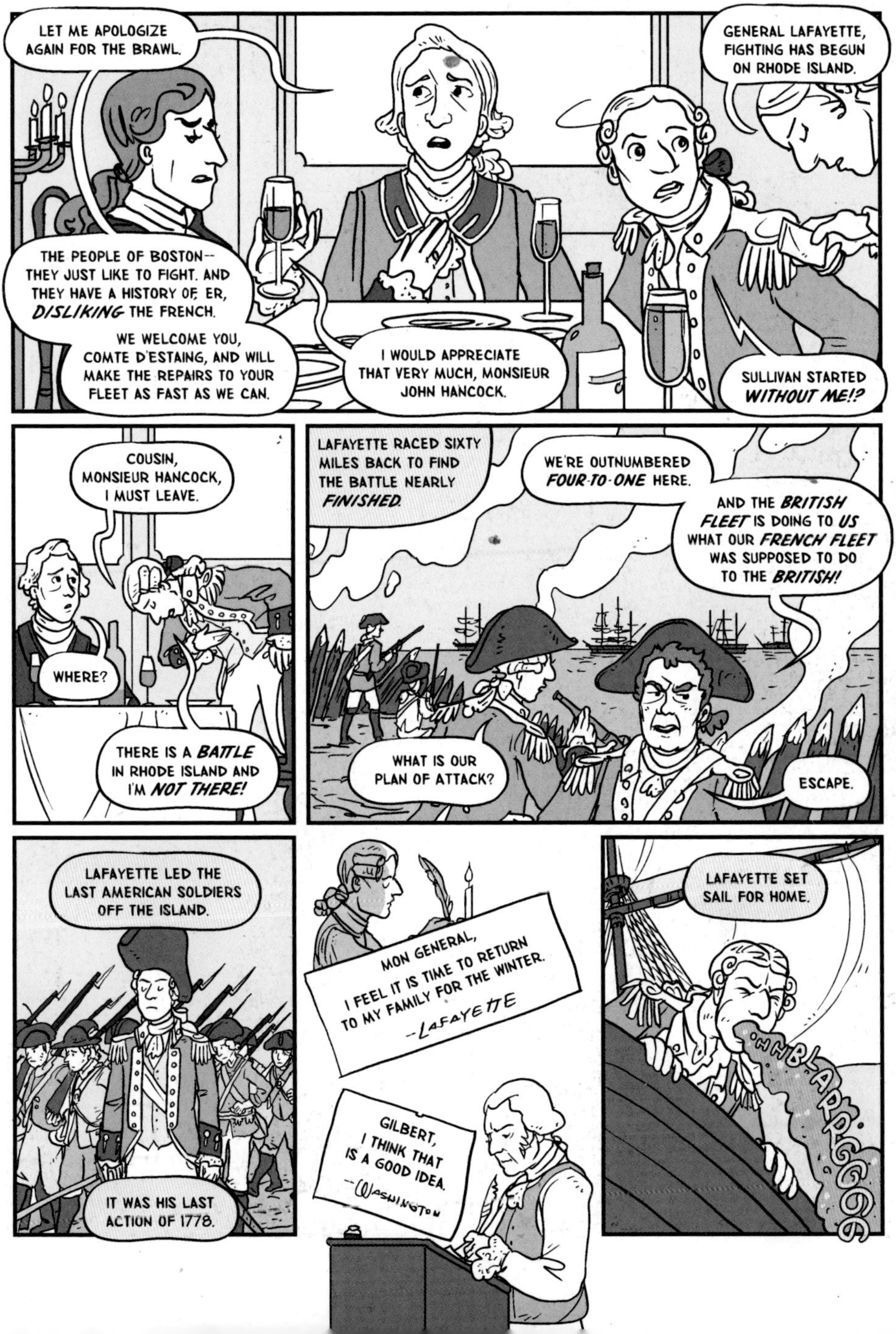
LET ME APOLOGIZE AGAIN FOR THE BRAWL.
THE PEOPLE OF BOSTON-- THEY JUST LIKE TO FIGHT. AND THEY HAVE A HISTORY OF, ER, *DISLIKING* THE FRENCH.
WE WELCOME YOU, COMTE D'ESTAING, AND WILL MAKE THE REPAIRS TO YOUR FLEET AS FAST AS WE CAN.
I WOULD APPRECIATE THAT VERY MUCH, MONSIEUR JOHN HANCOCK.
GENERAL LAFAYETTE, FIGHTING HAS BEGUN ON RHODE ISLAND.
SULLIVAN STARTED *WITHOUT ME!?*
COUSIN, MONSIEUR HANCOCK, I MUST LEAVE.
WHERE?
THERE IS A *BATTLE* IN RHODE ISLAND AND I'M *NOT THERE!*
LAFAYETTE RACED SIXTY MILES BACK TO FIND THE BATTLE NEARLY *FINISHED*.
WE'RE OUTNUMBERED *FOUR-TO-ONE* HERE.
AND THE *BRITISH FLEET* IS DOING TO *US* WHAT OUR *FRENCH FLEET* WAS SUPPOSED TO DO TO THE *BRITISH!*
WHAT IS OUR PLAN OF ATTACK?
ESCAPE.
LAFAYETTE LED THE LAST AMERICAN SOLDIERS OFF THE ISLAND.
IT WAS HIS LAST ACTION OF 1778.
MON GENERAL, I FEEL IT IS TIME TO RETURN TO MY FAMILY FOR THE WINTER. --LAFAYETTE
GILBERT, I THINK THAT IS A GOOD IDEA. --WASHINGTON
LAFAYETTE SET SAIL FOR HOME.
HHBLARRGGGG

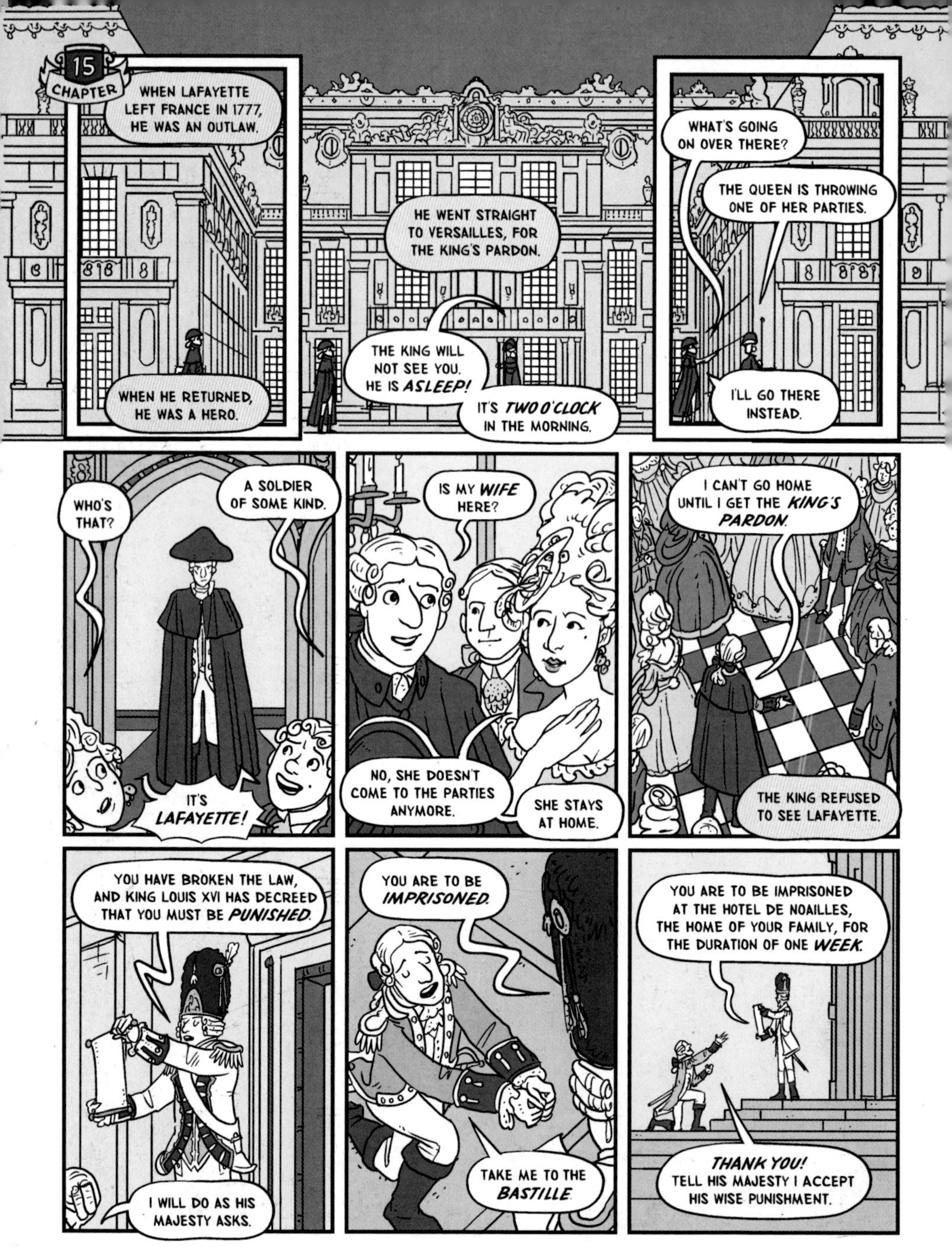
15
CHAPTER
WHEN LAFAYETTE LEFT FRANCE IN 1777, HE WAS AN OUTLAW.
WHEN HE RETURNED, HE WAS A HERO.
HE WENT STRAIGHT TO VERSAILLES, FOR THE KING'S PARDON.
THE KING WILL NOT SEE YOU. HE IS *ASLEEP!*
IT'S *TWO O'CLOCK* IN THE MORNING.
WHAT'S GOING ON OVER THERE?
THE QUEEN IS THROWING ONE OF HER PARTIES.
I'LL GO THERE INSTEAD.
WHO'S THAT?
A SOLDIER OF SOME KIND.
IT'S *LAFAYETTE!*
IS MY *WIFE* HERE?
NO, SHE DOESN'T COME TO THE PARTIES ANYMORE.
SHE STAYS AT HOME.
I CAN'T GO HOME UNTIL I GET THE *KING'S PARDON*.
THE KING REFUSED TO SEE LAFAYETTE.
YOU HAVE BROKEN THE LAW, AND KING LOUIS XVI HAS DECREED THAT YOU MUST BE *PUNISHED*.
I WILL DO AS HIS MAJESTY ASKS.
YOU ARE TO BE *IMPRISONED*.
TAKE ME TO THE *BASTILLE*.
YOU ARE TO BE IMPRISONED AT THE HOTEL DE NOAILLES, THE HOME OF YOUR FAMILY, FOR THE DURATION OF ONE *WEEK*.
THANK YOU! TELL HIS MAJESTY I ACCEPT HIS WISE PUNISHMENT.

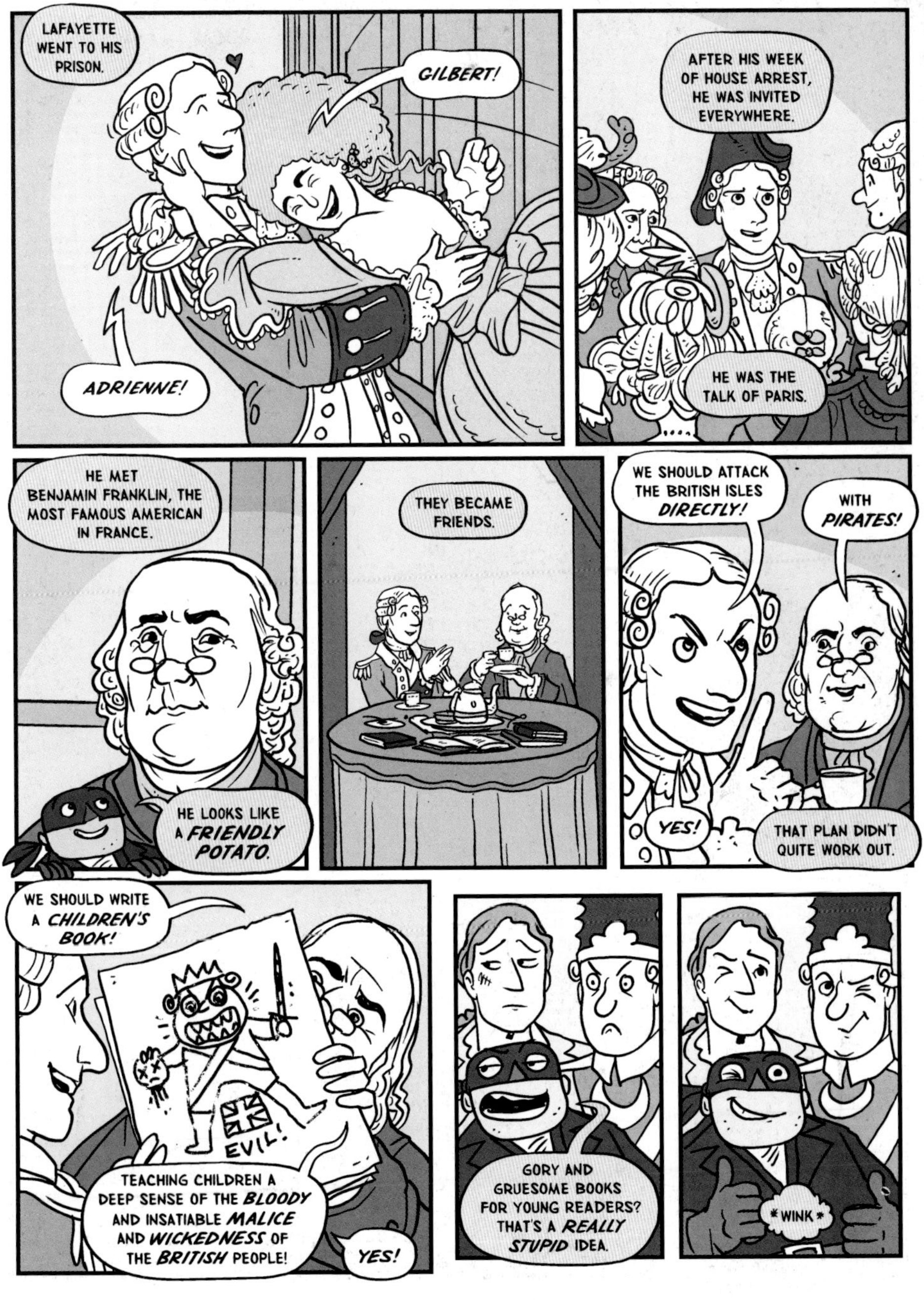
LAFAYETTE WENT TO HIS PRISON.
GILBERT!
ADRIENNE!
AFTER HIS WEEK OF HOUSE ARREST, HE WAS INVITED EVERYWHERE.
HE WAS THE TALK OF PARIS.
HE MET BENJAMIN FRANKLIN, THE MOST FAMOUS AMERICAN IN FRANCE.
HE LOOKS LIKE A FRIENDLY POTATO.
THEY BECAME FRIENDS.
WE SHOULD ATTACK THE BRITISH ISLES DIRECTLY!
WITH PIRATES!
YES!
THAT PLAN DIDN'T QUITE WORK OUT.
WE SHOULD WRITE A CHILDREN'S BOOK!
EVIL!
TEACHING CHILDREN A DEEP SENSE OF THE BLOODY AND INSATIABLE MALICE AND WICKEDNESS OF THE BRITISH PEOPLE!
YES!
GORY AND GRUESOME BOOKS FOR YOUNG READERS? THAT'S A REALLY STUPID IDEA.
WINK

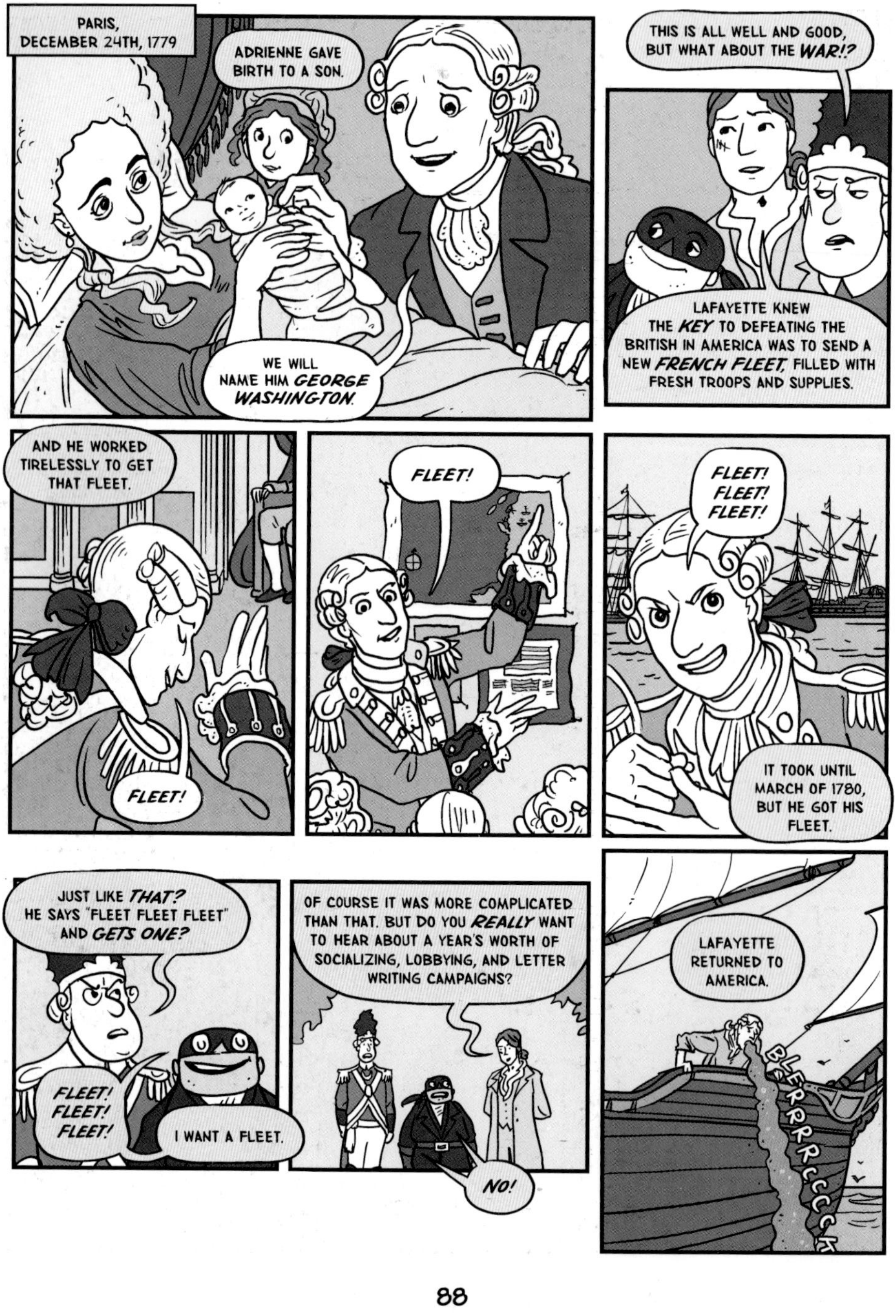
PARIS,
DECEMBER 24TH, 1779
ADRIENNE GAVE BIRTH TO A SON.
WE WILL NAME HIM GEORGE WASHINGTON.
THIS IS ALL WELL AND GOOD, BUT WHAT ABOUT THE WAR!?
LAFAYETTE KNEW THE KEY TO DEFEATING THE BRITISH IN AMERICA WAS TO SEND A NEW FRENCH FLEET, FILLED WITH FRESH TROOPS AND SUPPLIES.
AND HE WORKED TIRELESSLY TO GET THAT FLEET.
FLEET!
FLEET!
FLEET! FLEET! FLEET!
IT TOOK UNTIL MARCH OF 1780, BUT HE GOT HIS FLEET.
JUST LIKE THAT? HE SAYS "FLEET FLEET FLEET" AND GETS ONE?
FLEET! FLEET! FLEET!
I WANT A FLEET.
OF COURSE IT WAS MORE COMPLICATED THAN THAT. BUT DO YOU REALLY WANT TO HEAR ABOUT A YEAR'S WORTH OF SOCIALIZING, LOBBYING, AND LETTER WRITING CAMPAIGNS?
NO!
LAFAYETTE RETURNED TO AMERICA.
BLERRRRCCCK

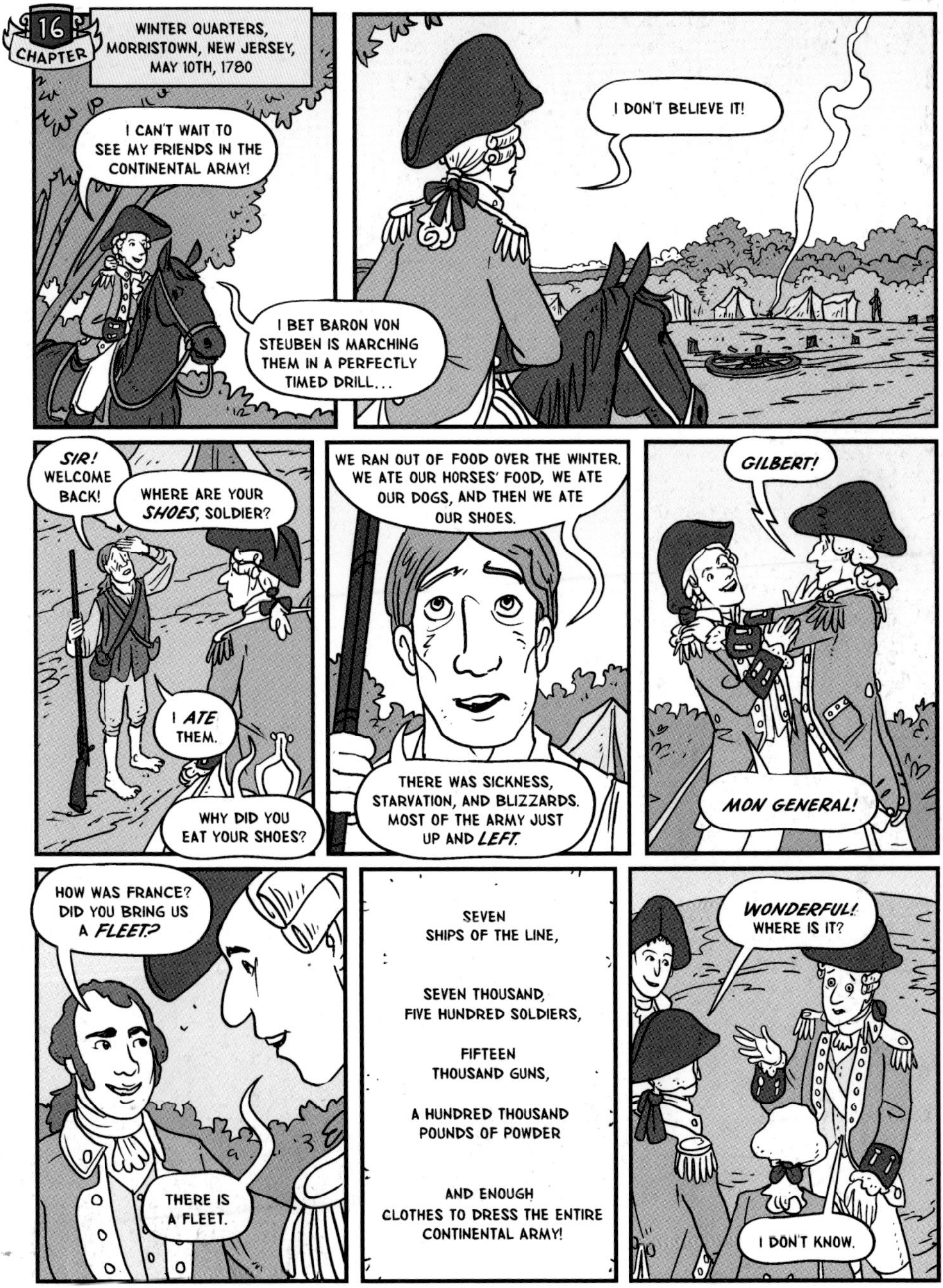
16
CHAPTER
WINTER QUARTERS, MORRISTOWN, NEW JERSEY, MAY 10TH, 1780
I CAN'T WAIT TO SEE MY FRIENDS IN THE CONTINENTAL ARMY!
I BET BARON VON STEUBEN IS MARCHING THEM IN A PERFECTLY TIMED DRILL...
I DON'T BELIEVE IT!
SIR! WELCOME BACK!
WHERE ARE YOUR SHOES, SOLDIER?
I ATE THEM.
WHY DID YOU EAT YOUR SHOES?
WE RAN OUT OF FOOD OVER THE WINTER. WE ATE OUR HORSES' FOOD, WE ATE OUR DOGS, AND THEN WE ATE OUR SHOES.
THERE WAS SICKNESS, STARVATION, AND BLIZZARDS. MOST OF THE ARMY JUST UP AND LEFT.
GILBERT!
MON GENERAL!
HOW WAS FRANCE? DID YOU BRING US A FLEET?
THERE IS A FLEET.
SEVEN SHIPS OF THE LINE,
SEVEN THOUSAND, FIVE HUNDRED SOLDIERS,
FIFTEEN THOUSAND GUNS,
A HUNDRED THOUSAND POUNDS OF POWDER
AND ENOUGH CLOTHES TO DRESS THE ENTIRE CONTINENTAL ARMY!
WONDERFUL! WHERE IS IT?
I DON'T KNOW.

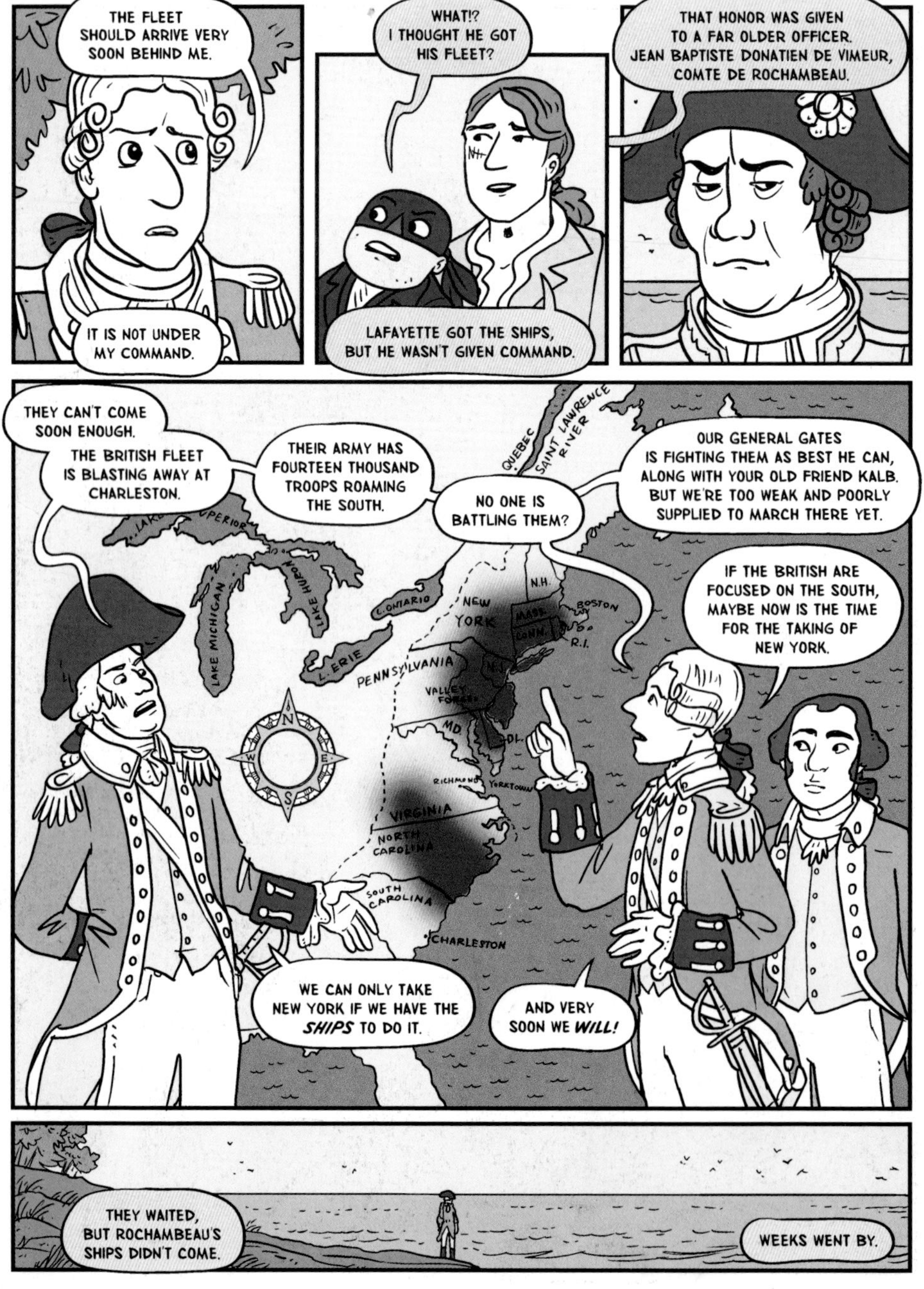
THE FLEET SHOULD ARRIVE VERY SOON BEHIND ME.
IT IS NOT UNDER MY COMMAND.
WHAT!? I THOUGHT HE GOT HIS FLEET?
LAFAYETTE GOT THE SHIPS, BUT HE WASN'T GIVEN COMMAND.
THAT HONOR WAS GIVEN TO A FAR OLDER OFFICER. JEAN BAPTISTE DONATIEN DE VIMEUR, COMTE DE ROCHAMBEAU.
THEY CAN'T COME SOON ENOUGH.
THE BRITISH FLEET IS BLASTING AWAY AT CHARLESTON.
THEIR ARMY HAS FOURTEEN THOUSAND TROOPS ROAMING THE SOUTH.
NO ONE IS BATTLING THEM?
OUR GENERAL GATES IS FIGHTING THEM AS BEST HE CAN, ALONG WITH YOUR OLD FRIEND KALB. BUT WE'RE TOO WEAK AND POORLY SUPPLIED TO MARCH THERE YET.
IF THE BRITISH ARE FOCUSED ON THE SOUTH, MAYBE NOW IS THE TIME FOR THE TAKING OF NEW YORK.
WE CAN ONLY TAKE NEW YORK IF WE HAVE THE *SHIPS* TO DO IT.
AND VERY SOON WE *WILL!*
QUEBEC
SAINT LAWRENCE RIVER
LAKE MICHIGAN
LAKE HURON
L. ONTARIO
L. ERIE
NEW YORK
N.H.
MASS.
CONN.
R.I.
BOSTON
N.J.
PENNSYLVANIA
VALLEY FORGE
MD
DL.
RICHMOND
YORKTOWN
VIRGINIA
NORTH CAROLINA
SOUTH CAROLINA
CHARLESTON
N
S
E
W
THEY WAITED, BUT ROCHAMBEAU'S SHIPS DIDN'T COME.
WEEKS WENT BY.

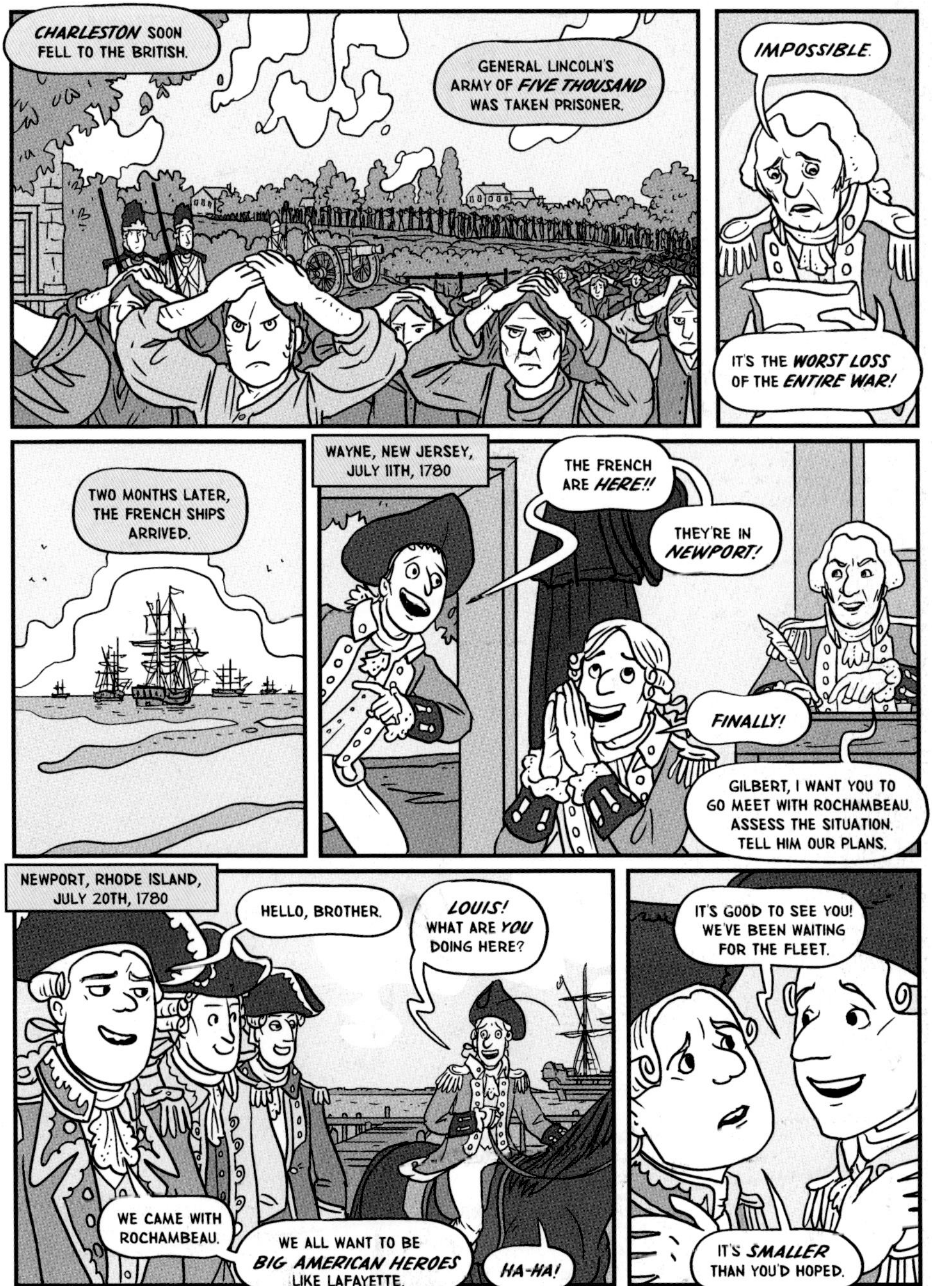
CHARLESTON SOON FELL TO THE BRITISH.
GENERAL LINCOLN'S ARMY OF FIVE THOUSAND WAS TAKEN PRISONER.
IMPOSSIBLE.
IT'S THE WORST LOSS OF THE ENTIRE WAR!
TWO MONTHS LATER, THE FRENCH SHIPS ARRIVED.
WAYNE, NEW JERSEY, JULY 11TH, 1780
THE FRENCH ARE HERE!!
THEY'RE IN NEWPORT!
FINALLY!
GILBERT, I WANT YOU TO GO MEET WITH ROCHAMBEAU. ASSESS THE SITUATION. TELL HIM OUR PLANS.
NEWPORT, RHODE ISLAND, JULY 20TH, 1780
HELLO, BROTHER.
LOUIS! WHAT ARE YOU DOING HERE?
WE CAME WITH ROCHAMBEAU.
WE ALL WANT TO BE BIG AMERICAN HEROES LIKE LAFAYETTE.
HA-HA!
IT'S GOOD TO SEE YOU! WE'VE BEEN WAITING FOR THE FLEET.
IT'S SMALLER THAN YOU'D HOPED.

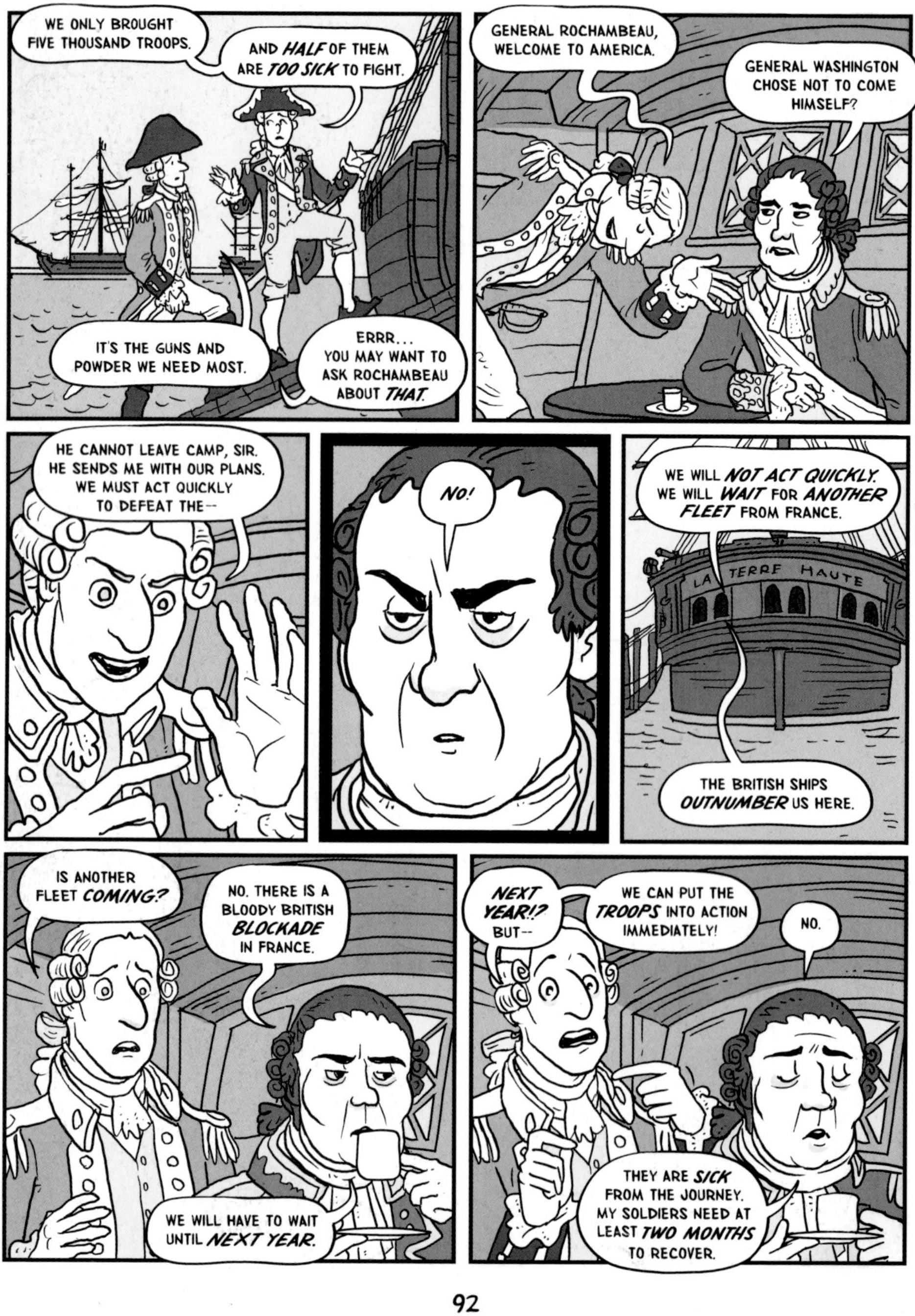
WE ONLY BROUGHT FIVE THOUSAND TROOPS.
AND HALF OF THEM ARE TOO SICK TO FIGHT.
IT'S THE GUNS AND POWDER WE NEED MOST.
ERRR... YOU MAY WANT TO ASK ROCHAMBEAU ABOUT THAT.
GENERAL ROCHAMBEAU, WELCOME TO AMERICA.
GENERAL WASHINGTON CHOSE NOT TO COME HIMSELF?
HE CANNOT LEAVE CAMP, SIR. HE SENDS ME WITH OUR PLANS. WE MUST ACT QUICKLY TO DEFEAT THE--
NO!
WE WILL NOT ACT QUICKLY. WE WILL WAIT FOR ANOTHER FLEET FROM FRANCE.
LA TERRE HAUTE
THE BRITISH SHIPS OUTNUMBER US HERE.
IS ANOTHER FLEET COMING?
NO. THERE IS A BLOODY BRITISH BLOCKADE IN FRANCE.
WE WILL HAVE TO WAIT UNTIL NEXT YEAR.
NEXT YEAR!? BUT--
WE CAN PUT THE TROOPS INTO ACTION IMMEDIATELY!
NO.
THEY ARE SICK FROM THE JOURNEY. MY SOLDIERS NEED AT LEAST TWO MONTHS TO RECOVER.

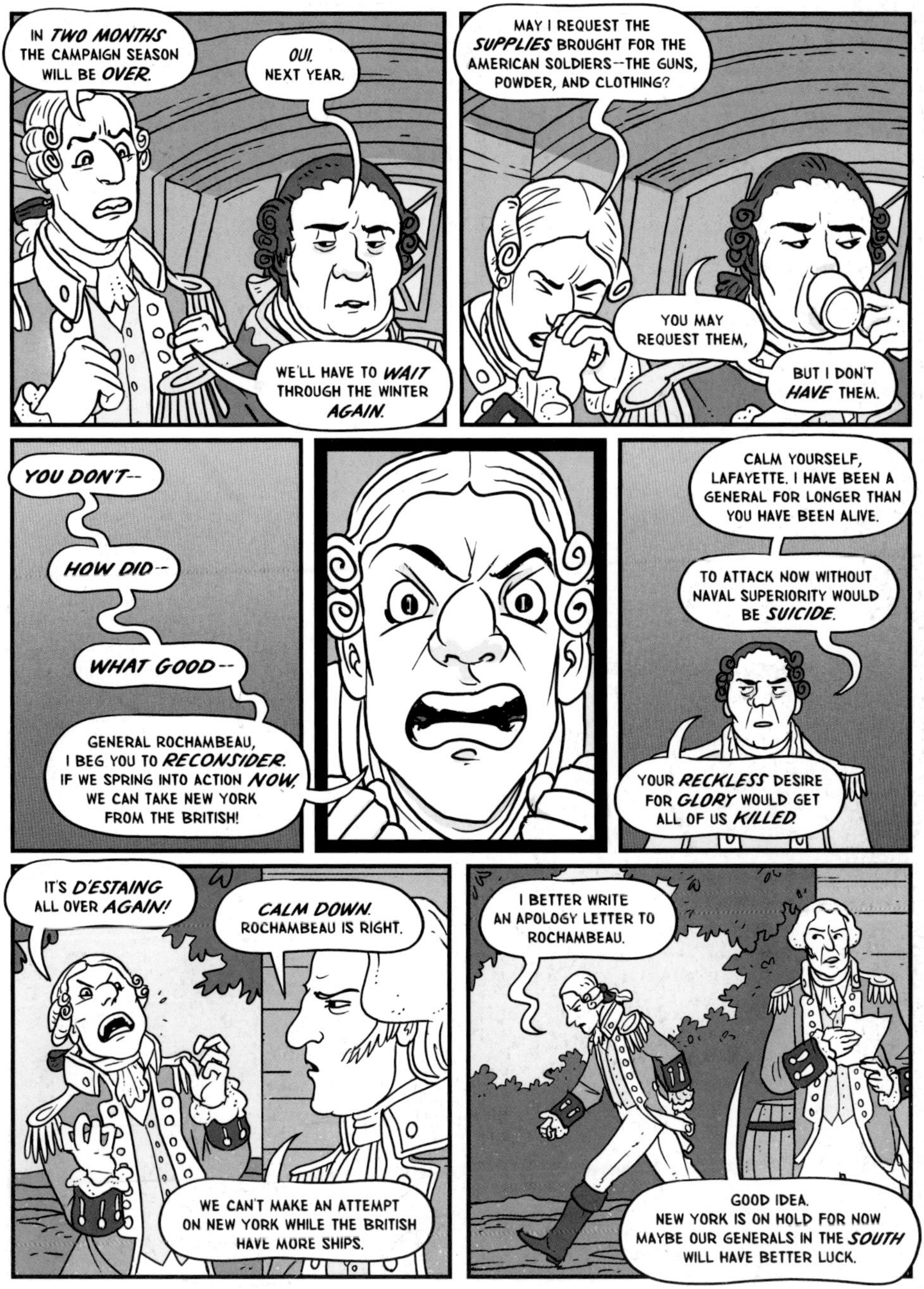
IN TWO MONTHS THE CAMPAIGN SEASON WILL BE OVER.
OUI. NEXT YEAR.
WE'LL HAVE TO WAIT THROUGH THE WINTER AGAIN.
MAY I REQUEST THE SUPPLIES BROUGHT FOR THE AMERICAN SOLDIERS--THE GUNS, POWDER, AND CLOTHING?
YOU MAY REQUEST THEM,
BUT I DON'T HAVE THEM.
YOU DON'T--
HOW DID--
WHAT GOOD--
GENERAL ROCHAMBEAU, I BEG YOU TO RECONSIDER. IF WE SPRING INTO ACTION NOW, WE CAN TAKE NEW YORK FROM THE BRITISH!
CALM YOURSELF, LAFAYETTE. I HAVE BEEN A GENERAL FOR LONGER THAN YOU HAVE BEEN ALIVE.
TO ATTACK NOW WITHOUT NAVAL SUPERIORITY WOULD BE SUICIDE.
YOUR RECKLESS DESIRE FOR GLORY WOULD GET ALL OF US KILLED.
IT'S D'ESTAING ALL OVER AGAIN!
CALM DOWN. ROCHAMBEAU IS RIGHT.
WE CAN'T MAKE AN ATTEMPT ON NEW YORK WHILE THE BRITISH HAVE MORE SHIPS.
I BETTER WRITE AN APOLOGY LETTER TO ROCHAMBEAU.
GOOD IDEA. NEW YORK IS ON HOLD FOR NOW. MAYBE OUR GENERALS IN THE SOUTH WILL HAVE BETTER LUCK.

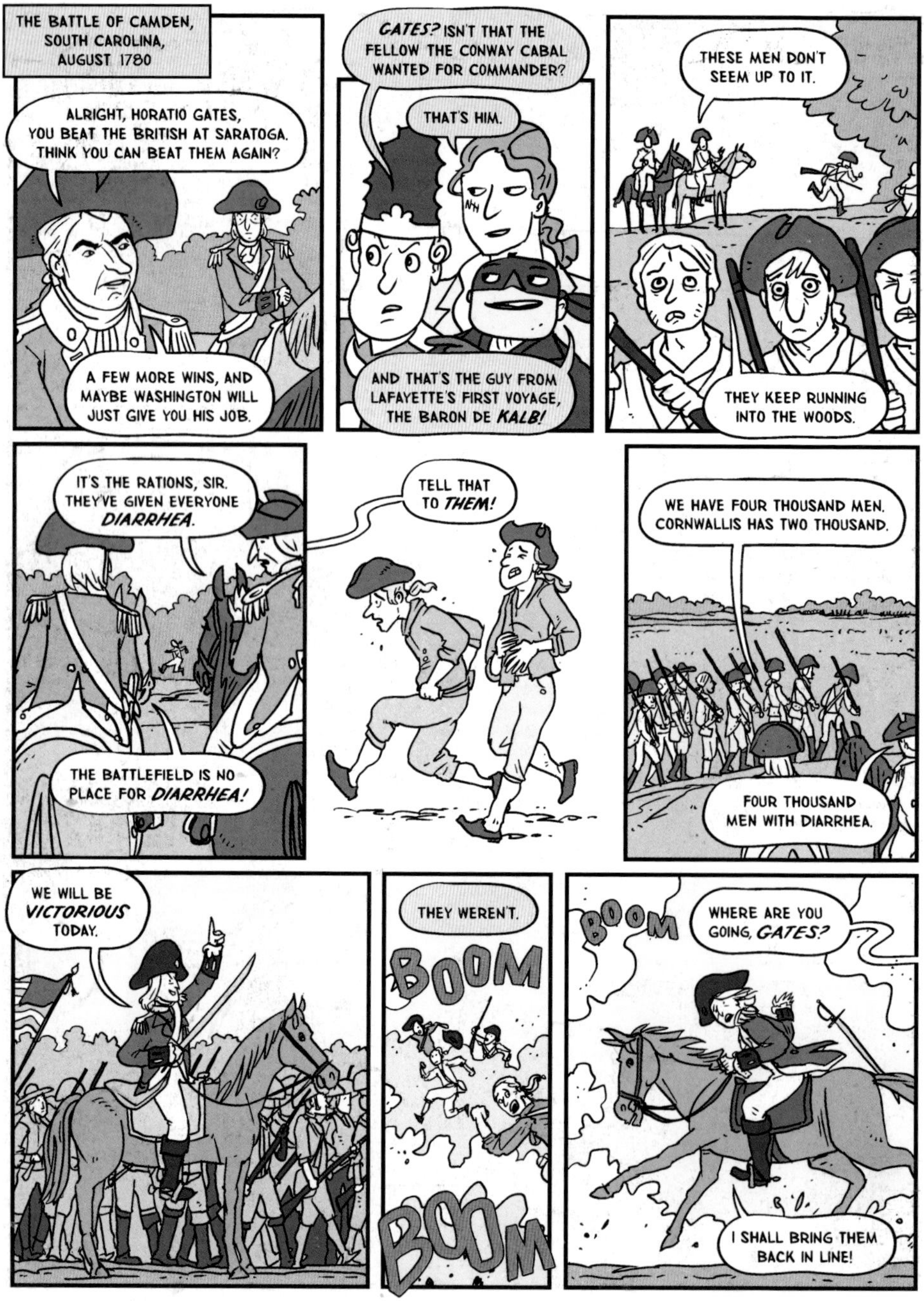
THE BATTLE OF CAMDEN, SOUTH CAROLINA, AUGUST 1780
ALRIGHT, HORATIO GATES, YOU BEAT THE BRITISH AT SARATOGA. THINK YOU CAN BEAT THEM AGAIN?
A FEW MORE WINS, AND MAYBE WASHINGTON WILL JUST GIVE YOU HIS JOB.
GATES? ISN'T THAT THE FELLOW THE CONWAY CABAL WANTED FOR COMMANDER?
THAT'S HIM.
AND THAT'S THE GUY FROM LAFAYETTE'S FIRST VOYAGE, THE BARON DE KALB!
THESE MEN DON'T SEEM UP TO IT.
THEY KEEP RUNNING INTO THE WOODS.
IT'S THE RATIONS, SIR. THEY'VE GIVEN EVERYONE DIARRHEA.
THE BATTLEFIELD IS NO PLACE FOR DIARRHEA!
TELL THAT TO THEM!
WE HAVE FOUR THOUSAND MEN. CORNWALLIS HAS TWO THOUSAND.
FOUR THOUSAND MEN WITH DIARRHEA.
WE WILL BE VICTORIOUS TODAY.
THEY WEREN'T.
BOOM
BOOM
BOOM
WHERE ARE YOU GOING, GATES?
I SHALL BRING THEM BACK IN LINE!

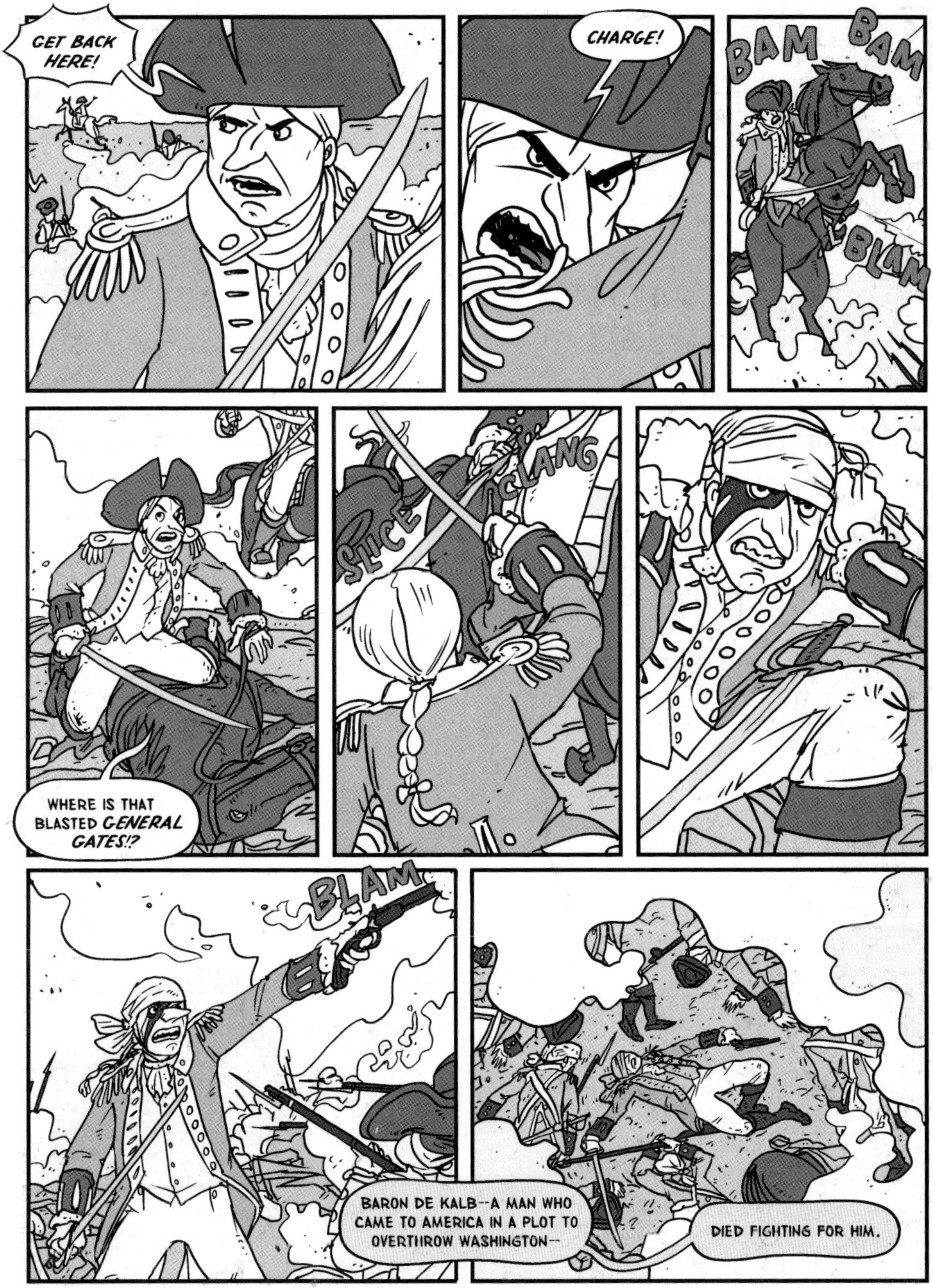
GET BACK HERE!
CHARGE!
BAM BAM
BLAM
SLICE
CLANG
WHERE IS THAT BLASTED *GENERAL GATES!?*
BLAM
BARON DE KALB--A MAN WHO CAME TO AMERICA IN A PLOT TO OVERTHROW WASHINGTON--
DIED FIGHTING FOR HIM.

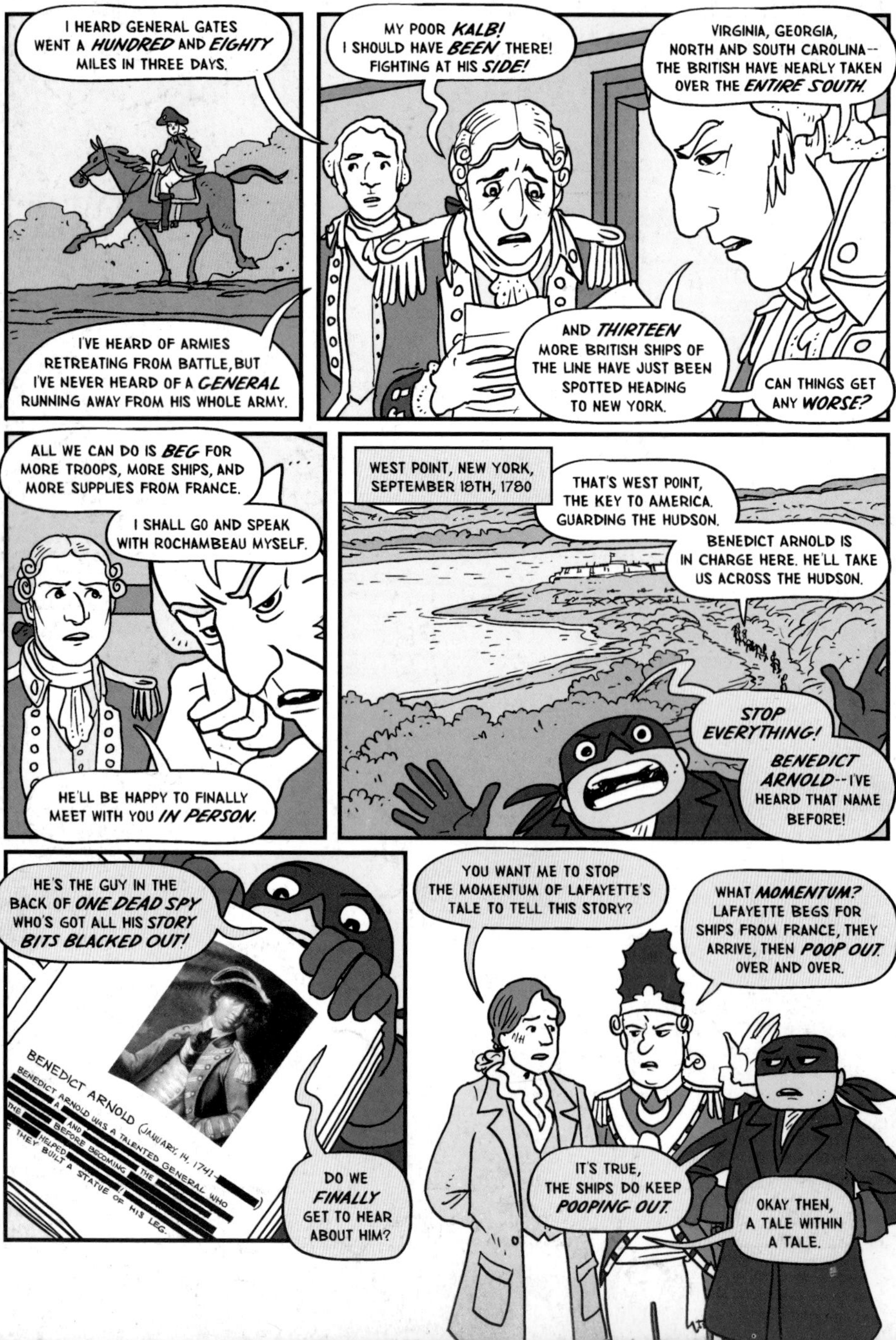
I HEARD GENERAL GATES WENT A HUNDRED AND EIGHTY MILES IN THREE DAYS.
I'VE HEARD OF ARMIES RETREATING FROM BATTLE, BUT I'VE NEVER HEARD OF A GENERAL RUNNING AWAY FROM HIS WHOLE ARMY.
MY POOR KALB! I SHOULD HAVE BEEN THERE! FIGHTING AT HIS SIDE!
VIRGINIA, GEORGIA, NORTH AND SOUTH CAROLINA-- THE BRITISH HAVE NEARLY TAKEN OVER THE ENTIRE SOUTH.
AND THIRTEEN MORE BRITISH SHIPS OF THE LINE HAVE JUST BEEN SPOTTED HEADING TO NEW YORK.
CAN THINGS GET ANY WORSE?
ALL WE CAN DO IS BEG FOR MORE TROOPS, MORE SHIPS, AND MORE SUPPLIES FROM FRANCE.
I SHALL GO AND SPEAK WITH ROCHAMBEAU MYSELF.
HE'LL BE HAPPY TO FINALLY MEET WITH YOU IN PERSON.
WEST POINT, NEW YORK, SEPTEMBER 18TH, 1780
THAT'S WEST POINT, THE KEY TO AMERICA. GUARDING THE HUDSON.
BENEDICT ARNOLD IS IN CHARGE HERE. HE'LL TAKE US ACROSS THE HUDSON.
STOP EVERYTHING!
BENEDICT ARNOLD--I'VE HEARD THAT NAME BEFORE!
HE'S THE GUY IN THE BACK OF ONE DEAD SPY WHO'S GOT ALL HIS STORY BITS BLACKED OUT!
BENEDICT ARNOLD (JANUARY 14, 1741–[redacted])
[redacted] BENEDICT ARNOLD WAS A TALENTED GENERAL WHO
THE [redacted] A [redacted] AND [redacted] BEFORE BECOMING THE [redacted]
[redacted] HELPED [redacted]!
E THEY BUILT A STATUE OF HIS LEG.
DO WE FINALLY GET TO HEAR ABOUT HIM?
YOU WANT ME TO STOP THE MOMENTUM OF LAFAYETTE'S TALE TO TELL THIS STORY?
WHAT MOMENTUM? LAFAYETTE BEGS FOR SHIPS FROM FRANCE, THEY ARRIVE, THEN POOP OUT. OVER AND OVER.
IT'S TRUE, THE SHIPS DO KEEP POOPING OUT.
OKAY THEN, A TALE WITHIN A TALE.

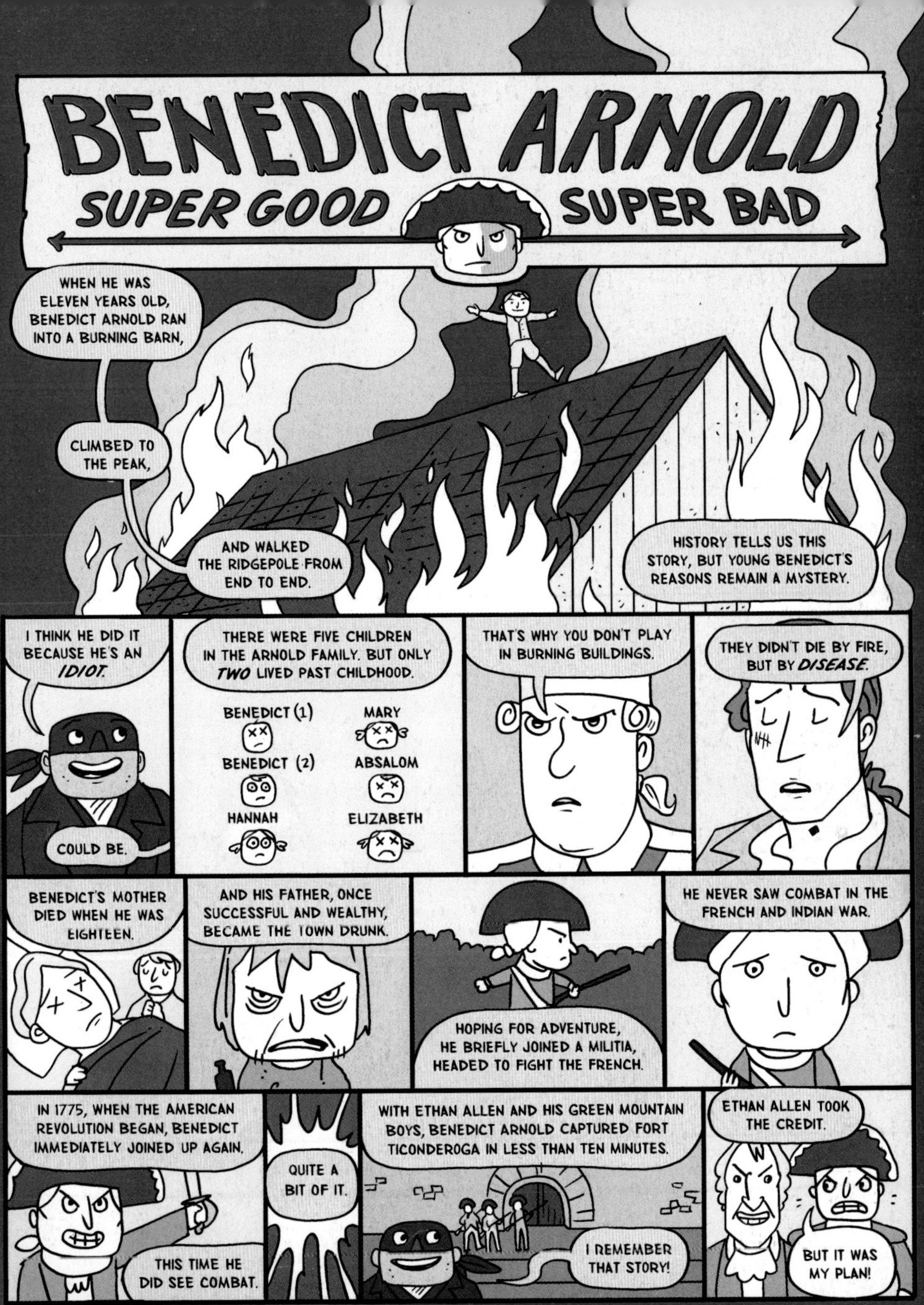
BENEDICT ARNOLD
SUPER GOOD
SUPER BAD
WHEN HE WAS ELEVEN YEARS OLD, BENEDICT ARNOLD RAN INTO A BURNING BARN,
CLIMBED TO THE PEAK,
AND WALKED THE RIDGEPOLE FROM END TO END.
HISTORY TELLS US THIS STORY, BUT YOUNG BENEDICT'S REASONS REMAIN A MYSTERY.
I THINK HE DID IT BECAUSE HE'S AN *IDIOT.*
COULD BE.
THERE WERE FIVE CHILDREN IN THE ARNOLD FAMILY. BUT ONLY *TWO* LIVED PAST CHILDHOOD.
BENEDICT (1)
MARY
BENEDICT (2)
ABSALOM
HANNAH
ELIZABETH
THAT'S WHY YOU DON'T PLAY IN BURNING BUILDINGS.
THEY DIDN'T DIE BY FIRE, BUT BY *DISEASE.*
BENEDICT'S MOTHER DIED WHEN HE WAS EIGHTEEN.
AND HIS FATHER, ONCE SUCCESSFUL AND WEALTHY, BECAME THE TOWN DRUNK.
HOPING FOR ADVENTURE, HE BRIEFLY JOINED A MILITIA, HEADED TO FIGHT THE FRENCH.
HE NEVER SAW COMBAT IN THE FRENCH AND INDIAN WAR.
IN 1775, WHEN THE AMERICAN REVOLUTION BEGAN, BENEDICT IMMEDIATELY JOINED UP AGAIN.
THIS TIME HE DID SEE COMBAT.
QUITE A BIT OF IT.
WITH ETHAN ALLEN AND HIS GREEN MOUNTAIN BOYS, BENEDICT ARNOLD CAPTURED FORT TICONDEROGA IN LESS THAN TEN MINUTES.
I REMEMBER THAT STORY!
ETHAN ALLEN TOOK THE CREDIT.
BUT IT WAS MY PLAN!

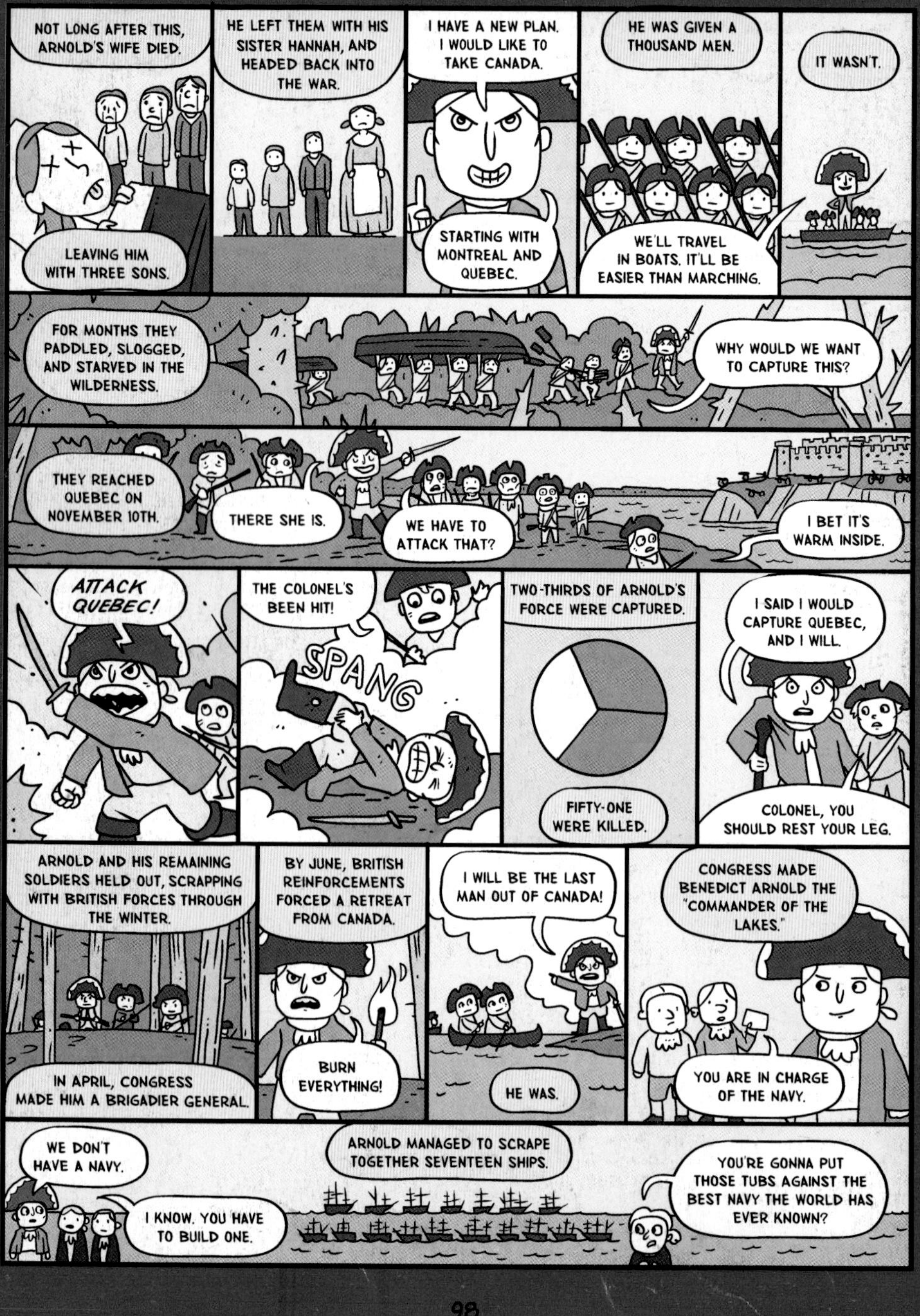
NOT LONG AFTER THIS, ARNOLD'S WIFE DIED.
LEAVING HIM WITH THREE SONS.
HE LEFT THEM WITH HIS SISTER HANNAH, AND HEADED BACK INTO THE WAR.
I HAVE A NEW PLAN. I WOULD LIKE TO TAKE CANADA.
STARTING WITH MONTREAL AND QUEBEC.
HE WAS GIVEN A THOUSAND MEN.
WE'LL TRAVEL IN BOATS. IT'LL BE EASIER THAN MARCHING.
IT WASN'T.
FOR MONTHS THEY PADDLED, SLOGGED, AND STARVED IN THE WILDERNESS.
WHY WOULD WE WANT TO CAPTURE THIS?
THEY REACHED QUEBEC ON NOVEMBER 10TH.
THERE SHE IS.
WE HAVE TO ATTACK THAT?
I BET IT'S WARM INSIDE.
ATTACK QUEBEC!
THE COLONEL'S BEEN HIT!
SPANG
TWO-THIRDS OF ARNOLD'S FORCE WERE CAPTURED.
FIFTY-ONE WERE KILLED.
I SAID I WOULD CAPTURE QUEBEC, AND I WILL.
COLONEL, YOU SHOULD REST YOUR LEG.
ARNOLD AND HIS REMAINING SOLDIERS HELD OUT, SCRAPPING WITH BRITISH FORCES THROUGH THE WINTER.
IN APRIL, CONGRESS MADE HIM A BRIGADIER GENERAL.
BY JUNE, BRITISH REINFORCEMENTS FORCED A RETREAT FROM CANADA.
BURN EVERYTHING!
I WILL BE THE LAST MAN OUT OF CANADA!
HE WAS.
CONGRESS MADE BENEDICT ARNOLD THE "COMMANDER OF THE LAKES."
YOU ARE IN CHARGE OF THE NAVY.
WE DON'T HAVE A NAVY.
I KNOW. YOU HAVE TO BUILD ONE.
ARNOLD MANAGED TO SCRAPE TOGETHER SEVENTEEN SHIPS.
YOU'RE GONNA PUT THOSE TUBS AGAINST THE BEST NAVY THE WORLD HAS EVER KNOWN?

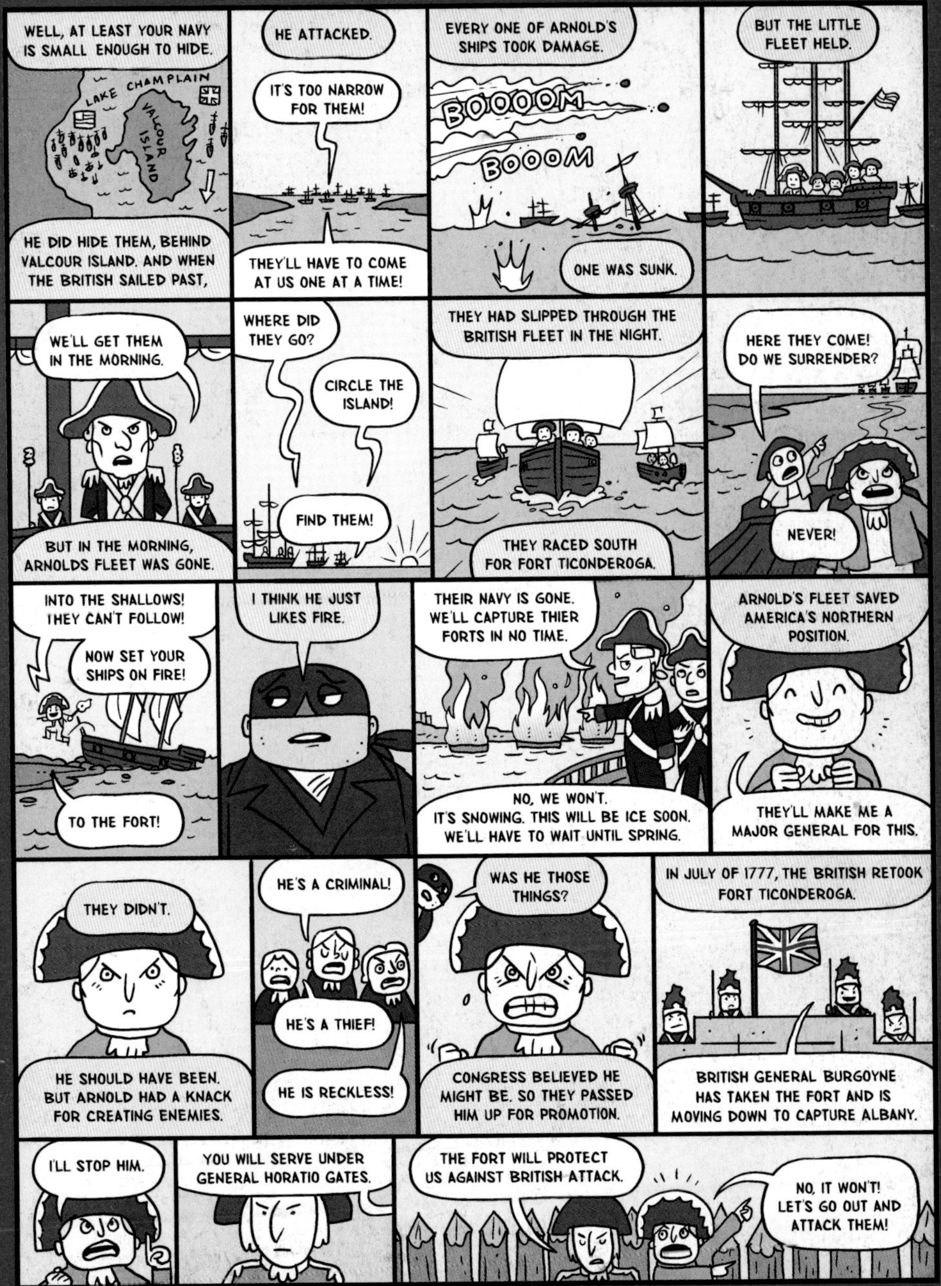
WELL, AT LEAST YOUR NAVY IS SMALL ENOUGH TO HIDE.
LAKE CHAMPLAIN
VALCOUR ISLAND
HE DID HIDE THEM, BEHIND VALCOUR ISLAND. AND WHEN THE BRITISH SAILED PAST,
HE ATTACKED.
IT'S TOO NARROW FOR THEM!
THEY'LL HAVE TO COME AT US ONE AT A TIME!
EVERY ONE OF ARNOLD'S SHIPS TOOK DAMAGE.
BOOOOM
BOOOM
ONE WAS SUNK.
BUT THE LITTLE FLEET HELD.
WE'LL GET THEM IN THE MORNING.
BUT IN THE MORNING, ARNOLDS FLEET WAS GONE.
WHERE DID THEY GO?
CIRCLE THE ISLAND!
FIND THEM!
THEY HAD SLIPPED THROUGH THE BRITISH FLEET IN THE NIGHT.
THEY RACED SOUTH FOR FORT TICONDEROGA.
HERE THEY COME! DO WE SURRENDER?
NEVER!
INTO THE SHALLOWS! THEY CAN'T FOLLOW!
NOW SET YOUR SHIPS ON FIRE!
TO THE FORT!
I THINK HE JUST LIKES FIRE.
THEIR NAVY IS GONE. WE'LL CAPTURE THIER FORTS IN NO TIME.
NO, WE WON'T. IT'S SNOWING. THIS WILL BE ICE SOON. WE'LL HAVE TO WAIT UNTIL SPRING.
ARNOLD'S FLEET SAVED AMERICA'S NORTHERN POSITION.
THEY'LL MAKE ME A MAJOR GENERAL FOR THIS.
THEY DIDN'T.
HE SHOULD HAVE BEEN. BUT ARNOLD HAD A KNACK FOR CREATING ENEMIES.
HE'S A CRIMINAL!
HE'S A THIEF!
HE IS RECKLESS!
WAS HE THOSE THINGS?
CONGRESS BELIEVED HE MIGHT BE. SO THEY PASSED HIM UP FOR PROMOTION.
IN JULY OF 1777, THE BRITISH RETOOK FORT TICONDEROGA.
BRITISH GENERAL BURGOYNE HAS TAKEN THE FORT AND IS MOVING DOWN TO CAPTURE ALBANY.
I'LL STOP HIM.
YOU WILL SERVE UNDER GENERAL HORATIO GATES.
THE FORT WILL PROTECT US AGAINST BRITISH ATTACK.
NO, IT WON'T! LET'S GO OUT AND ATTACK THEM!

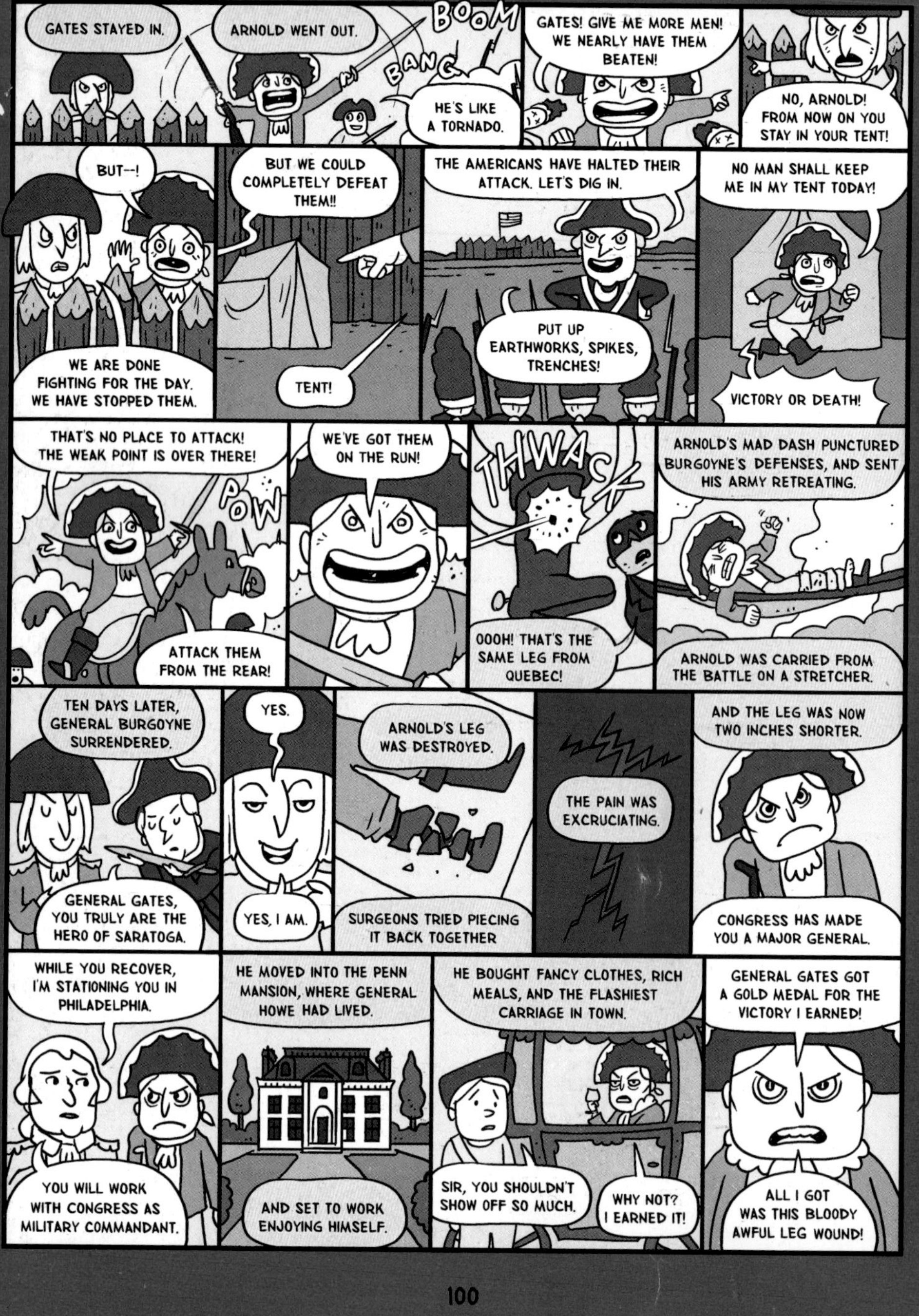
GATES STAYED IN.
ARNOLD WENT OUT.
BOOM
BANG
HE'S LIKE A TORNADO.
GATES! GIVE ME MORE MEN! WE NEARLY HAVE THEM BEATEN!
NO, ARNOLD! FROM NOW ON YOU STAY IN YOUR TENT!
BUT--!
WE ARE DONE FIGHTING FOR THE DAY. WE HAVE STOPPED THEM.
BUT WE COULD COMPLETELY DEFEAT THEM!!
TENT!
THE AMERICANS HAVE HALTED THEIR ATTACK. LET'S DIG IN.
PUT UP EARTHWORKS, SPIKES, TRENCHES!
NO MAN SHALL KEEP ME IN MY TENT TODAY!
VICTORY OR DEATH!
THAT'S NO PLACE TO ATTACK! THE WEAK POINT IS OVER THERE!
POW
ATTACK THEM FROM THE REAR!
WE'VE GOT THEM ON THE RUN!
THWACK
OOOH! THAT'S THE SAME LEG FROM QUEBEC!
ARNOLD'S MAD DASH PUNCTURED BURGOYNE'S DEFENSES, AND SENT HIS ARMY RETREATING.
ARNOLD WAS CARRIED FROM THE BATTLE ON A STRETCHER.
TEN DAYS LATER, GENERAL BURGOYNE SURRENDERED.
GENERAL GATES, YOU TRULY ARE THE HERO OF SARATOGA.
YES.
YES, I AM.
ARNOLD'S LEG WAS DESTROYED.
SURGEONS TRIED PIECING IT BACK TOGETHER
THE PAIN WAS EXCRUCIATING.
AND THE LEG WAS NOW TWO INCHES SHORTER.
CONGRESS HAS MADE YOU A MAJOR GENERAL.
WHILE YOU RECOVER, I'M STATIONING YOU IN PHILADELPHIA.
YOU WILL WORK WITH CONGRESS AS MILITARY COMMANDANT.
HE MOVED INTO THE PENN MANSION, WHERE GENERAL HOWE HAD LIVED.
AND SET TO WORK ENJOYING HIMSELF.
HE BOUGHT FANCY CLOTHES, RICH MEALS, AND THE FLASHIEST CARRIAGE IN TOWN.
SIR, YOU SHOULDN'T SHOW OFF SO MUCH.
WHY NOT? I EARNED IT!
GENERAL GATES GOT A GOLD MEDAL FOR THE VICTORY I EARNED!
ALL I GOT WAS THIS BLOODY AWFUL LEG WOUND!

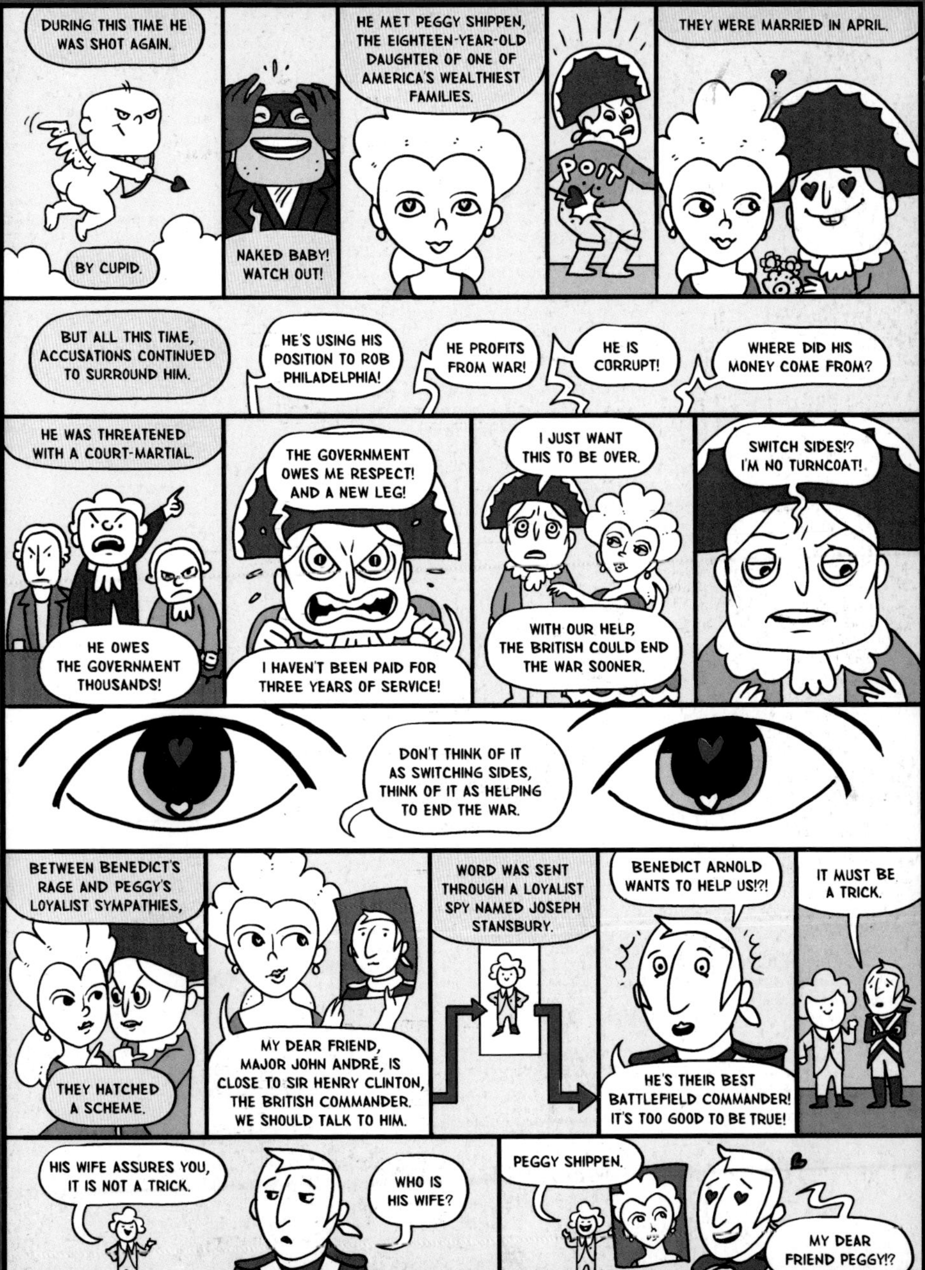
DURING THIS TIME HE WAS SHOT AGAIN.
BY CUPID.
NAKED BABY! WATCH OUT!
HE MET PEGGY SHIPPEN, THE EIGHTEEN-YEAR-OLD DAUGHTER OF ONE OF AMERICA'S WEALTHIEST FAMILIES.
POIT
THEY WERE MARRIED IN APRIL.
BUT ALL THIS TIME, ACCUSATIONS CONTINUED TO SURROUND HIM.
HE'S USING HIS POSITION TO ROB PHILADELPHIA!
HE PROFITS FROM WAR!
HE IS CORRUPT!
WHERE DID HIS MONEY COME FROM?
HE WAS THREATENED WITH A COURT-MARTIAL.
HE OWES THE GOVERNMENT THOUSANDS!
THE GOVERNMENT OWES ME RESPECT! AND A NEW LEG!
I HAVEN'T BEEN PAID FOR THREE YEARS OF SERVICE!
I JUST WANT THIS TO BE OVER.
WITH OUR HELP, THE BRITISH COULD END THE WAR SOONER.
SWITCH SIDES!? I'M NO TURNCOAT!
DON'T THINK OF IT AS SWITCHING SIDES, THINK OF IT AS HELPING TO END THE WAR.
BETWEEN BENEDICT'S RAGE AND PEGGY'S LOYALIST SYMPATHIES,
THEY HATCHED A SCHEME.
MY DEAR FRIEND, MAJOR JOHN ANDRÉ, IS CLOSE TO SIR HENRY CLINTON, THE BRITISH COMMANDER. WE SHOULD TALK TO HIM.
WORD WAS SENT THROUGH A LOYALIST SPY NAMED JOSEPH STANSBURY.
BENEDICT ARNOLD WANTS TO HELP US!?!
HE'S THEIR BEST BATTLEFIELD COMMANDER! IT'S TOO GOOD TO BE TRUE!
IT MUST BE A TRICK.
HIS WIFE ASSURES YOU, IT IS NOT A TRICK.
WHO IS HIS WIFE?
PEGGY SHIPPEN.
MY DEAR FRIEND PEGGY!?

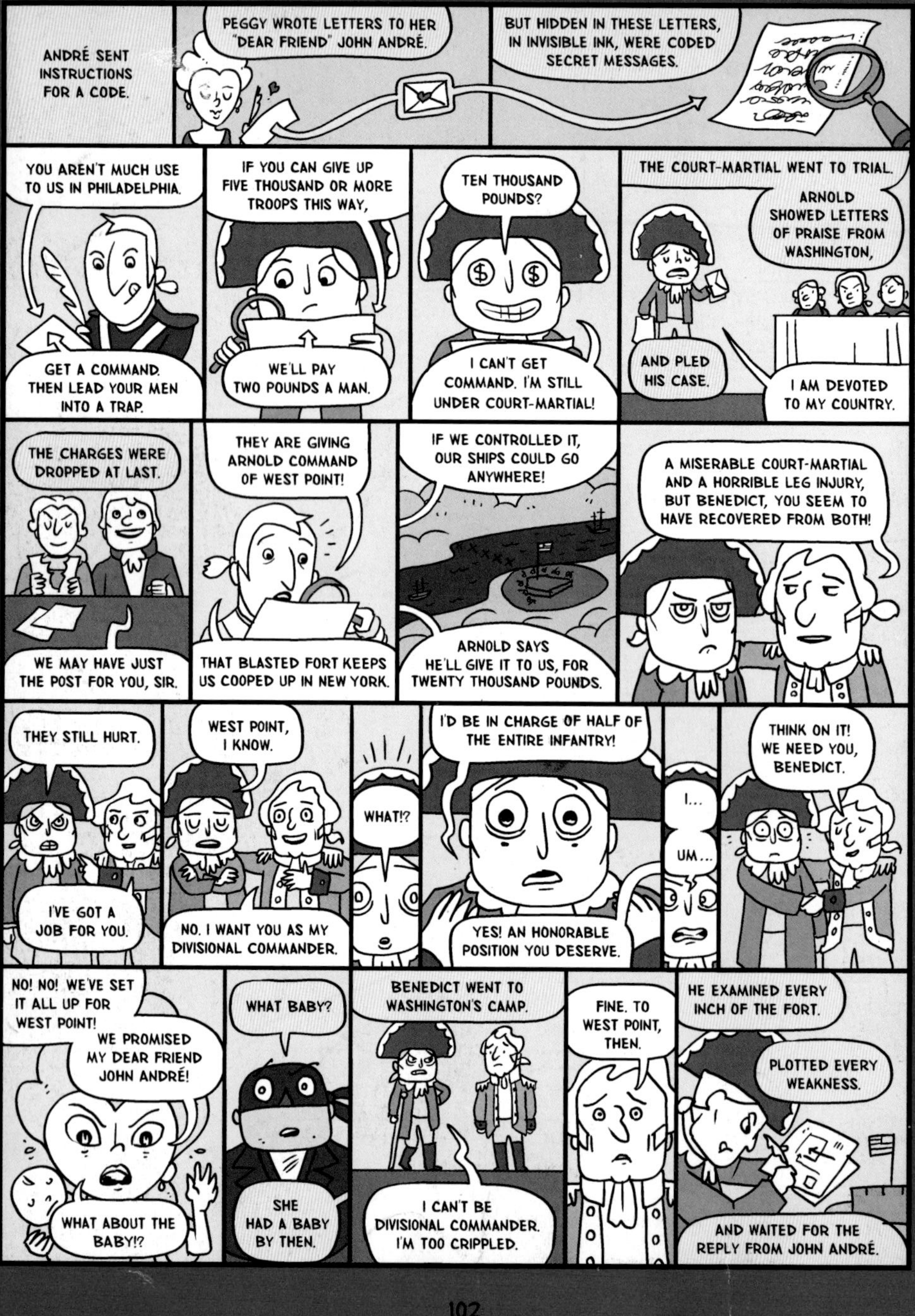
ANDRÉ SENT INSTRUCTIONS FOR A CODE.
PEGGY WROTE LETTERS TO HER "DEAR FRIEND" JOHN ANDRÉ.
BUT HIDDEN IN THESE LETTERS, IN INVISIBLE INK, WERE CODED SECRET MESSAGES.
YOU AREN'T MUCH USE TO US IN PHILADELPHIA.
GET A COMMAND. THEN LEAD YOUR MEN INTO A TRAP.
IF YOU CAN GIVE UP FIVE THOUSAND OR MORE TROOPS THIS WAY,
WE'LL PAY TWO POUNDS A MAN.
TEN THOUSAND POUNDS?
I CAN'T GET COMMAND. I'M STILL UNDER COURT-MARTIAL!
THE COURT-MARTIAL WENT TO TRIAL.
ARNOLD SHOWED LETTERS OF PRAISE FROM WASHINGTON,
AND PLED HIS CASE.
I AM DEVOTED TO MY COUNTRY.
THE CHARGES WERE DROPPED AT LAST.
WE MAY HAVE JUST THE POST FOR YOU, SIR.
THEY ARE GIVING ARNOLD COMMAND OF WEST POINT!
THAT BLASTED FORT KEEPS US COOPED UP IN NEW YORK.
IF WE CONTROLLED IT, OUR SHIPS COULD GO ANYWHERE!
ARNOLD SAYS HE'LL GIVE IT TO US, FOR TWENTY THOUSAND POUNDS.
A MISERABLE COURT-MARTIAL AND A HORRIBLE LEG INJURY, BUT BENEDICT, YOU SEEM TO HAVE RECOVERED FROM BOTH!
THEY STILL HURT.
I'VE GOT A JOB FOR YOU.
WEST POINT, I KNOW.
NO. I WANT YOU AS MY DIVISIONAL COMMANDER.
WHAT!?
I'D BE IN CHARGE OF HALF OF THE ENTIRE INFANTRY!
YES! AN HONORABLE POSITION YOU DESERVE.
I...
UM...
THINK ON IT! WE NEED YOU, BENEDICT.
NO! NO! WE'VE SET IT ALL UP FOR WEST POINT!
WE PROMISED MY DEAR FRIEND JOHN ANDRÉ!
WHAT ABOUT THE BABY!?
WHAT BABY?
SHE HAD A BABY BY THEN.
BENEDICT WENT TO WASHINGTON'S CAMP.
I CAN'T BE DIVISIONAL COMMANDER. I'M TOO CRIPPLED.
FINE. TO WEST POINT, THEN.
HE EXAMINED EVERY INCH OF THE FORT.
PLOTTED EVERY WEAKNESS.
AND WAITED FOR THE REPLY FROM JOHN ANDRÉ.

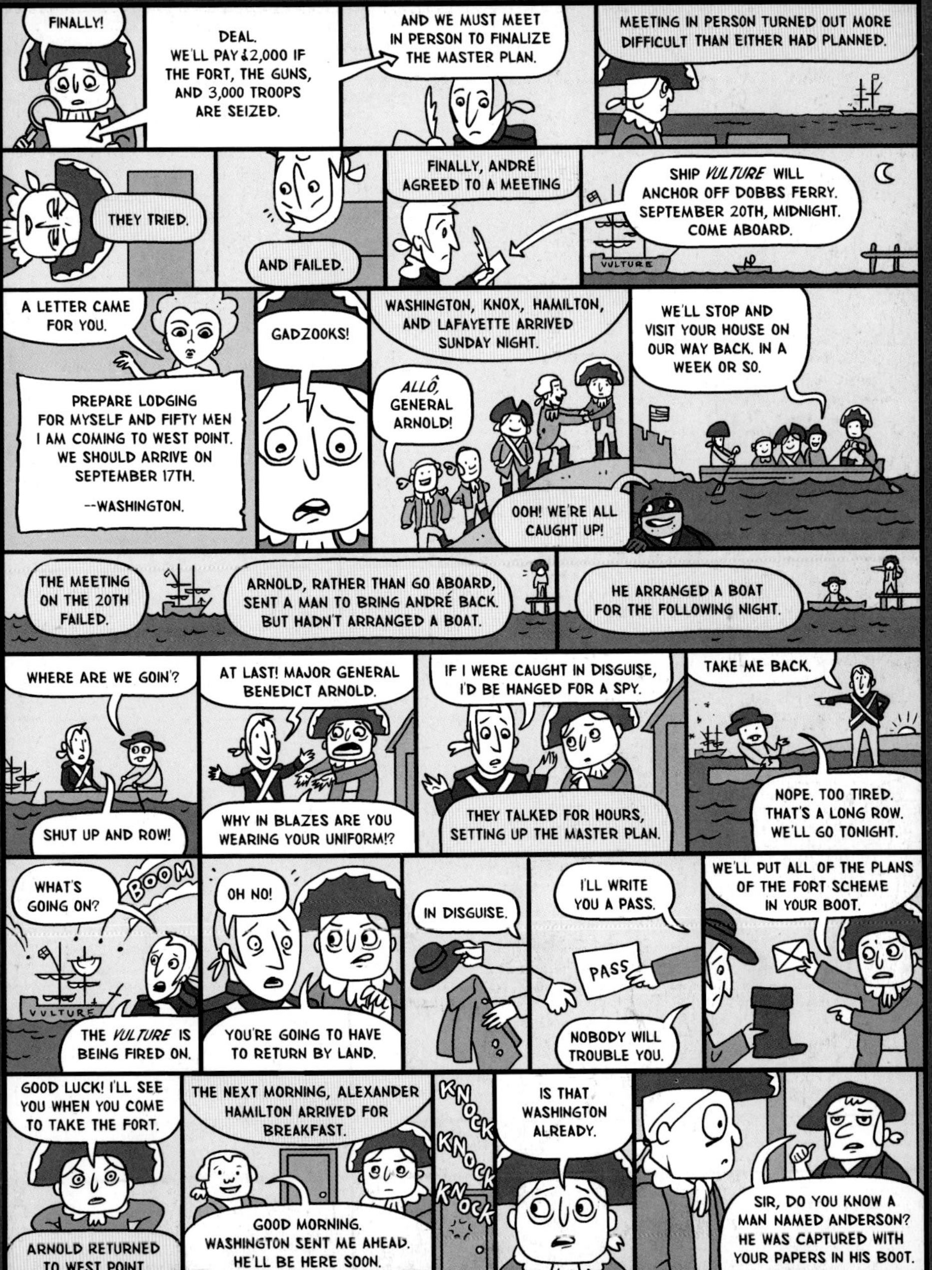
FINALLY!
DEAL. WE'LL PAY £2,000 IF THE FORT, THE GUNS, AND 3,000 TROOPS ARE SEIZED.
AND WE MUST MEET IN PERSON TO FINALIZE THE MASTER PLAN.
MEETING IN PERSON TURNED OUT MORE DIFFICULT THAN EITHER HAD PLANNED.
THEY TRIED.
AND FAILED.
FINALLY, ANDRÉ AGREED TO A MEETING
SHIP *VULTURE* WILL ANCHOR OFF DOBBS FERRY. SEPTEMBER 20TH, MIDNIGHT. COME ABOARD.
VULTURE
A LETTER CAME FOR YOU.
PREPARE LODGING FOR MYSELF AND FIFTY MEN I AM COMING TO WEST POINT. WE SHOULD ARRIVE ON SEPTEMBER 17TH.
--WASHINGTON.
GADZOOKS!
WASHINGTON, KNOX, HAMILTON, AND LAFAYETTE ARRIVED SUNDAY NIGHT.
ALLÔ, GENERAL ARNOLD!
OOH! WE'RE ALL CAUGHT UP!
WE'LL STOP AND VISIT YOUR HOUSE ON OUR WAY BACK. IN A WEEK OR SO.
THE MEETING ON THE 20TH FAILED.
ARNOLD, RATHER THAN GO ABOARD, SENT A MAN TO BRING ANDRÉ BACK. BUT HADN'T ARRANGED A BOAT.
HE ARRANGED A BOAT FOR THE FOLLOWING NIGHT.
WHERE ARE WE GOIN'?
SHUT UP AND ROW!
AT LAST! MAJOR GENERAL BENEDICT ARNOLD.
WHY IN BLAZES ARE YOU WEARING YOUR UNIFORM!?
IF I WERE CAUGHT IN DISGUISE, I'D BE HANGED FOR A SPY.
THEY TALKED FOR HOURS, SETTING UP THE MASTER PLAN.
TAKE ME BACK.
NOPE. TOO TIRED. THAT'S A LONG ROW. WE'LL GO TONIGHT.
WHAT'S GOING ON?
BOOM
VULTURE
THE *VULTURE* IS BEING FIRED ON.
OH NO!
YOU'RE GOING TO HAVE TO RETURN BY LAND.
IN DISGUISE.
I'LL WRITE YOU A PASS.
PASS
NOBODY WILL TROUBLE YOU.
WE'LL PUT ALL OF THE PLANS OF THE FORT SCHEME IN YOUR BOOT.
GOOD LUCK! I'LL SEE YOU WHEN YOU COME TO TAKE THE FORT.
ARNOLD RETURNED TO WEST POINT.
THE NEXT MORNING, ALEXANDER HAMILTON ARRIVED FOR BREAKFAST.
GOOD MORNING. WASHINGTON SENT ME AHEAD. HE'LL BE HERE SOON.
KNOCK KNOCK KNOCK
IS THAT WASHINGTON ALREADY.
SIR, DO YOU KNOW A MAN NAMED ANDERSON? HE WAS CAPTURED WITH YOUR PAPERS IN HIS BOOT.

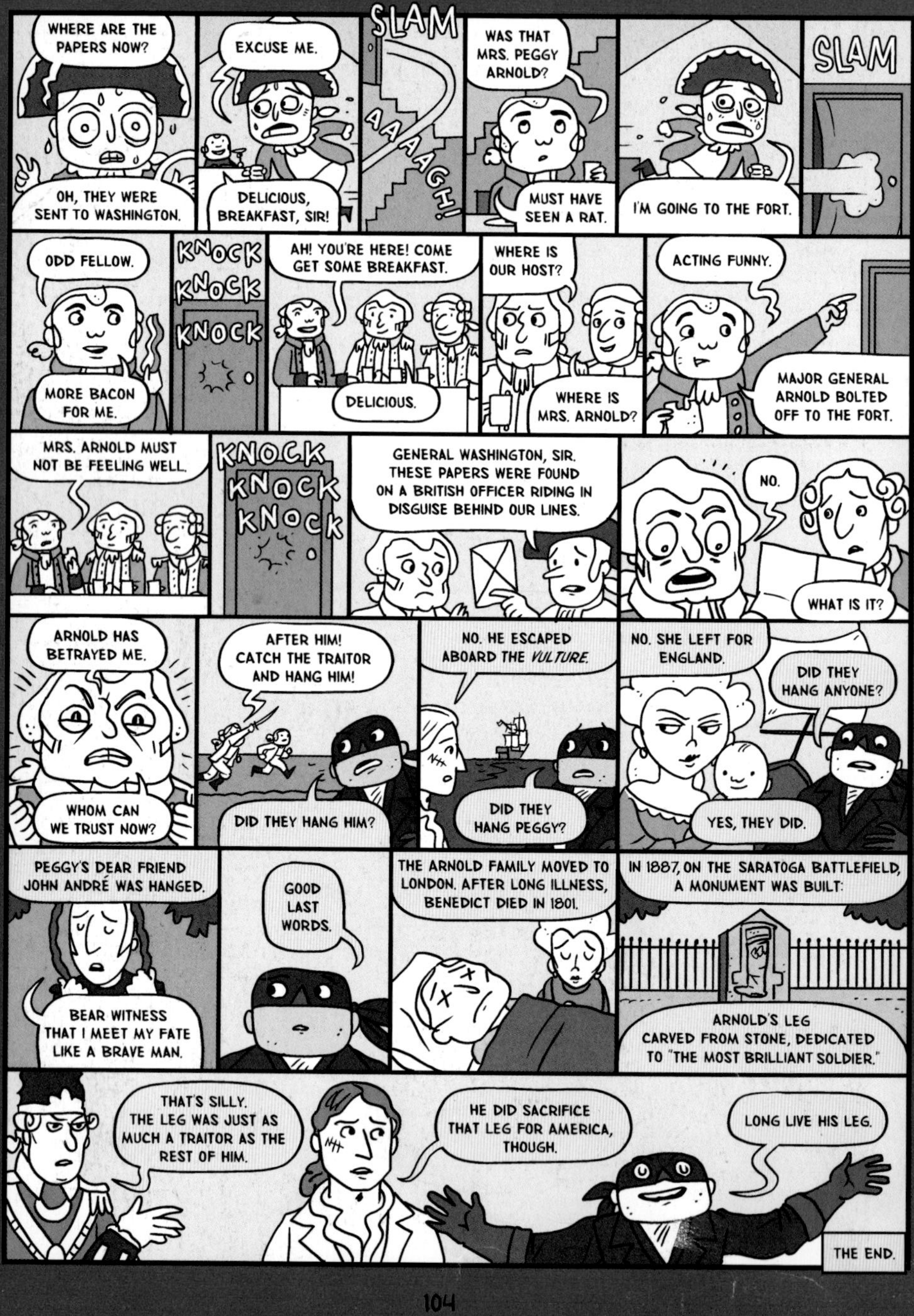
WHERE ARE THE PAPERS NOW?
OH, THEY WERE SENT TO WASHINGTON.
EXCUSE ME.
DELICIOUS, BREAKFAST, SIR!
SLAM
AAAAGH!
WAS THAT MRS. PEGGY ARNOLD?
MUST HAVE SEEN A RAT.
I'M GOING TO THE FORT.
SLAM
ODD FELLOW.
MORE BACON FOR ME.
KNOCK KNOCK KNOCK
AH! YOU'RE HERE! COME GET SOME BREAKFAST.
DELICIOUS.
WHERE IS OUR HOST?
WHERE IS MRS. ARNOLD?
ACTING FUNNY.
MAJOR GENERAL ARNOLD BOLTED OFF TO THE FORT.
MRS. ARNOLD MUST NOT BE FEELING WELL.
KNOCK KNOCK KNOCK
GENERAL WASHINGTON, SIR. THESE PAPERS WERE FOUND ON A BRITISH OFFICER RIDING IN DISGUISE BEHIND OUR LINES.
NO.
WHAT IS IT?
ARNOLD HAS BETRAYED ME.
WHOM CAN WE TRUST NOW?
AFTER HIM! CATCH THE TRAITOR AND HANG HIM!
DID THEY HANG HIM?
NO. HE ESCAPED ABOARD THE *VULTURE*.
DID THEY HANG PEGGY?
NO. SHE LEFT FOR ENGLAND.
DID THEY HANG ANYONE?
YES, THEY DID.
PEGGY'S DEAR FRIEND JOHN ANDRÉ WAS HANGED.
BEAR WITNESS THAT I MEET MY FATE LIKE A BRAVE MAN.
GOOD LAST WORDS.
THE ARNOLD FAMILY MOVED TO LONDON. AFTER LONG ILLNESS, BENEDICT DIED IN 1801.
IN 1887, ON THE SARATOGA BATTLEFIELD, A MONUMENT WAS BUILT:
ARNOLD'S LEG CARVED FROM STONE, DEDICATED TO "THE MOST BRILLIANT SOLDIER."
THAT'S SILLY. THE LEG WAS JUST AS MUCH A TRAITOR AS THE REST OF HIM.
HE DID SACRIFICE THAT LEG FOR AMERICA, THOUGH.
LONG LIVE HIS LEG.
THE END.

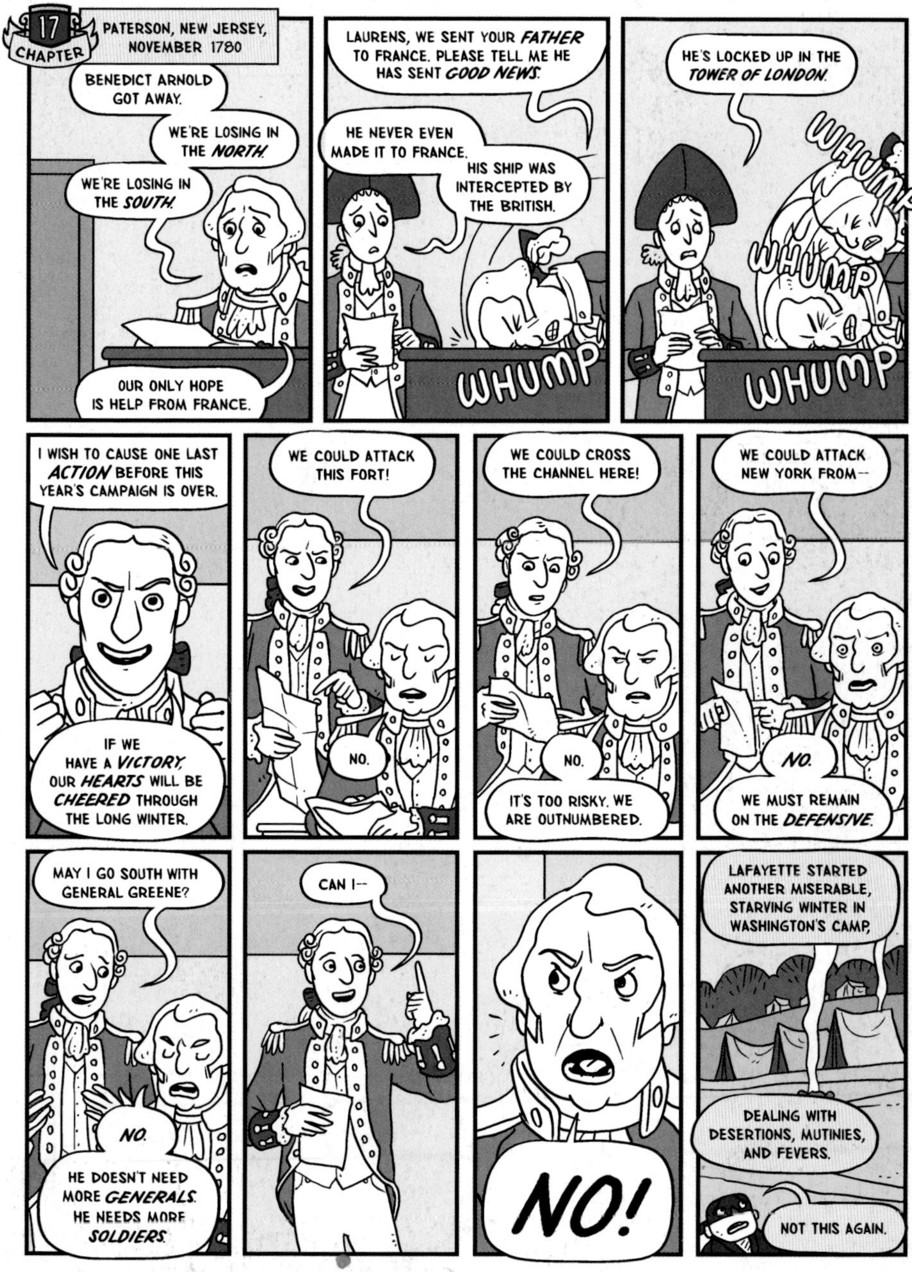
17 CHAPTER
PATERSON, NEW JERSEY, NOVEMBER 1780
BENEDICT ARNOLD GOT AWAY.
WE'RE LOSING IN THE NORTH.
WE'RE LOSING IN THE SOUTH.
OUR ONLY HOPE IS HELP FROM FRANCE.
LAURENS, WE SENT YOUR FATHER TO FRANCE. PLEASE TELL ME HE HAS SENT GOOD NEWS.
HE NEVER EVEN MADE IT TO FRANCE.
HIS SHIP WAS INTERCEPTED BY THE BRITISH.
WHUMP
HE'S LOCKED UP IN THE TOWER OF LONDON.
WHUMP
WHUMP
WHUMP
I WISH TO CAUSE ONE LAST ACTION BEFORE THIS YEAR'S CAMPAIGN IS OVER.
IF WE HAVE A VICTORY, OUR HEARTS WILL BE CHEERED THROUGH THE LONG WINTER.
WE COULD ATTACK THIS FORT!
NO.
WE COULD CROSS THE CHANNEL HERE!
NO.
IT'S TOO RISKY. WE ARE OUTNUMBERED.
WE COULD ATTACK NEW YORK FROM--
NO.
WE MUST REMAIN ON THE DEFENSIVE.
MAY I GO SOUTH WITH GENERAL GREENE?
NO.
HE DOESN'T NEED MORE GENERALS. HE NEEDS MORE SOLDIERS.
CAN I--
NO!
LAFAYETTE STARTED ANOTHER MISERABLE, STARVING WINTER IN WASHINGTON'S CAMP,
DEALING WITH DESERTIONS, MUTINIES, AND FEVERS.
NOT THIS AGAIN.

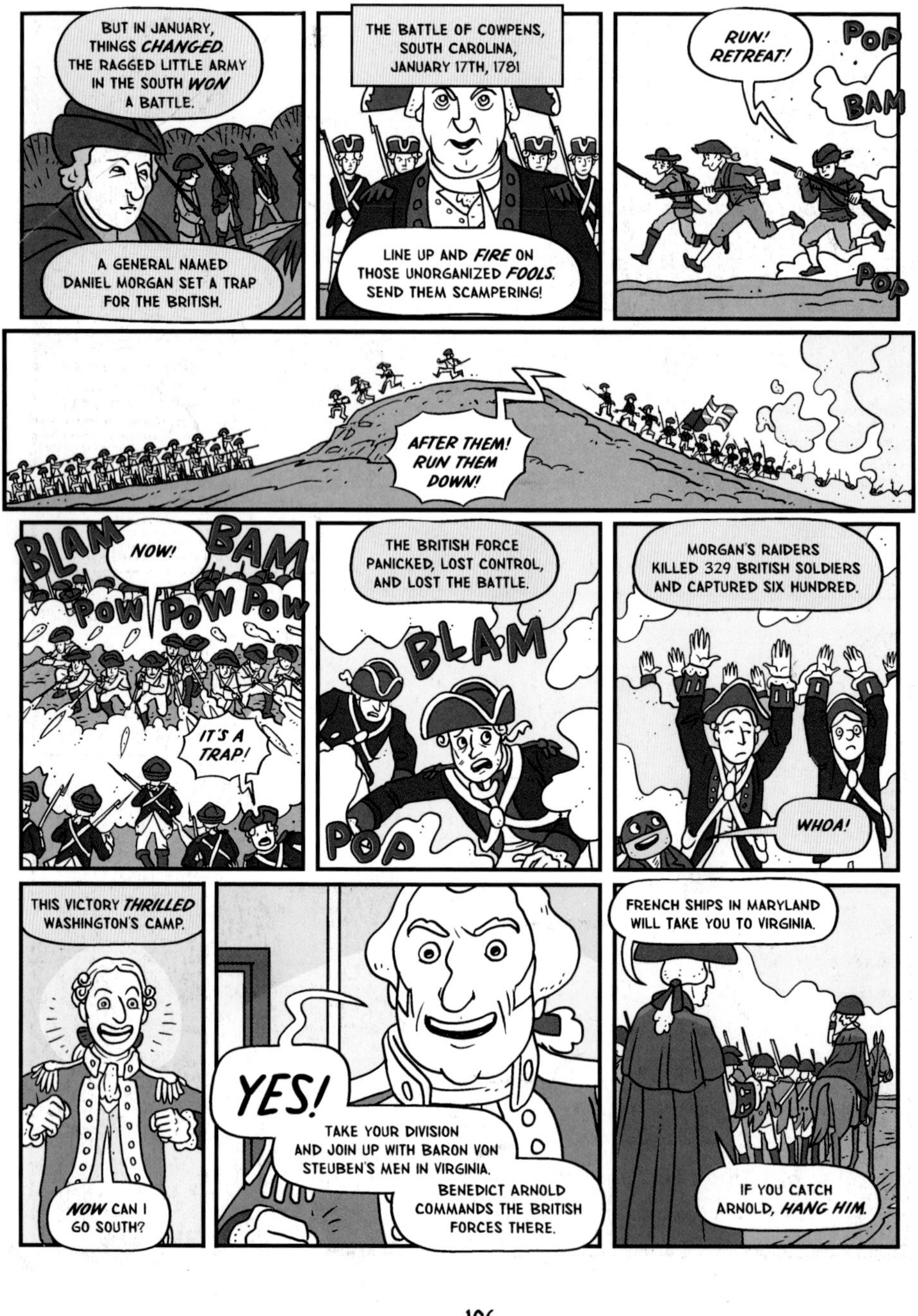

BUT IN JANUARY, THINGS CHANGED. THE RAGGED LITTLE ARMY IN THE SOUTH WON A BATTLE.
A GENERAL NAMED DANIEL MORGAN SET A TRAP FOR THE BRITISH.
THE BATTLE OF COWPENS, SOUTH CAROLINA, JANUARY 17TH, 1781
LINE UP AND FIRE ON THOSE UNORGANIZED FOOLS. SEND THEM SCAMPERING!
RUN! RETREAT!
POP
BAM
POP
AFTER THEM! RUN THEM DOWN!
BLAM
NOW!
BAM
POW POW POW
IT'S A TRAP!
THE BRITISH FORCE PANICKED, LOST CONTROL, AND LOST THE BATTLE.
BLAM
POP
MORGAN'S RAIDERS KILLED 329 BRITISH SOLDIERS AND CAPTURED SIX HUNDRED.
WHOA!
THIS VICTORY THRILLED WASHINGTON'S CAMP.
NOW CAN I GO SOUTH?
YES!
TAKE YOUR DIVISION AND JOIN UP WITH BARON VON STEUBEN'S MEN IN VIRGINIA.
BENEDICT ARNOLD COMMANDS THE BRITISH FORCES THERE.
FRENCH SHIPS IN MARYLAND WILL TAKE YOU TO VIRGINIA.
IF YOU CATCH ARNOLD, HANG HIM.

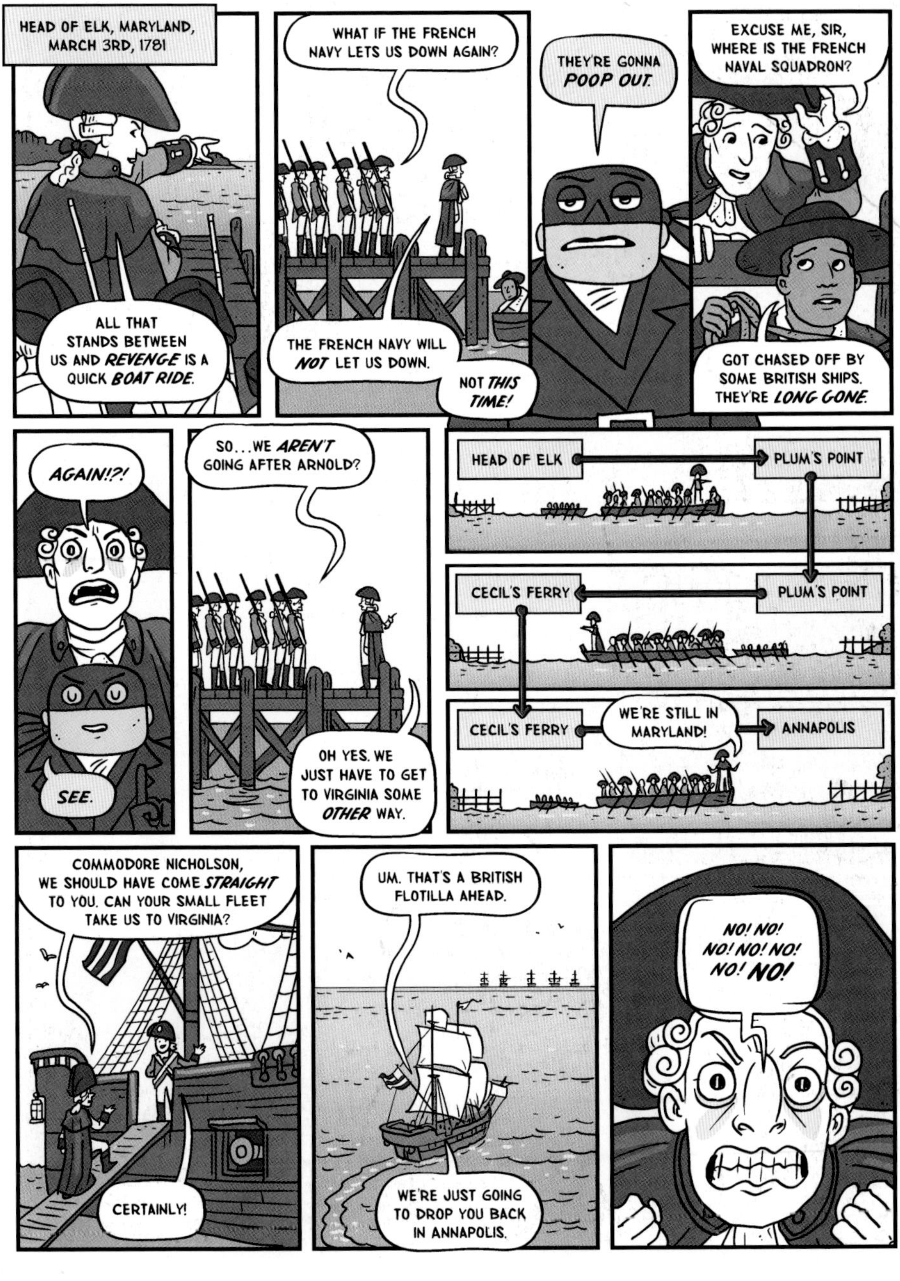
HEAD OF ELK, MARYLAND, MARCH 3RD, 1781
ALL THAT STANDS BETWEEN US AND REVENGE IS A QUICK BOAT RIDE.
WHAT IF THE FRENCH NAVY LETS US DOWN AGAIN?
THE FRENCH NAVY WILL NOT LET US DOWN.
NOT THIS TIME!
THEY'RE GONNA POOP OUT.
EXCUSE ME, SIR, WHERE IS THE FRENCH NAVAL SQUADRON?
GOT CHASED OFF BY SOME BRITISH SHIPS. THEY'RE LONG GONE.
AGAIN!?!
SEE.
SO...WE AREN'T GOING AFTER ARNOLD?
OH YES. WE JUST HAVE TO GET TO VIRGINIA SOME OTHER WAY.
HEAD OF ELK
PLUM'S POINT
CECIL'S FERRY
PLUM'S POINT
CECIL'S FERRY
WE'RE STILL IN MARYLAND!
ANNAPOLIS
COMMODORE NICHOLSON, WE SHOULD HAVE COME STRAIGHT TO YOU. CAN YOUR SMALL FLEET TAKE US TO VIRGINIA?
CERTAINLY!
UM. THAT'S A BRITISH FLOTILLA AHEAD.
WE'RE JUST GOING TO DROP YOU BACK IN ANNAPOLIS.
NO! NO! NO! NO! NO! NO! NO!

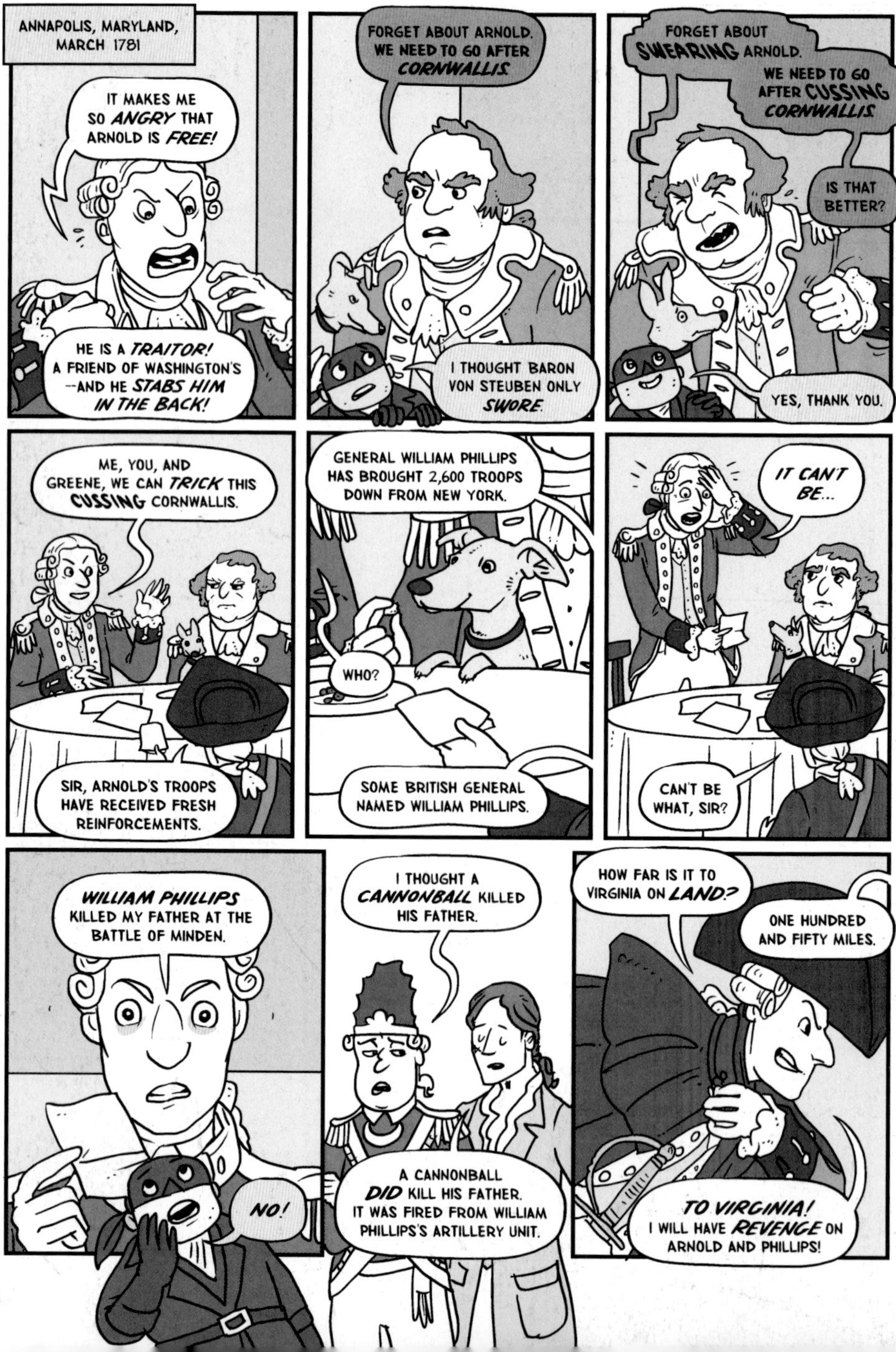
ANNAPOLIS, MARYLAND, MARCH 1781
IT MAKES ME SO ANGRY THAT ARNOLD IS FREE!
HE IS A TRAITOR! A FRIEND OF WASHINGTON'S --AND HE STABS HIM IN THE BACK!
FORGET ABOUT ARNOLD. WE NEED TO GO AFTER CORNWALLIS.
I THOUGHT BARON VON STEUBEN ONLY SWORE.
FORGET ABOUT SWEARING ARNOLD.
WE NEED TO GO AFTER CUSSING CORNWALLIS.
IS THAT BETTER?
YES, THANK YOU.
ME, YOU, AND GREENE, WE CAN TRICK THIS CUSSING CORNWALLIS.
SIR, ARNOLD'S TROOPS HAVE RECEIVED FRESH REINFORCEMENTS.
GENERAL WILLIAM PHILLIPS HAS BROUGHT 2,600 TROOPS DOWN FROM NEW YORK.
WHO?
SOME BRITISH GENERAL NAMED WILLIAM PHILLIPS.
IT CAN'T BE...
CAN'T BE WHAT, SIR?
WILLIAM PHILLIPS KILLED MY FATHER AT THE BATTLE OF MINDEN.
NO!
I THOUGHT A CANNONBALL KILLED HIS FATHER.
A CANNONBALL DID KILL HIS FATHER. IT WAS FIRED FROM WILLIAM PHILLIPS'S ARTILLERY UNIT.
HOW FAR IS IT TO VIRGINIA ON LAND?
ONE HUNDRED AND FIFTY MILES.
TO VIRGINIA! I WILL HAVE REVENGE ON ARNOLD AND PHILLIPS!

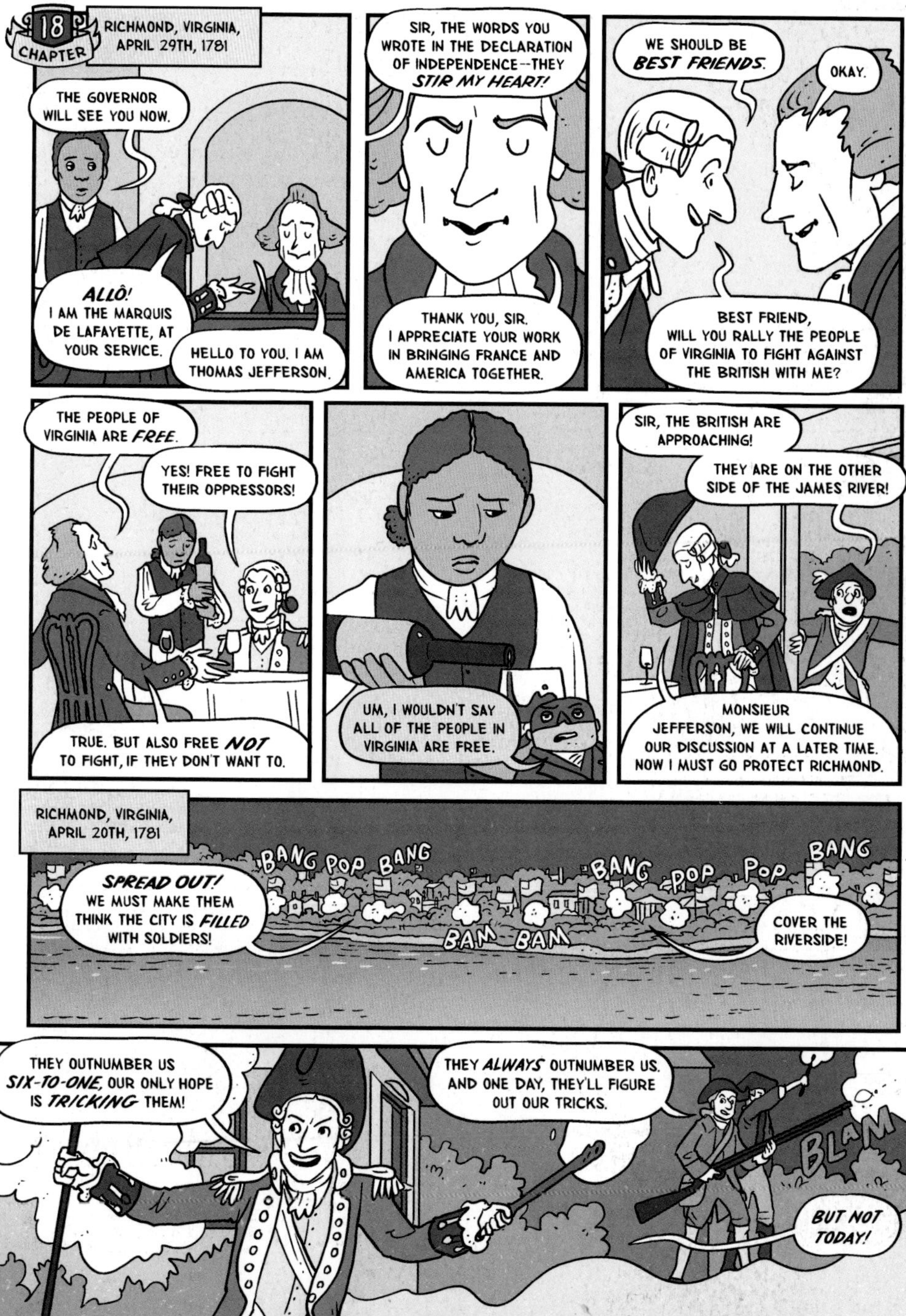
18
CHAPTER
RICHMOND, VIRGINIA, APRIL 29TH, 1781
THE GOVERNOR WILL SEE YOU NOW.
ALLÔ! I AM THE MARQUIS DE LAFAYETTE, AT YOUR SERVICE.
HELLO TO YOU. I AM THOMAS JEFFERSON.
SIR, THE WORDS YOU WROTE IN THE DECLARATION OF INDEPENDENCE--THEY STIR MY HEART!
THANK YOU, SIR. I APPRECIATE YOUR WORK IN BRINGING FRANCE AND AMERICA TOGETHER.
WE SHOULD BE BEST FRIENDS.
OKAY.
BEST FRIEND, WILL YOU RALLY THE PEOPLE OF VIRGINIA TO FIGHT AGAINST THE BRITISH WITH ME?
THE PEOPLE OF VIRGINIA ARE FREE.
YES! FREE TO FIGHT THEIR OPPRESSORS!
TRUE. BUT ALSO FREE NOT TO FIGHT, IF THEY DON'T WANT TO.
UM, I WOULDN'T SAY ALL OF THE PEOPLE IN VIRGINIA ARE FREE.
SIR, THE BRITISH ARE APPROACHING!
THEY ARE ON THE OTHER SIDE OF THE JAMES RIVER!
MONSIEUR JEFFERSON, WE WILL CONTINUE OUR DISCUSSION AT A LATER TIME. NOW I MUST GO PROTECT RICHMOND.
RICHMOND, VIRGINIA, APRIL 20TH, 1781
BANG POP BANG
BANG POP POP
BANG
SPREAD OUT! WE MUST MAKE THEM THINK THE CITY IS FILLED WITH SOLDIERS!
BAM BAM
COVER THE RIVERSIDE!
THEY OUTNUMBER US SIX-TO-ONE, OUR ONLY HOPE IS TRICKING THEM!
THEY ALWAYS OUTNUMBER US. AND ONE DAY, THEY'LL FIGURE OUT OUR TRICKS.
BLAM
BUT NOT TODAY!

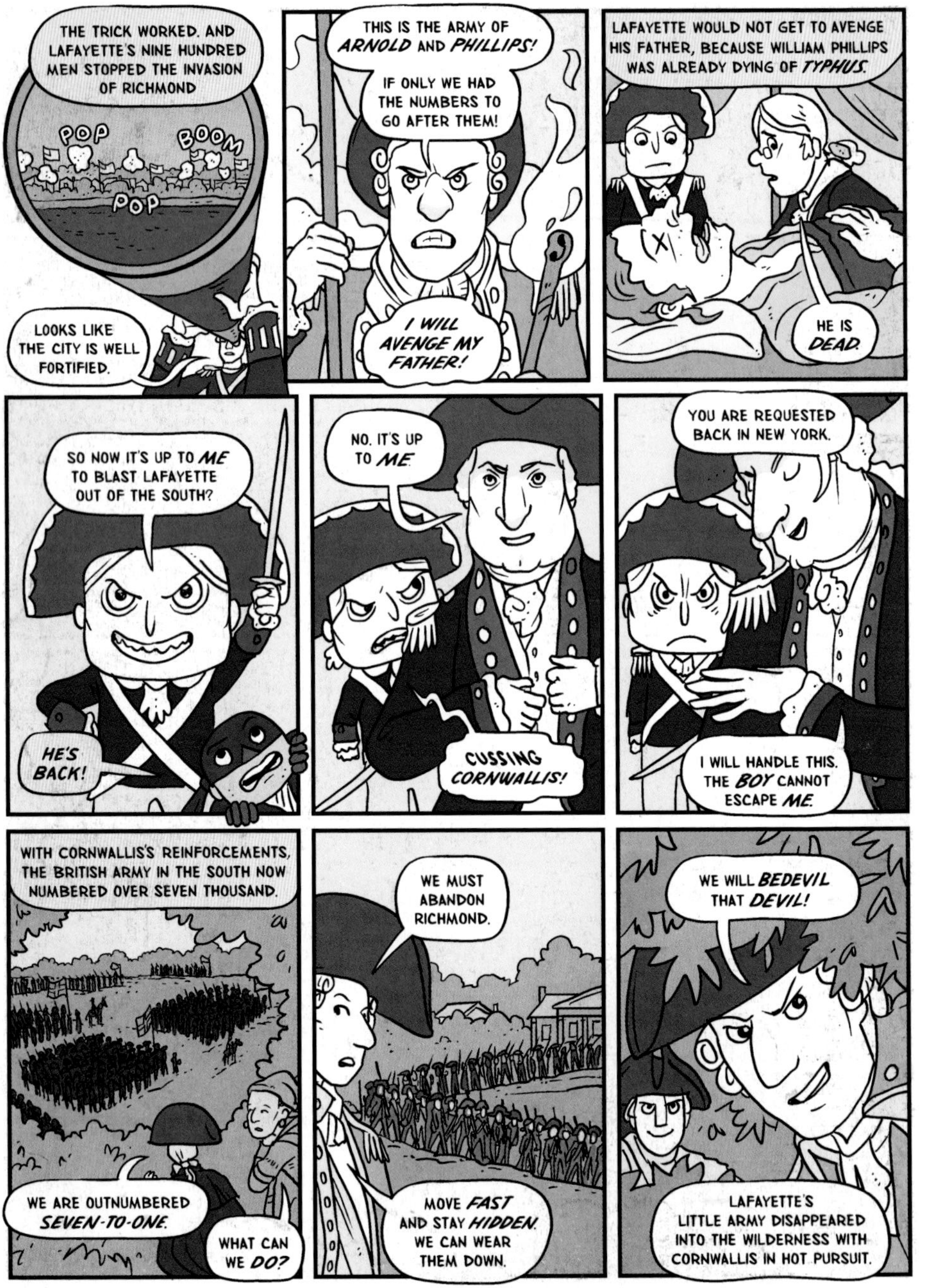
THE TRICK WORKED. AND LAFAYETTE'S NINE HUNDRED MEN STOPPED THE INVASION OF RICHMOND
POP
BOOM
POP
LOOKS LIKE THE CITY IS WELL FORTIFIED.
THIS IS THE ARMY OF ARNOLD AND PHILLIPS!
IF ONLY WE HAD THE NUMBERS TO GO AFTER THEM!
I WILL AVENGE MY FATHER!
LAFAYETTE WOULD NOT GET TO AVENGE HIS FATHER, BECAUSE WILLIAM PHILLIPS WAS ALREADY DYING OF TYPHUS.
HE IS DEAD.
SO NOW IT'S UP TO ME TO BLAST LAFAYETTE OUT OF THE SOUTH?
HE'S BACK!
NO. IT'S UP TO ME.
CUSSING CORNWALLIS!
YOU ARE REQUESTED BACK IN NEW YORK.
I WILL HANDLE THIS. THE BOY CANNOT ESCAPE ME.
WITH CORNWALLIS'S REINFORCEMENTS, THE BRITISH ARMY IN THE SOUTH NOW NUMBERED OVER SEVEN THOUSAND.
WE ARE OUTNUMBERED SEVEN-TO-ONE.
WHAT CAN WE DO?
WE MUST ABANDON RICHMOND.
MOVE FAST AND STAY HIDDEN. WE CAN WEAR THEM DOWN.
WE WILL BEDEVIL THAT DEVIL!
LAFAYETTE'S LITTLE ARMY DISAPPEARED INTO THE WILDERNESS WITH CORNWALLIS IN HOT PURSUIT.

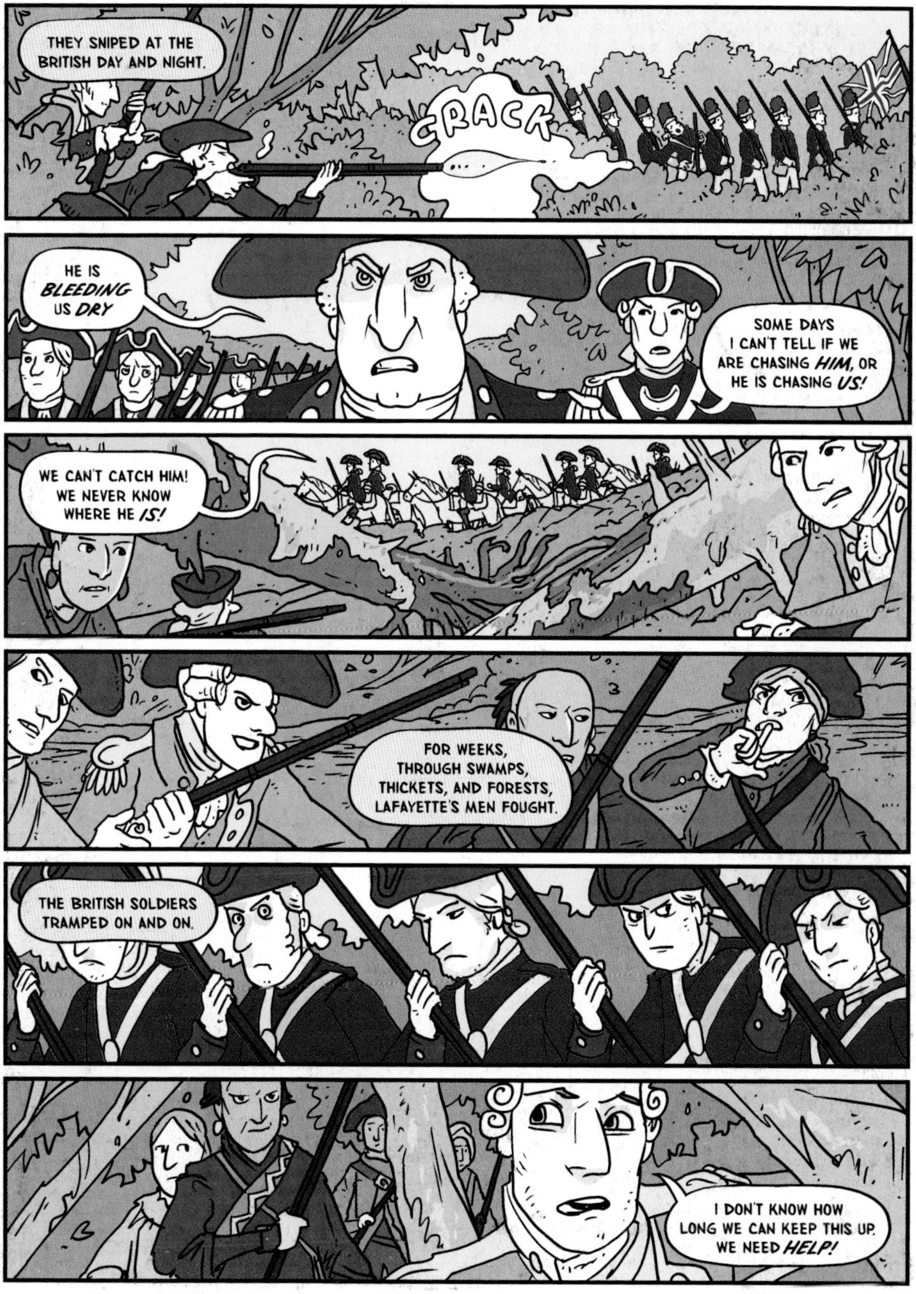

THEY SNIPED AT THE BRITISH DAY AND NIGHT.
CRACK
HE IS *BLEEDING* US *DRY*
SOME DAYS I CAN'T TELL IF WE ARE CHASING *HIM*, OR HE IS CHASING *US!*
WE CAN'T CATCH HIM! WE NEVER KNOW WHERE HE *IS!*
FOR WEEKS, THROUGH SWAMPS, THICKETS, AND FORESTS, LAFAYETTE'S MEN FOUGHT.
THE BRITISH SOLDIERS TRAMPED ON AND ON.
I DON'T KNOW HOW LONG WE CAN KEEP THIS UP. WE NEED *HELP!*

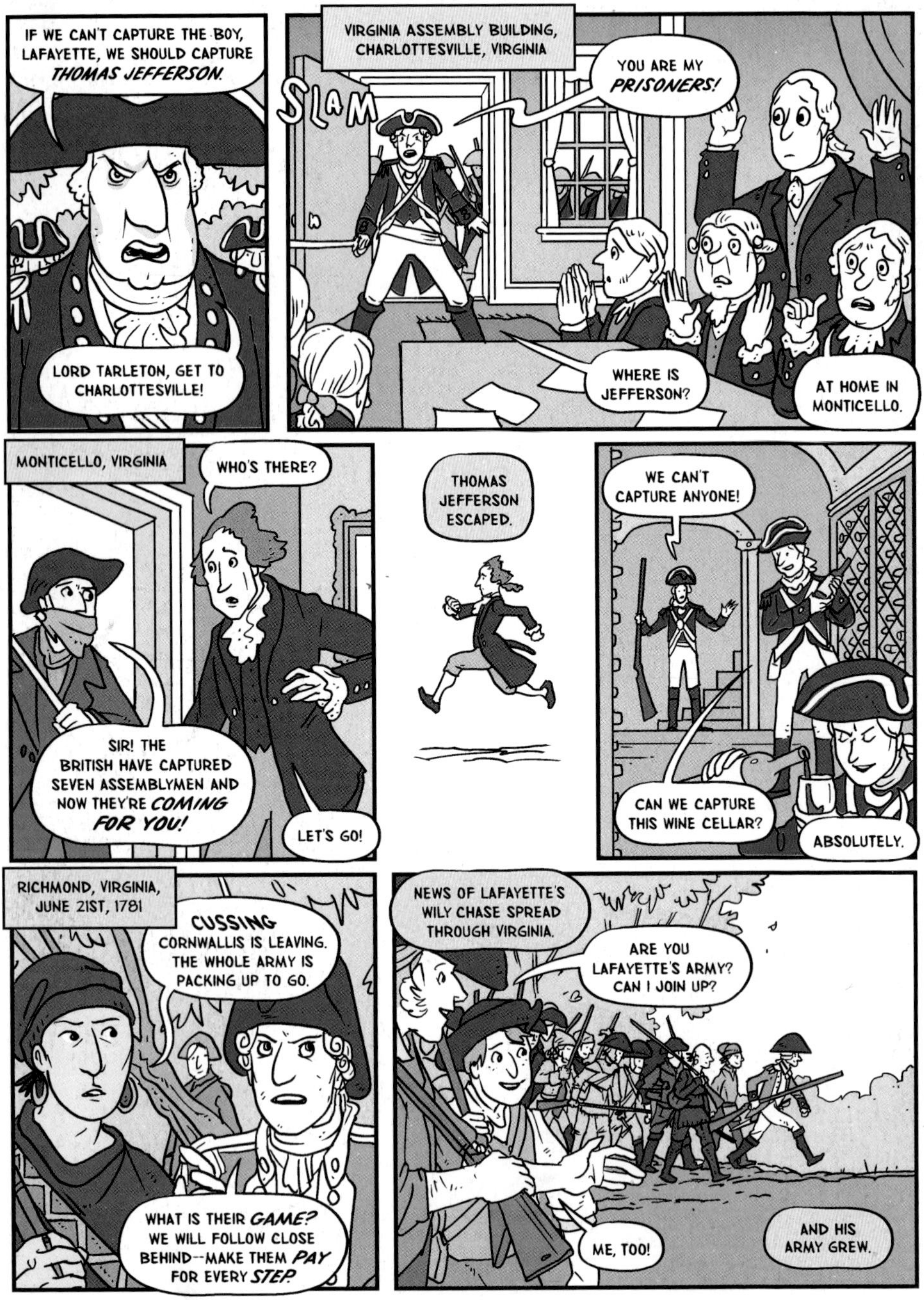

IF WE CAN'T CAPTURE THE BOY, LAFAYETTE, WE SHOULD CAPTURE *THOMAS JEFFERSON.*
LORD TARLETON, GET TO CHARLOTTESVILLE!
VIRGINIA ASSEMBLY BUILDING, CHARLOTTESVILLE, VIRGINIA
SLAM
YOU ARE MY *PRISONERS!*
WHERE IS JEFFERSON?
AT HOME IN MONTICELLO.
MONTICELLO, VIRGINIA
WHO'S THERE?
SIR! THE BRITISH HAVE CAPTURED SEVEN ASSEMBLYMEN AND NOW THEY'RE *COMING FOR YOU!*
LET'S GO!
THOMAS JEFFERSON ESCAPED.
WE CAN'T CAPTURE ANYONE!
CAN WE CAPTURE THIS WINE CELLAR?
ABSOLUTELY.
RICHMOND, VIRGINIA, JUNE 21ST, 1781
CUSSING
CORNWALLIS IS LEAVING. THE WHOLE ARMY IS PACKING UP TO GO.
WHAT IS THEIR *GAME?* WE WILL FOLLOW CLOSE BEHIND--MAKE THEM *PAY* FOR EVERY *STEP.*
NEWS OF LAFAYETTE'S WILY CHASE SPREAD THROUGH VIRGINIA.
ARE YOU LAFAYETTE'S ARMY? CAN I JOIN UP?
ME, TOO!
AND HIS ARMY GREW.

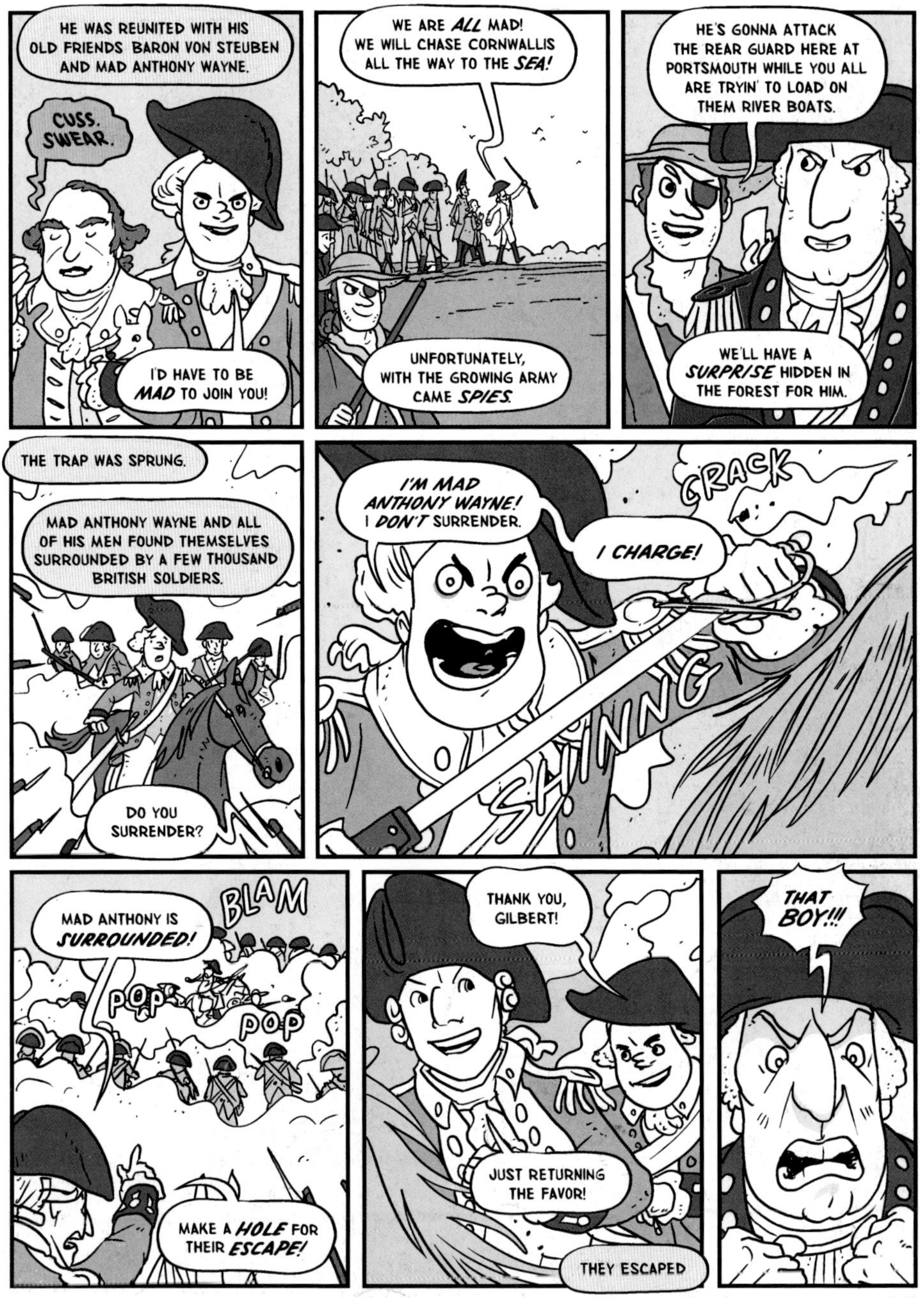
HE WAS REUNITED WITH HIS OLD FRIENDS BARON VON STEUBEN AND MAD ANTHONY WAYNE.
CUSS. SWEAR.
I'D HAVE TO BE MAD TO JOIN YOU!
WE ARE ALL MAD! WE WILL CHASE CORNWALLIS ALL THE WAY TO THE SEA!
UNFORTUNATELY, WITH THE GROWING ARMY CAME SPIES.
HE'S GONNA ATTACK THE REAR GUARD HERE AT PORTSMOUTH WHILE YOU ALL ARE TRYIN' TO LOAD ON THEM RIVER BOATS.
WE'LL HAVE A SURPRISE HIDDEN IN THE FOREST FOR HIM.
THE TRAP WAS SPRUNG.
MAD ANTHONY WAYNE AND ALL OF HIS MEN FOUND THEMSELVES SURROUNDED BY A FEW THOUSAND BRITISH SOLDIERS.
DO YOU SURRENDER?
I'M MAD ANTHONY WAYNE! I DON'T SURRENDER.
I CHARGE!
CRACK
SHIINNG
BLAM
MAD ANTHONY IS SURROUNDED!
POP
POP
MAKE A HOLE FOR THEIR ESCAPE!
THANK YOU, GILBERT!
JUST RETURNING THE FAVOR!
THEY ESCAPED
THAT BOY!!!

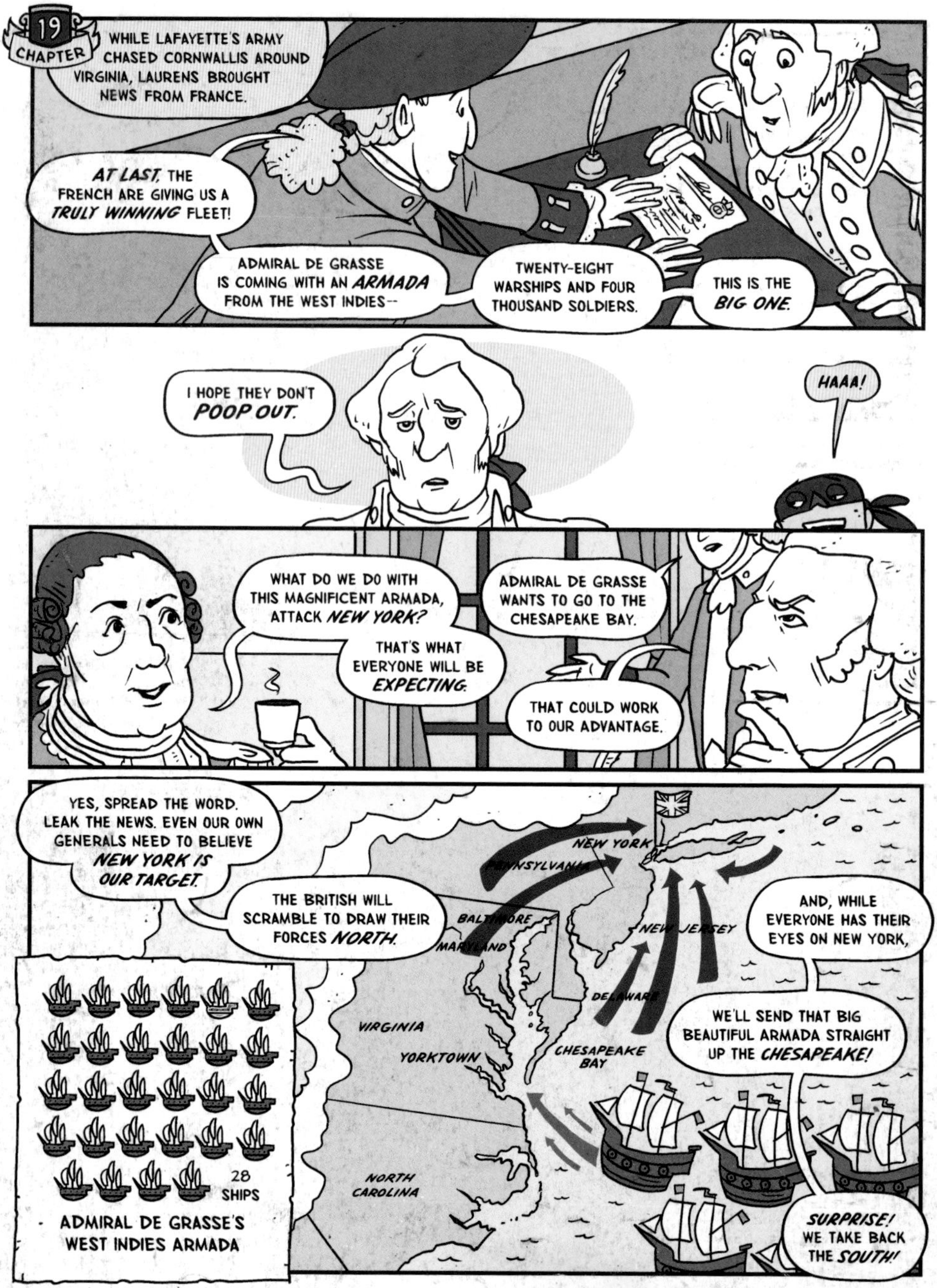
19
CHAPTER
WHILE LAFAYETTE'S ARMY CHASED CORNWALLIS AROUND VIRGINIA, LAURENS BROUGHT NEWS FROM FRANCE.
AT LAST, THE FRENCH ARE GIVING US A TRULY WINNING FLEET!
ADMIRAL DE GRASSE IS COMING WITH AN ARMADA FROM THE WEST INDIES--
TWENTY-EIGHT WARSHIPS AND FOUR THOUSAND SOLDIERS.
THIS IS THE BIG ONE.
I HOPE THEY DON'T POOP OUT.
HAAA!
WHAT DO WE DO WITH THIS MAGNIFICENT ARMADA, ATTACK NEW YORK?
THAT'S WHAT EVERYONE WILL BE EXPECTING.
ADMIRAL DE GRASSE WANTS TO GO TO THE CHESAPEAKE BAY.
THAT COULD WORK TO OUR ADVANTAGE.
YES, SPREAD THE WORD. LEAK THE NEWS. EVEN OUR OWN GENERALS NEED TO BELIEVE NEW YORK IS OUR TARGET.
THE BRITISH WILL SCRAMBLE TO DRAW THEIR FORCES NORTH.
NEW YORK
PENNSYLVANIA
BALTIMORE
MARYLAND
NEW JERSEY
DELAWARE
VIRGINIA
YORKTOWN
CHESAPEAKE BAY
NORTH CAROLINA
28 SHIPS
ADMIRAL DE GRASSE'S WEST INDIES ARMADA
AND, WHILE EVERYONE HAS THEIR EYES ON NEW YORK,
WE'LL SEND THAT BIG BEAUTIFUL ARMADA STRAIGHT UP THE CHESAPEAKE!
SURPRISE! WE TAKE BACK THE SOUTH!

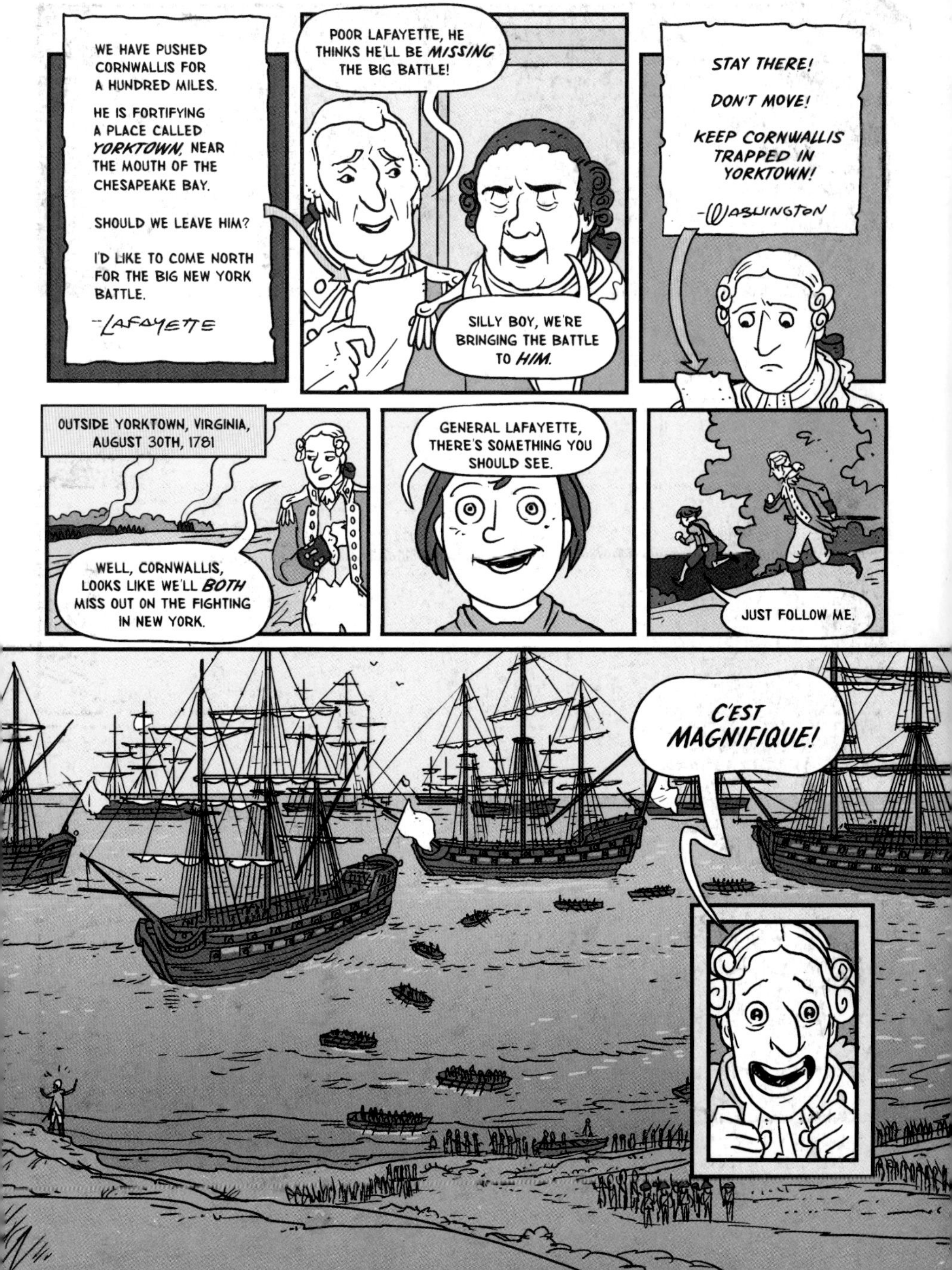
WE HAVE PUSHED CORNWALLIS FOR A HUNDRED MILES.
HE IS FORTIFYING A PLACE CALLED YORKTOWN, NEAR THE MOUTH OF THE CHESAPEAKE BAY.
SHOULD WE LEAVE HIM?
I'D LIKE TO COME NORTH FOR THE BIG NEW YORK BATTLE.
–LAFAYETTE
POOR LAFAYETTE, HE THINKS HE'LL BE MISSING THE BIG BATTLE!
SILLY BOY, WE'RE BRINGING THE BATTLE TO HIM.
STAY THERE!
DON'T MOVE!
KEEP CORNWALLIS TRAPPED IN YORKTOWN!
–WASHINGTON
OUTSIDE YORKTOWN, VIRGINIA, AUGUST 30TH, 1781
WELL, CORNWALLIS, LOOKS LIKE WE'LL BOTH MISS OUT ON THE FIGHTING IN NEW YORK.
GENERAL LAFAYETTE, THERE'S SOMETHING YOU SHOULD SEE.
JUST FOLLOW ME.
C'EST MAGNIFIQUE!

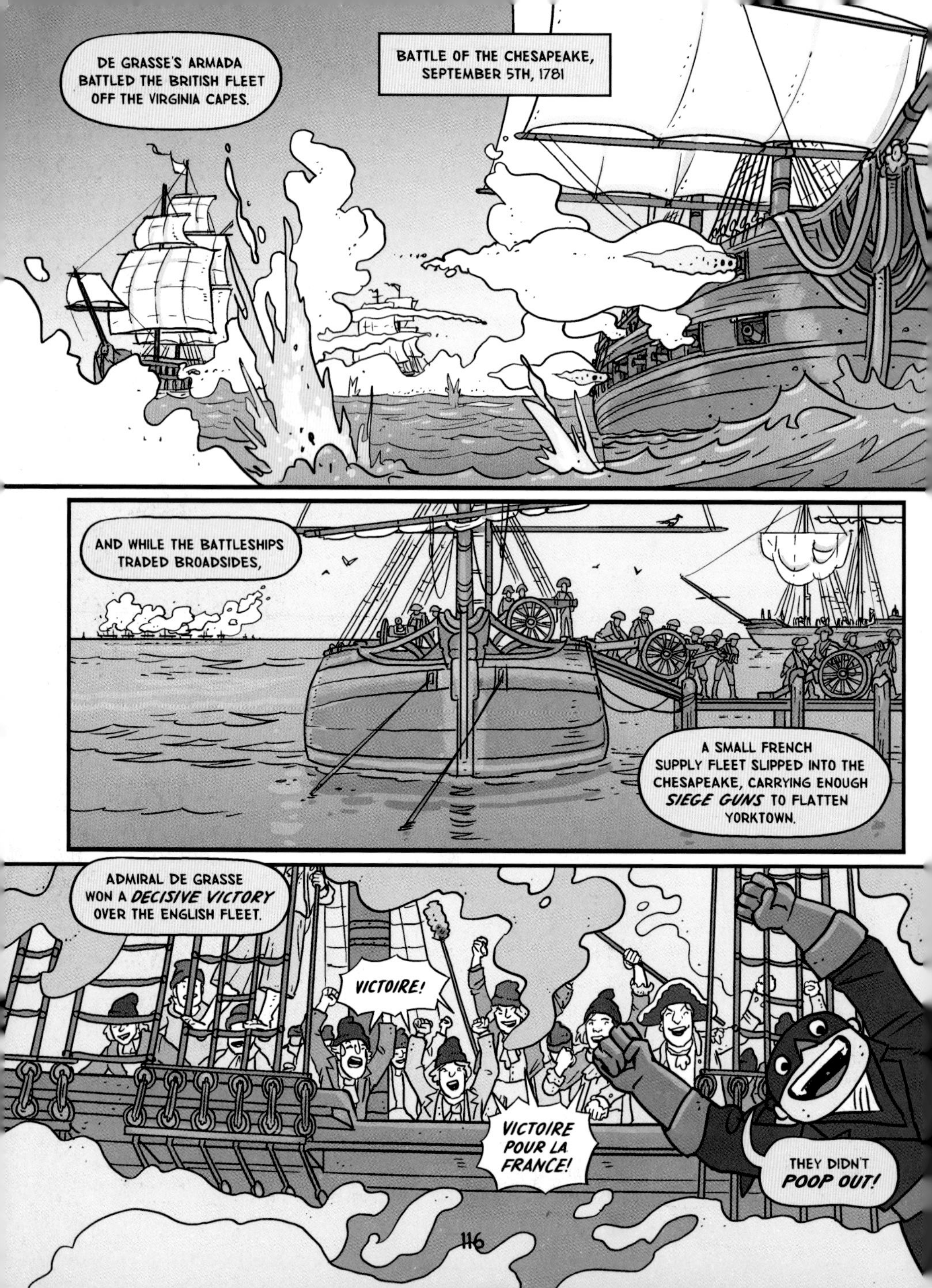

DE GRASSE'S ARMADA BATTLED THE BRITISH FLEET OFF THE VIRGINIA CAPES.
BATTLE OF THE CHESAPEAKE, SEPTEMBER 5TH, 1781
AND WHILE THE BATTLESHIPS TRADED BROADSIDES,
A SMALL FRENCH SUPPLY FLEET SLIPPED INTO THE CHESAPEAKE, CARRYING ENOUGH *SIEGE GUNS* TO FLATTEN YORKTOWN.
ADMIRAL DE GRASSE WON A *DECISIVE VICTORY* OVER THE ENGLISH FLEET.
VICTOIRE!
VICTOIRE POUR LA FRANCE!
THEY DIDN'T *POOP OUT!*

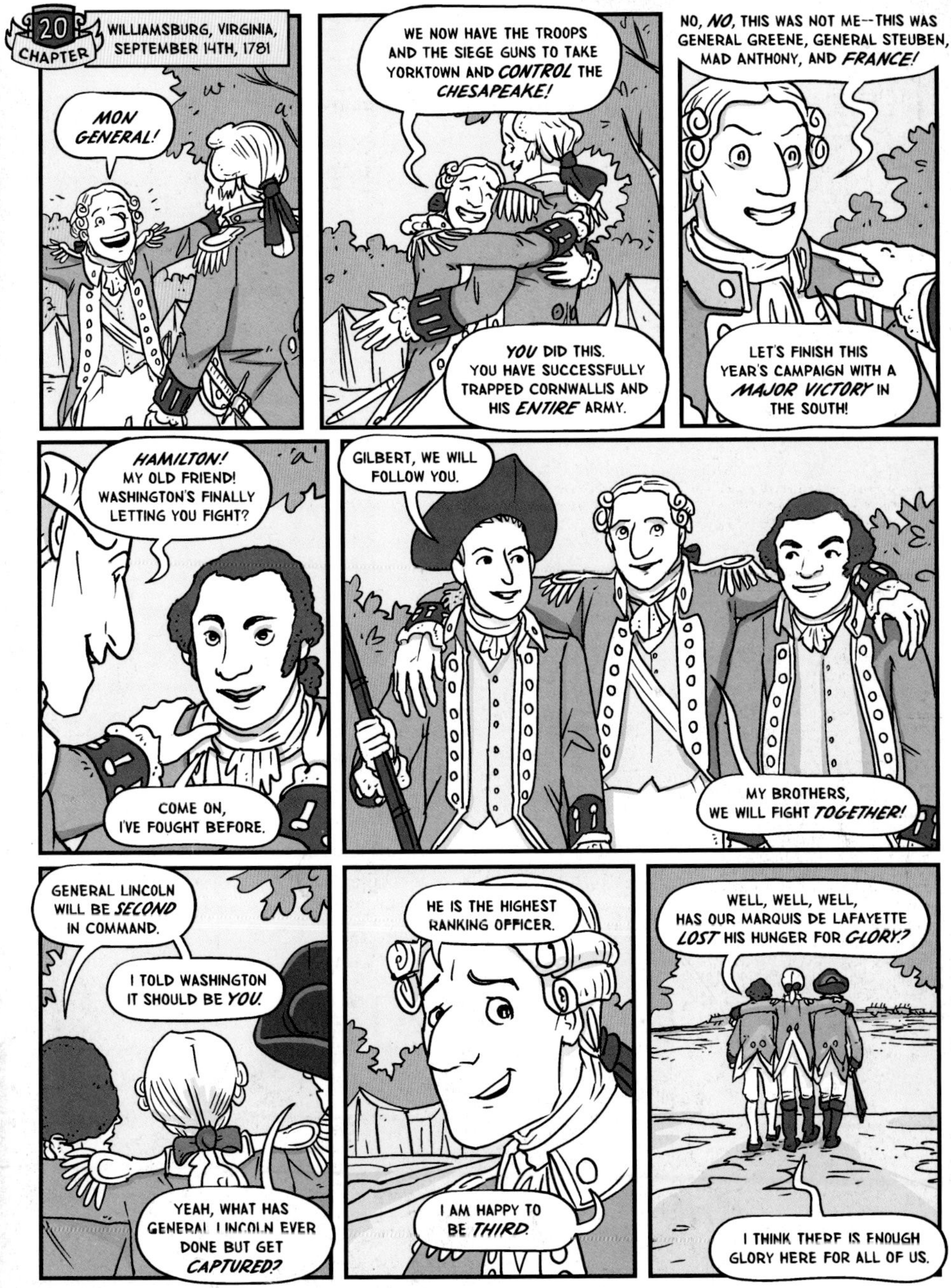
20 CHAPTER
WILLIAMSBURG, VIRGINIA, SEPTEMBER 14TH, 1781
MON GENERAL!
WE NOW HAVE THE TROOPS AND THE SIEGE GUNS TO TAKE YORKTOWN AND CONTROL THE CHESAPEAKE!
YOU DID THIS. YOU HAVE SUCCESSFULLY TRAPPED CORNWALLIS AND HIS ENTIRE ARMY.
NO, NO, THIS WAS NOT ME--THIS WAS GENERAL GREENE, GENERAL STEUBEN, MAD ANTHONY, AND FRANCE!
LET'S FINISH THIS YEAR'S CAMPAIGN WITH A MAJOR VICTORY IN THE SOUTH!
HAMILTON! MY OLD FRIEND! WASHINGTON'S FINALLY LETTING YOU FIGHT?
COME ON, I'VE FOUGHT BEFORE.
GILBERT, WE WILL FOLLOW YOU.
MY BROTHERS, WE WILL FIGHT TOGETHER!
GENERAL LINCOLN WILL BE SECOND IN COMMAND.
I TOLD WASHINGTON IT SHOULD BE YOU.
YEAH, WHAT HAS GENERAL LINCOLN EVER DONE BUT GET CAPTURED?
HE IS THE HIGHEST RANKING OFFICER.
I AM HAPPY TO BE THIRD.
WELL, WELL, WELL, HAS OUR MARQUIS DE LAFAYETTE LOST HIS HUNGER FOR GLORY?
I THINK THERE IS ENOUGH GLORY HERE FOR ALL OF US.

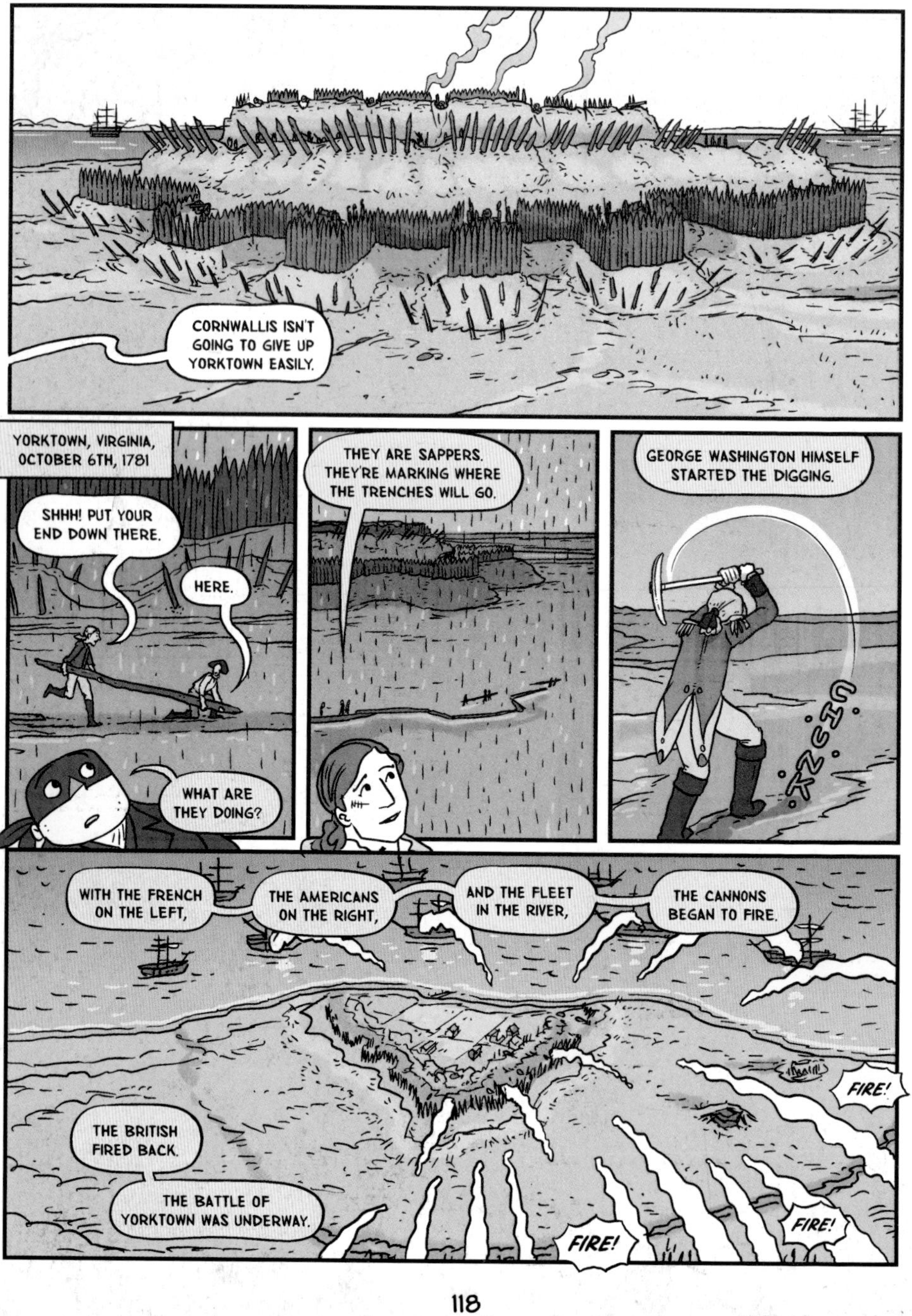
CORNWALLIS ISN'T GOING TO GIVE UP YORKTOWN EASILY.
YORKTOWN, VIRGINIA, OCTOBER 6TH, 1781
SHHH! PUT YOUR END DOWN THERE.
HERE.
WHAT ARE THEY DOING?
THEY ARE SAPPERS. THEY'RE MARKING WHERE THE TRENCHES WILL GO.
GEORGE WASHINGTON HIMSELF STARTED THE DIGGING.
WITH THE FRENCH ON THE LEFT,
THE AMERICANS ON THE RIGHT,
AND THE FLEET IN THE RIVER,
THE CANNONS BEGAN TO FIRE.
FIRE!
THE BRITISH FIRED BACK.
THE BATTLE OF YORKTOWN WAS UNDERWAY.
FIRE!
FIRE!

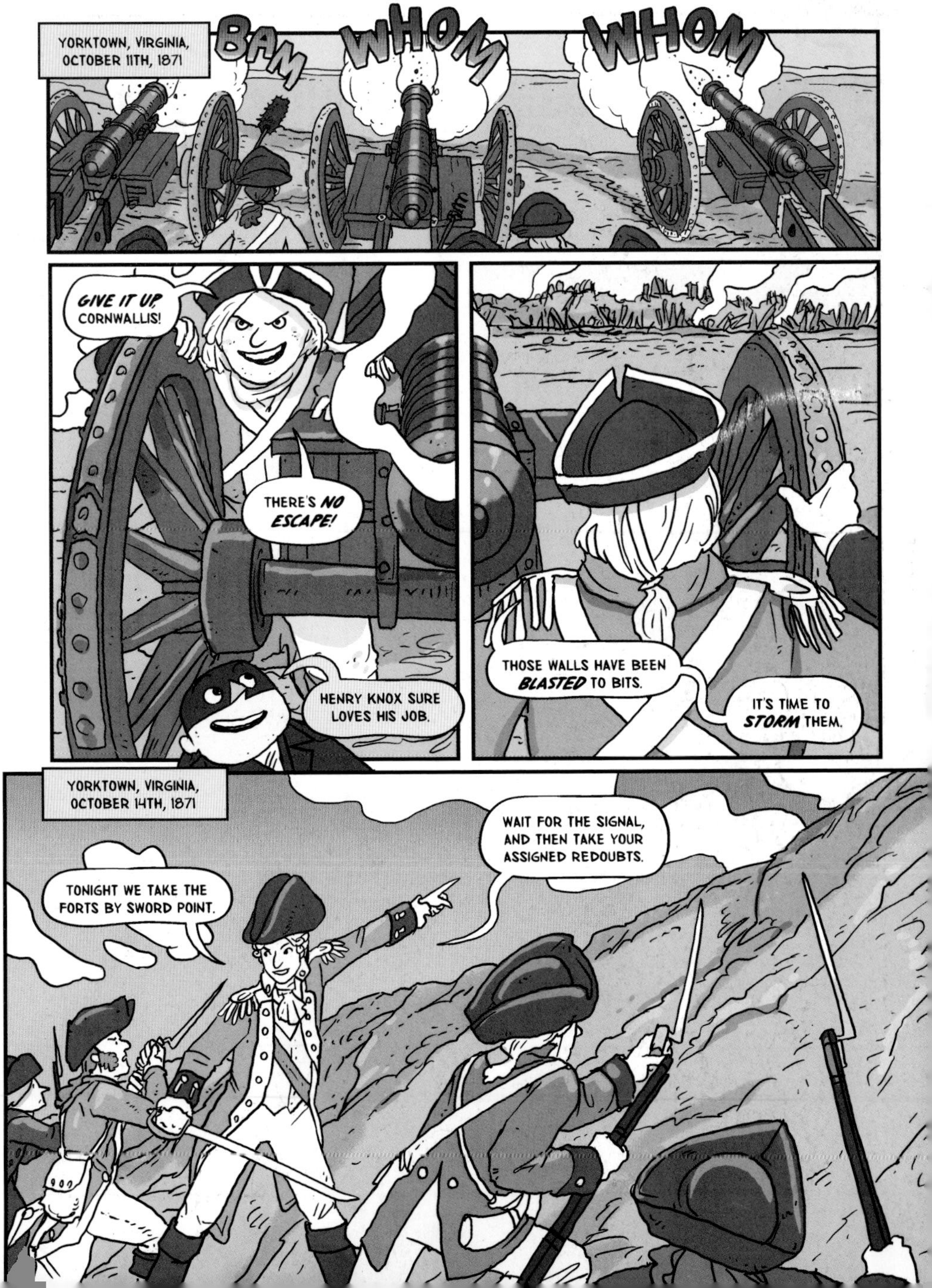

YORKTOWN, VIRGINIA, OCTOBER 11TH, 1871
BAM
WHOM
WHOM
GIVE IT UP, CORNWALLIS!
THERE'S NO ESCAPE!
HENRY KNOX SURE LOVES HIS JOB.
THOSE WALLS HAVE BEEN BLASTED TO BITS.
IT'S TIME TO STORM THEM.
YORKTOWN, VIRGINIA, OCTOBER 14TH, 1871
TONIGHT WE TAKE THE FORTS BY SWORD POINT.
WAIT FOR THE SIGNAL, AND THEN TAKE YOUR ASSIGNED REDOUBTS.

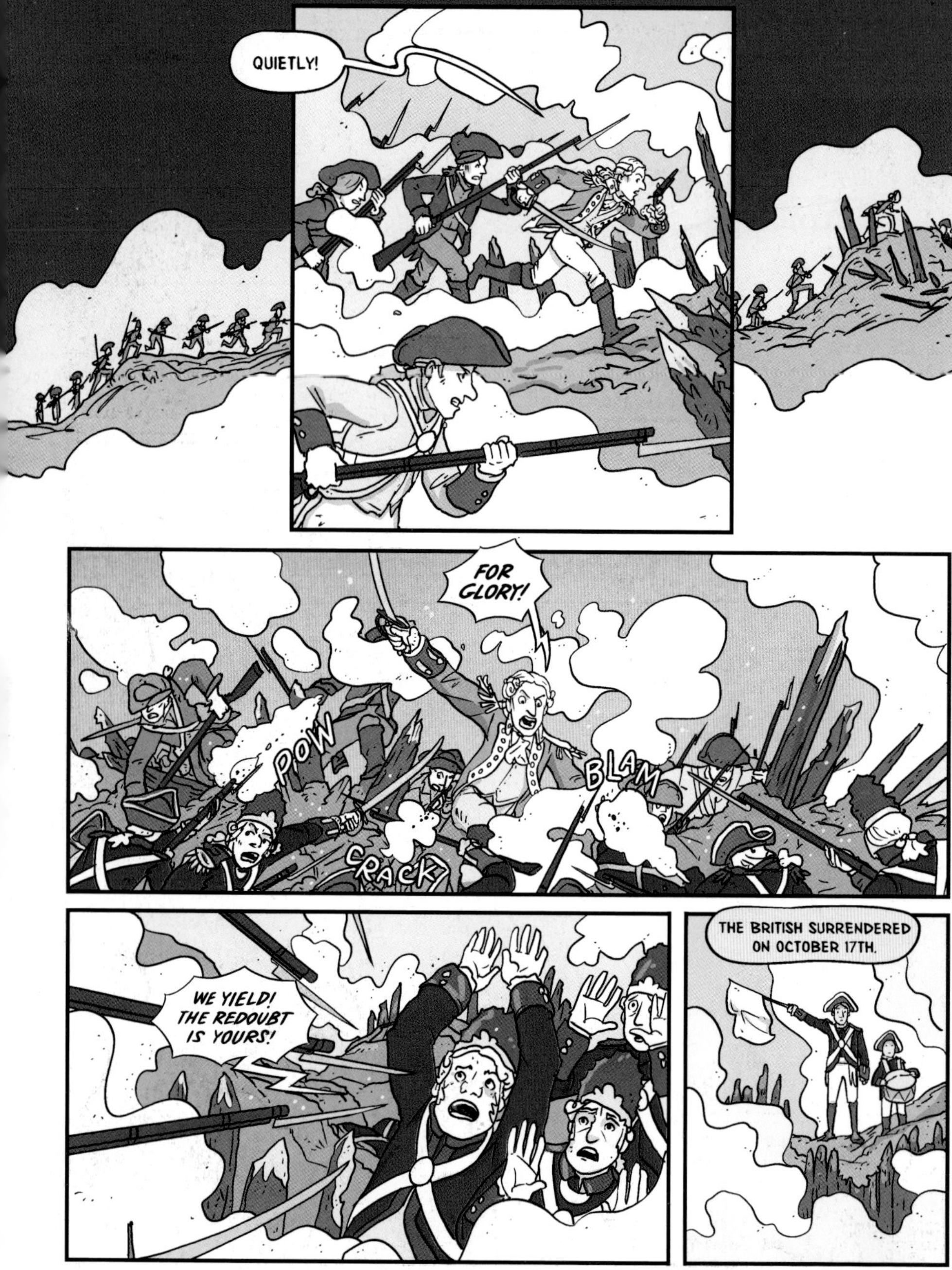
QUIETLY!
FOR GLORY!
POW
BLAM
CRACK
WE YIELD! THE REDOUBT IS YOURS!
THE BRITISH SURRENDERED ON OCTOBER 17TH.

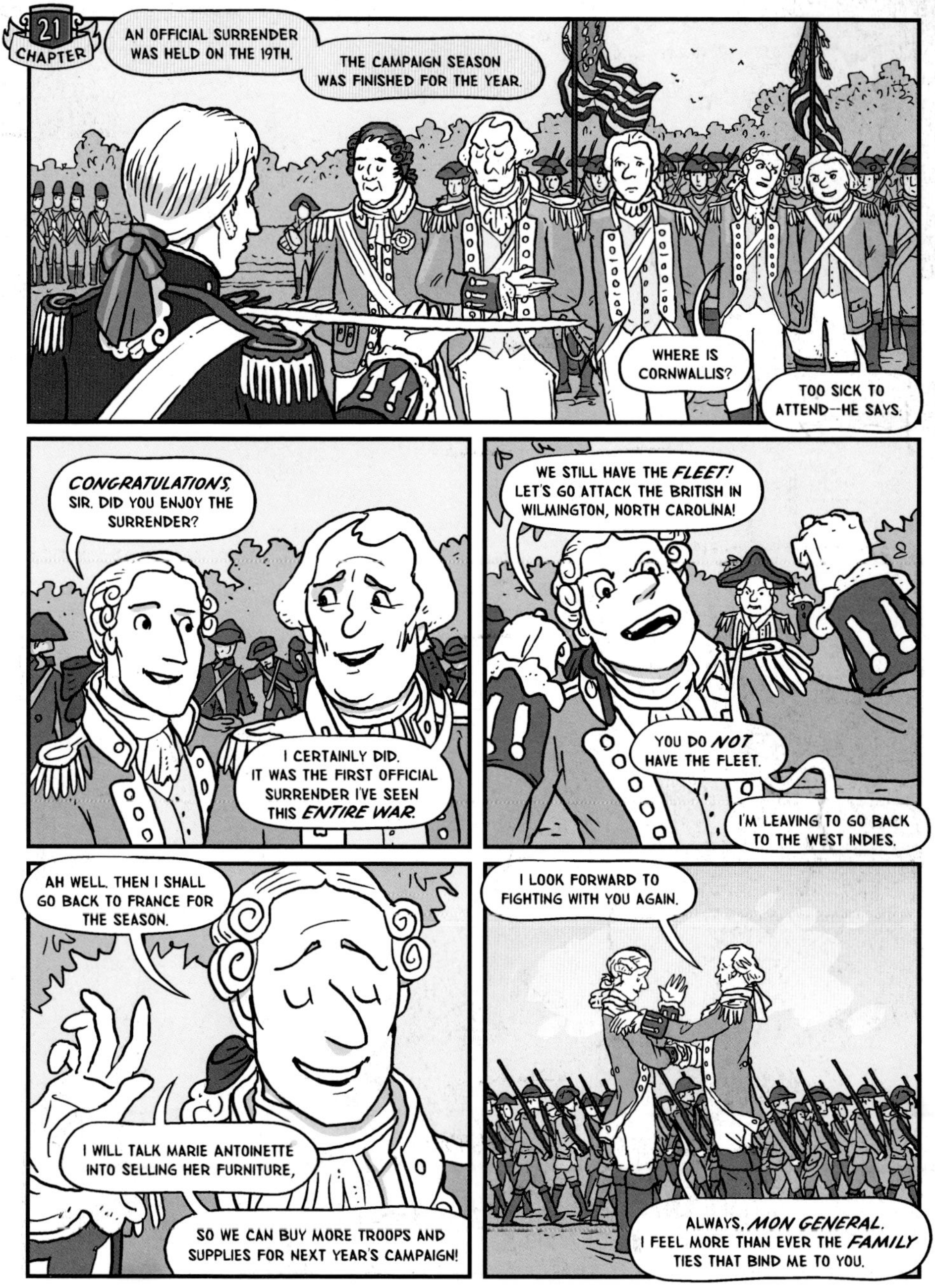
21 CHAPTER
AN OFFICIAL SURRENDER WAS HELD ON THE 19TH.
THE CAMPAIGN SEASON WAS FINISHED FOR THE YEAR.
WHERE IS CORNWALLIS?
TOO SICK TO ATTEND--HE SAYS.
CONGRATULATIONS, SIR. DID YOU ENJOY THE SURRENDER?
I CERTAINLY DID. IT WAS THE FIRST OFFICIAL SURRENDER I'VE SEEN THIS ENTIRE WAR.
WE STILL HAVE THE FLEET! LET'S GO ATTACK THE BRITISH IN WILMINGTON, NORTH CAROLINA!
YOU DO NOT HAVE THE FLEET.
I'M LEAVING TO GO BACK TO THE WEST INDIES.
AH WELL. THEN I SHALL GO BACK TO FRANCE FOR THE SEASON.
I WILL TALK MARIE ANTOINETTE INTO SELLING HER FURNITURE,
SO WE CAN BUY MORE TROOPS AND SUPPLIES FOR NEXT YEAR'S CAMPAIGN!
I LOOK FORWARD TO FIGHTING WITH YOU AGAIN.
ALWAYS, MON GENERAL. I FEEL MORE THAN EVER THE FAMILY TIES THAT BIND ME TO YOU.

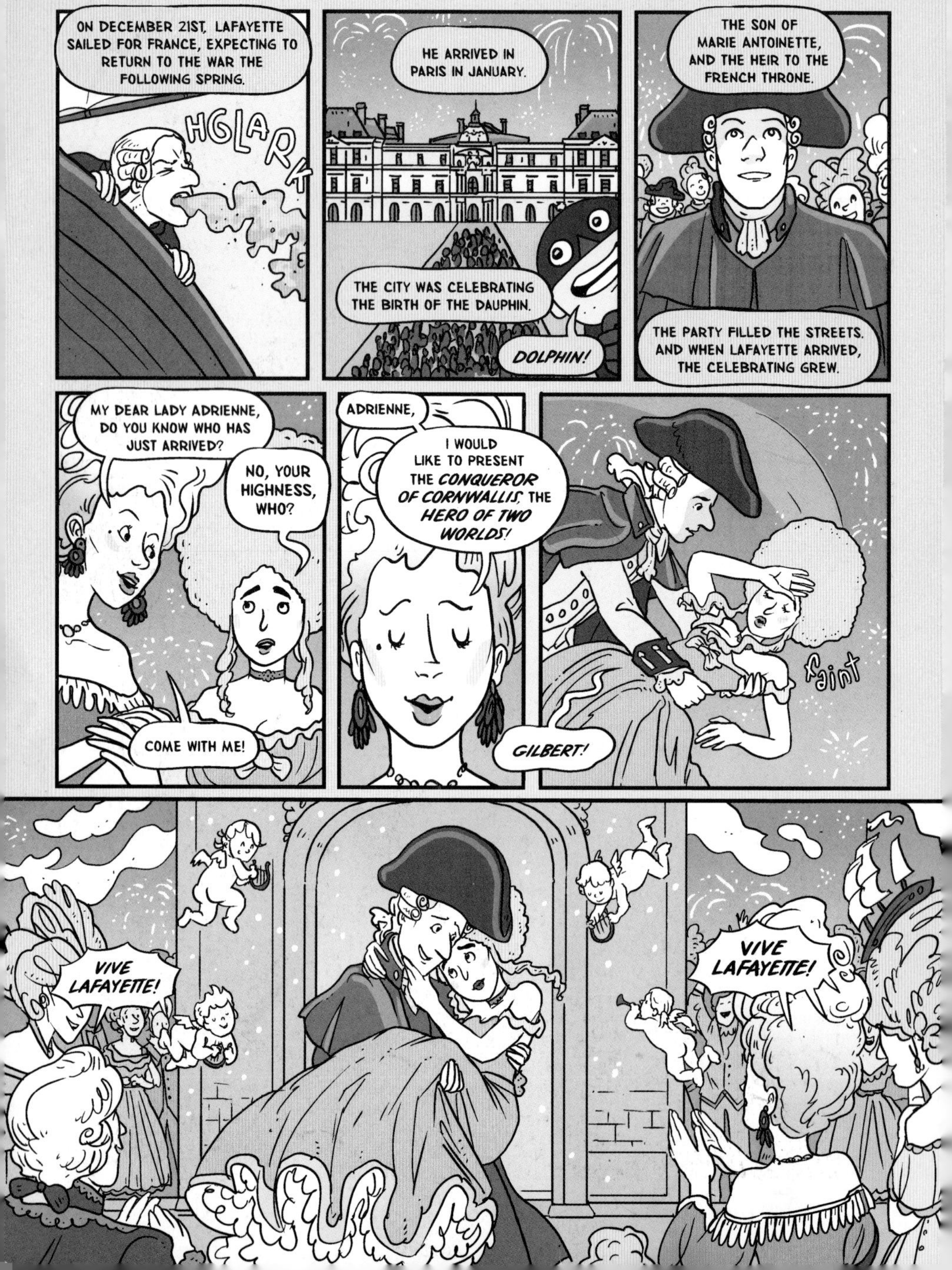
ON DECEMBER 21ST, LAFAYETTE SAILED FOR FRANCE, EXPECTING TO RETURN TO THE WAR THE FOLLOWING SPRING.
HGLARK
HE ARRIVED IN PARIS IN JANUARY.
THE CITY WAS CELEBRATING THE BIRTH OF THE DAUPHIN.
DOLPHIN!
THE SON OF MARIE ANTOINETTE, AND THE HEIR TO THE FRENCH THRONE.
THE PARTY FILLED THE STREETS. AND WHEN LAFAYETTE ARRIVED, THE CELEBRATING GREW.
MY DEAR LADY ADRIENNE, DO YOU KNOW WHO HAS JUST ARRIVED?
NO, YOUR HIGHNESS, WHO?
COME WITH ME!
ADRIENNE,
I WOULD LIKE TO PRESENT THE *CONQUEROR OF CORNWALLIS*, THE *HERO OF TWO WORLDS*!
GILBERT!
faint
VIVE LAFAYETTE!
VIVE LAFAYETTE!

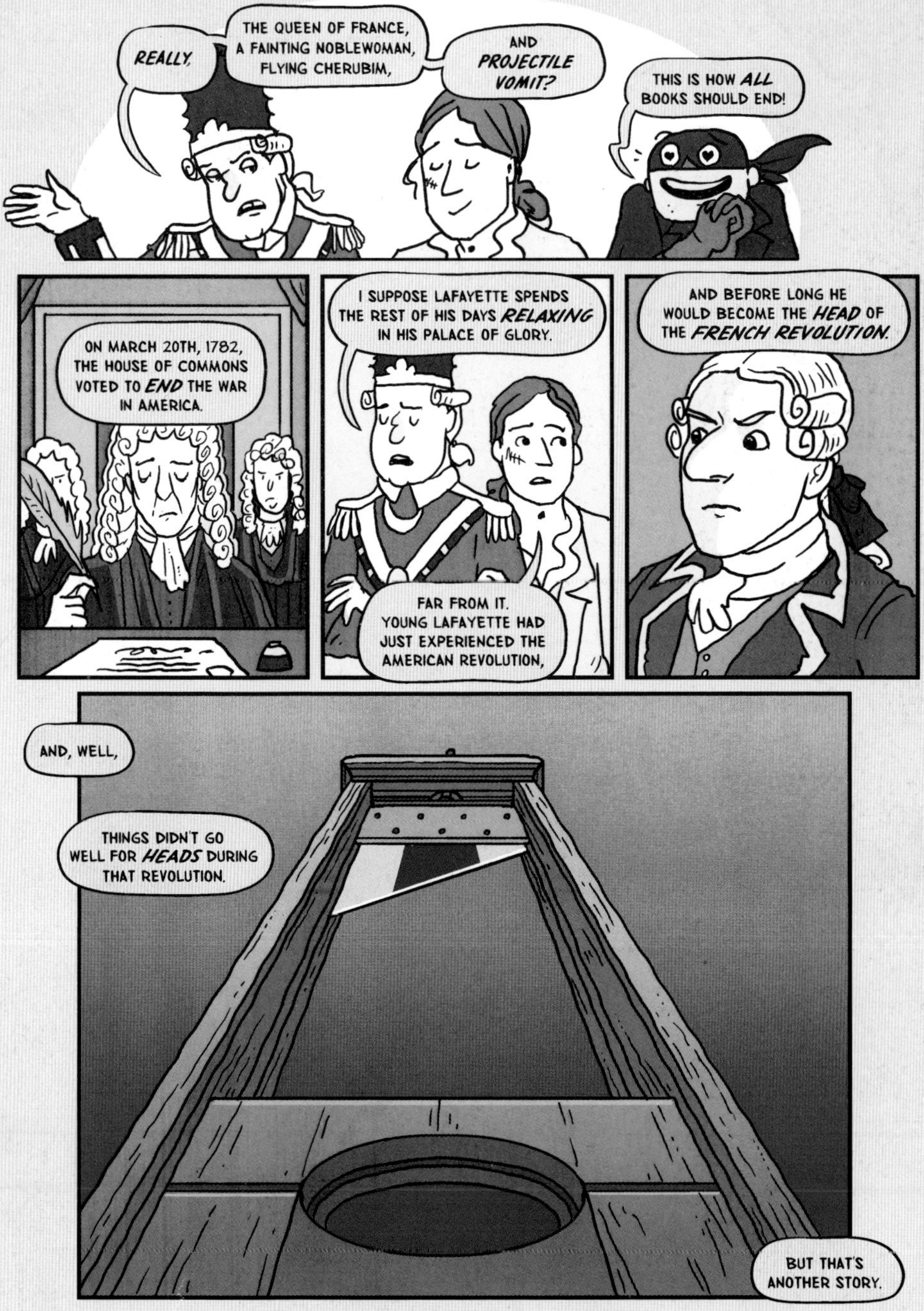
REALLY,
THE QUEEN OF FRANCE, A FAINTING NOBLEWOMAN, FLYING CHERUBIM,
AND PROJECTILE VOMIT?
THIS IS HOW ALL BOOKS SHOULD END!
ON MARCH 20TH, 1782, THE HOUSE OF COMMONS VOTED TO END THE WAR IN AMERICA.
I SUPPOSE LAFAYETTE SPENDS THE REST OF HIS DAYS RELAXING IN HIS PALACE OF GLORY.
FAR FROM IT. YOUNG LAFAYETTE HAD JUST EXPERIENCED THE AMERICAN REVOLUTION,
AND BEFORE LONG HE WOULD BECOME THE HEAD OF THE FRENCH REVOLUTION.
AND, WELL,
THINGS DIDN'T GO WELL FOR HEADS DURING THAT REVOLUTION.
BUT THAT'S ANOTHER STORY.

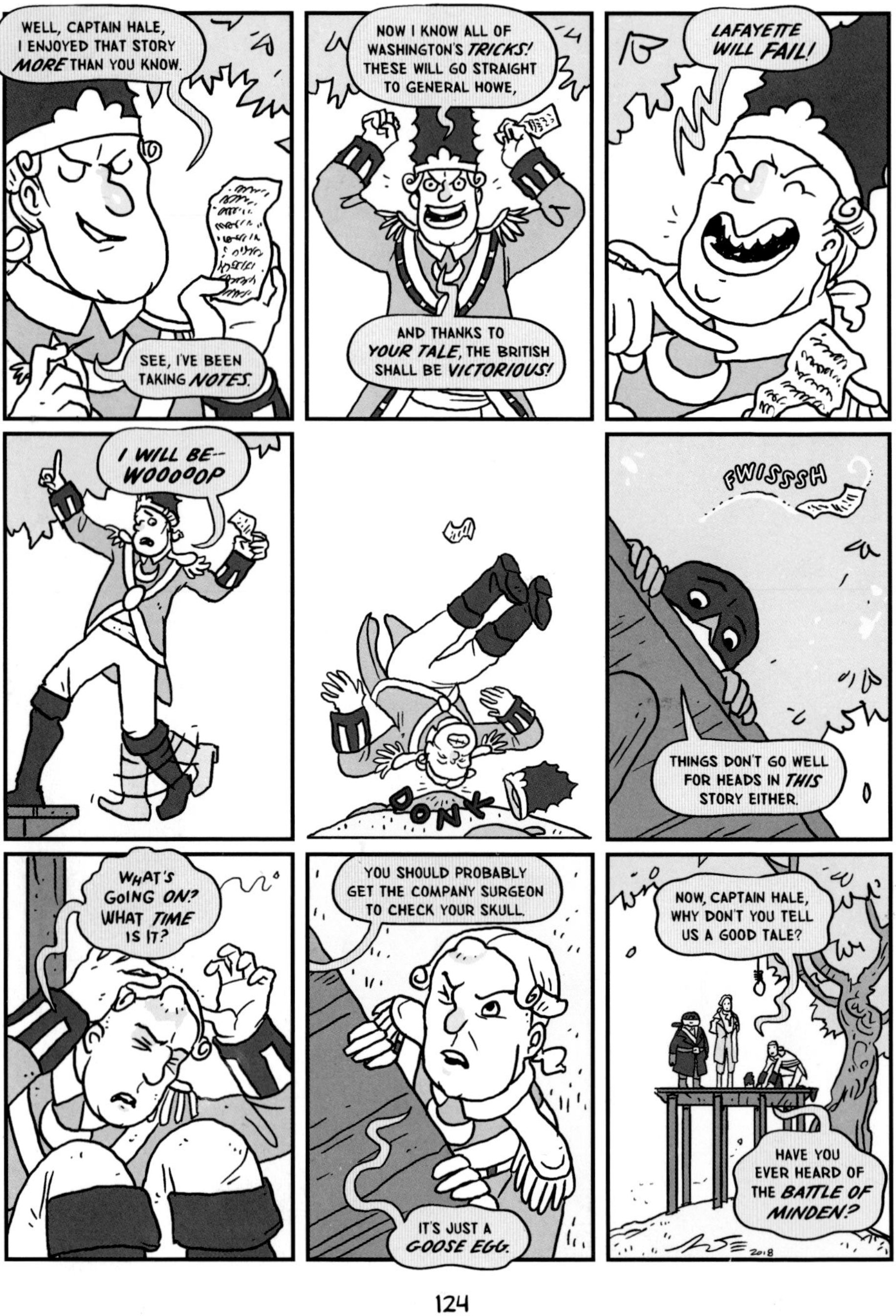
WELL, CAPTAIN HALE, I ENJOYED THAT STORY *MORE* THAN YOU KNOW.
SEE, I'VE BEEN TAKING *NOTES.*
NOW I KNOW ALL OF WASHINGTON'S *TRICKS!* THESE WILL GO STRAIGHT TO GENERAL HOWE,
AND THANKS TO *YOUR TALE,* THE BRITISH SHALL BE *VICTORIOUS!*
LAFAYETTE WILL FAIL!
I WILL BE-- WOOOOOP
DONK
FWISSSH
THINGS DON'T GO WELL FOR HEADS IN *THIS* STORY EITHER.
WHAT'S GOING *ON?* WHAT *TIME* IS IT?
YOU SHOULD PROBABLY GET THE COMPANY SURGEON TO CHECK YOUR SKULL.
IT'S JUST A *GOOSE EGG.*
NOW, CAPTAIN HALE, WHY DON'T YOU TELL US A GOOD TALE?
HAVE YOU EVER HEARD OF THE *BATTLE OF MINDEN?*
2018

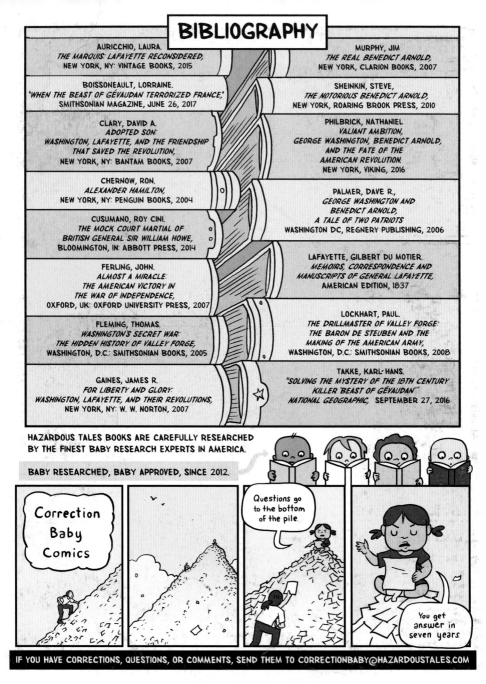

BIBLIOGRAPHY

AURICCHIO, LAURA. *THE MARQUIS: LAFAYETTE RECONSIDERED,* NEW YORK, NY: VINTAGE BOOKS, 2015

BOISSONEAULT, LORRAINE. *"WHEN THE BEAST OF GÉVAUDAN TERRORIZED FRANCE,"* SMITHSONIAN MAGAZINE, JUNE 26, 2017

CLARY, DAVID A. *ADOPTED SON: WASHINGTON, LAFAYETTE, AND THE FRIENDSHIP THAT SAVED THE REVOLUTION,* NEW YORK, NY: BANTAM BOOKS, 2007

CHERNOW, RON. *ALEXANDER HAMILTON,* NEW YORK, NY: PENGUIN BOOKS, 2004

CUSUMANO, ROY CINI. *THE MOCK COURT MARTIAL OF BRITISH GENERAL SIR WILLIAM HOWE,* BLOOMINGTON, IN: ABBOTT PRESS, 2014

FERLING, JOHN. *ALMOST A MIRACLE: THE AMERICAN VICTORY IN THE WAR OF INDEPENDENCE,* OXFORD, UK: OXFORD UNIVERSITY PRESS, 2007

FLEMING, THOMAS. *WASHINGTON'S SECRET WAR: THE HIDDEN HISTORY OF VALLEY FORGE,* WASHINGTON, D.C.: SMITHSONIAN BOOKS, 2005

GAINES, JAMES R. *FOR LIBERTY AND GLORY: WASHINGTON, LAFAYETTE, AND THEIR REVOLUTIONS,* NEW YORK, NY: W. W. NORTON, 2007

MURPHY, JIM *THE REAL BENEDICT ARNOLD,* NEW YORK, CLARION BOOKS, 2007

SHEINKIN, STEVE, *THE NOTORIOUS BENEDICT ARNOLD,* NEW YORK, ROARING BROOK PRESS, 2010

PHILBRICK, NATHANIEL *VALIANT AMBITION, GEORGE WASHINGTON, BENEDICT ARNOLD, AND THE FATE OF THE AMERICAN REVOLUTION.* NEW YORK, VIKING, 2016

PALMER, DAVE R., *GEORGE WASHINGTON AND BENEDICT ARNOLD, A TALE OF TWO PATRIOTS* WASHINGTON DC, REGNERY PUBLISHING, 2006

LAFAYETTE, GILBERT DU MOTIER. *MEMOIRS, CORRESPONDENCE AND MANUSCRIPTS OF GENERAL LAFAYETTE,* AMERICAN EDITION, 1837

LOCKHART, PAUL. *THE DRILLMASTER OF VALLEY FORGE: THE BARON DE STEUBEN AND THE MAKING OF THE AMERICAN ARMY,* WASHINGTON, D.C.: SMITHSONIAN BOOKS, 2008

TAKKE, KARL-HANS. *"SOLVING THE MYSTERY OF THE 18TH CENTURY KILLER 'BEAST OF GÉVAUDAN'"* *NATIONAL GEOGRAPHIC,* SEPTEMBER 27, 2016

HAZARDOUS TALES BOOKS ARE CAREFULLY RESEARCHED BY THE FINEST BABY RESEARCH EXPERTS IN AMERICA.

BABY RESEARCHED, BABY APPROVED, SINCE 2012.

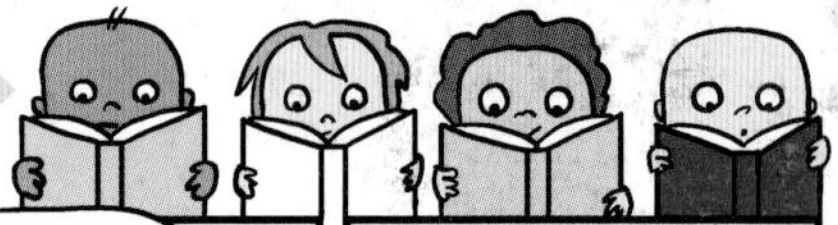

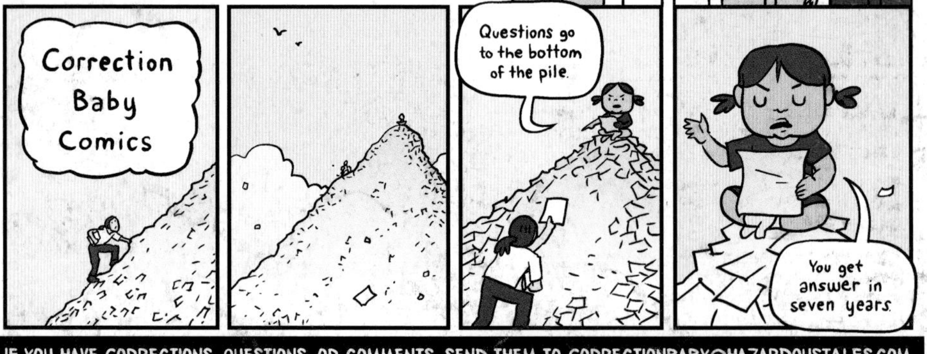

Correction Baby Comics
Questions go to the bottom of the pile.
You get answer in seven years.

IF YOU HAVE CORRECTIONS, QUESTIONS, OR COMMENTS, SEND THEM TO CORRECTIONBABY@HAZARDOUSTALES.COM

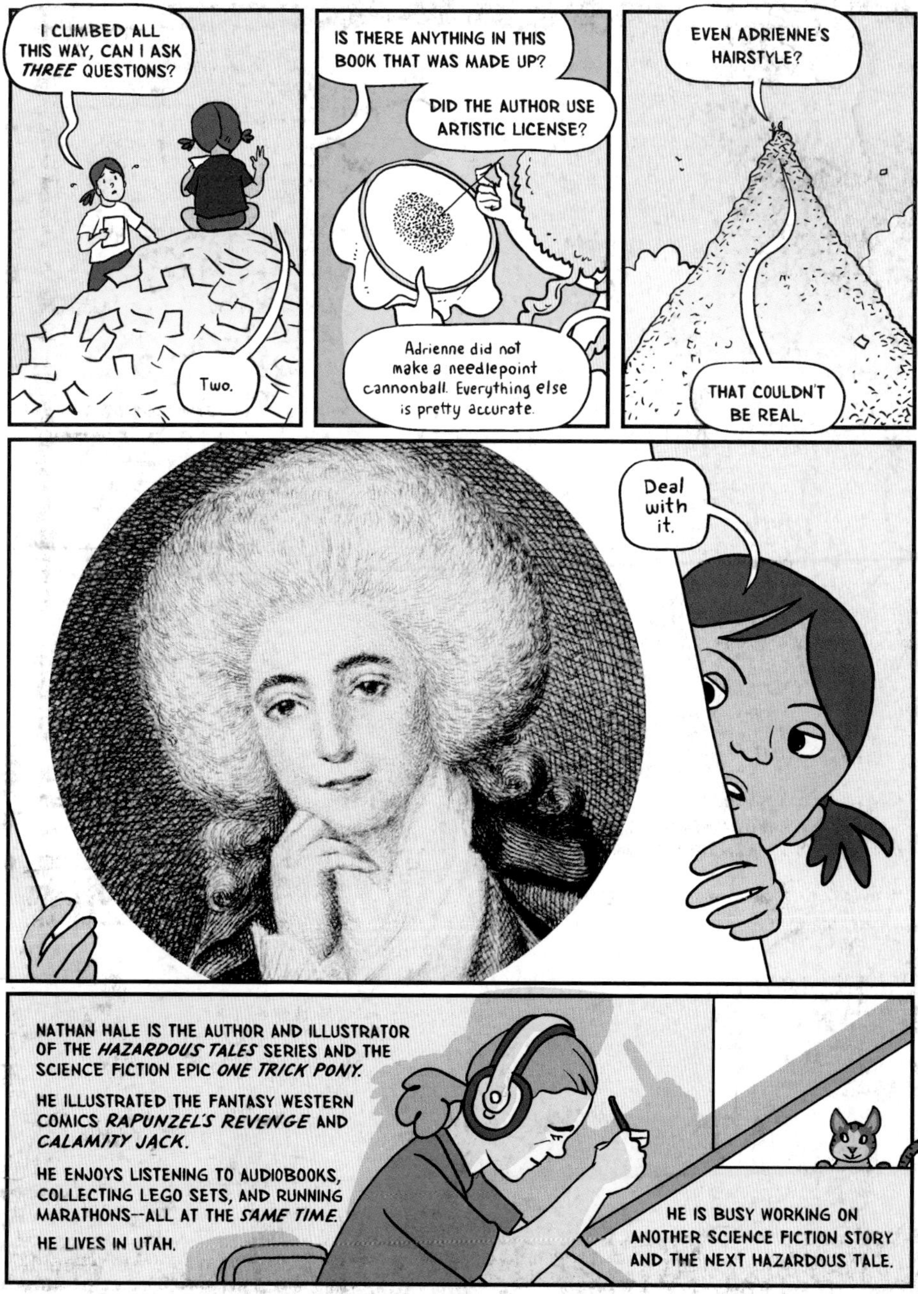
I CLIMBED ALL THIS WAY, CAN I ASK *THREE* QUESTIONS?
Two.
IS THERE ANYTHING IN THIS BOOK THAT WAS MADE UP?
DID THE AUTHOR USE ARTISTIC LICENSE?
Adrienne did not make a needlepoint cannonball. Everything else is pretty accurate.
EVEN ADRIENNE'S HAIRSTYLE?
THAT COULDN'T BE REAL.
Deal with it.
NATHAN HALE IS THE AUTHOR AND ILLUSTRATOR OF THE *HAZARDOUS TALES* SERIES AND THE SCIENCE FICTION EPIC *ONE TRICK PONY.*
HE ILLUSTRATED THE FANTASY WESTERN COMICS *RAPUNZEL'S REVENGE* AND *CALAMITY JACK.*
HE ENJOYS LISTENING TO AUDIOBOOKS, COLLECTING LEGO SETS, AND RUNNING MARATHONS--ALL AT THE *SAME TIME.*
HE LIVES IN UTAH.
HE IS BUSY WORKING ON ANOTHER SCIENCE FICTION STORY AND THE NEXT HAZARDOUS TALE.

MATCH THE NAKED CUPID BABY TO ITS CORRESPONDING BOOK!

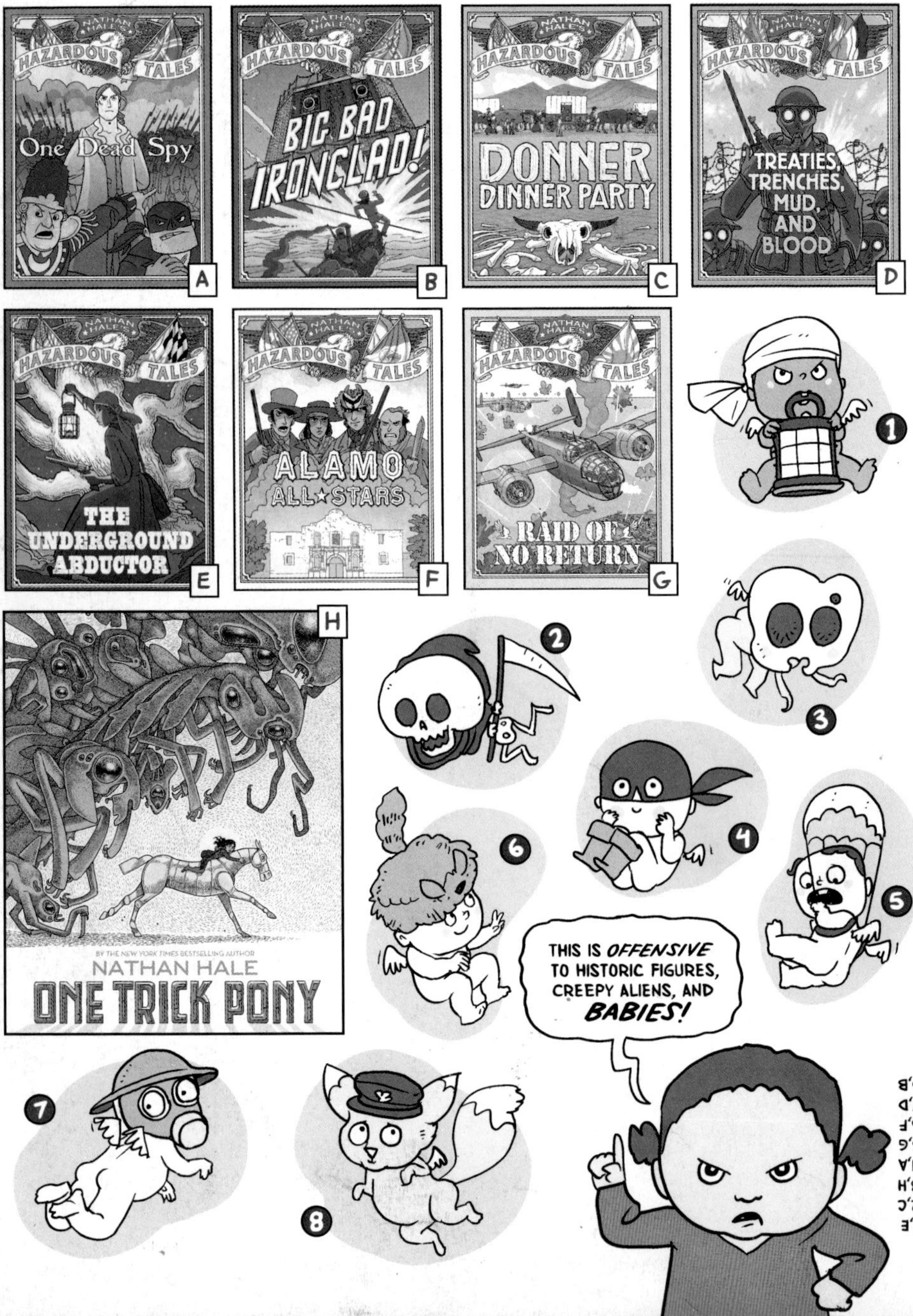
NATHAN HALE'S HAZARDOUS TALES
One Dead Spy
A
NATHAN HALE'S HAZARDOUS TALES
BIG BAD IRONCLAD!
B
NATHAN HALE'S HAZARDOUS TALES
DONNER DINNER PARTY
C
NATHAN HALE'S HAZARDOUS TALES
TREATIES, TRENCHES, MUD, AND BLOOD
D
NATHAN HALE'S HAZARDOUS TALES
THE UNDERGROUND ABDUCTOR
E
NATHAN HALE'S HAZARDOUS TALES
ALAMO ALL★STARS
F
NATHAN HALE'S HAZARDOUS TALES
RAID OF NO RETURN
G
H
BY THE NEW YORK TIMES BESTSELLING AUTHOR
NATHAN HALE
ONE TRICK PONY
1
2
3
4
5
6
7
8
THIS IS *OFFENSIVE* TO HISTORIC FIGURES, CREEPY ALIENS, AND ***BABIES!***

1,E
2,C
3,H
4,A
5,G
6,F
7,D
8,B

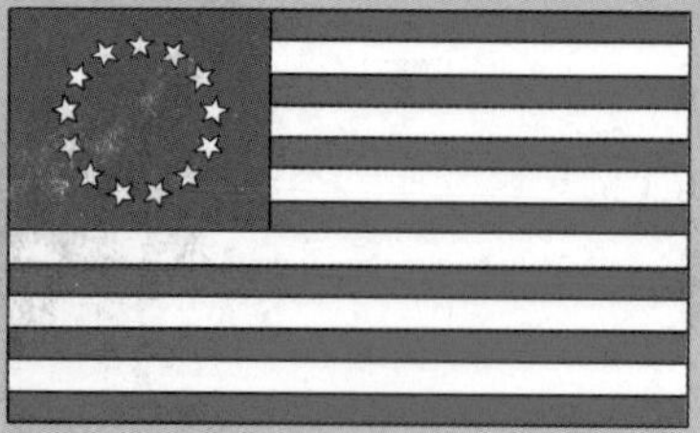

FLAG OF THE UNITED STATES OF AMERICA
1777–1795, BETSY ROSS VARIANT

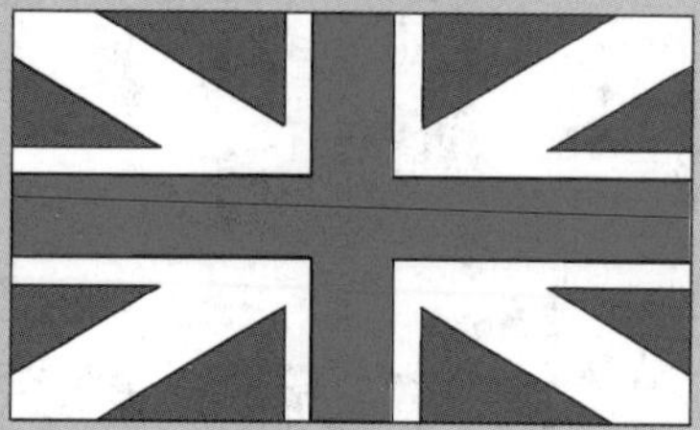

FLAG OF THE KINGDOM OF
GREAT BRITAIN, 1606–1801
NOTE: THE DIAGONAL RED STRIPES WERE
ADDED IN 1801 FOR IRELAND

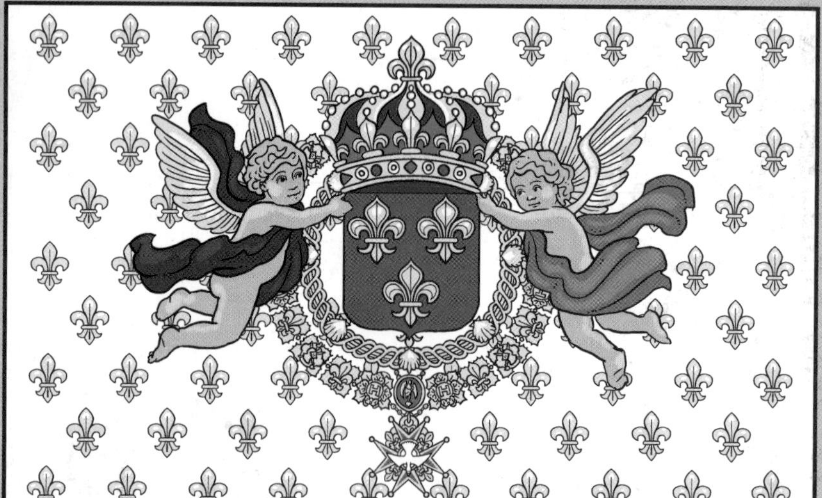

FLAG OF THE KINGDOM OF FRANCE, 1598–1790

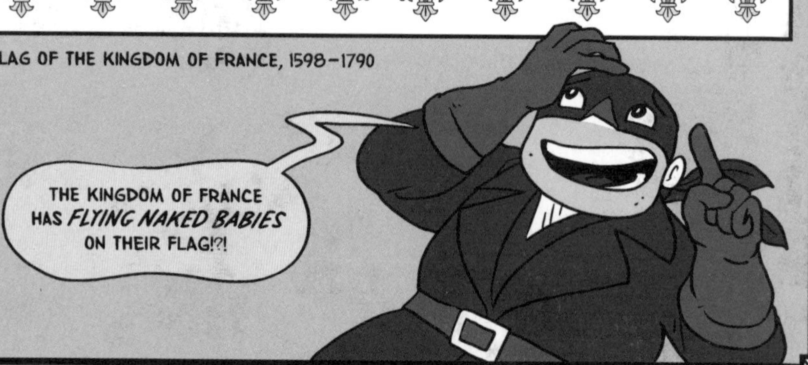
THE KINGDOM OF FRANCE HAS *FLYING NAKED BABIES* ON THEIR FLAG!?!

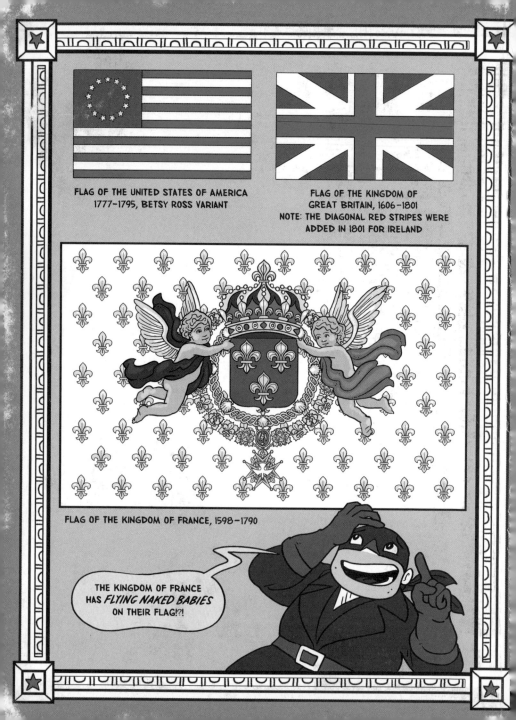